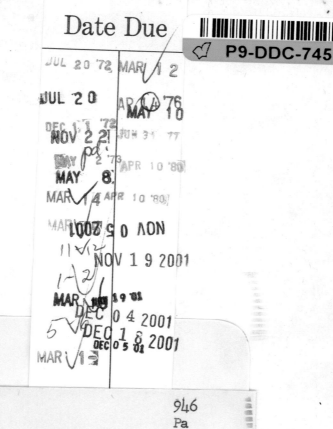

The Spanish Revolution

REVOLUTIONS IN THE MODERN WORLD

General Editor: JACK P. GREENE, *Johns Hopkins University*

ROGER L. WILLIAMS · The French Revolution of 1870–1871
STANLEY G. PAYNE · The Spanish Revolution

STANLEY G. PAYNE

University of Wisconsin

The Spanish

Revolution

 W·W·Norton & Company·Inc· NEW YORK

For my mother, Margaret Payne

Contents

MAPS

Preface

THIS BOOK WAS BEGUN at the invitation of Professor Jack P. Greene to prepare an account of the Spanish revolutionary experience of the 1930's for the series on "Revolutions in the Modern World." I was at first skeptical of the usefulness of such a study, but after further reflection and examination of the literature in the field came to agree that a fresh analysis of the topic was needed. This volume does not pretend to be a history of the Spanish Republic and Civil War, but is an account of the revolutionary left in modern Spain that concentrates primarily upon the convulsions of the 1930's. Hence I have not tried to treat fully the political history either of liberal moderates, or of the Spanish right in contradistinction to the left. Since much of the book is devoted to a discussion of leftist extremism, some may feel that equal emphasis should be given to the excesses of the radical right in Spain. That, however, would be another book—and one that I have already in large part composed in my *Falange* (1961) and *Politics and the Military in Modern Spain* (1967). In those volumes I have dwelt at considerable length on rightist extremism and felt no need to rewrite such material in composing a book on the left.

Considerable emphasis has been given to the development of the revolutionary movements in Catalonia, while Andalusian peasant anarchism has received considerably less attention despite the romantic appeal which the latter topic apparently has for readers in the English-speaking world. The reason for this is the much greater importance achieved by the working-class movement in industrial areas, particularly Catalonia, compared with the ultimate ineffectiveness of rural peasant anarchism. The latter has sometimes been stressed out of all importance to its genuine impact on the affairs of Spain, which were shaken by the industrial strike of 1917 and subsequent disorders in the industrial areas, but very little by the rural Andalusian *trienio bolchevique* of 1918–20. Rural agitation only acquired major importance after the growth of the Socialist UGT in the south-central and southwestern provinces in the early 1930's. In the treatment of the social and economic revolution during the Civil War, emphasis is placed on Catalonia because the revolution there was more thorough than in any other region of the Republican zone, and because the data for it are more complete and accessible. The rural revolution in the south-central provinces was also important, but since it has been extremely difficult to obtain data on this I have had to give it less attention than it perhaps deserves.

I want to thank my colleagues Juan J. Linz of Yale University and Edward E. Malefakis of Northwestern University for their criticism of the manuscript, and am also grateful to the editor of this series, Jack P. Greene of the Johns Hopkins University, and to Donald S. Lamm of W. W. Norton & Company, Inc. for their helpful editorial suggestions. It should scarcely be necessary to add that I am solely responsible for any shortcomings of style or interpretation.

STANLEY G. PAYNE

Madison, Wisconsin
March, 1969

Principal Personages

AGUIRRE Y LECUBE, José Antonio (1904–60). Leader of the Basque Nationalist party and president of the autonomous government of Euzkadi (the Basque provinces) created in October 1936.

ALCALÁ ZAMORA, Niceto (1877–1949). Wealthy Andalusian landowner and Liberal politician under the constitutional monarchy. Chairman of the Republican Committee in 1930–31 and first president of the Second Republic from 1931 until deposed by the Popular Front in April 1936.

ALVAREZ DEL VAYO, Julio (b. 1891). Socialist intellectual who became one of the most influential agents of the Comintern within the Spanish Socialist party. During the Civil War served as commissar-general of the People's Army and also as Republican foreign minister under Negrín. Eventually expelled from the Socialist party.

ARAQUISTAIN QUEVEDO, Luis (1886–1959). Perhaps the leading theorist of the revolutionary wing of the Spanish Socialist party. Served as Republican ambassador to France under Largo Caballero in 1936–37, and became profoundly disillusioned by the Bolshevization of Spanish socialism.

AZAÑA Y DÍAZ, Manuel (1880–1940). Outstanding prose stylist and principal leader of the Republican left in Spain. Served as prime minister from 1931 to 1933 and again in

1936, then became president of the Republic from 1936 to 1939.

BADIA, MIQUEL (1907–36). Sometime terrorist and leader of the militia of the protofascist Estat Català group under the Republic. Murdered in Barcelona in 1936, presumably by the anarchists.

BESTEIRO FERNÁNDEZ, Julián (1870–1940). Professor of logic at the University of Madrid and the outstanding intellectual of the Spanish Socialist party. Devoted to the social democratic principles of pre-Leninist Maxism, he was swept aside by the Bolshevizing trend of 1933–36. Helped lead the anti-Communist Republican revolt of March 1939 and was the only major leftist leader who did not flee from the country. After he died in prison in 1940, he became perhaps the only political figure in Spain whose moral stature was admitted by both sides.

CALVO SOTELO, José (1893–1936). Political leader of the monarchist opposition under the Second Republic. His murder by leftist Republican police in July 1936 was the final spark that set off the Civil War.

CAMBÓ BATLLE, Francesc (1876–1947). Millionaire Catalan financier and politician who was head of the moderate liberal Lliga Catalana that represented much of the Catalan middle and upper classes. Largely swept aside by the rise of left Catalanism after 1931.

CASADO LÓPEZ, Col. Segismundo (1893–1967). Professional army officer who supported the moderate left and held various important posts in the People's Army. Military leader of the anti-Communist Madrid revolt of March 1939 that ended the Civil War.

CASARES QUIROGA, Santiago (1884–1950). A leader of the Galicianist left and one of the most trusted lieutenants of Manuel Azaña. Minister of the interior from 1931 to 1933 and minister of war in 1936, he replaced Azaña as prime minister from May to July 1936.

CASTRO DELGADO, Enrique. Leading young Spanish Communist troubleshooter. Was an editor of *Mundo Obrero* (the official Communist daily), first commander of the Communist Fifth

Regiment, and also served as head of the Institute of Agrarian Reform. Later resigned from and bitterly denounced the Communist party.

COMORERA, JUAN. Before the war a leader of the Unió Socialista de Catalunya and after July 1936 the most prominent figure in the Communist party of Catalonia (PSUC).

COMPANYS JOVER, Luis (1883–1940). Lawyer and politician who succeeded Macià as leader of the Esquerra (the Catalanist left). President of the Catalan Generalitat from 1933 to 1939.

DENCÀS, JOSEP. Catalan physician who became the main leader of Estat Català in 1933 and 1934 and was the principal planner of the abortive Barcelona revolt of October 1934. Later expelled from Estat Català.

DÍAZ RAMOS, José. Onetime baker and CNT activist from Seville who switched to the Spanish Communist party and served as secretary general of the latter from 1932 until after the close of the Civil War. Apparently committed suicide in Baku in 1944.

DURRUTI, Buenaventura (1896–1936). One of the key leaders of the anarchist FAI and probably the best-known terrorist and insurrectionist in Spain. Killed leading anarchist militia on the Madrid front in November 1936.

FÀBREGAS, Juan. Economic theorist and writer of the CNT who became councillor of economics in the first regular Catalan government after the Civil War began and was the principal author of the Catalan collectivization decree of October 1936.

GARCÍA OLIVER, Juan (b. 1901). One of the most influential and capable anarchist leaders in Spain who served as minister of justice under Largo Caballero in 1936–37.

GIL ROBLES Y QUIÑONES, José María (b. 1898). Leader of the conservative Catholic CEDA, the largest middle-class party in Spain, and the outstanding conservative politician of the Republican period.

GIRAL Y PEREIRA, José (1880–1962). Professor of chemistry at the University of Madrid and political lieutenant of Manuel

Azaña. Served as wartime Republican prime minister from July to September 1936.

GONZÁLEZ PENA, Ramón. A leader of the UGT in Asturias and one of the directors of the insurrection of 1934. When released from prison in 1936, he opposed the Bolshevizing trend in the Socialist party and supported Prieto against Largo Caballero. He became president of the executive commission of the UGT in 1937.

HERNÁNDEZ TOMÁS, Jesús. One of the most active and important young Communist leaders in Spain. Served as minister of information in the Republican government during the Civil War.

IBARRURI, Dolores, known as "La Pasionaria" (b. 1895). Most powerful female politician in modern Spanish history. Member of the central committee of the Spanish Communist party since 1932 and during the Civil War perhaps the most influential single Communist leader because of the confidence placed in her by the Comintern.

IGLESIAS POSSE, Pablo (1850–1925). More than any other single man may be called the founder of the Spanish Socialist party, of which he was by far the most influential leader until his death.

LARGO CABALLERO, Francisco (1869–1946). Lifetime militant of the UGT and under the Republic became both president of the executive commission of the Socialist party and secretary general of the UGT. After 1933 became the leader of the revolutionary wing of the Socialist party and was hailed as "the Spanish Lenin." Served as minister of labor from 1931 to 1933 and as prime minister from September 1936 to May 1937. Ostracized from politics in the Republican zone after May 1937.

LERROUX GARCÍA, Alejandro (1864–1949). Leader of the Radical Republican party. In the early years of the century was the leading anticlerical demagogue in Spain but by the time of the Republic had become the representative of moderate middle-class liberalism. Served several brief terms as prime minister between 1933 and 1935.

MACIÀ Y LLUSÀ, Francesc (1859–1933). Professional army colonel who retired to become the leader of left Catalan nationalism. Founded the Catalan Esquerra and helped negotiated the Catalan autonomy statute of 1932, then became the first president of the Catalan Generalitat from 1932 to 1933.

MARTÍNEZ BARRIO, Diego (1883–1965). Former lieutenant of Lerroux who broke with the Radicals in 1934 to found his own Republican Union party that allied itself with Azaña's Republican Left. The most moderate of the Popular Front leaders, he failed in a tragic effort to form a compromise coalition government on July 19, 1936. Succeeded Azaña as president of the Republic in 1939.

MAURA Y GAMAZO, Miguel (b. 1887). First minister of the interior of the Second Republic and leader of a small liberal party. Urged restoration of order and formation of a "liberal Republican dictatorship" in June 1936.

MAURÍN JULIÀ, JOAQUÍN (b. 1896). A young leader of the CNT in Barcelona early in the 1920's. Subsequently worked with the Comintern. Broke with Spanish communism in 1930 and formed a separate Catalan Marxist party (BOC) that was later merged with Nin's Communist left to form the POUM in 1935. Captured by the Nationalists soon after the Civil War began.

MIAJA MENANT, Gen. José (1878–1958). Professional officer who commanded the Madrid front of the People's Army and became the most famous of the Republican military leaders.

NEGRÍN LÓPEZ, Juan (1889–1956). Professor of physiology at the University of Madrid and Socialist leader. Served as Republican prime minister from May 1937 until the end of the Civil War, relying heavily on the Communists.

NIN, Andrés. Founder of the small Trotskyist Communist Left group in 1930–31 that later merged with the BOC to form the POUM. After the start of the Civil War was the principal leader of the POUM, which opposed Stalinist communism and urged all-out revolution. Kidnapped and murdered by the NKVD in 1937.

ORLOV, Alexander. High-ranking NKVD officer who served as chief of Soviet security and counterintelligence in Spain from September 1936 until his defection in July 1938.

PEIRÓ, Juan (1887–1942). The leading theoretician of anarchosyndicalism in Spain during the 1930's. Served as minister of industry under Largo Caballero in 1936–37.

PESTAÑA, Angel (1881–1937). One of the most influential leaders of the CNT from 1917 to 1933. Founded a less inflammatory Syndicalist party in 1933 that engaged in normal political activity.

PRIETO, Horacio. Secretary of the national committee of the CNT in 1936 and opposed anarchist incendiarism.

PRIETO Y TUERO, Indalecio (1883–1962). Leader of the moderate nonrevolutionary wing of the Spanish Socialist party. Served as minister of public works from 1931 to 1933, minister of the navy from 1936 to 1937, and minister of defense from 1937 to 1938.

ROJO LLUCH, Col. Vicente (1894–1967). Professional officer who served as chief of staff of the People's Army from 1937 to 1939.

SÁNCHEZ ROMÁN Y GALLIFA, Felipe (1893–1956). Eminent jurist and leader of the small National Republican party. Though ultraliberal, a strict constitutionalist who refused to join the Popular Front and failed in his efforts to encourage moderation and compromise between May and July 1936.

SEGUÍ, Salvador. One of the principal leaders of the CNT between 1917 and 1923 and the most influential trade-union chief in Barcelona during that period. Opposed anarchist terrorism. Murdered in March 1923.

The Spanish Revolution

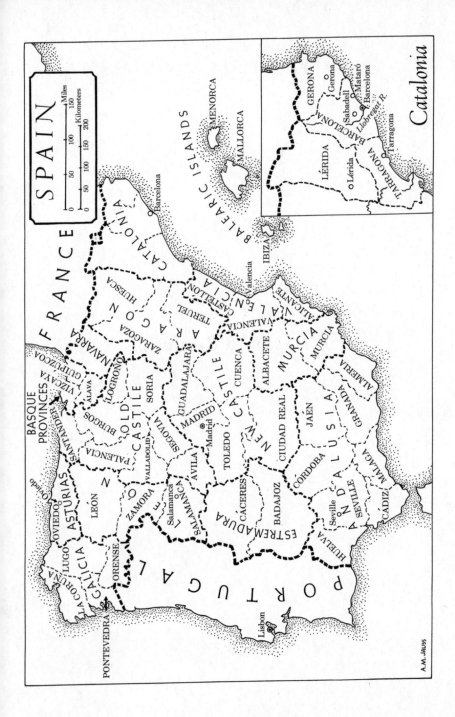

SPAIN

Miles
0 50 100 150
0 50 100 150 200
Kilometers

FRANCE

CATALONIA

Barcelona

BALEARIC ISLANDS

MENORCA

MALLORCA

IBIZA

Valencia

VALENCIA

CASTELLON

ALICANTE

TERUEL

ARAGON

HUESCA

ZARAGOZA

NAVARRA

GUIPUZCOA

VIZCAYA

BASQUE PROVINCES

ALAVA

LOGROÑO

SANTANDER

Oviedo

OVIEDO

ASTURIAS

LUGO

LA CORUÑA

GALICIA

PONTEVEDRA

ORENSE

LEON

ZAMORA

PALENCIA

BURGOS

OLD CASTILE

SORIA

VALLADOLID

SEGOVIA

MADRID

Madrid

GUADALAJARA

CUENCA

NEW CASTILE

ALBACETE

MURCIA

MURCIA

ALMERIA

GRANADA

JAEN

TOLEDO

AVILA

SALAMANCA

Salamanca

CACERES

ESTREMADURA

BADAJOZ

CIUDAD REAL

CORDOBA

ANDALUSIA

Seville

SEVILLE

MALAGA

CADIZ

HUELVA

PORTUGAL

Lisbon

Catalonia

GERONA

Gerona

Sabadell

Mataró

Barcelona

Llobrego R.

BARCELONA

LERIDA

Lérida

TARRAGONA

Tarragona

A.M. JAUSS

ONE *Social Tensions in*

Spanish History

T HE IDEA OF REVOLUTION has played a major role in modern secular utopian thought. As used in this book, "revolution" connotes drastic and usually violent changes not merely in the form of government, but also in the basis of political and economic power, in the organization of the economic system, and in the structure and values of society. The revolutionary idea has exerted particularly wide appeal in societies suffering severe crisis or profound obstacles to modernization. Its attractiveness has been enhanced by the decline of traditional religious conviction for, amid the resulting vacuum, some visionaries have sought to substitute the goal of an immanent, materialist utopia in modern society.

Events of the past century have shown that violent, thoroughgoing revolutions are probably only possible against comparatively weak governments and institutional systems based on relatively unproductive economies—that is, in nonwestern or at least nonmodernized countries. Conversely, even in times of great crisis, the type of radical solution to which modernized, industrialized countries have been likely to fall prey has not been a drastic, thoroughgoing "leftist" revolution that would profoundly alter the bases of government, economics, and society in the nominal interests of the lower classes. Rather, it has been a counterrevolution that promises to save most of constituted society and preserve national values. The fallacy of Marxist prophecy in this regard is now so well demonstrated by the examples of the countries of central and western Europe that it need not be belabored further. There have been, on the other hand, numerous examples of the relatively successful appeal to revolution as the route to accelerated development for backward societies under the aegis of authoritarian or totalitarian socialist systems.

Categories of "modernized" versus "underdeveloped" societies are purely relative, however. Compared with much of the rest of western Europe, most of Spain has been "underdeveloped" from the beginning of the Asturian monarchy in the eighth century down to the Franco regime in the mid-twentieth. The old saw that "Africa begins at the Pyrenees" would have it that Spain is not even a regular part of western civilization and so labors under a profound cultural handicap to modernization. But, in point of both geographical and cultural fact, Africa begins at the Strait of Gibraltar. Spain is a western country, yet it is a western country of a unique, peripherally distinctive kind. Spain has, with some lag, participated in all the religious, cultural, social, and economic developments of the western world (with the partial exception of the Reformation, which by no means swept all the West), but its participation has been individualized and incomplete.

Whether the relatively greater poverty and technical backwardness of Spain has resulted in greater social conflict than has been the case in the history of most western countries is not as yet altogether clear. Spanish historians, nationalists, and reformers are fond of harking back to what many of them like to describe as the "individualism" and "traditional democracy" of medieval and early modern Castilian society. Both these notions have been exaggerated, but they point to something important in Castilian social history, for it was true that in the Middle Ages the Castilian lower classes were somewhat freer than their counterparts in many regions of Europe. Classic medieval feudalism and serfdom never took root in Castile, in part because of the power of the monarchy—necessary to defend Christian territory from the Muslims—and even more because much of Castile was for long frontier territory and acquired something of the social characteristics of a military cooperative. To obtain volunteers to repopulate dangerous frontier districts, free land and relative social and economic autonomy had to be granted as well as, in some cases, the right of peasants to elect their overlord. As the Reconquest advanced, many new towns were founded with limited rights of self-government, and these communities played a part in the development of the first representative parliament in León at the end of the twelfth century.

Yet the effect of these conditions has frequently been exaggerated. Most Castilian peasants were technically free, and many communities enjoyed a fair degree of autonomy or at least had a strong sense of local rights and interests, but Castilian society did not clearly generate a modern notion of political constitutionalism. This society was in many ways a unitary one, whose members were so bound together by religious and cultural ties that they almost constituted a caste. Such increasingly intense, ultimately absolute, ethnoreligious identification resulted in a society with a strongly homogeneous ethos. Stress upon military values led to extreme overemphasis on the military style of life and the cavalier temper which provided its leadership, so that the aristocratic class achieved great preponderance in late medieval Castile. Eventually, with a greater degree of urban social differentiation and the development of more dynamic economic interests, an uncertain attempt was made to implant representative semiparliamentary government through the Comunero revolt of 1519–20. This attempt was choked off and never recurred.

Though middle-class elements in Spanish society have never been so few proportionately as many foreigners assume, they have not filled the same function as the enterprising middle classes of the more advanced regions of western Europe in the early modern period. They have customarily been more oriented toward status, security, and bureaucratic employment than their counterparts in northwest Europe. A sense of profit seeking has seldom been lacking in Spanish society, but the ideal of innovation and enterprise has been much rarer.

With the exception of a few large cities, the urban sector of the Spanish population was until the nineteenth century comparatively less significant than that of the northwest European countries. As late as the mid-nineteenth century, the peasantry comprised nearly 75 percent of Spanish society. Through the first third of that century well over half the arable land was held in *señorio,* or feudal economic domain, by the aristocracy and the Church. Only a very small portion was actually owned by the peasantry, but in much of northern Spain nominally large estates had for long been broken up into small family rental farms so that there already existed a sizable class of de facto smallholders. Hence the paradox that in northern "feudal" Spain a formerly partially enserfed peasantry came to constitute a relatively well-balanced rural society in the modern period.

The situation in much of the south was different. The large southern territories taken over in the great Reconquest of the thirteenth century were not resettled with partially autonomous peasant communities as in much of Castile. There most of the land was granted directly to the nobility, the Church, and the military orders, who turned their territory over to pasture or cultivated it in large units with hired laborers. In much of the south the new Castilian immigrants never had an opportunity to set themselves up as individual farmers, though for long this lack produced little resentment. At first farm laborers' wages were fairly high, declining only with the large increase in the southern population during the late Middle Ages. Before the sixteenth century part of the ordinary population had become a sort of rural proletariat, yet this development was not accompanied by the sense of servility or degradation that might be expected. The farm laborers of Andalusia and Extremadura were miserably poor, but they participated in the general ethno-caste sense of Castilian society and, like most of the Castilian lower classes, were given to imitating at least a part of the value system of the aristocracy. The fact that the Castilian nobility was itself an open group frequently broadened by new plebeian entrants helped discourage radical class resentment. Especially in the sixteenth century, a few of the more adventurous and lucky of the southern peasantry, who provided a disproportionate number of the followers of the American conquistadores, managed to climb to the top echelons of society. Moreover, conditions varied greatly from village to village and from estate to estate. Most towns still had *tierras concejiles* or common lands to relieve the plight of ordinary peasants.

Another set of conditions existed in northeastern Spain, in the lands of the crown of Aragon. Catalonia and Aragon were the only parts of Spain that developed a degree of feudalism equal to that of France. Similarly, only in Catalonia—and its sociocultural offshoot, Valencia—was there a fully active and resourceful urban society in the late Middle Ages. Medieval Catalonia was by far the most "European" part of Spain, and developed one of the most fully articulated and representative constitutions in late medieval Europe. But feudalization, urban growth, and the development of keen political consciousness were accompanied by considerable social stratification. In the countryside, aristocratic feudalization led to a greater degree of enserfment than in any other part of Spain save in the northwest.

The first major social revolts in Spanish history occurred during the fifteenth century. They constituted one aspect of the tensions attending the transformation of medieval society, having counterparts in peasant *Jacqueries* in France and the great religious and social rebellion of the peasantry in Bohemia. The Spanish revolts began with the rising of the *irmandades* (brotherhoods) of peasants and townspeople in Galicia to shake off the social and economic domination of the regional aristocracy. The main *irmandade* revolt took place between 1465 and 1469; its efforts to check the power of the upper nobility were encouraged by the Crown and supported by some of the lesser nobles as well. After the Crown eventually managed to impose order, most of the legal remains of feudalism were abolished, but the economic position of the peasantry improved only slightly. The peasants of Galicia have remained more impoverished than those of any other part of northern Spain.

A better known and more successful social revolt was the

"serf war," or *guerra de remenças,* that sputtered and sometimes
flared violently in Catalonia between 1462 and 1484. When it
began, over 100,000 peasants, more than one-fourth the total
population of Catalonia, were still restricted by vestiges of serfdom, a central aspect of which was the requirement to make
remença (redemption) payments for leaving the land, and which
might prohibit altogether the leaving of at least one son or
daughter. In addition, other sectors of the peasantry were still
subject to various kinds of feudal dues or requirements, known
colloquially as *malos usos.* When the Crown granted *remença*
peasants the right to form a syndicate to represent their interests,
some 60,000 signed up in a matter of months. Their demands
soon went beyond elimination of *remença* servitude and *malos
usos* to include revolutionary proposals of property division for
outright ownership by the peasantry. Meanwhile, the lower
classes in Barcelona and other large Catalan towns were carrying
on a vigorous struggle for democratization of municipal government. The Catalan civil war of the 1460's, like the Spanish
Civil War of 1936, was touched off by a resort to arms by the
upper classes in the face of a strong latent revolutionary threat
from the peasants and urban workers. The conflict was resolved
by the Crown largely in the interest of the lower classes. Through
the famous sentence of Guadalupe (1484), Ferdinand the Catholic
arbitrated a settlement that abolished *remença* payments and
most of the *malos usos* and renegotiated most peasant rental fees
at a moderate level. Municipal government in Barcelona was
also reformed to permit greater popular representation.

The *remença* struggle was paralleled by vicious class war in
the Balearics, mainly on the island of Mallorca. Most property
there was either owned or worked in small holdings, but population increase, commercial decline, shortage of credit, and
political and financial domination by the urban oligarchy had
placed the Mallorcan peasantry in severe straits by the mid-
fifteenth century. Their lands were saddled with an impossible
load of debt and were increasingly taken over by the upper
classes. The goals of the *foráneo* or smallholders' revolts of
1451–53, 1462–66, and 1521 were both political and social, aiming
at democratization of government and more egalitarian distri-

bution of property. Though the first rebellion was very nearly successful, taking over all the island save the capital, each was ultimately drowned in blood, bringing severe reprisals and no social reform.

Even more radical was the rebellion of the Germania of Valencia in 1519 and 1520. The Germania (brotherhood) was originally a militia group of the Valencian lower classes authorized by the Crown to help defend the coast from attack by Muslim pirates. It developed into a social revolutionary force which took over control of the Valencia region, insisted on the forced Catholicization of the local Moors and generated radical ideas about the division of property. The Germania defeated one royal army before it was put down by the Crown. In toto, the revolutionary movements in greater Catalonia constituted the most far-reaching struggle for change in their age, exceeding even the radical aspects of the Bohemian uprising—save in the religious dimension, in which the Catalans and their fellows were thoroughly orthodox. Not without reason have some Catalan historians suggested that the notion of revolution in the modern sense first emerged in late medieval Catalonia. Yet these outbursts were not paralleled in Castile—which contained 80 percent of the population of the Spanish kingdoms—except in the one frustrated effort of the Comuneros in the years 1519 and 1520.

During the imperial age of the sixteenth century, identification with the Crown and with the military aristocracy was general throughout most social classes and helped reduce any sense of conflict. Severe social strife did not reappear in Spain until the psychological and economic crisis of the seventeenth-century decadence. The Catalan revolt of 1640 was essentially a political rebellion; social conflict did emerge among the rebels, however, and ultimately weakened Catalan resistance to the Hapsburg Crown. In seventeenth-century Castile, social strife mainly took the form of blind, spontaneous riots—the "poor" against the "rich"—such as the outbursts at Córdoba in 1652 and a longer-lived rampage at Seville two years later. These sudden urban *Jacqueries* passed almost as soon as they came and had little organization or rationale: the trough of the Castilian economic decadence, which came in the early 1680's, was not marked by special social tensions. It possibly affected the lower classes less than the inflation of earlier years and was not interpreted as the result of any specific exploitation or manipulation. In most parts of Castile the relatively unitary sense of society survived fairly intact into the nineteenth century. Aristocratic values and adherence to tradition prevailed, for there was little to encourage identification with alternative goals.

The advent of the Bourbon dynasty and the subsequent phase of enlightened despotism had scant immediate impact on Spanish society. The peasant-artisan structure of the lower classes and their place in the economic system remained relatively unchanged until the latter part of the eighteenth century. The civil struggles of the Succession War (1701–14) seem to have had a social dimension only in Valencia and Catalonia—in the former region because of the dissatisfaction of the poorer sectors of the peasantry whose position had worsened during the preceding century.

The guild system of the urban artisan classes underwent little modification, though it was disappearing in the more advanced countries. The first textile factories were created by the Crown in Castile (1719) and by private enterprise in Barcelona (1738), but these efforts only began to form a modern proletarian nucleus in the Barcelona region in the last quarter of the century. Even in Catalonia, the typical male urban worker was a *menestral* (artisan) who usually owned his own tools and frequently held at least partial control of his business. Compared with earlier generations, most sectors of the population did not fare badly. Real wages of the urban working force declined significantly—by at least one-third—in the second half of the century, but this was a gradual process and for various reasons, not all of which are clear, does not seem to have been felt as sharply as one might expect. The experience was not unique to Spain, but was part of the effects of the general price rise in western Europe. The living standards of the peasantry seem definitely to have improved with the rise of agricultural prices, especially in the last third of the century. Though there were tensions between landlords and renters or laborers in several of the regions where properties were most poorly distributed, these did not become severe. The only direct urban labor disputes on record occurred in the royal textile factories at Guadalajara and Ávila, which housed two of the largest individual labor concentrations in Spain. The difficulties seem to have developed following efforts to increase the working day of the already comparatively well-paid textile operatives.

The most profound changes in modern Spanish social and economic relations were not effected by the pseudoabsolutism of the eighteenth century but by the liberal regime established after 1833. Parliamentary government under constitutional monarchy, together with the economic alterations brought in its wake, was almost exclusively the work of the upper and middle classes. It established the political rule of an oligarchy of fluctuating composition and removed many of the traditional barriers to individual enterprise. The right of entail was eliminated and seigneurial jurisdiction abolished, with almost revolutionary social and legal effects in the countryside. An across-the-board agrarian disamortization was gradually carried out between 1836 and the 1890's. This step involved forced confiscation by the state and sale or private distribution of nearly all the landed property of the Church as well as most of the municipal and common lands of the local communities—the latter having been held under communal ownership since the Reconquest. In Spain as elsewhere nineteenth-century liberalism initiated an individualistic *sauve qui peut* pursuit of personal profit. The lands opened up by disamortization were for the most part snatched off by middle- and upper-class people who had the capital and know-how to take them over. Though some of the municipal and common lands were originally divided up among the local peasants as private properties, comparatively little was retained by the rural lower classes, most of whom lacked the capital, training, or understanding to function as petit-bourgeois agrarian entrepreneurs. Altogether, approximately 35 percent of the arable land in Spain changed ownership during the long process of disamortization and, by the end of the century, nearly all the real property in the country was in private hands. The old rural oligarchy of the aristocracy had given way to a new semi-bourgeois oligarchy with even greater political and economic power.

There seems little doubt that the economic situation of much of the southern peasantry deteriorated. Population mounted more rapidly than ever before, but production and income scarcely kept pace. Much of the southern peasantry had no means of livelihood other than seasonal employment on large estates at minimal subsistence wages. Only a minority were able to take advantage of the new system as individual entrepreneurs, for even among those who owned a little land or farming equipment, it was usually necessary to seek alternative employment part of the time. These conditions, which were worst in parts of Andalusia, Extremadura, and La Mancha, gave rise to intense social resentment, which some commentators later called the "endemic socialism of Andalusia." What Andalusian peasants came to understand as "socialism" had nothing to do with collectivism, but simply meant the *reparto*—the equal division of land either as private property or on reasonable terms of rent. The first major explosions occurred in Seville province in 1857 and at nearby Loja in 1861.

It should be kept in mind, however, that, while nearly all the Spanish peasantry was poor and backward, conditions in most areas were not so bad as in the worst parts of the south. Even in portions of Andalusia and Extremadura, there were stable groups of smallholders, more satisfactory rental conditions, or a broader distribution of agrarian capital—at least in the form of livestock. In much of northern Spain, a little more of the disamortized land went into the hands of the peasantry, and the proportion of secure renters or smallholders was much higher, though again there were significant exceptions in provinces such as Ávila and Salamanca, where latifundia were more frequent. The northwestern region of Galicia was given over almost entirely to family farms, but mostly held on terms of *foros*, or leases, which in turn were subdivided (as *subforos*) into ever more tiny plots at proportionately higher rates as the population grew. The overcrowding of the land, the uneconomic size of units of exploitation, and the onerous terms of the *foros* left Galician living conditions scarcely any higher than in the worst parts of the south, save that in Galicia there was more security, a more dependable climate, and outlets in fishing and in emigration. Intensive, irrigated agriculture was practiced only in the east—in Valencia,

Murcia, and sectors of the Ebro valley. There the size of property was small and the rural population even more middle class in outlook than in parts of the north.

The urban population only began to expand rapidly after the 1840's, and was increased in part because of the pressure from underemployment and poverty in the countryside. Urbanization in Spain was not exactly a product of industrialization, but to a certain extent preceded it. By the middle of the nineteenth century the only region that had any significant industrial concentration was Catalonia, and this was still confined to the textile (largely cotton) plants in the area around Barcelona. Only in the greater Barcelona district was there anything that might be called a "proletariat" (in the classical sense of a capitalless working force employed exclusively by middle-class entrepreneurs). In the other larger cities the lower classes were still composed for the most part of petty artisans in small shops, not factory proletarians. The breakup of the guild system had, however, deprived the latter of the modicum of security they had earlier enjoyed. In Madrid there was a large servant and petty bureaucrat population.

Even by the standards of that day, the living conditions of the nineteenth-century Catalan textile workers were very low, lower than those of probably the majority of the Catalan peasant farmers who held long-term leases. But the great increase in the Catalan rural population during that century—an increase of more than 100 percent—made it impossible to absorb the excess population into the countryside, and left little alternative save the larger towns. The expanding Catalan textile industry of the mid-nineteenth century lived in mortal fear of French and British competition and recognized that by comparison its operations were relatively inefficient. Catalan enterprise was mostly small-scale family business built up by the most niggardly acquisitive practices. Turnover was small in any one enterprise, and capital for plant modernization was limited. To Catalan entrepreneurs industry was a very personal struggle in which they, the social elite of their region and country, had invested their life, sweat, and blood. To prosper, it was necessary to hold costs down and that meant keeping wages at a minimum. The notion that Catalan entrepreneurs looked on their working force as "subhuman" is somewhat exaggerated, for a fair number of entrepreneurs had risen from the artisan class themselves. But they did look on industrial relations as a strict business competition in which they could afford no concessions. Semiskilled workers and artisans normally drew fairly good wages so long as they had employment, but the women and children who at first made up the bulk of the textile labor force were paid mere pittances and had little alternative. Their real wages were probably lower than those of similar workers at Manchester and Lyons even in the blackest phase of British and French industrialization.

Even worse than the plight of the poorly paid workers was that of the new immigrants from the countryside, without skills and, except in boom periods, usually without obvious employment. The worst social problems were created not so much by the regular working force as by this lumpenproletariat, or "rabble," as the middle classes called the permanently semiunemployed. Vagabonds and beggars had constituted a social problem in Spain for at least four hundred years, but expanding rural population and disamortization greatly increased their numbers in the mid-nineteenth century.

Public affairs were almost exclusively the preserve of the middle and upper classes, but in years of political effervescence the more advanced liberals—the Progressives of the 1830's and 40's, the Democrats of the 1850's and the Federal Republicans of the 1860's and 70's—attempted to rally the urban lower classes round their banner. The rural population was almost immovable because of its ignorance, traditionalism, and political confusion. Its only initiative came from the conservative peasantry of the northeast who turned out in the tens of thousands for Carlism in the major civil wars of the century. Carlism championed the traditional authoritarian monarchy, traditional local rights, and church privileges in opposition to modern centralism and parliamentary monarchy. The Carlist peasants were opposed to anticlericalism, urban financial control, and the terms of the disamortization. The great bulk of the peasantry, however, stood by apathetically. Even the Progressives were opposed to universal suffrage, but it usually proved possible to mobilize most of the urban lower classes—mostly artisan—in support of the more advanced liberal causes in intermittent outbursts from the mid-1830's on.

During the First Carlist War, these outbursts gave way to bloody political and anticlerical riots in quite a number of the larger towns. The riots of 1835 to 1837 were not really so much an index of social war, however, as of the sharpness of political and ideological division in the country and, insofar as they had any goal or leadership, were used for the purposes of the basically oligarchic Progressives. Nonetheless, the turmoils of the decade 1833–43, followed by the larger European outbursts of 1848–49, frightened the possessing classes. Under the rule of the Moderates, a loose coalition of ultraoligarchic liberals from the upper-middle and upper classes dominated the government for most of the quarter-century 1843–68 and maintained rigid centralized control of politics.

Fray Magín Ferrer, one of the better Spanish social observers of the early nineteenth century, termed the lower classes a "passive people that knows no more than to keep quiet and obey and can only be moved for three goals: religion, the crown and the independence of the country." This judgment was largely correct, but by the middle of the century no longer applied to the urban society of the larger and more active cities. The first efforts to form workers' associations, or incipient trade unions, were among Barcelona textile workers in the mid-1830's. The first briefly successful trade union was an apolitical Mutual Society formed in 1839 that carried out two strikes and temporarily received legal recognition. In 1842 the city government of Barcelona helped it to borrow credit to establish a new collective textile factory. After the establishment of the Moderate regime, however, all workers' societies were banned (1844). The holding of a labor identification card was required in Catalonia and later for all Spanish industrial workers (1846), and the collective factory went bankrupt in 1848.

Several small workers' aid groups were formed in Madrid in the 1830's and 40's, but they were not genuine trade unions. The much smaller size of the industrial force in the capital, together with the concentration of political activity there, tended to divert the attention of the lower classes from economic issues per se. Both the Progressives and the subsequent Democratic party concentrated workers' attention on civil rights and the suffrage rather than on social reform.

Yet, as the labor force in the Barcelona region continued to grow in the 1840's and 50's, economic disputes and self-consciousness increased. There was much resentment against the labor cards, including a number of small quasispontaneous strikes, and the government and employers never managed to enforce the original decree. Among the remnants of the Barcelona and Valencia artisan class, resentment was particularly high against the new textile machinery and there were a number of Luddite-type outbursts in these two cities between 1835 and 1855, including the burning of Barcelona's most modern steam-powered cotton fabric factory in 1835.

The first major opportunity for worker organization came after the temporary overthrow of the Moderate regime in 1854. Even before the change of government, a major strike had been initiated against the most technologically advanced textile factory in Barcelona, which had been introducing new machinery and lowering wages. Feeling against mechanical looms or *selfactinas* (self-actings) was intense, and the strike spread to other factories and led to large street demonstrations. By the end of the year a major union, the Union of Classes, was organized out of the semisecret groups that had persisted during the previous decade, and soon numbered half the textile workers in Barcelona province. It demanded freedom of trade union organization, higher wages, and regulation of female and child labor and government initiative in forming labor arbitration tribunals. The semi-Progressivist government in Madrid took no action on these demands but instead eliminated most of the existing restraints on individual industrial enterprise and the importation of machinery. A wave of strikes in Barcelona was met by a series of lockouts. By July 1855, 50,000 workers—over half the industrial labor force—were on strike in Barcelona province. The government had authorized volunteer workers' welfare associations and was encouraging arbitration commissions, but it refused to legalize dues-collecting trade unions, and this soon became the major issue of the strike as demonstrating workers carried banners read-

ing "Association or Death!" In December 1855, 39,000 workers—
22,000 of them from Catalonia—signed a petition to the Cortes
asking for free trade unions to exercise moral and economic
suasion on employers, but the government refused.

The beginnings of organized worker activity in nineteenth-
century Spain were almost exclusively apolitical and economically
reformist, without ideological sectarianism or revolutionary overtones. Before 1868 there were only a few individual representatives of socialist ideology in Spain, and their contact with the
workers was minimal. Nevertheless, during the disturbances of
1854 and 1855, Catalan industrialists and some other Spanish
large-property owners were sure that they stood on the brink of
violent social revolution. During the post-1856 Moderate reaction,
the government took measures to dissolve even volunteer cooperative and welfare organizations in Catalonia (1861). By the
1860's, the country appeared to be securely in the grip of a small
middle- and upper-class oligarchy. The peasant majority was
cowed and mute, save in the Carlist regions, and the urban lower
classes were without organization or representation.

There was nothing uniquely Spanish in this situation, for the
general direction of Spanish social evolution through the mid-
nineteenth century paralleled the norm of western and central
Europe. What was different in Spain was the slower rhythm of
development, leaving much of the population in greater misery,
compounded by the absence of those autonomous groups that
provided meliorative facilities in England and a few of the more
advanced countries.

TWO *Origins of the Anarcho-syndicalist Movement*

NOMINAL PARLIAMENTARY DEMOCRACY was first introduced in Spain after the overthrow of the Bourbon dynasty in 1868. A new constitution written the following year provided for representative government on the basis of universal male suffrage. Under an Italian prince, the new system functioned as a constitutional monarchy from 1870 to 1873, when it collapsed from the effects of corrosive factionalism. Power was then seized by the Federal Republican movement, which proved unable even to control its own provincial groups. Under the Federal Republic of 1873–74 the country faced absolute chaos. As provincial capitals tried to proclaim complete autonomy, the Carlists rose in full-scale civil war and anticolonial revolt simmered in Cuba. Peace and order were finally restored when the Army brought back constitutional monarchy under the regular Bourbon dynasty. The constitution of 1876 provided for a parliamentary system based on limited suffrage, though not so narrow as that which existed prior to 1868.

During this period of democratization, confusion, and, ultimately, reaction, Spain's first revolutionary working-class movement was born. Its founders were several small nuclei of middle-class intellectuals and professional men, together with a few trade-union organizers. They were inspired by the First Workingmen's International, founded in London in 1864, and even more concretely by the semisecret International Alliance of Social Democracy, organized by supporters of the Russian anarchist Mikhail Bakunin in 1866.

The ideology of Bakuninist anarchism posited the goal of complete personal liberty, to be achieved through the total destruction of organized government and the existing social and economic system. Hierarchical authority and private wealth were to be replaced by free collective associations of workers that would federate on the regional, national, and international levels. Bakunin himself did not insist on a communistic form of organization for the new society: though all instruments of production were to be owned collectively, personal enterprise and differential rates of income were not to be prohibited. The main difference between the new society and the old would be the absence of coercion: no one would be forced to join the collectives, and each local group would be free to conduct its affairs unhindered. Harmony would be achieved by equality and cooperation for, when rightly instructed, all men would realize that no one could be free and happy unless all enjoyed the same freedom and opportunity.

In addition to abolishing the state and capitalism, the anarchists were determined to destroy religion and all feelings of exclusivist patriotism. They stressed repeatedly that men could not be free until they had overthrown the tyranny of priestly authority and outworn myths. Noncoercive collectivism would also liberate men from the deceptions of patriotic antagonisms engendered by the state and the upper classes, so that universal brotherhood might be realized. Altogether, anarchist ideology was soon being summarized by the capsule formula: "In politics —anarchist; in religion—atheist; in economics—socialist [or collectivist]."

Anarchist doctrine was very explicit concerning tactics, for everything save direct revolutionary action was rejected. Anarchist groups would not participate even in the functioning of parliamentary democracy, for the latter was held to be merely another more sophisticated form of political and economic oppression. The existing system, they believed, had to be destroyed through direct action—which meant strikes and violence on a large scale. Later, after the first anarchist effort had failed, the doctrine of "propaganda by the deed"—individual acts of terrorism and assassination—was accepted by some anarchist circles. Many anarchists came to hold that acts of revolutionary violence had a profoundly moral quality, for they dramatized social oppression, revealed the personal commitment and self-sacrifice of anarchists, and hastened the day of revolution.

Anarchist proselytizers at first drew more attention from artisans, intellectuals, and professional men than from the rather small Spanish urban working classes, but they gained a foothold among the latter as well. After the government granted freedom of association in 1868, Spanish trade unions expanded rapidly. In Catalonia, where three-quarters of the trade union members were located, some 195 shops representing nearly 25,000 workers were organized within a year. The problem for anarchist agitators was that Spanish trade unionism, or syndicalism, was for the most part nonideological, nonrevolutionary, and oriented toward economic reformism. In Barcelona many workers were influenced by the individualist philosophy of the Democrats and their successors, the Federal Republicans, who were becoming the only important popular force in the towns of eastern and southern Spain. In 1869 one of the most active anarchist leaders, Rafael Farga Pellicer, wrote that the majority of Catalan workers were hostile to the notion of revolutionary collectivism, which they considered a denial of individual freedom. Indeed, it seems that a majority of the members of the first anarchist group in Barcelona were Andalusian immigrants from the artisan and middle classes. Yet within the next few years the doctrine of spontaneous, apolitical revolutionary activity began to win converts among a minority of trade union leaders and some of their more militant followers. A number of the nominally moderate trade unions of Barcelona eventually joined the anarchist-dominated Spanish section of the International.

The Spanish Regional Federation of the Workingmen's

International was officially organized in 1870 at a congress in Barcelona attended by representatives of some 15,000 unionists, nearly half of Spanish organized labor. One month earlier small groups of intellectuals and workers from cities of eastern and southern Spain had formed a separate anarchist Alliance of Social Democracy, whose purpose was to assure anarchist predominance in the establishment of the Federation. This goal was achieved, for the Barcelona congress adopted a basically anarchist program that pledged abstention from regular political activity with the aim of completely destroying the existing politicoeconomic order.

The term "anarchist" was not in common use among members of the Spanish Federation when it was formed, and the explicit doctrine of anarchosyndicalism was not propagated until after 1900, but the main features of the twentieth-century anarchosyndicalist movement were present in the Spanish Federation of 1870. Structurally, the Spanish Federation was to be composed of craft syndicates, each of which was to federate on the national level. The union of all the craft federations made up the Spanish Federation as a whole, but each craft syndicate was nominally autonomous and not under the control of the Federation's national committee. Though the subsequent theory of the great revolutionary general strike had not yet been clearly formulated, strikes by the sections of the Federation were to be an important weapon in destroying the existing system, so long as strikes were used for revolutionary goals and not for mere collective bargaining. Finally, although it was not officially recognized, the actual cement that held the nonauthoritarian trade union Federation together was the tutelage of the anarchist Alliance, which was able to control most policy decisions of the Federation leadership. Henceforth such direction by a special anarchist elite became characteristic of the syndicalist movement in Spain, and was continued by the regional anarchist groups of the next generation and the organized Iberian Anarchist Federation (FAI) of 1927, which dominated the syndicalist movement in the 1930's. Elitism is an inevitable quality of violent revolutionary movements, for little can be accomplished by mass proletarian spontaneity, no matter what the claims of ideology may be. Bolshevism later solved the problem by the fiction of "democratic centralism"; the anarchists persistently tried to counterbalance the organizational weakness of libertarian syndicalism by private committees of anarchist purists, who pulled the strings. In the early 1870's, the Spanish Federation, with a growing syndical base, comprised the largest revolutionary group within the First International. Later, in September 1872, following the split between Marx and Bakunin, the all-anarchist international congress declared its approval of "the Spanish [form of] organization, which is the best to date."[1]

By that time the Spanish Federation had approximately doubled its following, thanks in large measure to the fact that it had decided not to make agreement on all doctrinal points a test of membership. Recognizing that many—perhaps most—syndicate members did not understand or accept the full anarchist revolutionary program, the 1870 congress had decided that members would be free to participate in the existing political system on an individual basis if they so desired. Hence a large proportion of the Federation's rank and file actively supported the Federal Republican movement, which was socially reformist but essentially lower middle class and not a proponent of economic revolution.

The social and political failure of the democratic monarchy (1870–73) encouraged radicalization. The functioning of the parliamentary system was perverted almost before it began; Federal Republicans rose in armed rebellion as early as 1869, while the middle-class liberals in control of government had no intention of losing power to the left, either by fair means or foul. Fraud, discrimination, and intimidation by strong-arm gangs was common.

During the abortive Federal Republic that followed, many members of the Spanish Federation played an active role in the regional cantonalist rebellions, which were partly inspired by the Paris Commune. Yet the Federation's leaders never endorsed the new regime. Their position, as expressed by *La Federación* of Barcelona, was to reject any kind of political compromise by means of parliamentary government and any kind of reformist

1. Maximiano García Venero, *Historia de las Internacionales en España* (Madrid, 1956), I, 217.

economic arbitration. The Federal Republic was termed "the last bulwark of the bourgeoisie," and was supposed to give way to a direct revolutionary confrontation with the possessing classes in which the winner would take all.

Despite its rapid growth between 1870 and 1873, the Federation was completely unable to organize itself as an effective force. It aroused intense fear and hatred among the middle-class parties, and the restored monarchy of 1875 drove it underground. After a few years, little more than a hard core of fanatics remained in most areas where the Federation had formed syndicates. Yet the skeletal structure, the ideas and sympathies, remained. The network sprang back to life repeatedly during the four decades that followed, until it finally emerged as a powerful mass movement.

The persistent strength of anarchosyndicalism in Spain can best be discussed in terms of the structural and cultural characteristics of certain parts of the country, and also in terms of the eventual failure of liberal representative government under the restored constitutional monarchy of 1875 to 1923. The failure of parliamentary liberalism in Spain is one of the major unexplored problems of modern western European history. The most common explanation is that liberal government in Spain was a fraud, dominated by boss rule, electoral corruption, and oligarchic exploitation of the economy. That description, if correct, makes Spain sound like much of Britain, France, and the United States during a large part of the nineteenth century, yet these are the only large countries in the world in which liberal representative government has been successful. In fact, the negative qualities so frequently mentioned have characterized most modernizing countries. Instead of wondering at their presence in Spain, it might be more useful to inquire how Spain compared with other countries at similar stages, and what was unique in the Spanish situation.

From this point of view, it might be argued that a primary difficulty experienced by Spanish liberalism was that it was induced prematurely. Whereas the economically and culturally powerful German middle classes were unable to take over the government of their country until after 1918, a small middle-class elite imposed a liberal parliamentary system in Spain before

society was prepared to sustain it. Spain enjoyed nominal universal male suffrage from 1869 to 1874 and after 1889, though
at first nearly two-thirds of the adult population was illiterate.
In no large country of the western world was political democracy
introduced at so early a stage of civic development.

Thus it is not altogether surprising that under the constitutional monarchy public affairs were dominated by an oligarchy and political activity mostly controlled by local bosses
(caciques). In most parts of the country elections were rigged with
little protest from the citizenry. It is certainly true that dissidents
were excluded, discriminated against, and occasionally beaten up
by hired thugs, particularly in the early years, but it is not at
all clear that such practices were followed where the dissident
minority was as large as 10 or 15 percent. Whenever a sizable
minority of local voters showed a determination to have responsible elections, it became very difficult, and eventually impossible,
to rig the contests. Even in Barcelona, however, no more than
25 percent of the electorate showed interest in voting until after
the turn of the century. In some provinces, the local political
leaders and bosses were genuinely accepted by the majority
of people as representatives of local interests, and in many
others they were tacitly accepted without a struggle by a society
in which mutual concern and cooperation beyond the family
group was not a strong cultural value. Caciquismo was a corollary
of Spain's level of civic development in the latter part of the
nineteenth century.

The fundamental questions are why the political system
subsequently showed less capacity to reform itself than did those
of more successful countries, why it failed to incorporate broader
segments of the population after 1900, and why it was unable
to muster talent and energy to face social and economic problems
more effectively. Initially, the two alternating parties (Liberals
and Liberal Conservatives) represented most, if not all, of the
major economic interests of the country. After the turn of the
century, with increased industrialization in the north and more
rapid urbanization in other centers, they became less and less
representative. The two established parties ceased to grow, stagnating at the level of rural and small-town politics of the 1870's

and 1880's. With their leadership mortally divided by personal and factional disputes, they relied on the allegiance of the rural and small-town middle classes, who were morbidly concerned with security and status. The growth-oriented middle classes of the north and east increasingly turned against the two established parties, though they were not strong enough to supplant them. Instead of finding allies to support their interests, they split along regional lines (especially in the cases of Catalan and Basque nationalism) or simply withdrew into political abstention. The industrial and progressive north and east were severely out of phase with the conservative, rural center and south, yet not sufficiently united or politically creative to take control of the country. The unequal rhythm of development, regional separatism, and intense social division within individual regions, along with a profoundly subjective personalism that has been deeply imbedded in Spanish character and militates against civic cooperation, sapped the strength of the Spanish middle classes and made it difficult for them to act successfully as a modernizing elite. The question of timing was also important. The expansion of the working-class movement into mass proportions occurred after 1917 when the Spanish economy had still made only modest achievements in industrialization. The working-class movement sometimes clashed with other reformist sectors and was handicapped in serving as a force for constructive change because it made radical demands drawn from the examples of the most advanced countries. What might conceivably have been a powerful reformist coalition was splintered between Republicans and reformist monarchists, rival regionalists and radical working-class movements. Largely as a consequence, the two official parties of the 1870's—though split by a myriad of internal factions, out-of-date in their programs, and ineffective as instruments of legislation and leadership—continued to dominate the seats of parliament until, to the relief of much of the population, the parliamentary system was finally suspended by military coup in 1923.

Anarchosyndicalism eventually gained a strong foothold in parts of a society living under the theory of liberal democracy and individual civic freedom but never achieving the substance of it. The Spanish economy had adjusted to a system of capitalist individualism. Yet, despite a slow, steady increase in living standards for most, it had not developed the industry and technology to realize the full benefits which the system was supposed to bring. In a more completely backward society anarchosyndicalism might have been less appealing, but Spanish society was far enough evolved to have developed the ideal of personal freedom and plenty without reaching the degree of complexity that might have discouraged simplistic revolutionary notions of how to achieve it.

In Catalonia, however, only a minority of organized labor was influenced by anarchist doctrine until after the turn of the century. Probably no more than half the Barcelona syndicates joined the Federation in the early 1870's, and under the restored monarchy independent nonpolitical trade unions were left alone so long as they did not cause much trouble. The 1876 constitution recognized the right of association, though not the right to strike, and in 1877, 22 moderate syndicates in Barcelona organized themselves as a Federative Center of Workers' Societies with the main goal of winning government recognition of the labor regulations that had been passed under the Federal Republic. During the following decade the Barcelona Center expanded, and the local textile workers' industrial union (the Tres Clases de Vapor) became the only really effective trade union in Spain. It numbered 14,000 by 1890 and provided the best—for long the only —workers' medical insurance system in the country.

During the first fifty years of the revolutionary syndicalist movement in Spain, its real base was not among the country's only large industrial proletarian force, the Catalan workers, but among the landless peasants, renters, sharecroppers, and smallholders of Andalusia. In the late nineteenth and early twentieth century, Spain offered the only example in Europe of a semiorganized mass peasant revolutionary force. The appeal of revolutionary anarchism to the Andalusian peasantry is usually explained in terms of the latter's poverty and ignorance. In a general sense, this is more or less correct, but care must be exercised not to overgeneralize about Andalusia as a whole, for the region contains widely varying social and economic districts. While some sections are abysmally poor and sub-European, there are parts of other provinces where the peasant standard of living is much higher, as in certain districts of Córdoba, Seville, and Granada.

Though sizable sectors of the Andalusian peasantry were in miserable circumstances, so were millions of peasants in eastern Europe among whom revolutionary syndicalism never developed. It is important to remember the atmosphere of partially frustrated freedom and expectation created by Spanish liberalism in the nineteenth and early twentieth centuries. The possessing classes of Andalusia had played a major role in the development of minoritarian parliamentary government in Spain, perhaps because the region's economic backwardness helped them assume disproportionate power in their local districts. It might also be remembered that even in the Middle Ages the Andalusian lower classes had been legally free of serfdom and had fully developed the sense of personalism so strong in Spanish history. Economic backwardness, social frustration, nominally advanced politicojuridical instructions, and rising expectations all combined to encourage radical discontent.

There is little doubt that the rudimentary nature of anarchist collectivism as propagated by unsophisticated agitators was well adapted to the social psychology of illiterate peasants who were capable of great bursts of enthusiasm but lacked tenacity to pursue complex social endeavors. The messianic notion of the revolutionary *reparto*—even though peasant understanding of it rarely approximated Bakuninist orthodoxy—was much more satisfying emotionally than tedious Marxist teachings of slow economic transformation. Anarchist agitation seemed to suggest that little more was needed to inaugurate the millennium than syndical solidarity and a farm laborers' strike.

The role of revolutionary syndicalism as a substitute religion was also important among relatively simple people no longer influenced by the Church. Much of the peasantry lived in a great spiritual void and was filled with social and economic resentment against the clergy, who were identified with the upper classes. The revolutionary myth gave them a new object of faith, however vague, and a means of channeling social hatreds in a legitimized fashion. For the *obreros conscientes,* or awakened, responsible workers, the moral teachings of anarchism replaced the moral doctrines of religion in encouraging chastity, seriousness, and the avoidance of alcohol. By the turn of the century, as anarchist doctrines spread farther and assumed more eccentric forms, anarchism also took the place filled by faddism and cultism in more advanced countries; a minority of followers of the movement began to embrace notions of vegetarianism, or, in larger towns, free love.

Since even the middle classes tended to regard politics as corrupt and unworthy, it was not surprising that illiterate peasants embraced an apolitical creed. The lure of revolutionary syndicalism was all the greater because it not merely denied the need for political work, but largely eschewed any sort of precise planning and organization. Even at the heights of activist frenzy, peasant syndicates remained poorly organized. They rested more on a common social psychology of solidarity than on disciplined membership; their strength lay much more in mystique than in technique. In the great peasant strikes of the early twentieth century, there was almost no rational planning of strike activity and goals. The revolutionary apocalypse was left to do its magical work almost unaided by human hands or brains. It was largely for this reason that, despite the support of tens of thousands of peasants, revolutionary syndicalism in Andalusia could never become a serious menace to the established order.

It should not be concluded, however, that revolutionary peasant syndicalism was the blind reaction of a miserable helotry. Peasant syndicalism was usually stronger in the more prosperous sectors, often with a little capital of their own, than among the poorest peasants. Strikes ordinarily occurred in times of prosperity, as in most countries. In his classic work on Córdoba province, Juan Díaz del Moral has shown that the movement was strongest in areas where conditions were improving rapidly in the early twentieth century. By contrast with more prosperous Córdoba and Seville, the movement was extremely weak in some of the most wretched parts of Andalusia, such as Almería. And, as mentioned in the previous chapter, the doctrine of revolutionary collectivism never really sank in among the peasants. Almost all of them believed that the triumphant revolution would bring the individual *reparto,* a democratic disamortization, not collective farming. Andalusian peasant syndicalism was not a slave revolt, but part of the revolution of rising expectations.

In 1881 the Spanish government removed the ban on opposition organizations and the fragments of the former Federation reorganized themselves as the Federation of Workers of the Spanish Region (FTRE), reaffirming their revolutionary program. The FTRE claimed more than 50,000 members, two-thirds of them in Andalusia. The renewal of the movement, however, raised serious questions of tactics and principles. The main controversy was between Catalan syndicates that wanted to emphasize the economic goals of trade union activity and the leaders of the Andalusian groups who stood for the apocalypse. Another question was the exact relationship of the genuine anarchists to the syndicalist movement, whose mass organization, however decentralized, conflicted with the theoretical beliefs of many individualist anarchists. Moreover, the FTRE, like its predecessor, did not make explicit anarchist doctrine a test of membership and hard-core anarchists feared that their creed would be submerged by mere reformism. The question of reformism and/or organized political activity versus apoliticism and "direct action," and the question of the relationship of individualist anarchism to organized syndicalism troubled the movement throughout its turbulent history. In 1883 the worst fears of hard-core anarchists were realized when a general congress of the FTRE at Valencia officially announced its willingness to work within the bounds of legality so long as these permitted the achievements of the working classes' aims.

The hopeful phase of the FTRE lasted only three years. Alarm over a serious strike in Cádiz province, which followed the murder of two informers by local anarchists (the much-exaggerated "Mano Negra" affair), led to severe police repression that broke up most of the flimsily organized syndicates in Andalusia. Only the separate anarchist cells survived intact, ready to submerge and spring back again when opportunity permitted.

In urban Spain living conditions improved slowly during the 1880's. After the Barcelona stock market crash of 1886, wages ceased to rise in most industrial areas but prices for some commodities were declining and comparative living conditions in the textile and metallurgical centers may have continued to improve until a marked downturn in wages occurred after 1900. Most urban workers' syndicates associated with the FTRE were wanting in militancy, and in 1888 the Federation was dissolved. During the last years of the century, Spanish trade unions remained autonomous local organizations that in most cases devoted themselves to practical problems and were free of ideological overtones.

Local anarchist cells put together a new Anarchist Organization of the Spanish Region, affiliated with the anarchist International Workers' Alliance that had been formed in London in 1881. The Anarchist Organization lacked a syndical base, but tried to maintain contact with syndical groups through loose "Pacts of Union and Solidarity." Local peasant riots or strikes flared almost yearly in parts of Andalusia, but lacked consistent organization and comprehensive goals.

Discouraged by the difficulty of mobilizing active support, anarchist circles in the late 1880's and 1890's concentrated their energies on two tasks. Their primary activity was propaganda, for in the anarchist concept of human nature men do evil primarily because of ignorance. Once they have been told the truth, they are supposedly set free and can scarcely fail to respond. Hence, the anarchists put massive effort into propaganda in the late nineteenth and early twentieth centuries. The historian García Venero has counted at least 19 different journals or weekly papers published by Spanish anarchists in the 1880's, and these were supplemented by a steady stream of thousands of pamphlets and simple hortatory tales. Printed labors were accompanied by the personal and verbal prosleytization of anarchist agitators who worked directly among illiterate Andalusian peasants or Catalan workers. During this period anarchist propaganda was also influenced by the publications of French anarchist culture, which helped to raise somewhat its theoretical and intellectual tone.

The second notable aspect of anarchist activity in the 1890's, even though carried on by only a handful, was "propaganda by the deed," or direct terrorism. The last part of the nineteenth century was the heyday of anarchist terrorism throughout Europe; in geographical extent it reached from St. Petersburg, where a Tsar was assassinated, to Buffalo, where an American president was murdered. Belief in the efficacy of terrorism was present as a theoretical value in the anarchist movement from the beginning. The first efforts to assassinate the king of Spain occurred in 1878 and 1879, and sporadic acts of fiery economic sabotage were common from that time on. But it was not until the 1890's that the anarchists employed systematic murder in the wave of bomb-throwing in Barcelona between 1893 and 1895. The goal was to kill symbolic figures of authority or, failing that, to destroy members of the upper classes in general, so as to terrorize the existing order into accelerated collapse. The incident that aroused greatest horror was the throwing of a bomb onto the crowded main floor of the Barcelona opera house; a score of people were killed. The city was placed under marital law for months, since Barcelona, like large urban centers in Spain and elsewhere, had grown very rapidly and lacked the facilities to cope with its problems. The police were comparatively few in number, poorly organized, and inefficient. On the other hand, a pamphlet in 1894 claimed that in Barcelona there were 300 hardcore anarchist cells (or conversation groups?) with a following of several thousand people. Unable to identify exactly and repress the anarchist activists, the police—and then the military authorities under martial law—began to pull in ordinary trade union militants with whom anarchists were known to have contacts. Few of the guilty were arrested, but a good many trade unionists, whose only crime was association with the anarchists, were imprisoned and sometimes tortured. The brutality of prison conditions in Barcelona was widely publicized and sometimes exaggerated. It was nominally in revenge for the Barcelona repression that the Italian anarchist Angiolillo assassinated Cánovas del Castillo, the prime minister and architect of the restored constitutional monarchy, in 1897.

The events in Barcelona had a fateful effect on social relations and the subsequent history of the working-class movement in Catalonia, for they substantially widened the gulf between working-class people on the one hand and the authorities and "respectable society" on the other. To that extent, the whole series of episodes constituted a victory for the anarchists in their effort to split society and bring it to the edge of cataclysm. Work-

ers afterward did not easily forget how all proletarian elements
had been lumped together and brutalized by the police.

This was the more fateful and ironic in that the first significant steps toward social reform were being taken by the Spanish
government during this period. In 1887 charitable and mutual-
assistance activities of unions were finally given complete legal
authorization. Jury trials for many offenses were introduced in
the Spanish courts the following year. A modest law requiring
that workers be given small indemnities for certain kinds of industrial accidents was approved in 1900, and a royal decree of 1901
recognized the right of railroad personnel to strike in terms that
implied similar recognition for most other Spanish workers. An
attempt was made by the government to create local labor arbitration councils in 1908, but this effort was not completed. In the
following year the Conservative administration carried through
full legal recognition of the right to strike by unions, so long
as the latter were properly registered and gave several days' notice
of their intentions. The same law also recognized employers'
rights to call a lockout. Parliament had set up a committee to
investigate social problems early in the 1880's, and in 1903 this
was given official status as the Institute of Social Reforms. During
the next twenty years it collected a great deal of information
on social problems and helped to encourage new regulations. In
1908 a National Insurance Institute was created to foster local
efforts.

By the beginning of the twentieth century the urban labor
force in Spain was still proportionately smaller than in most other
western countries, but it was slowly becoming the major déclassé
group in the country. Though the three-quarters of a million
urban workers were somewhat less numerous than the total number of landless rural laborers in Spain, the urban proletariat
was much more concentrated, more easily aroused and organized,
and in a stronger position potentially to assert its influence.

Yet, with the possible exception of the mining and metallurgy industry in the Basque provinces, the Spanish industrial
expansion of the late nineteenth and early twentieth century
was still in the small-shop phase and had not graduated to the
large-scale, concentrated industry to be found in the United

States, Germany or even Great Britain, and (in some instances) Russia. There were definite similarities between the pattern and rate of development of France, Italy, and Spain. France obviously led the way among the Latin countries and revealed more complex patterns by 1910. Italy came second, while Spain was a lagging third.

An earlier trend toward concentration in Catalonia's principal industrial sector—textiles—was never completed. Most of Catalan industry was dispersed amid a multiplicity of small shops. The personalized conditions of Catalan shops, which only slowly overcame the artisan phase of production, obviously made it easier for the anarchist form of syndical action, with its emphasis on the individual and the local unit, to strike root amid workers in times of major social conflict. Moreover, despite a somewhat higher general standard of living than in the rest of Spain, Catalan workers were not well educated, even by Spanish standards. Throughout the early twentieth century, the literacy rates in Barcelona province and neighboring regions were lower than in the stable, conservative, lower-middle-class rural provinces of northern and north-central Spain, where land and capital were fairly evenly divided. As complex, highly organized heavy industry began to develop in the Basque country and Asturias, anarchists had notably less success in influencing the working-class movement there than they did in Catalonia.

At the turn of the century a considerable divergence of emphasis was evident in Spanish anarchist thinking. Some hard-core anarchists would have nothing to do with syndicalism. Some were interested only in plotting magnicide, while others relied on vegetarianism and meditation. Ricardo Mella, one of the most widely read theorists, recognized the justice of private property cooperatives in his *La cooperación libre* (1900). The main trend, however, was in the direction of anarchosyndicalism, a doctrine given its most coherent formulation by French revolutionary theorists. The intent of anarchosyndicalism was to provide a way of organizing mass support for revolution. Anarchist individualism was forced to recognize the need for syndical organization in order to forge an economic weapon. The organizational goal of revolutionary anarchosyndicalism was to bring together all the working class in trade unions, not for collective bargaining and economic improvement—which was held to be absolutely futile under capitalism—but to give the workers control of the economy. Trade unions formed by spontaneous worker initiative on the local level would federate together regionally and nationally, and their actions would be coordinated by regional and national committees chosen directly and indirectly by a series of workers' assemblies and their representatives on each level. Strikes might be employed, but only as a means of direct action, to increase the workers' strength and raise their morale, not for mere financial improvement. The final weapon of anarchosyndicalism was the great revolutionary general strike that would cripple the entire economy and transfer power to the workers. Once that had been achieved, the temporary contradictions involved in syndical organization would be resolved and free individual association would reign. The new society as envisioned by the anarchosyndicalists of the early twentieth century differed somewhat from that of the anarchists of the 1870's, for the doctrine of "libertarian communism" won increasing acceptance. This doctrine went somewhat farther than Bakuninist collectivism in proposing commnual ownership of all tools and capital, and equal distribution of all rewards. But there was some disparity of opinion among theorists as to how rigidly communal and equalitarian libertarian communism must be. More important was the continued stress on noncoerciveness, for each person was to be free to join or leave a libertarian commune as he preferred, and each commune was to be autonomous vis-à-vis its fellows. Though anarchosyndicalism relied on violence in consummating this revolution, it never posited a transitional "dictatorship of the proletariat."

During the first years of the twentieth century, several abortive efforts were made to form new regional syndical organizations. A number of local general strikes were attempted. None achieved much success, though, in spite of the intentions of some of the strike organizers, the strikes did occasionally score an economic triumph for the workers.

Aside from the small trade union group associated with the Socialist party, the first enduring effort to draw together a regional labor federation occurred in 1907, when 70 Barcelona craft unions joined in a new organization called Worker Solidarity. It was not a specifically anarchosyndicalist group, and its avowed aim was to advance the social and economic interests of the workers while avoiding political involvement. The leaders of Worker Solidarity came from various sectors: some were anarchists, some were Radical Republicans, a few were Socialists, and others were trade unionists pure and simple, but the first two elements predominated.

The organization had been founded in part as a working-class response to the union of moderate and conservative middle-class Catalanist groups of Catalan Solidarity, which swept the 1907 elections in Catalonia. If the latter was the main regional enemy of Worker Solidarity, the main competitor was the well-organized Radical Republican party led by Alejandro Lerroux. The Radicals were a vulgar, violent, demagogic group who appealed to democratic republicanism and anticlericalism in order to attract lower-class votes. They paid some lip service to social reform and maintained a series of "Houses of the People" in working-class districts to serve as community centers. By the spring of 1909 Worker Solidarity had only 15,000 members, whereas the Radicals polled 20,000 votes in working-class districts during municipal elections. There were 88,000 male industrial workers in Barcelona province, but little more than 15 percent belonged to trade unions.

The business recession of 1908–09 brought new hardships for some of the syndicates in Worker Solidarity in the form of lay-offs and wage reductions. As conditions worsened, trade union leaders became more receptive to the notion of attempting a general strike. In this situation there occurred a callup of reserves for the Spanish Army's colonial duties in Morocco. Radical leaders, anarchists, and trade union chiefs seized the opportunity to proclaim a general strike, which the Radicals quickly diverted toward incendiary anticlericalism. The result was Barcelona's "Tragic Week" of July 1909, in which one-third of the city's churches and monasteries were set ablaze and more than 100 people killed in street fighting.

In the aftermath, the anarchosyndicalist elements won control of Worker Solidarity and took the lead in calling a national workers' congress in Barcelona in 1910. Most of the representatives in attendance came from Worker Solidarity, and by a heavy majority agreed to set up a National Confederation of Labor (CNT) to be composed of all syndicates regardless of ideology that were willing to join. It was recommended that affiliates pay dues of from 30 to 50 *céntimos* per week. Regular strike funds were not, however, anticipated, for anarchosyndicalist ideology precluded the use of the strike as a nominal economic weapon and collection of money might weaken reliance upon direct action.

The anarchosyndicalist tone of the founding congress of the CNT was made clear in its formal resolutions that the Confederation had been formed

to hasten the integral economic emancipation of the entire working class through the revolutionary expropriation of the bourgeoisie, as soon as syndicalism is strong enough numerically and intellectually prepared to carry out the expropriation . . . and provide for the subsequent direction of production.

Another accord stated that "the general strike must be essentially revolutionary" and "violent," specifying that

A general strike should not be called to win an increase in wages or a slight reduction in the working day, but only to achieve a total transformation. . . . The strike will be general in the true sense of the term, when all the workers of the entire country lay down their tools at the same time. . . .

Yet the emphasis on the general strike was substantially modified in the same resolution, which went on to declare that

Nevertheless there are cases in which the bourgeoisie or the government force the workers to declare a general strike in a certain locality or region [alone]. In these situations the local committee is authorized to resolve the problem and determine how far the strike should be extended. . . .

In the future, political leaders who assault any one of our sister federations with armed force will be met not by tears but by the resolute action of the entire Confederation. It is not necessary to define future policy precisely, for the road must be left open to carry out the strongest and most vigorous protest, according to the scope of the injury.[2]

2. Maximiano García Venero, *Historia de los movimientos sindicalistas españoles* (Madrid, 1961), 345–48.

Between 1908 and 1910 the anarchosyndicalists had taken over the major part of the working-class movement in Spain's principal industrial region. They would never entirely lose control of it until finally ground down by military defeat in 1939. A unique feature of the CNT was that it was a working-class movement founded almost exclusively by working-class people. Few middle-class intellectuals were associated with Spanish anarchosyndicalism, which had a crude, anti-intellectual, decidedly proletarian tone.

Labor disputes reached a new high in urban Spain during 1911. Though the CNT specifically disavowed partial strikes, its member syndicates soon found themselves involved in quite a number of them. In October 1911 the organization was outlawed by the Spanish courts as a subversive organization and was not allowed officially to reconstitute itself for four years. In the meantime, a new effort was made to federate the revolutionary peasant syndicates of Andalusia; the resulting National Federation of Agricultural Workers of Spain was ultimately absorbed into the CNT in 1919.

The second decade of the twentieth century saw the height and incipient decline of revolutionary peasant syndicalism during the socalled *trïenio bolchevista* of 1918–20. The commercial prosperity enjoyed by neutral Spain during the First World War brought profits to many landowners, but trapped farm laborers in an inflationary price squeeze. News of revolutionary Russia aroused veritable ecstacies among Andalusian anarchists in 1918–19. They took seriously Bolshevist propaganda about "all power to the Soviets," which they interpreted as libertarian assemblies. "All land to the peasants" and similar slogans made it sound as though the great revolutionary *reparto* had finally been completed on the other side of the continent. Bolshevist agitation was nonexistent in the Andalusia of 1918, but the contradictory economic situation that was developing in Spain, combined with news from abroad, revitalized the energies of village anarchists.

Peasant strikes in 1918 diverged from the anarchist norm by demanding moderate, concrete economic goals, many of which were won. These victories built excitement and enthusiasm for more extensive activity in 1919, which coincided with the largest industrial strikes seen thus far in the northern towns. Yet, true to form, the great agrarian strikes of 1919 lacked unity and clear revolutionary goals, despite the euphoric expectations of many participants. Martial law was declared in parts of Andalusia but as it turned out there was no widespread violence. Andalusian peasant syndicalism, unlike its urban counterpart, had little stomach for political murder, and the authorities also acted with relative restraint. Perhaps a score of people were killed in the south, nearly all in individual shootings. The "farm burnings" that took place consumed mostly hayricks, not farmhouses. The government used coercive, though not brutal, tactics to end the strike and several thousand syndicalists were arrested, including even a few members of anti-revolutionary Catholic peasant unions.

There was nothing "Bolshevist" about the "Bolshevist triennium" in Andalusia but the name. Possibly as many as 150,000 peasants participated in the strikes, but the volume dropped off greatly in 1920. Though peasant conditions improved slightly, the general scheme of things remained the same. Despite widespread fears among the middle classes, anarchosyndicalism was unlikely to become an effective revolutionary force among largely illiterate peasants. Its future depended primarily on its success among the industrial workers of the northeast.

THREE *The Social Struggle in*

Barcelona, 1917-1923

D URING THE FIRST QUARTER of the twentieth century, Catalonia was the focus of political and social attention within Spain. Its small territory contained the most active sector of the Spanish middle classes and the most powerful part of the working-class movement. After 1907 official Catalan politics were largely dominated by middle-class regional nationalists, organized under the Lliga Regionalista, probably the only Spanish political group of its time with a modern party structure. The goals of middle-class Catalanism were to wrest regional autonomy from the centralized Spanish parliamentary system, protect and advance the region's economic interests, and encourage the modernization of Spain. To the main group of middle-class Catalanists, the working-class movement was a menace that divided Catalan society and, if it should gain enough strength, would threaten the existing structure of Catalan industry and commerce. When the CNT swelled into a mass movement, the stage was set for revolutionary confrontation.

During the four years that the organization was officially outlawed, individual CNT unions remained active. A Barcelona textile strike in the summer of 1913 took at least 24,000 workers off the job and prompted a Royal Decree from Madrid that reduced the work week in the textile industry by 10 percent to a maximum of 60 hours. Similar regulations had already been decreed for the mining industry.

Catalan textile manufacturers were infuriated by the government's "illegal coercion" and considered countermeasures. They began to perceive that revolutionary syndicalists and Socialists had hope for eventual victory if they could organize the working classes, for Spanish capitalists and industrialists were not well organized and had difficulty acting in concert. Medium and large-scale landowners in most parts of Andalusia were similarly disunited; they had hastily to throw together provincial resistance groups in the face of mass peasant strikes. Though several regional associations of entrepreneurs joined to form a Spanish Employers' Confederation in 1914, this organization did not generate strong support, and small producers and shopkeepers were even more poorly organized. Spanish entrepreneurs were not accustomed to spending time and money on cooperative professional endeavors unless faced by dire necessity. Employers' associations thus tended to be local and limited, for these groups lacked the money and influence of their American, German, or even French and Italian counterparts.

Although the Barcelona police had maintained since the 1890's a special "political section" to deal with the activities of anarchists and trade unionists—whom they tended to lump together—they had never been notably successful or efficient. Between 1902 and 1909 they failed to apprehend any single one of those responsible for some 40 bomb explosions in the city—a failure which led the left to charge that such deeds were the work of provocateurs who sought to provoke animosity against the left. At any rate, in 1913 the local Barcelona employers' association decided to supplement the political section by setting up a private employers' police squad which was immediately labeled "murderers' band" by the CNT. Since the first anarchist wave of the 1890's the Barcelona police had compensated for their inefficiency by periodic brutality, dealing bloody beatings and occasionally more refined mistreatment to syndicalist prisoners. The new employers' police was charged with further excesses toward CNT militants that resulted in at least one death.

Though the economic effects of the First World War brought Catalonia the greatest prosperity it had ever known, it eventually left domestic tragedy in its wake. After most west European industry was diverted to war production, Catalan producers found themselves swamped with export orders. Industrial activity in this region and certain other parts of Spain reached previously unimagined heights. Employment rolls expanded dramatically as thousands of illiterate and semiliterate ex-peasants were pulled into new jobs. Wages increased, but not so rapidly as profits and prices. By 1916–17 profiteering in Barcelona and other key centers was enormous, and conspicuous consumption was flaunted by middle-class nouveaux riches on every hand.

TABLE 3.1 *General Spanish Price and Wage Index, 1913–22*

	Men's wages	Women's wages	Price index	Normal length of working day
1913	100	100	100	10 hours
1914	98.2	93.8	106.9	10 "
1915	107.4	100	113.8	10 "
1916	107.8	105.3	120.3	9–10 "
1917	110.6	108.4	136.1	9–10 "
1918	125.6	135.1	161.8	8–9 "
1919	146.9	135.1	180	8 "
1920	179.3	167.9	202.6	8 "
1921–22	207.1	167.9	193	8 "

SOURCE: Instituto de Reformas Sociales, *Movimiento de los precios al por menor durante la guerra y postguerra 1914–1922* (Madrid, 1923), in Albert Balcells, *El sindicalisme a Barcelona (1915–1923)* (Barcelona, 1965), 170.

Economic prosperity was accompanied by considerable maldistribution of income in which many sectors of the lower and lower middle classes suffered. Army officers felt the stress as much as many others, and responded by forming independent "juntas" that placed heavy pressure against the government. These conditions encouraged renewed efforts toward far-reaching political reform. Leaders of the Catalan Lliga and other small liberal groups called an independent assembly in Barcelona in mid-1917 to reform the Spanish constitution. But the reform movement of 1917 was supported mainly by middle-class Catalans and lower-middle-class Republicans from the more active cities of northern and eastern Spain. It failed to carry a majority of the middle classes, and government remained in the hands of the established cliques. Similarly, when the small Socialist movement attempted a revolutionary general strike (as will be seen in the next chapter), it could not rally broad support. Even the CNT responded halfheartedly.

By bringing rapid expansion of the working class, wartime prosperity enabled the CNT to become Spain's first proletarian mass movement. By 1918 the urban working class had become the largest single social group in Catalonia, outnumbering the peasantry in an individual region of Spain for the first time. Crowded conditions, new economic pressures and opportunities, and the active labors of syndical organizers brought a notable rise in working-class self-consciousness. During 1918 the CNT's membership in Catalonia shot up dramatically. It is not possible to give precise membership totals for any date in the CNT's history, because of the organization's loose, locally autonomous structure, but by the end of that year the Catalan sector of the CNT may have numbered 200,000 or more—approximately one-third of the region's total labor force. This growth was made possible in part by the decision taken at the June 1918 meeting of the CNT's Regional Confederation of Catalonia to adopt the organizational form of the *sindicato único*—the "sole" or industrial union—to enroll all the workers in a given industry regardless of craft specialty. The expansion was also the result of increasing use of strong-arm tactics in union organization, but the *sindicato único* proved so effective that at the close of 1919 the CNT adopted it as the mandatory form of organization for the entire movement.

The 1918 congress of the Catalan Regional Confederation reaffirmed the CNT's "obligatory" commitment to "direct action" whenever possible, but in fact there was considerable diversity of views among Catalan *cenetista* leaders and militants concerning ideology and tactics. The two main forces in the CNT were the anarchosyndicalists and those who propounded a less violent course of revolutionary syndicalism. The genuine anarchosyndicalists had little or no interest in what would be normally thought of as trade union activity; for them the syndicates existed only as vehicles for mobilizing large numbers of workers for "direct action" against capital that would ultimately bring total conflict, a general strike, and successful revolution. Because of their militancy, the anarchosyndicalists had always held a central place in the CNT. Prior to 1918, however, they had not been joined by all the hard-core anarchists of the local anarchist clubs and cells of Catalonia, some of whom could not reconcile mass syndicalism with individualist anarchism. A general conference of anarchosyndicalists and individualist anarchists was held at Barcelona in October 1918 to resolve the problem, and there was wide if not unanimous agreement to accept the means of syndicalism to achieve anarchist revolution.

The other main element in the CNT leadership, the revolutionary syndicalists, agreed with the anarchists on the ultimate goal of a revolutionary transformation to achieve a decentralized, confederated society of free collectives and communes, but opposed the constant stress on direct action and bloody, all-or-nothing conflict with capital. The revolutionary syndicalists placed great value on the syndical organization in its own right and wanted to use strikes and syndical unity to achieve practical improvements in the short run, believing that a successful revolution would be impossible until the syndical movement had developed the maturity, training, and scope that would enable it to assume the direction of society. The chief revolutionary syndicalist, Salvador Seguí, was the most influential labor leader in Barcelona from 1917 to 1923.[1]

1. Victor Serge has penned a graphic portrait of Seguí at the time of his participation in the abortive revolutionary strike of 1917:

> A worker, and usually dressed like a worker coming home from the job, cloth cap squashed down on his skull, shirt-neck unbuttoned under his cheap tie; tall, strapping, round-headed, his features rough, his eyes big, shrewd and sly under heavy lids, of an ordinary degree of ugliness, but intensely charming to meet and with his whole self displaying an energy that was lithe and dogged, practical, shrewd, and without the slightest affectation. To the Spanish working-class movement he brought a new role: that of the superb organizer. He was no anarchist, but rather a libertarian, quick to scoff at resolutions on "harmonious life under the sun of liberty," "the blossoming of the self," or "the future society"; he

Despite all the rhetoric expended on the "individualism" exhibited by the Spanish anarchosyndicalist movement, the CNT membership was, like nearly all Spanish groups, a mass that exhibited considerable conformity and little in the way of independent ideas save among the top leadership. Among the grass-roots union membership and even among the lowest echelon of leaders, however, might be found a great many people most easily identified as simple trade unionists, with only the haziest sort of ideas about a different kind of society, but concerned to achieve a better future and support their fellow workers. As the Catalan anarchist José Prats wrote in 1919:

> The masses easily give up two pesetas in dues for "the cause," but have no clear idea what that is. There is a great deal of shouting, but little understanding or none at all. Generally the masses are moved because a small minority [*unos cuantos*] pushes them forward, but are not impelled by internal convictions. Hence the ignorance, contradictions, lack of logic, mistakes, vacillations and fumbling. The masses are both heroic and herdlike, rebellious one day and submissive the next. In general, the syndicalist masses are like all mass groups, in which strong individual personalities are not very numerous. . . .[2]

Hence the hard-core anarchists and activist anarchosyndicalists espoused a consciously elitist theory no less willful than that of Russian Bolshevists, according to which it was the duty of the self-identified anarchists to lead, and if necessary to force, the syndicalist mass toward the cause.

At the end of 1918, with the CNT leadership still teetering uncertainly between serious syndicalism and anarchist incendiarism, the organization launched a nationwide propaganda campaign that coincided with a new membership drive and increased strike agitation. The government responded by suspending constitutional guarantees, shutting down the CNT's official news-

---

presented instead the immediate problems of wages, organization, rents, and revolutionary power. The anarchists would not hear any talk of the seizure of power. They refused to see that if the Comité Obrero was victorious, it would be the Catalan government of tomorrow. Seguí saw this, but, afraid of starting a clash of ideas that would have isolated him, dared not talk of it. And so we went into battle, as it were in the dark. *Memoirs of a Revolutionary 1904–1941* (London, 1963), 56.

2. Quoted in Palmiro Marbá, *Origen, desarrollo y transcendencia del movimiento sindicalista obrero* (Barcelona, 1931), 8.

paper, *Solidaridad Obrera,* closing some syndical headquarters, and arresting a number of key leaders.

The opposition of Catalan employers to revolutionary pressures was axiomatic, but they showed only slightly greater willingness to accept labor reforms of a moderate and practical nature. At the beginning of 1919 most of Spanish industry was still riding the wave of wartime prosperity; the export decline did not become serious until the second half of 1920. Industrial profit margins were large enough and the attitude of public authorities flexible enough to have permitted sizable gains in wages and working conditions. Syndical leaders in Barcelona pressed a minimum program that included retention of all previous wartime benefits, as well as an eight-hour day, injury compensation, reforms in the treatment of juvenile employees, and full recognition by all employers of the CNT syndicates. As was frequently the case, revolutionary anarchosyndicalists accepted these goals, not because of their concern to raise the workers' living standards, but simply as agitational incentives to spur the workers into direct confrontation with employers. The first big strike of 1919 against the power industry in Barcelona (the *canadiense* strike) expanded into a general industrial walkout under conditions of martial law. It resulted in a victory for the CNT, which won several concrete demands, including recognition of the union shop in Barcelona.

After the initial settlement, however, the military authorities in Barcelona refused to release without trial a dozen CNT leaders who had violated the terms of martial law. This issue, which might have been settled by negotiation, provided the anarchosyndicalists with the opportunity to bring the CNT out in a general strike at Barcelona on March 24. It lasted nearly three weeks, and was seconded for shorter periods in a number of other Spanish cities. Contrary to anarchist ideology, some of the syndicates were able to pay modest strike allotments during the first week of this walkout. Employee censorship also enabled the CNT to control briefly what was published in some newspapers.

Meanwhile, the government responded with steps of its own to improve workers' conditions. On April 3 parliament passed a bill making a maximum eight-hour day mandatory in Spanish industry on October 1, 1919. A seven-hour day was subsequently decreed for coal mines. On May 13 the government directed that measures be taken to encourage the creation of local "mixed commissions" representing labor and management to solve disputes.

The general strike in Barcelona was not a success. Though the CNT in this period normally collected dues of 10 *céntimos* per month, these were not enough to build up large strike funds. Normally payments were made only to the families of militants who had been arrested; otherwise the custom was to take up special collections among syndicates or in towns whose workers were not on strike to assist those off the job. The CNT's tactics were not equal to a prolonged general industrial strike, and lack of funds brought most Barcelona industrial workers back to their shops by mid-April.

TABLE 3.2. *Incidence of Strikes in Spain, 1916–29*

	Number of strikes	Workers on strike	Number of days lost
1916	237	96,882	
1917	306	71,440	
1918	463	109,168	
1919	895	178,496	
1920	1,060	244,684	7,261,762
1921	373	83,691	2,802,299
1922	484	199,417	2,672,567
1923	465	120,568	3,027,026
1924	165	28,744	604,512
1925	181	60,120	839,934
1926	96	21,851	247,223
1927	107	70,616	1,311,891
1928	87	70,024	771,013
1929	96	55,567	313,065

SOURCE: Spanish Ministry of Labor, Commerce, and Industry.

But the general strike of the spring of 1919 was a turning point, for it showed the strength of anarchosyndicalist influence in the CNT. Economic reforms were considered secondary, resulting in the loss of some of the wage gains made during the past year. The attitude of Catalan employers hardened; they determined to break the CNT. A general federation of Barcelona industrialists (Federación Patronal Barcelonesa) was organized through the initiative not so much of the older, established entrepreneurs as of the owners of the smaller wartime-built factories, many of whom were from the lower middle class or even in some cases were former skilled workers. The nouveaux riches were easily threatened and had no intention of losing their new-found status and prosperity. A Catalan financial crisis in mid-1919 shrank industrial and commercial credit, and increased the anxieties of the entrepreneurs. Many Spanish employers had been enraged by the new labor legislation passed in the Cortes, and there were strong protests against the government's decision to be affiliated with the new International Labor Office in Geneva. When conflict occurred with Barcelona construction workers, a lockout was declared which spread to other industries. By August 1919 over 100 firms in the Barcelona area were idle and at least 40,000 employees were out of work. From that point the situation steadily deteriorated.

Police pressure against the syndicates often resulted in the arrest of some of the most prominent and responsible union leaders, leaving their places to be taken by anarchist agitators who more successfully eluded the police. Moreover, the *sindicato único* industrial union form of organization had swamped the more moderate and practical skilled workers with a larger number of unskilled quasi-illiterates who were more easily stirred up to follow a radical line. From the middle of 1919 the Catalan CNT was increasingly dominated by anarchosyndicalist radicalism that relied on terrorist methods. Syndicalist writers and sympathizers have customarily presented events in Barcelona between 1919 and 1923 as the result of brutal harassment by the police and employers which forced the CNT to take justice into its own hands. Foreign commentators, most of whom are favorable to the left, have often taken these claims at face value, though the facts of the situation were not so simple.

Barcelona experienced intermittent disorders throughout the nineteenth century and seemed to breed its own self-sustaining ethos of revolutionary violence, but the number of attacks on persons increased steadily after the great riots of 1909. Though the customary CNT justification for what Spanish criminologists of the period called *atentados sociales* [3] was revenge against police and employer brutality, the majority of the victims were neither policemen nor employers. Most of the assaults by CNT strong-arm men were made on antagonistic workers who refused to be carried along by revolutionary syndicalism. In this respect the pattern of anarchosyndicalist terrorism resembled that of nationalist terrorists in Cuba (1895–98), Algeria, or Cyprus who chose the greater share of their victims from among their own compatriots who refused to support them.

In 1917, when tension mounted, a new head was appointed for the political section of the Barcelona police department. This man, Francisco Bravo Portillo, became the most controversial figure in the Catalan social struggle. It is not clear that Bravo was personally committed to any one goal or cause; circumstantial evidence leads to the conclusion that he was probably a corrupt psychopath out for all that he could gain. So long as the World War lasted, the most lucrative single source of bribery in Barcelona was the German secret service, which carried on a large-scale propaganda campaign through mercenary sectors of the press and was eager to disrupt the Catalan economy, one of the main sources of Entente supplies among the neutral powers. The subsequent judicial investigation refused to release its evidence, but the best-informed sources largely agree that Bravo accepted bribes from agents in the German consulate to collect information on shipments from the port of Barcelona and to carry out acts of provocation in Catalan labor relations. To this end he organized a private gang of gunmen paid for by German money.

German agents were also subsidizing the other side. At one point in 1917 the mouthpiece of the CNT, *Solidaridad Obrera,* accepted regular payments from the Germans, who were as willing to foment revolutionary outbursts in Catalonia as in Russia. Moreover, corrupt CNT leaders were bribed to hire gunmen to murder Catalan industrialists. The most spectacular incident was the killing of Antonio Barret, a Barcelona factory

3. Literally, "social crimes," but "political crimes" would be a more accurate equivalent.

owner who manufactured mortars for the French Army and was an ·outspoken pro-Entente liberal.

Reprisals against the CNT were then carried out by Bravo Portillo's private gang, which also levied extortion on local businessmen. Operations of the gang were not fully exposed until a more dedicated group of revolutionaries took over direction of *Solidaridad Obrera,* rejected further overtures from German agents, and published a detailed account of Bravo Portillo's relations with the latter.[4] This and other evidence was so damning that Bravo was suspended and then placed under arrest in June 1918. Yet powerful influences in Barcelona felt that they could not afford to have any part of the police discredited. Some of the evidence was suppressed; the trial was suspended and Bravo was released on "provisional liberty." The only measure taken to improve the police was to expand the Somatén, a militia of middle-class Catalan volunteers that helped maintain order in times of severe disturbance.

Meanwhile, CNT terrorism began to take the form of professional organization. By 1918, if not before, some CNT leaders were paying special gangs of *pistoleros* out of union dues to carry out "reprisals against" or to "make examples of" employers, policemen, strikebreakers, and in many instances ordinary workers who refused to go along with the *sindicatos únicos.* One of the most responsible of the revolutionary syndicalist leaders, Angel Pestaña, later concluded that the increase in terrorism could be traced to three main factors: the anarchist tradition that had taken deep root, the callous attitude of employers, and the Russian Revolution.

We who occupied positions of responsibility in the CNT in that period and saw how the idea of assassination gained ground in our group, poisoning the youth with completely mistaken ideas about what could be achieved by such acts, know how much young people in the CNT were influenced by the news about the Russian revolution that arrived in Spain.[5]

4. Angel Pestaña, the new editor of *Solidaridad Obrera,* later wrote that Eduardo Ferrer, head of the CNT metallurgists' syndicate and the man responsible for arranging the Barret murder, was subsequently slain by CNT gunmen for betraying the organization. *Lo que aprendí en la vida* (Madrid, 1934), 172–74.
5. *Ibid.,* 166.

According to Manuel Buenacasa, the secretary general of the CNT in this period, by 1919

half a million dues-payers were filling the syndicate treasuries in Catalonia alone. The ambitious, the hotheads, the criminal saw that the time had come to turn things to their own profit. Thus we all soon found ourselves caught up in a whirlwind, unable to control the profiteers and opportunists who dominated the situation. Then began the murder on a large scale of employers, foremen, policemen, and scabs, the organization finding no way to prevent unnecessary violence being converted into a system. Very few of the thousand or so terrorist deeds carried out in Barcelona could be termed "revolutionary acts." The syndicates simply could not get rid of the gunmen who were soon demanding a wage for their "work" and even in a few scattered instances managed to take over the leadership of important syndicates. Then there followed with vertiginous haste court prosecution of the most eminent and responsible leaders of anarchism and the worker organization, whom the courts had in almost every case to release for lack of evidence. But that is explained by the fact that the police, who could not identify the real authors of terrorist deeds, simply arrested the comrades most conspicuous for their advanced ideas. Therefore the CNT which, in the beginning, with a little courage on the part of its [more responsible] anarchist elements, could have prevented so much damage by energetically facing up to the gangsters who dishonored it, later found itself forced to defend the worst crimes, because the majority of those accused were innocent.[6]

Pestaña explained that

If the organization never really met to plan the *atentados,* everyone [in it] was convinced that the authors of the *atentados* were paid and protected by the organization and that their victims fell after having been marked for the gunmen by those interested in their death. There were isolated instances in which this was not the case, but these were the minority. Most of the killings were paid for at so much per head.

The usual arrangement was an agreement between the "action group" that charged for its deeds and a group of two or three individuals, sometimes only one, who gave the orders.

However hard or painful it may be for us to admit it, we must state that the men who did the killing—the moral authors, who induced them, and the material authors, who pulled the triggers—came from our midst, lived in anarchist and syndicalist circles, were visible members of our organization and enjoyed in the general opinion of the workers as much respect and consideration as anyone might deserve.[7]

6. *El movimiento obrero español, 1886–1926* (Barcelona, 1928), 78–79.
7. *Lo que aprendí en la vida,* 79–80, 163.

In September 1919 a colonel of the Civil Guard named Arlegui was appointed police chief in Barcelona. Shortly before, Bravo Portillo had been reappointed "special agent," giving him opportunity to reorganize his private gang, which was well subsidized by the Employers' Federation. With the approval of police authorities and many industrialists, Bravo's henchmen took the offensive against the CNT, and the rate of violence increased. As Pestaña said, this escalation (*primer desdoble*) or "second phase in the period of terrorism was inaugurated by the employer class," though "to be strict in telling the truth, we must confess that this was the means used by employers to oppose the terrorism of the working class." [8]

The series of lockouts imposed by Catalan employers in 1919 and 1920 were as effective as the strong-arm tactics of union organizers in increasing CNT membership still further. If workers were reluctant to pay their modest dues, these were forcibly extorted in public view, and in a meeting on October 15, 1919, one CNT spokesman boasted that the organization had already paid out 428,000 pesetas in strike benefits that year, including 57 pesetas per week for the families of those in jail. Police reports indicated that some CNT leaders preferred partial strikes affecting only specific industries rather than general strikes because the former enabled them to collect dues from workers still on the job. [9]

By the latter part of 1919 most CNT leaders had lost hope of any immediate chance to engineer a nationwide general strike, because of the government's use of martial law, resistance to the CNT in industrial areas outside Catalonia, and the manifest weakness of the French left, with whom Spanish anarcho-syndicalists were in frequent contact. The more practical business leaders in Barcelona urged that a distinction be made between the anarchists and syndicalists in the CNT, in order to work constructively with the latter. Furthermore, on October 11, 1919, the government approved a law requiring *sindicación forzosa,* or organized labor representation, throughout Spanish industry.

8. *Ibid.,* 80.
9. Manuel Burgos y Mazo, *El verano de 1919 en el Ministerio de Gobernación* (Cuenca, 1921), 460.

What this law actually required was vague, and no machinery was provided to assure its execution. Yet, even though sizable sectors of the Spanish economy would remain untouched by labor organization for years to come, measures such as this did help to take the initiative from the strong-arm organizers of the CNT.

The uncertain balance between compromise and violence in the CNT was affected by the obvious efforts of national and local government to play fair with labor during the summer and fall of 1919. Moreover, the fact that middle-class political opinion tended to place much of the blame for the existing disorder in Catalonia on the Catalan industrialists themselves, and the regionalist politics which the latter supported, was also a factor in encouraging the moderates to try to see that the CNT did not overplay its hand. Finally, on November 2, Barcelona CNT leaders signed an accord under local government auspices promising to act within the bounds of legally authorized syndical activity, if the Employers' Federation would do likewise.

The Employers' Federation replied that the *sindicatos únicos* had already violated a previous agreement to postpone further complaints and work stoppages until after the proposed mixed arbitration commissions began their work, and declared a general lockout in Catalan industry save for food and public services. This lockout began on November 3 and lasted 19 days, further solidifying the ranks of much of Catalan labor in a closed, hostile attitude. When the Undersecretary of the Interior complained that most of the workers thus made to suffer were innocent of any wrongdoing, the Employers' Federation replied that, next to the anarchists, the government was most at fault:

Let it be known that the employer federations will not change their attitude until the sacred responsibility of government power rests on men capable of exercising it without any other ideals than the well being and tranquility of the fatherland, placed in grave peril by the subversive action of all the political parties without exception, since they all contributed to converting the function of government into the indulgence of shameful appetites.[10]

10. García Venero, *Internacionales*, II, 287–88.

When the moderate reformist government then in power at Madrid collapsed, its successor lacked vigor and support to deal with the social struggle. After another outburst of bombings, the lockout was resumed three days later on November 25.

The main achievement of CNT gunmen during those months was the killing of the police counterterrorist Bravo Portillo. His murder, however, did not break up the provocateur gang, for a new figure stepped forward to take it over. This was the nefarious "Baron Koenig," a German national of Belgian origin and a Barcelona underworld figure, who had worked as agent for both the Germans and the Entente during the war. He had gotten in touch with Bravo Portillo and the strong-arm clique while engaged in espionage in 1917 and retained his contacts. Yet when he took over the gunmen's gang of the "employers' police" in the fall of 1919, he did not enjoy the confidence of the Employers' Federation to the extent that Bravo had. He soon resorted to crude extortion, which led to the breakup of the gang and his expulsion from the country early in 1920.

The Employers' Federation developed a new tactic by supporting antianarchist militants among the workers. Since the mid-nineteenth century there had been a handful of ultra-Catholic pro-Carlist worker associations in Barcelona, and in 1919 the Carlists claimed to be administering approximately twenty small labor centers in that province. Many of the small minority of religiously devout workers could not stomach the militant atheism of anarchosyndicalism and its encouragement of private "rationalist schools," while others rebelled against the violent monopoly of labor and forcible collection of dues imposed by the *sindicatos únicos*. On October 10, 1919, approximately 100 ultra-Catholic workers assembled in a Carlist center in the Barcelona suburbs to form a new syndicate similar in structure to the Catholic trade unions of Belgium. They decided to eliminate official religious statements from their statutes in order to gain broader support and were soon joined by an independent association of cooks and waiters. The new group was officially registered with the authorities as a Sindicato Libre (Free Syndicate) on December 11, 1919. Its proclaimed goals were opposition to capitalism and practical action to improve the condition of workers. It approved strikes and boycotts but rejected sabotage and terrorism.[11]

But the Sindicato Libre had great difficulty making headway in the turbulent atmosphere of Barcelona. Its organizers were mostly men of mature years, in contrast to many of the young anarchosyndicalist leaders and militants who were in their twenties. Some who joined them already had records as "scabs" or were for other reasons on bad terms with the CNT. The fact that the Employers' Federation soon showed interest in smoothing the path of the new group seemed only to confirm the suspicion of *cenetistas* that the anticapitalist program of the Sindicato Libre was mere pretense. There were frequent clashes between Libre activists and CNT toughs, and the Employers' Federation indicated willingness to contribute to a defense fund to protect the Sindicato Libre, which soon was able to organize its own squads of gunmen to deal with those of the anarchists. *Pistoleros* on both sides were drawn from approximately the same elements of the Barcelona underworld. Moreover, both the CNT and its enemies were infected with double agents, and charges of provocation were doubtless sometimes true.

During the winter of 1920 the incidence of terrorism increased. After an apparent attempt on the life of Felix Graupera, the ex-worker nouveau riche head of the Employers' Federation, martial law was again declared in Barcelona on January 9, 1920, and later extended to other provinces. When the employers' lockout was lifted on January 24, the CNT declared a general strike in Catalonia.

After severe economic losses for both sides, which were sometimes harder on small businessmen that on workers, an uncertain economic peace returned to Catalan industry in the spring of

11. There were already at that time two different Catholic trade union movements in Spain, but neither was represented in Barcelona. One group was begun by Severino Aznar and the social reformist priests Maximiano Arboleya and Antonio Vicent in 1913, and officially reorganized in 1919 as the Confereración Nacional de Sindicatos Católicos. A smaller group, led by the Dominican monks Pedro Gafo and Pedro Gerard, placed less official stress on religion and was called the Sindicatos Católicos-Libres. It later fused with the Sindicato Libre movement in Barcelona. The Confederación Nacional de Sindicatos Católicos enjoyed only limited success and may never have had more than 50,000 members.

1920.[12] Yet the volume of terrorism rose, not merely in Catalonia, but in other large urban centers—Bilbao, Madrid, Seville, Valencia, and Zaragoza. By 1920 a general citizens' militia was organized in several northern provinces on the model of the Catalan Somatén to help maintain order and basic services during strikes. But it proved impossible to control the violence by normal police action. In Barcelona there had been 107 "political crimes" during 1919, with 22 deaths. In 1920 there were approximately 300, bringing 57 fatalities. Of the latter, 23 were anti-CNT workers, 5 were *cenetistas,* 15 were employers, and 14 were police or unaffiliated persons. Very few people were arrested for these assaults and, of the handful apprehended, only eight were convicted, all receiving comparatively light sentences. Juries in Barcelona refused to convict for fear of reprisals against themselves and their families, and the structure of constitutional justice broke down. The place of the now defunct "employers' police" in counterterrorism was taken by the gunmen of the Sindicato Libre, heavily subsidized by the Employers' Federation. Hard-core anarchist activists set up several special anarchist groups in Barcelona (Los Solidarios, El Crisol) and other towns to provide unity and direction in their constant struggle against reformist syndicalists within the CNT so that the stress on violence and revolutionary goals would be maintained.

Most of the political bosses and factional leaders who dominated the Cortes (national parliament) in Madrid were men of moderately liberal spirit, willing to concede mild reforms and not displeased to see Catalonia, whose middle-class regionalism had only recently been creating severe political stress, completely distracted by its internal labor problems. The national government made feeble gestures of conciliation toward the syndicates in the spring of 1920. During the summer, however, strikes and disorders spread into mining areas and large cities outside Catalonia. The cabinet was reorganized and a hard line imposed. In August 1920 the jury system was temporarily suspended in Barcelona to expedite prosecution of terrorists. Three months later the national government accepted the Army's ouster of the civil governor of Barcelona province and ratified

12. See tables in Appendix to this chapter. pp. 59–61.

the appointment of the local garrison commander, General Martínez Anido, in his place.

As chief civil authority in Barcelona, Martínez Anido completely endorsed Arlegui's police policy. Within a matter of days most of the top CNT leaders were arrested and syndical headquarters closed down. By fomenting the counterterrorism of the Sindicatos Libres, Arlegui did manage to reduce somewhat the activity of the CNT gunmen and change the balance of killings sharply against the anarchosyndicalists. Under the *ley de fugas* ("shot while attempting to escape"), an undetermined number of CNT militants were handed over to the vengeance of their syndical adversaries.

The most spectacular anarchist response did not occur in Barcelona but in Madrid in March 1921, when three CNT gunmen firing from a motocycle and sidecar assassinated the prime minister, Eduardo Dato. After one of the killers was arrested, he avowed, "I did not fire against Dato, but against the prime minister who authorized the *ley de fugas*." [13] This was the third time that a Spanish prime minister had been murdered by anarchists within a quarter century. There had been at least four other attempts on prime ministers or the king.

As the CNT was driven underground during 1921 and 1922, the Sindicatos Libres gained members. In mid-1922 they won over several Barcelona *sindicatos únicos* that were sick of violence and by that time they formed unions of different professions in 11 cities claiming a total membership of approximately 150,000. The Employers' Federation lost much of its interest in the Sindicatos Libres after the latter refused to act as mere company unions in economic disputes, but in Barcelona the provincial government offered further encouragement, especially in the street battle against CNT gunmen.

According to Pestaña, until the coming of Martínez Anido and the Sindicatos Libres, the former employers' police had killed only "a few" *cenetistas*. Losses shot upward in 1921 and 1922. Thousands of CNT members were forced to leave Barcelona province in the six-year yeriod 1917–1923, and during the rule

13. There is no evidence that Dato "authorized" the *ley de fugas,* but the government did tolerate it.

of Martínez Anido several hundred were sent on *conducciones* (forced marches) that sometimes extended all the way to southern Spain and broke the health of some of those forced to undergo them.

During 1921, the big year of the Martínez Anido repression, available evidence indicates 49 *cenetistas* were killed in shootings in Barcelona, and 21 were wounded. Among the Sindicato Libre there were 13 fatalities and 18 wounded. At least 20 other people —police or nonconformist workers—were killed that year in Barcelona, and 63 more wounded. In 1922, after the repression achieved control, the number of shootings dropped by approximately 75 percent, and casualties were divided as follows: [14]

	Killed	Wounded
CNT	8	1
Sindicato Libre	6	15
Police	2	7
Employers	1	1
Undetermined	7	28

By 1922, many of the direct-action militants in the CNT had given up and gone back to their jobs, and the postwar economic crisis in Catalonia was leveling out. But the hard-core anarchist gunmen had no occupation other than that of thug; with the CNT syndicates in disarray, their fees and salaries could no longer be paid out of dues, and so they had to finance themselves directly. They turned to *atracos* (armed robberies) against banks and other businesses and communications. Though this was pure criminality, not dissimilar to the post-1905 operations of Russian Bolshevists, the CNT leaders still refused to disown the *pistoleros*. Even though more was spent in legal fees to defend captured *atracadores* than was ever brought in from the robberies,[15] it was widely argued that the gunmen had been driven to this expedient by the repression and were still serving the cause.

14. F. de P. Calderón, *La verdad sobre el terrorismo* (Barcelona, 1932). The difference in the ratio of killed to wounded among the CNT casualties and the police and Sindicato Libre casualties is explained by application of the *ley de fugas* to the former, which made it easy to "finish the job." But the CNT gunmen had to hit and run in their attacks on the police and on their rivals, and frequently missed.

15. Pestaña, *Lo que aprendí*, p. 90.

Nonetheless, much of the syndicalist leadership was weary of violence and interested in orienting CNT activity toward more constructive channels. After martial law was finally raised, a national congress of the CNT met at Zaragoza in June 1922 to try to repair syndicalist organization. Though the classic goals of revolutionary syndicalism were reaffirmed, recent experience with martial law and police repression had convinced many leaders of the desirability of a more favorable attitude on the part of the authorities. Moreover, there were frequent contacts between the CNT and lower-middle-class radicals of the "Catalanist left," who frequently provided defense attorneys for syndicalists in court. Left Catalanist radicals hoped to win CNT support for an autonomous, socially "progressive" Catalonia. The Zaragoza congress agreed that CNT members might henceforth vote in political elections for the most liberal candidates if civil liberties were in danger, which came close to a tacit admission that apolitical direct action by itself did not suffice. A few sections of the CNT were even willing to cooperate with honest elements in the Sindicatos Libres. There is evidence that Salvador Seguí, the main syndicalist leader in Barcelona and a supple tactician with broad political contacts, was working to dissociate the syndicates from the murder squads altogether and adopt a practical laborite policy when he was shot down in March 1923, apparently by gunmen of the Sindicatos Libres.

During the period of 1921 to 1922 the national government had passed more social reform legislation than ever before. The scope of the jury system was extended, accident indemnities and maternity compensation were established, a new decree outlined machinery to create labor arbitration commissions throughout Spain, and a parliamentary committee prepared a new bill establishing obligatory retirement and old-age compensation. Yet these changes were slow to take effect and some were not observed immediately. Meanwhile, after an especially provocative employment of the *ley de fugas* in October 1922, the Madrid government finally deposed Martínez Anido and appointed a conciliatory governor to Barcelona to curtail police repression.

The notion that an end to police counterterrorism would also encourage the terrorists to desist seems to have failed in application. In 1923, especially after the death of Seguí, the anarchist incendiaries and gunmen gained almost complete control of the CNT. During the nine-month term of the liberal García Prieto administration (December 1922–September 1923) *atentados* reached an all-time high; 154 were killed throughout Spain and at least 90 more wounded. The Cardinal-Archbishop of Zaragoza, Soldevila, who encouraged Catholic syndicalism, was murdered by members of the anarchist society Crisol. Even the gunmen of the Sindicatos Libres began to lie low.

The anarchosyndicalists who dominated the CNT in mid-1923 stressed continuation of *atracos* in order to collect funds to organize a revolutionary general strike. It is difficult to judge to what extent this was an excuse for criminal profiteering, for the anarchosyndicalist movement was in no position to attempt any kind of nation-wide strike. At its peak in 1919 the CNT had perhaps three-quarters of a million members—and briefly may have enjoyed an even larger following [16]—yet this was only a comparatively small minority of the total Spanish labor force of more than 4 million. The Socialist trade union movement was, as will be seen in the next chapter, minuscule. At about the same time the National Catholic Agrarian Confederation claimed that nearly 600,000 peasant families were associated with it. Whether or not the figure was exaggerated, it gave some indication of the countervailing force of northern peasant conservatism among Spain's lower classes. The CNT had not repaired the organizational damage inflicted by the repression of 1920–22, and in 1923 it was much weaker than it had been three years earlier.

Terrorism had nearly destroyed the movement, increasing opposition among the middle classes and provoking antipathy among some of the workers. The insecurity generated by prolonged terrorism was an important factor in encouraging public opinion in some parts of Spain to accept a military dictatorship under General Primo de Rivera that seized power in September

16. The December 1919 national congress of the CNT reported 715,000 members. The anarchosyndicalist leader Eusebio Carbó later claimed that the actual figure had at that time reached 1,282,000. "Espagne. Notre situation" (manuscript essay, Perpignan, Feb. 2, 1925), International Institute of Social History, Amsterdam.

1923. Though the frustration and humiliation of Spain's military policy in Morocco was the major single influence in precipitating the dictatorship, the middle and lower-middle classes were very tired of seeing a combination of political immobilism and leftist extremism block constructive domestic change. Many were willing to have public affairs mended by an "iron surgeon." The CNT made a feeble effort to call a general strike in Barcelona that was easily suppressed by the military. Angel Pestaña later confessed, "The dictatorship put an end to a state of affairs that had become intolerable." [17]

17. *Lo que aprendí en la vida*, 100.

APPENDIX

Appendix Tables 1–5 have been adapted from data in the study by the criminologist José María Farré Moregó, *Los atentados sociales en España* (Madrid, 1922).

TABLE 1. *The Incidence of Political Violence in Major Spanish Cities, 1917–21*

	Number of political crimes per year					
	1917	1918	1919	1920	1921	Total
Barcelona	49	93	109	304	254	809
Bilbao	9	1	14	84	44	152
Valencia	5	6	41	77	22	151
Zaragoza	4	12	8	69	36	129
Madrid	5	6	66	37	13	127
Seville	0	7	22	63	12	104

TABLE 2. *Objects of Political Crimes, 1917–22*

	Barcelona			Bilbao	Zaragoza	Madrid	Valencia	Seville
	1910–17	1917–22	Total					
Against employers	25	126	151	7	10	7	16	3
Against foremen, etc.	8	58	66	8	4	3	5	5
Against workers	164	279	443	83	21	47	17	40
Group fights	0	4	4	6	0	0	2	0
Against CNT	0	49	49	5	0	0	5	0
Against Free Synd.	0	14	14	3	0	0	9	0
Against public officials	0	7	7	3	3	1	4	2
Against police, etc.	5	73	78	8	10	10	31	2
Against factories, etc.	52	119	171	22	21	26	39	22
Against the public	7	104	111	11	14	1	18	8

TABLE 3. *Means Employed in Political Crimes, 1917–22*

| | Barcelona | | | | | | | |
	1910–17	1917–22	Total	Bilbao	Zaragoza	Madrid	Valencia	Seville
Armed robbery	1	11	12	1	1	2	0	0
Firearms	90	344	434	50	23	29	61	15
Knife	13	32	45	5	1	7	1	7
Explosives exploded	9	150	159	8	24	3	55	31
detected	0	190	190	43	17	0	11	8
Beating	30	47	77	15	5	11	3	8
Stoning	46	10	56	3	9	6	7	3
Acid	2	1	3	0	1	0	0	4
Major sabotage	84	56	140	2	17	39	11	15
Major coercion	1	13	14	4	21	16	8	8
Looting	0	6	6	0	0	7	12	0
Kidnapping	0	0	0	0	0	1	0	0
Ley de fugas *	0	10	10	0	0	0	8	0

* Men released from jail and shot by Free Syndicate gunmen with police compliance.

TABLE 4. *Results of Political Violence, 1917–22*

		Barcelona			Bilbao	Zaragoza	Madrid	Valencia	Seville
		1910–17	1917–22	Total					
Against employers	Killed	1	25	26	0	2	2	6	1
	Injured	8	40	48	1	4	1	4	0
Against foremen	Killed	1	23	24	2	3	1	3	1
	Injured	7	27	34	3	3	1	2	3
Against non-union workers	Killed	11	95	106	7	8	5	27	9
	Injured	119	328	447	87	26	45	60	36
Against bystanders	Killed	1	21	22	9	0	0	5	1
	Injured	16	121	137	23	13	18	29	3
Against CNT or Free Synd.	Killed	0	57	57	2	7	0	7	0
	Injured	0	45	45	9	0	0	8	0
Against police	Killed	0	20	20	1	3	0	9	0
	Injured	7	15	22	13	5	7	17	0

BARCELONA: 255 Dead, 733 Injured   BILBAO: 24 Dead, 145 Injured   ZARAGOZA: 23 Dead, 51 Injured
VALENCIA: 57 Dead, 120 Injured   MADRID: 8 Dead, 62 Injured   SEVILLE: 12 Dead, 42 Injured

TABLE 5. *Proportionate Incidence of Political Crimes*

	Number of political crimes, 1917–22	Population, 1920	Percentage per inhabitant
Bilbao	152	114,351	0.00132
Barcelona	809	710,335	0.00113
Zaragoza	129	141,350	0.00091
Valencia	151	239,800	0.00062
Seville	104	205,527	0.00050
Madrid	127	751,852	0.00016

FOUR

Spanish Socialism to 1930

THE MAIN REVOLUTIONARY RIVAL of the anarchosyndicalist movement was Marxist socialism, but the Spanish Socialist party was very slow in taking form. The first Marxist organization in Spain was a little group called the New Madrid Federation, set up by nine Madrid Socialists on July 8, 1872. Approximately one month earlier, this circle had denounced the fact that the semisecret anarchist Alliance had ignored orders of the Marxist-dominated International and, far from dissolving itself, still held sway over the Spanish Federation. At issue was the question of serious organization and practical political work versus spontaneous revolutionary action. The overwhelmingly pro-anarchist leadership of the Spanish Federation expelled the dissenters, and the New Madrid Federation gained the support of no more than a dozen small trade unions in the Madrid district. After a few years it expired altogether.

Whereas anarchism spread quickly among radical intellectuals and syndicate leaders, Spanish Marxism developed very slowly and was largely identified with one figure, a Galician typesetter named Pablo Iglesias Posse (1850–1925). Iglesias was a man of cautious temperament. He had had a bitterly meager childhood and suffered all his life from poor health. He was devoted to his mother, living in her dingy apartment until her death and marrying only in middle age. Iglesias possessed great patience and emphasized the need to prepare carefully whatever was done.

The nucleus of what eventually became the Spanish Socialist party was constituted by some 40 Marxist Socialists in Madrid in 1879. Their base was the Madrid typesetters' union (Asociación del Arte de Imprimir). Only six were middle-class intellectuals, while more than half were ordinary typesetters—literate, mostly self-educated, among the elite of the Spanish working class of their day.

Iglesias and his coworkers were sometimes called "reformists" in later years, but they conceived their strategy as orthodox Marxist revolutionism based on the concrete conditions of Spanish society. Given the political influence of those elements somewhat inaccurately described as the "oligarchy," the timidity of the lower middle classes, the backwardness of the economy, and the weakness of the proletariat, they saw no chance for an early victory of socialism in Spain—an attitude which paralleled that of Marx himself. As José Mesa, one of Iglesias' principal colleagues, wrote to Engels in 1873, "Any effort to move immediately toward a proletarian revolution in Spain will end in a massacre." [1] The founders of Spanish socialism, like their counterparts in nearly all other Marxist parties, believed that a long, slow process of work, organization, education, and sociopolitical change would be necessary to build the strength of socialism and achieve the dictatorship of the proletariat.

Hence Spanish Socialists embarked on a program of practical reform to advance the social and economic interests of the workers. Instead of leaping into wildcat strikes and threatening the bourgeoisie with immediate destruction, the Socialists stressed civic reforms to increase the influence of the lower classes. They were willing to engage in any kind of organized political activity that did not infringe their principles or require them to take responsibility for the existing system. The immediate goals of the first organized Socialist group in 1879 were universal suffrage, establishment of a full-fledged jury system,

---

1. Josep Termes Ardèvol, *El movimiento en España: La Primera Internacional, 1864–1881* (Barcelona, 1965), 79.

freedom of religion, complete freedom of association and political organization, and elimination of all censorship.

The propaganda of Spanish socialism during its first half-century was consistently low-keyed. Iglesias' attitude was that

> Shrill, insulting, reckless propaganda is used only by feeble political and economic movements that are here today and gone tomorrow, and invokes scant respect and less fear among those who tyrannize the working class.
>
> In propaganda one must reject the tactic of shrill oratory, of threats and of insults. . . . Nothing is gained by curses, threats and personal attacks against the exploiters or their supporters, and the discontent of the workers is not satisfied by arousing or sharpening hatred against management and its defenders.[2]

In 1884, when reformist elements in the government succeeded in establishing a Commission of Social Reforms at Madrid to gather information about social problems, the Socialist leadership accepted an invitation to appear before the new agency. Iglesias reiterated the group's doctrinaire Marxist position, but emphasized that it would always press for the most practical reforms possible in any given situation. The responsibility of government, he said, was to ensure the freedom that would enable the class struggle to be conducted in a peaceful and evolutionary manner, at least until the "final battle."

The first effort to establish a Socialist trade union network ended in failure. The Socialists seemed dull, colorless, materialistic, and authoritarian compared with the anarchosyndicalists of the FTRE, who were engaged in extensive propaganda work. Though anarchosyndicalist activity was irregularly organized and always financed on a shoestring, it reached tens of thousands. The anarchosyndicalist mystique was already fullblown and had developed its own myths and poetry, its own martyrology and hall of fame, from Spartacus to Tom Paine through all the figures of the French Revolution and the leftist currents of the nineteenth century. Some 25 anarchist and anarchosyndicalist journals had already been published before the first Socialist newspaper, *El Socialista,* appeared as a weekly in Madrid in 1886. Though Socialist propaganda increased during the 1890's,

2. García Venero, *Internacionales,* I, 283.

when a total of approximately 20 other publications were begun irregularly, the official weekly achieved a printing of only 2,000 to 3,000, compared with the 18,000 weekly copies of the main anarchist journal, *Tierra y Libertad,* that were being published at the turn of the century.

Expansion was so slow that the formal Spanish Socialist Workers' party (PSOE) was not organized until 1888, when the initiative was prompted by the need to have an officially constituted party to participate in the new Socialist International that was being formed abroad. In the same year a Socialist trade union system was founded. It was called the General Union of Laborers (UGT), and was composed of 27 craft unions with a total of 3,355 members, located mainly in Madrid and Catalonia. Over half the total membership was drawn from the typographical federation, which might be called the founder of the UGT. The UGT was nominally independent of the PSOE and adopted a platform of apoliticism so as to concentrate on workers' grievances. For the first eleven years its headquarters were in Barcelona and a majority of the members of the original national committee were Catalans. As indicated in Table 4.1, the UGT's growth during the next decades was very slow.

TABLE 4.1. *Growth of UGT Membership, 1890–1920*

1890	3,900	1910	41,000
1893	8,500	1911	78,000
1896	6,200	1913	148,000
1899	15,000	1916	76,000
1900	26,000	1917	100,000
1904	56,900	1918	90,000
1907	30,000	1920	211,000

SOURCES: *Unión Obrera* (April 1909); Francisco Largo Caballero, *Presente y futuro de la Unión General de Trabajadores de España* (Madrid, 1925), 226–27.

By the time that the CNT had ballooned into a mass organization of three-quarters of a million or more, the UGT had difficulty passing the 100,000 mark. In the process, it completely lost influence in the country's largest industrial concentration—Catalonia—where by force and suasion the CNT at one point seemed about to acquire a monopoly of trade union support. The appeal of anarchosyndicalism to the workers of Catalonia was to some extent reinforced by the parallel dissidence of the anticentralist middle classes, who turned to Catalan regionalism. The centralizing policy of the Socialists proved an almost impossible handicap in the Catalan milieu.

The appeal of the Socialists was also limited by their general disinterest in the peasantry, typical of most European Marxist parties of the early twentieth century. The anarchists laid much more stress on peasant syndicalism. Moreover, the CNT, as explained in the previous chapter, broadened the base of industrial syndicalism by adopting the industrial union, while the UGT doggedly clung to the craft union form of organization.

Neither Spanish revolutionary movement was very much involved with intellectuals, but the anarchists did make efforts to attract the collaboration of writers and a few scientists in their journals, and won the sympathies of certain marginal groups of Spanish intellectuals. They also established a few small "rationalist schools." The Socialists, by contrast, ignored intellectuals almost altogether until about the time of the First World War.

The anarchist appeal to direct action and terrorism created for them an attractive aura among militant workers, while the Socialist emphasis upon legality and organization seemed in comparison tepid and spiritless. During its first years the UGT called few strikes and lost most of those. At its second national congress (1890), the UGT leadership came out strongly against the doctrine of the general strike that was being propounded by revolutionary syndicalism. The Socialists steadfastly condemned anarchists for frivolity and irresponsibility, for lacking a seriously analyzed program. They refused to participate in anarchist-inspired efforts at general strikes in 1891, 1901, and 1902, denying that anarchosyndicalist action was revolutionary in any real sense. Iglesias explained after the 1902 episode, "If it had been a truly revolutionary movement, seriously organized to destroy the institutions that we mortally hate, then we would have seconded the strikers and those who encouraged them." [3]

The discipline and restraint demanded by the UGT led

3. García Venero, *Historia de los movimientos sindicalistas españoles* (Madrid, 1961), 317.

many Spanish workers to reject Marxism as authoritarian. More-over, the Socialist party was not altogether democratic in structure. The president of the party's executive commission was chosen by majority vote of delegates at party congresses, but the other members of the commission were chosen by the vote of the Madrid membership alone, which was dominated by Iglesias and his close associates. Election of the entire executive commission was not extended to the party membership as a whole until 1914. The narrow rule of Iglesias and a party elite preserved orthodoxy and won the party a reputation for rigid incorruptibility at a time when similar claims could scarcely have been made by any other political organization in the country. But this aura of moral superiority by no means overcame the aversion felt by many workers to a centralized, "authoritarian" organization of "Spanish Prussians."

Socialist electoral strength grew very slowly. A city councilman was elected in Bilbao in 1891. Ten years later the Socialists only held a total of 8 city council seats in Bilbao and 27 elsewhere. Their vote in national elections increased from 7,000 in 1893 to 25,000 in 1901.

The most striking political support among the working classes in the first years of the twentieth century was won by the Radical Republicans in Barcelona. The Radicals' Casas del Pueblo in the industrial suburbs provided social and political centers for the lower classes, and this title was taken over by the Socialists in 1908 as the name for their own worker centers in other cities. In elections for the labor representatives on the board of the Institute of Social Reforms, the Socialists normally won nearly all the seats, but this was mainly for lack of competition. Indeed, the elections of 1907 showed that the party was stagnating politically, its vote falling to less than 20,000. The UGT also began to lose membership. The electoral decline was largely accounted for by the rise of the Radicals and the coalescence of other Republican factions into a "Republican Union."

This posed more seriously than ever before the question of cooperation with middle-class Republican liberalism. In 1881 the original Socialist nucleus in Barcelona had split off from the Madrid group to cooperate with Catalan Republicans, following

a course roughly parallel to the pragmatic Broussist social democrats in France. In 1888 there had appeared briefly an "opportun-
ist" Catalan Socialist party and a moderate, short-lived Social
Democratic party in Madrid. Yet the regular Socialist party had
persistently denounced the pro-Republican political illusions
that had captured the attention of the urban lower classes in
the 1870's, and had specifically refused to endorse the republican
form of government per se, though casually stating that it preferred a republic to constitutional monarchy. In the Madrid
district a temporary tactical alliance was formed in 1899 with
one of the most socially progressive of the old Republican leaders,
Pi y Margall, but four years later local Socialist groups elsewhere
rejected a national electoral alliance with the Republican Union
by a vote of more than two to one.

Their electoral decline and the anticonservative alliance of
Liberal and Republican middle-class parties in 1910 led the
Socialists to change their position. An electoral alliance with the
Republicans in Madrid gave the Socialists their first Cortes seat,
won by Pablo Iglesias. Compared with this lone Socialist triumph,
the Republican factions gained 40 seats, and three years later
the party leadership had to beat back the first attempt by reformists to take over direction. A group of pro-Republican writers
and intellectuals temporarily gained control of *El Socialista,* the
party organ, but the orthodox leadership soon reasserted itself
on the basis of its strength in the Madrid section. In 1914, however, local Socialist sections voted 157 to 17 in favor of retaining
the electoral alliance with the Republicans and for the first time
the party officially declared in its statutes the desirability of
eliminating the monarchy in favor of a democratic republic.

The UGT meanwhile achieved a record of moderate success
in developing workers' cooperatives and medical centers, especially in Madrid, Bilbao, and Asturias. The First World War's
economic boom and attendant price squeeze encouraged the most
militant stand yet taken by the movement. In 1916 the UGT
signed the first working agreement with the CNT in its history to
protest the cost-of-living increases that were sharply felt in most
parts of Spain.

In March 1917 the two trade union movements made another

pact for joint action to raise wages, lower living costs, obtain amnesties for those convicted of "political crimes," and dramatize their determination with a general strike. At approximately the same time, the Socialist leaders made a secret agreement with the heads of the small Reformist Republican party to plan a revolutionary strike. The goal would be establishment of a new provisional government that would hold elections for a constituent assembly, repudiating the monarchy and drawing up the constitution for a democratic republic. In so doing, the Socialists by no means categorically endorsed a parliamentary republic, for they rejected collaboration with the potentially largest Republican group, the Radicals of Alejandro Lerroux. During the early years of the century, Lerroux had been the leading petty-bourgeois anticlerical demagogue in Spain. Though he thundered vaguely of revolution, Lerroux's reputation for corruption, his penchant for compromise, and his lack of commitment to genuine social reform all made him anathema to Socialists. The leaders of the small Reformist party, however, convinced the Socialists of their democratic integrity and their intention to face social problems. They were deemed genuine "bourgeois progressives." Conversely, it was difficult to draw the CNT into the plan. Even the nonanarchist CNT leaders such as Seguí and Pestaña were repelled by the organized, regimented Socialist party. Hence the dealings of the CNT were always with the UGT, and not with the party directly, but it was the CNT that made the most direct preparations for revolutionary action, spending union dues to store up pistols and street bombs.

Political dissidence was encouraged by the barracks revolt of the Spanish Army that broke out into the open in June 1917. Thousands of resentful officers, organized into Military Defense Juntas, protested low pay and favoritism and placed severe pressure on the Madrid government. In this atmosphere, with parliament prorogued and the government unwilling to consider constitutional reform, an independent "Parliamentary assembly" of liberal reformist representatives was convened at Barcelona in mid-July. The Socialist party's executive commission authorized Iglesias to accept a seat in the cabinet of any Republican provisional government that might be formed—a decision that infuriated the CNT directors. The Republican-Socialist agreement provided that if the Barcelona assembly had no effect it would be followed by a general strike, with which the UGT would make every effort to associate the CNT. The Barcelona assembly was closed by police almost as soon as it opened, but not before anarchists and Republicans had provoked a large-scale strike in the Catalan capital. Socialist railway workers joined the walk-out without the official consent of their union. The strike was soon broken, yet, since it had not been conducted according to legal regulations, the railway company refused to rehire approximately 35 of the workers involved.

This circumstance was seized by the Socialists as justification for the revolutionary general strike that had been talked about for months. They were in agreement with some of the key Republican leaders and had maintained liaison committees with the CNT in several provinces since midspring. Most of the Socialists seem to have calculated that the split in the ranks of the parliamentary liberals and the rise of dissidence in the Army presented a sudden opportunity for revolutionary transformation of government. Pablo Iglesias, who remained cautious to the end of his days, apparently disagreed and tried to limit the movement to a mere protest strike. He was overruled by Julián Besteiro and other leaders; the UGT strike manifesto of August 12, 1917, presented the effort as a revolutionary general strike whose goal was a new provisional government and elections to a constituent assembly.

The response to the strike was very uneven. It lasted from three to six days in most of the larger urban and industrial areas, and somewhat longer in the mining districts of Asturias and León. There the workers were more unified; connections with peasant relatives in the surrounding countryside gave them greater economic flexibility and they received more direct support from middle-class Republicans. The national government declared martial law almost immediately and there were a number of bloody incidents, in which perhaps as many as 70 workers altogether were killed. Support from the CNT, which did not officially sign the strike manifesto, was erratic, as was that of some Republicans. Afterward Socialist writers found it convenient to blame the strike's ultimate failure on the "betrayal" of the middle-class Republicans, but this charge was considerably exaggerated. In general, the latter did about as much as had been expected of them. The first element to officially desert the revolutionary front was the UGT's railway workers' federation, whose secretary was subsequently expelled from the union.

The Army stood firm, and the hollowness of the merely abstract comparison drawn by some Socialists between Spain and revolutionary Russia was soon apparent. Spanish society was not exhausted by world war, but merely discontented about the uneven distribution of wartime prosperity. The Military Defense Juntas were almost the very opposite of Soviets. Rather than revolutionary councils, they were elite committees of officers that aimed not at overturning the system but mainly at increasing the rewards and influence of army officers within the existing framework. The grumbling lower middle classes and the syndicates of white-collar bureaucrats that had been formed wanted more money for genuine middle-class status, not egalitarian revolution.

The failure of the strike was due not so much to the weakness of organized labor—nearly half a million members in a land of some 20 million—as to overestimating the support that might have been expected from the lower middle classes and most of all from the military. No serious effort had been made to undermine army morale or win over disaffected junior officers.

The entire UGT strike committee was jailed and at the end of September a military court sentenced its four principal members to life imprisonment. Lesser colleagues were condemned to twelve years' detention. Hundreds of ordinary followers were also rounded up and many workers were fired.

Failure of the strike abruptly ended Socialist interest in direct action, and the party reverted to pursuit of limited goals. Its immediate aim was to win amnesty for the hundreds of party and union members in jail. Perhaps partially as a result of the recent pressure, the elections of February 1918 were the freest and most honest held in Spain up to that time. The exercise of male suffrage was democratic in all the larger towns and in the more literate rural regions as well. In electoral alliance with

Republicans, the Socialists made their major effort in Madrid, Barcelona, Bilbao, Oviedo, and Valencia. In addition to retaining Iglesias' seat, they managed to elect the leaders who remained in jail as deputies from Barcelona, Oviedo, Valencia, and Bilbao, bringing their release.

The new statutes of the UGT, adopted in 1918, declared:

> The aim of those who aspire to overthrow this regime and establish another of greater equity and justice . . . ought to be to avoid shedding the blood of the working class needlessly, striving to carry out the transition as humanely as possible, letting all the responsibility for bloody clashes between the working class and the capitalists or their representatives fall on those who struggle blindly to close the path to new ideas. . . .
>
> But this labor cannot be carried out exclusively by manual workers; the collaboration of intellectual workers is indispensable to give scientific validity to the empirical task of building a new society.
>
> The Congress therefore resolves that the National Committee should solicit, in the form it deems most fitting, the individual or collective collaboration of intellectual workers who are in agreement with aims and tactics of the UGT, to prepare immediate socio-economic reforms and future methods of administration.

This was the most explicit official statement of a moderate, evolutionary approach to the transition to a socialist society that the UGT had ever made. Moreover, this was drafted during October 1918, in the last weeks of the world war, at a time when the revolutionary tide seemed to be rising throughout Europe. The Socialist leaders had no intention of repeating the mistake of 1917.

During 1919 and 1920 UGT membership more than doubled, rising to 210,000, but this increase was much less than that of the CNT. The Socialists were running a calculated risk of being altogether outdistanced in competing for worker support so long as they held to their cautious program of building constructively. In 1918 the UGT congress proposed a unity-of-action pact with the CNT for syndical action to improve social and economic conditions but this did not interest the anarchosyndicalist leaders. At the time of the Catalan employers' lockout in the summer of 1919 the UGT proposed another unity-of-action pact with plans for an ultimate fusion of the federations and a UGT general strike in support of the CNT, but the anarchosyndicalists refused to work with the Socialists, whom they always suspected of maneuvering for position to gain dominance over the much larger, much looser CNT. When the first open general congress of regional delegates of the CNT met at Madrid in December 1919, it rejected the UGT's proposal by a margin of two to one.

After the CNT's national committee was reorganized in 1920, the nonanarchist leaders, headed by Seguí and Pestaña, carried a vote in favor of a new unity-of-action agreement with the UGT, but this was repudiated by a subsequent conference of CNT regional leaders. The decision was reversed once more by a national plenum of CNT leaders in October 1921, but the failure of the UGT to support the anarchosyndicalists' abortive, ill-planned attempt at a general strike to protest military rule in Barcelona put an end to negotiations.

Meanwhile, the emergence of international communism had repercussions on the working-class movement in Spain as elsewhere. The first news of the Bolshevist coup d'état had aroused enthusiasm among both Socialists and anarchosyndicalists. Strong sympathy persisted throughout the years of the Russian Civil War, though the more reflective Socialist leaders had grave hesitations about the course of Bolshevist rule. To many Socialists, however, Lenin's regime was the first example of the dictatorship of the proletariat that was supposed to be the common goal of all Marxists. During 1918–19, paradoxically, the enthusiasm was if anything greater among anarchosyndicalists. To explain this, it is necessary to understand the effectiveness of Lenin's manipulation of the revolutionary soviets (workers' councils) in Russia. The impression was created that Communist Russia was governed by democratic soviets; this hoax was at first accepted by syndicalists not merely in Madrid and Barcelona, but in Berlin, Budapest, and other centers.

While the Socialists waited with their customary circumspection, the CNT delegates at the 1919 congress vigorously debated Lenin's initiative in forming a Third International. Most of the revolutionary anarchosyndicalists favored affiliation. Furthermore, their speeches revealed the development of a new trend that Gerald Meaker has called "syndicalist communism," for several of the anarchosyndicalist spokesmen endorsed the concept of the dictatorship of the proletariat. The congress approved by acclamation a resolution that "the National Confederation of Labor of Spain declares itself a firm defender of the principles of the First International supported by Bakunin and second declares that it joins provisionally the Communist International because of the latter's revolutionary character."

A small delegation was dispatched to Moscow, but only Angel Pestaña managed to arrive. There he pledged the CNT's support to the Comintern, but soon saw enough to change his mind. Composition of the CNT's national committee changed greatly during the police repression of 1921 and the "syndicalist communists," led by Joaquín Maurín and Andrés Nin, temporarily gained control. They led a CNT delegation to the meetings of the new Communist international trade union organization in Moscow.

Nevertheless, CNT adherence to the Third International remained a dead letter. Even at the 1919 congress, the non-anarchist syndicalists led by Seguí had shown no illusions about Bolshevism. During the following year, most of the individualist anarchist circles in Catalonia also lost whatever sympathies they may have had for the Leninist regime. Lenin's publication of his Twenty-One Conditions of Comintern membership made the nature of Bolshevism much clearer, and the CNT ultimately repudiated its impulsive gesture of 1919. By the time of the mid-1922 CNT leaders' conference at Zaragoza, the practical reformists were considerably stronger and the ultrarevolutionaries at least temporarily in a minority. By the end of that year the small minority of "syndicalist communists" withdrew from the CNT altogether.

The relationship of the Spanish Socialist party to communism was inevitably more complicated. Only three days after the overthrow of the Russian Provisional Government, *El Socialista* criticized the Bolshevist coup for being "inopportune and . . . perhaps regrettable," since the main concern of progressive forces was supposed to be the defeat of central European militarism. The Spanish Socialist leaders rejected various aspects of the new Bolshevist regime, but they did not denounce it on the same moral grounds used by leaders of the German and French Socialist parties.

A special congress of the Socialist party met at Madrid in December 1919, at the same time that the CNT decided upon nominal adherence to the Comintern. Besteiro explained the position of the Socialist leadership:

> Like the Russian maximalists [Bolshevists], the Spanish Socialist Party believes that the dictatorship of the proletariat is indispensable for the triumph of socialism. Nonetheless, it should not be thought that the dictatorship of the proletariat must necessarily take the same form in every country.[4]

He went on to quote Trotsky to the effect that the Russian Revolution had been made possibly only because of Russia's exhaustion from the world war, and that after the collapse the only other significant force the Bolshevists had to combat was that of the agrarian populists. Hence a socialist dictatorship had been comparatively easy to install in Russia, but that would not be the case in Spain, where the Socialist party still had to follow moderate, evolutionary tactics. The motion to remain in the Second International was, however, approved by only a small margin—14,010 to 12,497.

The strongest support for communism came from young activists in the party. After several months of fretting, the national committee of the Federation of Socialist Youth was persuaded on April 15, 1920, to declare that it was henceforth reconstituted as the Communist party of Spain, affiliated with the Comintern. The regular Socialist leadership managed to retain control of a majority of the local sections of the Socialist Youth, but there was so much muttering among the rank and file that a second congress of the party had to be called in June 1920. At that time the party claimed nearly 53,000 regular members, but the representatives of only about 15,000 attended the congress. Despite the pleas of the leaders of the executive commission, 8,269 votes were cast at this assembly in favor of joining the Comintern, and only 5,016 against. The pro-Communists also gained several seats on the executive commission, although the

4. Eduardo Comín Colomer, *Historia del Partido Comunista Español* (Madrid, 1965), I, 46.

delegation dispatched to Moscow to consider precise terms of entry into the Third International was composed of one pro- and one anti-Communist. The congress had agreed that affiliation would not be consummated until full autonomy for the Spanish party was assured, and even Daniel Anguiano, the pro-Communist representative on the delegation, was not altogether reassured by what he found in Russia. Opposition was strengthened by the outcome of the UGT congress, which met only a few days after the party congress. As in other countries, the Socialist trade union organization was politically more moderate than was the party itself. Representatives of the UGT cast 110,902 votes to 17,919 in favor of remaining affiliated with the trade union federation of the Second International.

A definitive decision on the party's relationship to the Comintern was delayed until a third congress met in April 1921. Besteiro, who made the most coherent statements on behalf of the executive commission, pointed out that some of the men most active in trying to orient the party toward Bolshevism had the most unstable political records; seven years earlier some of them had been energetic revisionists. Without attacking Bolshevism directly, he dismissed it as impossible and irrelevant for Spain. Besteiro denied that there was a clear-cut distinction between evolution and revolution in socialist tactics, because any activity that hastened the coming of a socialist society, however unspectacular, was a revolutionary deed. This time the resolution opposing entry into the Comintern drew 8,808 votes, and the one in favor, 6,025.

Feeling that the last major opportunity had been lost, a small group of pro-Communist extremists split off and founded its own Spanish Communist Workers' party, so that briefly there were two separate Communist parties in Spain. They were brought together at a Madrid conference in November 1921, whence emerged the unified Communist party of Spain (PCE) as a section of the Third International. Its structure was roughly similar to that of the Socialist party, based on local groups organized into regional federations. Nascent Spanish communism's only significant following lay among former Socialists in the industrial regions of Vizcaya and Asturias. Its only trade union support came from the Vizcaya Miners' Syndicate, perhaps the strongest single trade union in Spain. Though it remained within the UGT, it was dominated by Communist leaders for the next few years. This made it possible to carry out a number of violent strikes as well as various terrorist acts against the police and Socialist leaders in Bilbao between 1921 and 1923.

By the close of 1921 the Communist split had cost the Socialist party more than half its membership, which sank to 21,000. Only 95,000 workers were represented at the UGT congress the following year, though Socialist spokesmen claimed that their trade unions actually had more than 200,000 members. For the first year or two the Communist party may have had almost as many members as its parent organization, but the Socialists retained most of their small but compact following among labor as well as the support of lower-middle-class and lower-class sympathizers who voted for but never joined the party. The Spanish Communist party found itself isolated and impotent in the elections of 1923, whereas the Socialists increased their vote somewhat and won 10 seats in parliament. In the meantime the party had reaffirmed its ambiguous position halfway between social democracy and communism by joining the more militant Vienna Reconstructionist International before the latter finally merged with the old (Second) Socialist International once more.

By 1923 non-Communist Socialist parties had achieved considerable political strength in central and western Europe, with the major exception of Fascist Italy. The Spanish Socialists had failed to do this, but could take satisfaction from the fact that at least the newly established Primo de Rivera dictatorship was not a fascist regime. Its main thrust was against anarchosyndicalism; aside from one or two isolated incidents the country was surprisingly quiet by the end of 1923. Primo deprived all the political parties of any further field for activity, but made no move to proscribe the UGT, whose discipline, moderation, and practicality he admired.

The dictatorship did not develop a trade union system of its own. Though Catholic syndicates prospered among conservative peasants, the Sindicatos Libres in the industrial areas declined without the rival pressure of the Sindicatos Unicos to galvanize the antileftist workers and win employer support. This gave the UGT an opportunity for expansion that was not wasted. One of its major leaders, Francisco Largo Caballero, accepted appointment as a Spanish Councillor of State and in 1926, when the regime set up machinery for the election of state labor arbitration committees (*comités paritarios*), the Socialists agreed to participate. The UGT expanded from about 200,000 in 1927 to 277,000 at the beginning of 1930, most of its gains coming in New Castile, Extremadura, Granada, and rural Aragon.

Yet the history of UGT activity under the dictatorship was not exactly one of unalloyed cooperation with official labor policy, as has often been charged. Unauthorized strikes by local sections of the UGT in 1927 brought the temporary closing of numerous local syndicate headquarters.[5] Delegates at the 1927 UGT special congress voted not to send representatives to Primo de Rivera's new corporate National Assembly as they were entitled to do under the law and also went on record in favor of political protest against the arbitrary structure of the regime. After these events have been taken into consideration, it nevertheless remains true that the Socialist party and the UGT did nothing of importance to combat the regime directly, and engaged in little more than a certain amount of sporadic strike activity.

Opposition to the practical Socialist attitude of political quietism and general cooperation in labor affairs came from the two extremes of the party—the social democratic right and the revolutionary left, who stirred up considerable dissent at the 1928 party congress. The most active leader of the social democratic sector of the party, Indalecio Prieto, lamented that Socialist acquiescence in the dictatorship merely compounded the party's mistake in combating the preceding parliamentary regime: "We have played the fool, as before us the silly Communists, who were to a certain degree responsible, together with us and the anar-

5. Enrique Santiago, *La UGT ante la revolución* (Madrid, 1932), 50, in Svetlana P. Pozharskaya, *Sotsialisticheskaya Rabochaya Partiya Ispanii 1931–1939 gg.* (Moscow, 1966), 9, stated that 150 local UGT trade union headquarters were temporarily closed under the dictatorship.

chosyndicalists—through their excesses—for the coming of the dictatorship." [6] But the orthodox center remained strong enough to prevent any change in the party's position.

The experience of the CNT under the dictatorship was almost exactly the reverse. Police pressure forced CNT leaders to dissolve the Confederation nominally in May 1924, but local nuclei remained in loose contact throughout Spain. They participated in several military-backed conspiracies against the regime and retained much of their grass-roots strength among previously organized workers, so that later it was comparatively easy to reconstitute the Confederation in 1930. Angel Pestaña, the most moderate of the CNT leaders, hoped to reorient the Confederation in the direction of constructive trade union and political activity, but the anarchists had such a tight grip on the clandestine national committee that they forced him off that body in 1927.

The hard-line anarchists were also on guard against Communist efforts to infiltrate the disorganized cadres of the CNT. It was to block such tactics and ensure anarchist dominance that a secret conference of anarchist representatives at Valencia in 1927 formalized the network of anarchist cells that had existed for years by organizing an Iberian Anarchist Federation (FAI). This organization was to serve as the ideological preceptor and organizational elite of the CNT, guaranteeing that when the Confederation sprang back to life the predominance of revolutionary anarchosyndicalism would be secure.

The Spanish Communist party dwindled to insignificance, rent by internal splits and arrests. Equally disruptive was the determination of the Comintern to gain complete control of the party in Spain as elsewhere, which led to the destitution of various leaders and the split of one of the most important nuclei. Russian financial assistance did not offset the debilitating effect of foreign control, which imposed rigid policies unsuited to Spanish conditions and drove away most of the original following. The organized following of the Spanish Communist party declined to less than 1,000 members by 1929.

Comintern policy during the 1920's was predicated on the

6. García Venero, *Internacionales*, III, 423.

struggle of "class against class" in which the "only genuine revolutionary party of the proletariat" (the Communists) must eschew all cooperation with the "social fascists" (Socialists) and "petit-bourgeois pseudorevolutionaries" (CNT), while trying to attract as many of their members as possible. The only Communist success vis-à-vis the CNT occurred in Seville, where in 1927 the Communists won over the leaders of at least half the CNT shadow syndicates, including such key groups as the dock, transport, and metallurgical workers. This was the only achievement of any note by the Spanish Communist party during the dictatorship, but it did give the Communists a trade union foothold in Andalusia for the first time. This was used as the basis for a Conference of Syndicalist Reconstruction that convened in Seville in the spring of 1930 only a few months after the Primo de Rivera regime had been ousted. Its object was to win over as much as possible of the formerly large CNT following in Andalusia, but aside from the Seville nucleus only a few minor gains were registered in Málaga and Almería. No serious effort was made to penetrate the countryside.

The first important organizational division in the Spanish Communist party came in 1930, when the leadership of the Catalan-Balearics regional federation was expelled from the party and declared the independence of its regional group in reply. The main figure was Joaquín Maurín Juliá, a young former schoolteacher from the hill country of northeastern Aragon, who had been a CNT delegate to Moscow in 1921 and was one of the early leaders of Spanish communism. Maurín was an independent and imaginative young revolutionary ideologue who sympathized with the Workers' Opposition in the Soviet Union and found it impossible to accept the tactical policy imposed on the Spanish party by the Comintern. He believed that Marxist revolutionaries would greatly multiply their strength and the opportunity for an early revolution by cooperating with other working-class groups, the left-wing sectors of the middle classes, and the left-wing sectors of the regionalist movements, especially in Catalonia, where "left Catalanism" was gaining support because of social and cultural changes under the dictatorship. He became one of the earliest advocates of a Popular Front, and the Catalan-Balearic federation was by 1931 converted into a Worker-Peasant Bloc (Bloc Obrer i Camperol—BOC) that operated almost exclusively in the Catalan-speaking provinces. It hoped to exploit the revolutionary possibilities created by the collapse of the monarchy by cooperating with the newly organized lower-middle-class Esquerra Catalana (Catalan left).

Yet another focus of revolutionary Marxist dissidence was created by Andrés Nin, a former CNT militant who had served as an international official of the Comintern in the mid-1920's and espoused Trotsky's doctrine of the "permanent revolution." The defeat of Trotsky in Russian Communist politics eventually brought Nin's arrest in the Soviet Union, but his Spanish nationality enabled him to leave the country together with his Russian wife and children. In Barcelona he founded in 1931 a minuscule, openly Trotskyist Communist Left group, dedicated to pragmatic exploitation of all opportunities for revolution as soon as possible. These splits further weakened the Marxist extreme left at the very time that the collapse of the monarchy opened an enormous political vacuum in Spain.

FIVE   *The Republican Left and*

the Socialists 1930-1933

I F THE SPANISH working class movement was until 1917 distinguished primarily by its insignificance, the same might be
said of Spanish Republicanism until 1930. Discredited by the
excesses of 1874–75, the small Republican cliques of the early
twentieth century were ignored by most of the middle classes.
Though some support came from sectors of the urban workers
and the lower middle classes, Republicanism was further weakened by personal and programmatic division among its leaders
and by the centralist-regionalist controversy. Hence except for a
few years after the turn of the century there was no such thing
as a united Republican party.

In general, Spanish Republicanism split between two tendencies: incendiary extremism and liberal moderation. On the
one hand there were proponents of the armed *pronunciamiento,*
paralleled by demagogues who encouraged class hatred, violent
anticlericalism and in some regions flirted with anarchism. Indeed
in Catalonia and Andalusia the line between extremist Republican and anarchist sometimes blurred. But on the other hand
were Republican moderates, divided between centralist constitutional democrats and practical regionalists.

The principal expression of responsible Republicanism under the monarchy was the Reformist Republican party whose leader from 1914 to 1923 was Melquiades Alvarez. The Reformists were not so much interested in the question of monarchy versus republic as in responsible democratic government—no matter what the form of the executive—and practical social and cultural reform. The Reformists rejected federalism in its extreme mode and unlike many Republicans did not make a fetish of anti-clericalism. They understood that tax reform, economic progress, social legislation, and technical education were more important that closing down religious orders or running the king out of Spain. The Reformists attracted the elite of politically minded Spanish intellectuals in the decade before 1923, but they never became an influential national party. Their only strongholds were in Asturias and a few large towns where they drew the vote of the workers and the ultraliberal sectors of the middle classes. Rural districts were usually too conservative or ignorant to be interested, whereas the Reformists were denied most of the vote of the more industrial regions because of clerical strength, regionalist influence, or strong local personalities. Alvarez himself symbolized the tragedy of democratic liberalism in Spain for, as he grew older, he was bypassed by the extremist trend in Spanish politics and finally murdered by the left after the Civil War began.

None of the reformists or revolutionaries was able to alter the existing configuration of parliamentary government under the monarchy, but the whole political system was swept away by Primo de Rivera's *pronunciamiento* in 1923. During its first months the dictatorship enjoyed genuine popularity, for it seemed to be accomplishing changes that had previously been impossible. Even after it became apparent that Primo had no plans to restore representative government, most of the middle classes continued to accept his rule. The Primo de Rivera regime was not a "fascist" dictatorship; it had no ideology, no program, and no clear idea about how to institutionalize itself. It was frank and defensive about its authoritarianism, attempted to stimulate the economy, and even tried to promote social reform. But it was unable to offer Spain a regular alternative to representative government. The regime professed to be no more than an interim caretaker, and after six years most of the country's elite elements grew restive. Intellectuals were almost unanimously hostile and were becoming strongly republican. The beginning of economic difficulties in 1929 left business leaders uneasy. The king was impatient and much of the Army turned against the dictator, yet after Primo was forced to resign in 1930 the Crown found that there was no one with whom to replace him. The old pre-1923 political parties had been destroyed and the former constitutional system could not be raised from the dead. The monarchy itself was blamed for ratifying authoritarianism and the Republican factions gained broad popular support for the first time in decades.

The election of Republican councillors by nearly all the larger towns in the municipal voting of April 12, 1931, precipitated collapse of the monarchy but did not mark the emergence of a new consensus. It revealed instead a political vacuum without precedent in western countries since 1871. The former political parties had been discredited and destroyed, but there were no new organized parties in their place, with the exception of the Socialists.

The difficulty that Spain faced in achieving stability and a reasonable degree of consensus under liberal democracy in the early 1930's might be better understood if the relative level of cultural, social, and economic modernization of the country at that time is considered. On the basis of civic culture, literacy rates, and economic development, it might be hypothesized that by 1930 Spain was at the level of England in the 1840's and 50's or France in the 1860's and 70's. Neither mid-nineteenth-century England nor even France at the beginning of the Third Republic had to face such severe political tests as Spain underwent in the 1930's. Early Victorian England lived under a controlled system of modernizing oligarchy. France, after emerging from the second Bonapartist dictatorship, was faced with revolutionary insurrection in only one large city, and that was suppressed with a ferocity exceeding anything by either side in the Spanish Civil War (or in earlier Spanish revolutionary confrontations). Aside from the equivocal episode of the Commune, the working-class movement scarcely existed in France during the first decades of the Third Republic, but at a similar stage of development Spanish political society was subjected to severe mass plebiscitarian and revolutionary pressures.

In 1931 three political sectors were able to take advantage of the vacuum in which the Second Republic was established: the Socialists, the moderate Republican liberals, and the Republican left.[1] The Reformist party, like nearly all the pre-1923 parties, had nearly disintegrated. Under the dictatorship its younger leaders and activists had moved to more advanced positions. One of them, Manuel Azaña, a bureaucrat and frustrated belle-lettrist who was president of the Madrid Ateneo, helped found a small group called Republican Action. The Reformists' chief republican rival, the Radical party, had also split; the younger and more extreme elements founded a new group, the Radical Socialists, in 1929. These new parties, together with the lower-middle-class Catalanist left (Esquerra) and the radical Galicianists (ORGA), formed the basis of the Spanish Republican left of 1931 to 1936.

The Republican left was produced in part by a moral reaction to the failures of the monarchy and the imposition of the dictatorship. Having been constituted under authoritarian regimes in 1929–31, it had been formed along strictly ideological lines and did not in the beginning have to face the exigencies of practical politics. Its pattern was that of moralistic French ideological politics rather than the conciliatory Anglo-Saxon empiricism of the former official parties and the Reformists. For most leaders of the Republican left, the modern political world began with the French Revolution and anticlericalism was the ideological keystone of politics.

The anticlerical fixation of the new Republican left of 1931

1. The term "liberal" will be used to denote individuals and groups who stood for democratic constitutional government, protection of private property, individualistic society, and equal civil rights for all. The terms "Republican left" or "middle-class left" will be used to refer to individuals and groups who took a more doctrinaire, exclusive position and proposed to limit the scope of liberal democratic government so as to exclude the rights of certain groups to which they were opposed, as well as advocating more extensive social reform. Because of the broad leftward trend of Spanish politics and the systematic perversion of political vocabulary, the liberals were frequently referred to as moderates or conservatives and the middle-class left as liberals.

may be interpreted in large measure as the reaction of middle-class radicalism to the resurgence of Catholicism in much of middle- and upper-class society during the late nineteenth and early twentieth centuries. Liturgical reforms, expanded church education, and active laymen's associations, such as Catholic Action, had enabled the church to regain much of the influence among the "respectable" classes of Spanish society that had been partially lost during the first half of the nineteenth century. Though feeble efforts at "social Catholicism" among the workers mostly failed, the Catholic peasant syndicates of northern Spain (CONCA) had more members than any of the revolutionary movements.

The middle-class left saw religious belief and clerical influence as the main obstacles to "freedom" and "progressivism." They believed that the collapse of the monarchy signaled the irrevocable decline of conservative principles and that the tide of Spanish politics and culture had begun to move strongly against Catholic values. It should be kept in mind that most sectors of the Spanish intelligentsia had just begun to enter the west European cultural milieu of the late nineteenth or twentieth centuries where the question of religion was as much or more one of indifference as of controversy. Many leaders of the Republican left had received an early religious education and remained preoccupied with religion even when in rebellion against it. Some of the most ardent anticlericals were themselves religious men, albeit of a secularized, rationalistic, or Deistic sort, who wanted to establish a purified religion after their own notions. A different kind of influence was also provided by two examples which would have passed unnoticed in most European countries—the Portuguese and Mexican revolutions of 1910, both of which inaugurated a degree of persecution of the previously established religion.

Another touchstone was insistence on ideological purity in the tradition of European radicalism. This ideological moralism resulted in an antipolitical stance; compromise and practical adjustment were adjudged a sellout of principle. The moralistic, ideological, antipolitical orientation of left Republicanism was a major manifestation of reaction to the monarchy and dictatorship which had been "immoral" and "political." Alvaro de Albornoz, one of the two top leaders of the Radical Socialists, eulogized civil war as the only true "moral conflict."

The other main aspect of the left Republican program was social reform, which was to include labor regulation and agrarian reform, with the breakup of the large estates. But social problems did not attract the attention of left Republicans nearly as much as did intellectual ideals of liberty and ideological problems related to religion and the authority of conservative institutions.

By contrast, the major force of moderate Republicanism was the Radical party led by Alejandro Lerroux. Lerroux had tempered his ways from his demagogy of two decades earlier. Gone were class hatred and the extremes of anticlericalism. By 1931 the sexagenarian aspired to the leadership of national middle-class Republican liberalism, and his Radical party, which had managed to establish sections in most parts of the country, was to play much the same role in Spanish affairs of the next four years as its Radical Socialist counterpart did in France.

It took considerable pulling and hauling to bring the Socialists into the coalition that formed the Republican provisional government. The social democratic leaders Indalecio Prieto and Fernando de los Ríos had ignored party discipline to sign the so-called "Pact of San Sebastián" of September 1930, by which a self-appointed committee of Republican leaders agreed in principle with Catalanist representatives about the form of a democratic republic that would prepare for the regional autonomy of Catalonia as well as full civic liberty and equality. There was sharp division of opinion in the Socialist leadership even after the decision to collaborate had been ratified; the UGT failed to bring off a general strike during the disturbances of December 1930 that attended an abortive pro-Republican military revolt. However, the main UGT leaders associated with Largo Caballero eventually decided in favor of participation, and the chief party theoretician, Julián Besteiro, tentatively agreed that the Socialists ought to participate in the government during its early stages to help stabilize a progressive Republican regime. At first only a small minority of revolutionaries completely opposed this strategy.

Of three seats held by the Socialists in the provisional government, the most important was Largo Caballero's tenure of the Ministry of Labor, which he used to carry out rapid, positive reforms. A decree of May 1931 revived the *comités paritarios* in the form of *jurados mixtos* (mixed juries) to resolve labor disputes, and before the calling of the first election a series of measures were imposed to correct regulation of labor affairs. Fifteen years later, Largo wrote,

> From this collection of laws I only want to point out two: the new Law of Workers' Associations and that of Labor Inspection. The first, ill-understood by the National Confederation of Labor, took all jurisdiction over the right of association from the Ministry of the Interior and the police, giving it to the inspectors of the Ministry of Labor. This was an important innovation for the working class, and had already been introduced in other countries. The second created a Corps of Inspectors selected by examination, with salaries substantial enough to protect them from bribery, entrusted with the fulfillment of social legislation.[2]

The steps taken during Largo's first months in office had measurable effect in improving the lot of Spanish workers, both urban and rural. The *jurados mixtos* frequently went beyond fairness, however, since tie votes on arbitration issues were broken by the ballot of the government-appointed chairmen, who under Largo were invariably prolabor. This resulted in major improvements in wages and working conditions, though occasionally more than the partially depressed Spanish economy of 1931 to 1933 could afford.

Most of the Socialist party were quite satisfied with the results of the first phase of government collaboration, and in many provinces the Socialists formed alliances with the Republican left for the elections to the constituent Cortes that were held in June 1931. Formation of broad provincial alliances was encouraged by the terms of the voting regulations, which were designed to avoid the fragmentation of small single-party candidacies. The list of candidates with the largest number of votes in each province won from 67 to 80 percent of the seats for that province, while the second highest list received from 20 to 33 percent of the seats.

2. Largo Caballero, *Mis recuerdos* (Mexico City, 1954), 123–24.

The electoral results revealed that the Socialist party had become the largest organized political group in the country. Representation in the constitutent Cortes by party was as follows:

117	Socialists
93	Radicals
59	Radical Socialists
32	Catalanist left
27	Republican Action
27	Progressives (moderate Republican liberals)
26	Agrarian party
16	ORGA (Galician regionalist Republican left)
14	"Al Servicio de la República" (liberal intellectuals)
14	Basque nationalists
3	Lliga Catalana (Catalanist liberals)
1	Monarchists
18	Miscellaneous liberals and moderate left
10	Independents

Of the 457 deputies, the left had 251, the liberals 155, and the conservatives no more than 41.

This lopsided victory was due to two main factors: a gust of enthusiasm for Republican progressivism that swept the country and the almost complete disorientation of the conservative sectors of Spanish politics, which had still not recovered from the shock of the sudden collapse of the monarchy. They had failed to organize and for the most part did not contest the elections. Consequently one of the most striking features of the constituent Cortes was the lack of continuity with the last parliament of 1923. Nearly all of the 49 political organizations that participated in the elections were newly organized, and only a handful of the deputies that were elected had ever sat in parliament before. This is in sharp contrast to the rebuilding of representative government in more mature countries, such as in France after 1944 or in Italy, Austria, and West Germany following long periods of dictatorship. As a result, the representatives who drew up the Republican constitution did not reflect the full range of values and commitments of Spanish society. This led to a somewhat artificial policy that helped set the stage for the great conflicts of the next five years.

The new constitution was nonetheless in most respects a sound document. The chairman of the parliamentary drafting commission, the Socialist professor Luis Jiménez de Asúa, subsequently labeled it "a leftist constitution but not a Socialist one." Though the constitution defined Spain as a "republic of workers of all classes" (to the satirical amusement of anarchists and Communists), its main provisions guaranteed liberal democratic parliamentary government based on the equal rights of individuals. Article 44, which legalized "socialization" and "nationalization" of property without compensation when in the national interest, passed by only one vote, and further provided that confiscation of property could "in no case" be imposed as an individual political penalty. This article was especially pleasing to the Socialists because it seemed to mark the first step toward a smooth transition to a socialist system.

The tenents of liberal democracy were clearly violated by the anti-Catholic provision, Article 26. Separation of Church and state was long overdue, but the provision for outlawing Catholic orders and prohibiting Catholic education save in the training of priests constituted basic restrictions of religious freedom. This was a conscious effort on the part of the left to stifle traditional Spanish culture and provoked the resignation of the two moderate liberals in the cabinet.

Insofar as one man was responsible for pushing such legislation through and setting the tone of Republican politics, it was Manuel Azaña, a fifty-year-old writer and bureaucrat who had never had a regular political post prior to the coming of the Republic. Azaña was a prose stylist of great purity and rigor, but he had never achieved major literary fame. He had recently risen to prominence as head of the literary Ateneo and as a leading spokesman for radical intellectuals. Azaña's determination, incorruptibility, parliamentary vigor and rhetorical eloquence made him the "political revelation" of 1931 and lifted him to the premiership in October. Left Republican ideals were shared by the heads of a dozen other factions, but only Azaña seemed able to provide the forceful direction that could complete a program. His very coldness and misanthropy was fundamental to his power, for they helped arm him with a personal and intellectual discipline that his more superficial, gregarious associates lacked.

Azaña also provided a left Republican style—cold, sneering,

sarcastic, sectarian, and often brilliantly eloquent. His liberal col-
league Miguel Maura recalled that

> The oratory of Azaña resembled no other. It was cold, hard, incisive,
> monotonous, and lacking in tonalities of voice or gesture, but was
> nevertheless crushing and fascinating. How many times listening to him
> from the front benches of congress did I say to myself, "How can the
> oratory of this man convince, conquer and captivate the masses?" I
> never figured it out.[3]

What Azaña said was sometimes not so important as the way he
said it; he spoke as much to wound the opposition as to rally the
faithful. Maura recalled, "I once asked him the reason for his
mania of wounding simply in order to wound, of never losing an
opportunity to pour scorn on the opposition, and he replied, 'I do
it because it amuses me.' I am sure that was correct."[4]

Azaña's political norms were derived from his intellectual
ideals, his moral convictions, and his esthetic sense. He was opposed to authority in its traditional forms, which he considered
irrational and arbitrary. He proposed instead to establish a new
authority based on a pure ideological thesis, a sort of platonic idea
of the perfect Spanish constitutional system.

Azaña was opposed to the notion that politics was the art of
the possible. Professor Juan Marichal has written in his introduction to Azaña's *Obras completas* that

> For Azaña the tragedy of Spanish liberalism . . . had been its tendency
> to transaction and compromise. . . . The duty of true liberals is, then,
> very clear: it is what he calls intransigence. He wrote on December 29,
> 1923, " . . . It will be necessary to restore doctrines in their purity and
> shield oneself against compromise. Intransigence will be symptomatic
> of integrity."

Alfonso XIII, a tolerant man who believed in compromise, resigned when threatened with potential civil war in 1931. Five
years later Azaña refused the same course. His insistence on
"pure" liberalism was so extreme that it led him to illiberal
positions. To the end of his life Azaña liked simply to define himself as a "liberal," yet soon after the Republic began he got

3. Miguel Maura, *Así cayó Alfonso XIII* (Mexico City, 1964), 229.
4. *Ibid.*, 230.

at least a glimmering of the contradiction involved, and when his faction was reorganized it called itself the "Republican Left."

In a well-publicized speech of October 13, 1931, Azaña maintained that "Spain has ceased to be Catholic" and specified two main activities of the Catholic Church that must be proscribed. He warned that "I know that I am going to displease the liberals," but stressed that since Catholic charities also encouraged religious proselytization, the charitable work of Catholic orders must be outlawed. "The other decisive restriction that will displease the liberals" was the demand to outlaw Catholic schools, save for the training of priests. He recognized the illiberal nature of this denial of Catholic rights, but held that a true Republic could only be constructed in a non-Catholic society. Hence his remark, "Let no one say to me that this is contrary to liberty, for it is a question of public health."[5]

Azaña's position as leader of the middle-class left enabled him to play the crucial role of master of the terrain separating the revolutionaries from the nonrevolutionaries. During the first Republican biennium, when the Socialists only pressed their minimum demands, Azaña's program was in some respects quite moderate. Since the middle-class left was much more concerned about the questions of authority and religious influence than about economic problems, there was no radical assault on the structure of property itself. However, Azaña's government explicitly rejected a policy of consensus or coexistence with Catholic conservatism—or even with reformist Catholic liberalism—whose representatives were told they had no right to share power or participate in government decisions. After the middle-class left had isolated itself with the revolutionaries, Azaña's course became increasingly sectarian and arbitrary. His enormous pride—which he disguised with public boasting of his "stoicism" and lack of ego investment in worldly vanity—together with his intense scorn for mediocre contemporaries, made it almost impossible that he admit he had been mistaken or had gone too far. Only after the final cataclysm began did he to some extent repent and admit that it might have been better to have accepted at least a degree

5. *Obras completas* (Mexico City, 1966), 56–57.

of coexistence with the opposition, however much less enlightened they were than his ideals. Azaña's career became a classic case of *hubris* and of the nemesis of public power.

Azaña did not make the mistake of assuming that the middle-class left alone could rally the majority of the population, and relied upon alliance with the Socialists to remain in power. Initially, most Socialist leaders seemed willing enough, but the exact presuppositions of Socialist participation in power had never been made explicit. Ever since the first agreement to form a government with Republicans in 1917, the Socialist party had tended more and more toward a pragmatic, reformist, non-doctrinaire position similar to that of its French and German counterparts. The Socialist leadership refused, however, to define its policy clearly in those terms. The exact relationship of Socialist policy to doctrinaire Marxist revolutionism was left increasingly vague; most leaders seemed to find it convenient to ignore the problem and talk exclusively in terms of immediate tactics. The original decision to participate in the government of a parliamentary Republic had caused a serious problem, but this had been gotten around on the grounds that the Socialists would participate only so long as it was necessary to protect the new regime from the right. This was an artificial excuse, since an organized political right was nonexistent in 1931.

Judging from their statements, most Socialist leaders—and their followers—accepted the Republic as the beginning of a steady leftward evolution in Spanish affairs. They expected it to bring rapid, sweeping social reform, the progressive education of the Spanish electorate, and before too very long a Socialist Republic. But there is no indication of concrete planning as to how this process was to be brought about. The main current of Socialist opinion seems to have merely assumed that the natural trend of events was almost inevitably moving in this direction.

Only one major Socialist figure questioned the wisdom of committing the party to continued participation without setting specific limits. At a Socialist congress in July 1931, Julián Besteiro warned of the frustrations and dilemmas that would eventually have to be faced:

I have said before that if we remain in the government we shall in the long run either have to let ourselves be led by other elements who abuse our good will or have to show a strong hand and become dictatorial. I fear a Socialist dictatorship more than a bourgeois dictatorship. We could defend ourselves against the latter, but with the former we would destroy ourselves.[6]

During 1931 both the party and the UGT seemed to be profiting greatly from their association with the Republic. Party membership, which had dropped to less than 15,000 under the dictatorship shot up to more than 71,000 by April 1932, giving the party the largest number of organized participants of any political association in Spain. For the first time in its history, the UGT expanded more rapidly than the CNT, benefiting in some provinces from the assistance of mediators and Labor Ministry appointees. By mid-1932 the UGT numbered 1,041,539 members, making it the largest trade union organization in Spanish history. The bulk of this increase came in the new farm workers federation (FNTT), set up as a branch of the UGT in 1930. The FNTT concentrated especially on the poorer regions of south central and southwestern Spain, and by 1932 had enrolled 445,000 members.

Government participation reinforced the Socialists' commitment to practical restraint and legal evolutionary tactics, whereas anarchosyndicalists used the return of civil guarantees to reactivate the CNT as an instrument of libertarian revolution. Socialist politicians and labor leaders alike were appalled by the immediate resumption of street murders and pseudo-revolutionary violence by the anarchists, and made clear their determination not to tolerate it. *El Socialista* declared on June 13, 1931, "We do not hesitate to say it: All the gangsterism, all the crimes that have been committed in Barcelona, including the *ley de fugas,* are the indirect work of the Sindicatos Unicos. The National Conferation of Labor is a worker organization based on gunmen." And on July 9:

When the dictatorship came, Catalonia—and especially Barcelona, including the workers—applauded the dictator, because they saw in the new situation the only way of freeing themselves from those dishonor-

6. Quoted by Gabriel Morón, *La ruta del socialismo en España* (Madrid, 1932), 45–46.

able deeds. Soon after the dictatorship and the monarchy disappeared violence broke out again. In Barcelona everyone is armed; the syndical- ists are given to every kind of excess. Where will this situation lead Barcelona?

Under the new Republic, the country was almost immedi- ately enveloped in disorder more severe than that of 1923. To Azaña, anarchist gunmen were common criminals. Neither he nor the Socialist leaders were willing in 1931–32 to have the nascent regime discredited and weakened by street anarchy. A special new urban police force, the Assault Guard, was formed by the Minister of the Interior, and on October 29, 1931, a temporary new Law for the Defense of the Republic provided for the sus- pension of constitutional guarantees and facilitated police con- trol. Anarchists soon reflected on the bitter paradox that the left Republican regime was harder on them than some of the more liberal monarchist ministries had been.

The strong line that had been adopted on public order some- times made the Socialists uneasy, especially after the more radical sections of the FNTT became involved in riots and barn burn- ings, but the party leaders at first stood resolutely beside the government despite the fog of demagogic propaganda and the persistent accusations of police brutality. The party did take the position that the heavyhanded rural constabulary, the Civil Guard, ought to be dissolved in favor of a more moderate form of police, but this was not made a matter of parliamentary confidence.

The ultimate success of the first phase of the Socialists' participation in government depended on the nature and result of the agrarian reform law that was prepared in 1932. This was even more important than the labor administration of Largo Caballero, for the peasantry remained the largest single social class in Spain and the plight of nearly 1 million landless peasants was still the country's most grievous social problem. The mal- distribution of property in the latifundist provinces and the ills generated by the social and economic structure of those areas were by that time admitted even by many conservatives. After the advent of the Republic, the question was not whether there would be an agrarian reform, but whether it should be thoroughgoingly radical or moderate, whether it should set up individual family farms or adopt a socialist program for cooperatives and collective agriculture. When the Republic was introduced, conditions in the southern countryside were extremely agitated and there was fear of an outright peasant revolt. In his first months as Minister of Labor, Largo had acted to ease the peasant's plight: benefits of the pre-1923 industrial accidents' law were extended to farm workers; it was decreed that farm renters could be expelled for no reason other than failure to cultivate their land or pay rent; a *términos municipales* law prohibited employment of workers from outside the employers' district, reserving local jobs for local labor; an eight-hour day for farm laborers was decreed and the *jurados mixtos* extended to argiculture. The *términos municipales* law enormously increased the bargaining power of organized farm labor and was the main factor behind the spectacular rise of the FNTT in 1931 and 1932. Labor Ministry–appointed chairmen enabled labor interests to dominate most *jurados mixtos* in rural areas, as in the cities. This influence, plus the local labor monopolies created by the *términos municipales,* brought a rapid increase in farm laborers' wages. While the prices of farm products declined in the face of the international depression, farm laborers' wages in Spain nearly doubled between 1931 and 1933. Spiraling production costs did not hurt latifundists so badly as they did the owners of small- and medium-sized properties who used hired labor.

The left Republican leaders were slow in presenting an agrarian reform bill, in part because they had given the matter little thought. Most of them were opposed to drastic social revolution, and some thought that Largo Caballero had already gone too far in stacking the cards against landowners in arbitration disputes. If all the landless peasants were to be given farms of their own, nearly one-third of the arable soil of Spain would have to be expropriated. Few of the left Republicans thought of a change of such magnitude. Moreover, it was agreed that whatever was expropriated would have to be paid for, and the government had little money to devote to the project.

The Socialists demanded that a significant portion, though not necessarily all, of the soil thus made available be turned into agrarian collectives supervised by the FNTT. In support of the latter proposition, they could point to the failure of east European reforms that had allotted minuscule plots to backward peasants without capital or technical preparation and so merely redistributed poverty. The left Republican leadership would not concede the maximal Socialist demands and Lerroux' Radicals, the number two party in the Cortes, came out in opposition to the first compromise proposals with the slogan, *"Reforma agraria si; reforma agraria socialista no."*

The bill bogged down altogether during the spring and summer of 1932. The middle-class left was so reluctant to attack medium properties or commit a major share of government resources that little might have been done had it not been for the small, abortive, monarchist-military revolt of August 1932, which temporarily swung the political balance to the left once more. Azaña himself set the new tone by a speech on September 8, 1932, which affirmed that the "Republic" was, after all, "revolutionary" and would have to adopt revolutionary standards of justice.

The resulting law was extremely complicated. The minimal plots of land exempt from expropriation varied, depending on location and the nature of the land, from 10 to 1,000 hectares, or a maximum of one-fifth of the assessed land in any municipality. Moreover, the property of owners who held land in several districts was counted individually, so that such an owner might altogether retain several times the minimum individual total. The totals were not cumulative, and nonarable land was largely exempt.

Four types of land were to be expropriated in their entirety: land originally held under *señorío* rights (medieval aristocratic tenure); badly cultivated land; land in irrigated zones that had not been converted to irrigation; and land that had been leased continually for a period of not less than twelve years. Moreover, the proportion liable to confiscation was raised especially high in *ruedo* districts (strips bordering inhabited villages) that might easily be converted to peasant use, and all leased land beyond 1,000 pesetas annual taxable income (about 25 hectares) was also made liable to confiscation. Since it was mainly small-medium and medium holders who owned soil in *ruedo* districts, and since medium holders leased a significant amount of their property, they constituted the great majority of those affected. Of a total of 80,000 owners liable to partial or total confiscation, only 10,000 to 12,000 were large holders, and approximately 60,000 were small-medium and medium holders from northern and central Spain, not the latifundist regions. Only rentiers were affected, however, for anyone who farmed his own land was specifically exempt.

The provisions affecting small-medium and medium owners were included by the middle-class left as a favor to the Socialists in return for the exclusion of state-financed collectives. Only two concessions were made to socialization: Title to all expropriated land would be retained by the state; individual peasant farmers granted private use would only enjoy emphyteutic rights, while paying annual rent equivalent to 4 percent of the assessed value. Secondly, after landless peasants, preference for distribution would be given to "legally constituted peasant societies that have been in existence for at least two years." This qualification was so worded that only the FNTT could currently meet its terms. The Socialists, however, wanted to make the scope of expropriation as broad as possible and were greatly disappointed with the dimensions of the program. On the other hand, the bill's unbalanced effects, which would in most instances hurt small-medium owners more than latifundists, discredited the reform among moderates and made it easy to rouse strong opposition. The most politically effective measure would have been a reform aimed specifically at reduction and transformation of the latifundia, which could have been presented as a crusade against overweening wealth and social injustice.

The bill was voted on September 15, 1932, but its machinery was slow to go into effect. There were violent disturbances among FNTT peasants in the southwest during October, and Communist agitators seized the opportunity to organize a revolutionary strike in 11 villages in Badajoz province. Increasing tension led the government to enact an emergency measure on November 1, the "intensification of cultivation" decree. It provided for the temporary settlement of landless peasants for up to two years at nominal rent on uncultivated portions of large estates in eight southern and western provinces. This was a moderate but specific act that was carried out immediately and vigorously. Within less than six months 40,100 peasant cultivators were settled on land totaling 123,000 hectares.

Much less progress was made in implementing the main reform law. Its administrative arm, the Institute of Agrarian Reform, was directed by a technical council whose diverse membership made prompt action extremely difficult. The most decisive restriction was budgetary: in the beginning, funds were limited to 1 percent of the national budget. During the first two years of the agrarian reform law, only 12,000 families received land. Meanwhile, after passing the original bill, Azaña devoted most of his time in the months which followed to his anticlerical campaign. A new religious associations act supplemented Article 26 of the constitution by requiring the closure of all ordinary Catholic schools within one year. The resultant controversy and bitterness diverted attention from social reform.

Aside from the reduction in the size of the Army, the other major efforts of the Republican government during its first two years centered on the areas of public finance, public works, and public education. The scant interest of the middle-class left in sweeping social and economic reform was best revealed by the government's emphasis on orthodox financing and its lack of concern to reform the highly unjust Spanish tax structure, which relied mainly on excises and failed to tap the resources of the wealthy. Instead, the budget was nearly balanced and the customary annual increase in the national debt almost eliminated, even though significant new projects were undertaken in construction, irrigation, and hydroelectric development.

One of the proudest achievements was the great expansion of primary and secondary education from 1931 to 1933. The dapper young Socialist Rodolfo Llopis—called the "Rudolph Valentino of pedagogy"—became director of primary education, presiding over the most extensive school construction program in Spanish educational history up to that time. Yet all the new schools built from 1931 to 1933 would not have made up for the number of classrooms that were scheduled to be eliminated by the religious associations act.

Anticlericalism was the fetish of the middle-class left and also, it might be added, of the anarchists, but it did not rank as high on the Socialist list of priorities. Indeed, one of the Socialist ministers, the reformist social democrat De los Ríos, had at first tried to speak out on behalf of the Catholic Church. Failure to carry through the major part of the social reforms that had been expected left the Socialists increasingly restive.

Nevertheless, the thirteenth congress of the Socialist party met at Madrid in October 1932 and did not lead to any change in the party's position. Though voices were raised in protest against the rejection of revolutionary tactics, moderates warned that withdrawal from the government might open the way to rightist reaction. A resolution by Prieto in favor of continuing participation on a temporary basis, with the intention of withdrawing from responsibility in the middle-class regime "as soon as circumstances permit," was carried by a large majority.

The principal opposition to the Socialist–left Republican government in the months that followed did not come from the right, but from anarchosyndicalists and dissident liberals. The wave of unprecedented anarchist disorders continued throughout 1932 and into 1933, bringing political strikes and shootings. For the most part, these were met with restraint, but at the height of outbreaks police atrocities did occur, the worst of which was the murder of some 18 peasant prisoners by the Assault Guard after a local insurrection in Andalusia in January 1933 (the Casas Viejas affair). As the wave of strikes, explosions, and political *atracos* persisted, the government arrested thousands of CNT militants and enacted new laws to regulate firearms, check vagrancy, and expand the police. The Socialist ministers sometimes took a sterner attitude toward disorder than did leaders of the middle-class left.

Meanwhile, opposition among middle-class liberals increased. Lerroux' Radicals were not represented in the government, but they had largely supported it until the beginning of 1933, when Lerroux went into outright opposition because of the cabinet's concessions to the Socialists and its handling of recent disorders. The small pro-Catholic Republican parties of the president, Alcalá Zamora, and of Miguel Maura were also in opposition,[7] as were Spain's leading intellectuals—José Ortega y Gasset, Miguel de Unamuno and Gregorio Marañón—who had been elected to the constituent Cortes and hoped to collaborate in the building of a liberal democratic Republic. Ortega's best-remembered comment was the contrast he drew between the broad enthusiasm for civic renewal in 1931 and the sectarian Azaña regime of 1932–33: *¡No era eso!* (It wasn't that!).[8]

More damaging were the results of the first local elections under the Republic, held in the spring of 1933. These were to choose new municipal councils for some 2,600 villages and small towns in northern Spain whose election of monarchists in April 1931 had been arbitrarily annulled by the new regime. The Socialists and the middle-class left combined won only about one-third the seats, while the Radicals and the conservative

7. Maura's most sweeping critique of the first Republican biennium was published in *El Sol* on June 23, 1936:

> We were mistaken in convening the constituent Cortes and undertaking the labor of writing the new state constitution only a few months after the establishment of the new regime, for it was inevitable that inexperience in government on the one hand and the revolutionary tension of the masses on the other result in a fundamental law plagued with errors in its organizational structure and laden with sectarianism and demagogy in its postulates. . . .
>
> We were wrong to deny dialogue and coexistence to political adversaries, because this falsified the function of parliament, perverted its mission and opened the way for the justified protest of opinion that created the ambiguous, enervating avalanche of 1933. Above all this undermined the prestige of parliament itself, making public opinion lose confidence in it. . . .
>
> We were wrong to have consented to and even encouraged the relaxation of the reins of authority, and with this lowering the prestige of the organs charged with maintaining it, instead of considering the maintenance of public order a responsibility common to all the parties in the regime.

8. Ortega, Marañón, and the novelist Pérez de Ayala were the leaders of a loose association of intellectuals, writers, and professional men that labeled itself the Agrupación al Servicio de la República, and Unamuno was elected under the column of the small middle-class Progressive party. Though Ortega disclaimed political ambition or talent, his speeches in the Cortes of 1931–33 were the most lucid, telling, and far-sighted delivered in that body. He correctly foretold the failure of the Republican regime if it continued to

Agrarians won about 20 percent each. Azaña tried to dismiss these results as the work of "rotten boroughs." His comparison convinced few, for the areas involved had comparatively high literacy rates and were among the most self-reliant in Spain.

All the moderate liberal groups believed that the Republic had moved too far too fast and that the time had come to retrench. Even sectors of the middle-class left began to waver. Azaña had accomplished most of his goals and offered no further aims than to complete the writing of certain constitutional laws and carry out the reforms already legislated. The largest party of the middle-class left, the Radical Socialists, was restive and divided. It had ridden the crest of the Republican wave in the hope of establishing a mass social democratic party. The Radical Socialists stood for a federal but not confederate Republic, with considerable regional autonomy under a system of central unity and law. In addition to the institutional changes in the military, the police, and the Church demanded by their allies, they also stood for tax reform, direct representation of the economic interests of all classes, and sweeping social reforms. By May 1933 they claimed to have a total following greater than any other organized party in the country.[9] Yet the Radical Socialists were hopelessly divided by doctrinal and personal disputes. Their leading figures, sobered by domestic disorder, the problem of political unity, and the dilemma of economic reform, came more and more to fear the loyalty and ultimate intentions of the Socialists. They finally

---

pursue a policy based on ideological sectarianism.

Ortega's principal criticisms concerned economic and religious policies and the need for compromise with moderates and conservatives. He warned against the tendency to think about economic programs in terms of ideologico-moral abstractions rather than the complicated problems of twentieth-century society. It was not a matter of "capitalism" versus "collectivism," Ortega said, but of technical knowledge and public and private planning to increase the productivity of an increasingly industrial economy.

Ortega was appalled by the attempt to stifle Catholic culture, and doubted that the vital forces of Spanish Catholicism had declined to the extent that Azaña supposed. He warned that the anti-Catholic legislation constituted an "armed cartridge" that might produce a "delayed detonation."

9. A nominal membership of 126,585 was claimed in the party secretary's report, *Texto taquigráfico del cuarto congreso nacional ordinario del Partido Republicano Radical Socialista de España* (Madrid, 1933), 121. The criteria of party membership were, however, vague and probably unreliable.

demanded that the Socialists either put an end to sporadic disorder by the UGT and support the government fully, or else withdraw altogether in favor of a cabinet composed exclusively of left and liberal Republicans. In reaction to this trend, radical young intellectuals and activists in the extreme left wing of the party, led by Eduardo Ortega y Gasset (brother of the philosopher) and Ramón Franco (younger brother of the general), split off to form a Left Radical Socialist party. After the moderates gained the ascendancy in the main group, the center of the former party also walked out to set up an Independent Radical Socialist party that favored continued collaboration with the Socialists. The main body of Radical Socialists, like Lerroux' Radicals, hoped to attract support from the principal politically unrepresented group on the left, the trade unionists of the CNT. The latter were thoroughly alienated from the Azaña-Socialist government, but Radicals and Radical Socialists alike calculated that a reorganized democratic cabinet might win part of the rank-and-file syndicalists away from the apolitical revolutionary dogmas of the CNT leadership.

The Republican parties tended toward extreme fragmentation. Between 1929 and 1934 they were organized under the following groups:

1929: "Republican Alliance," composed of the
  Radical Republican party
  Federal Republican party
  Republican Action group

1931: The seven preceding parties were joined by two new regionalist groups:
  Basque Nationalist party
  ORGA (Galicianist left)

1930: In addition to the three existing parties, four new ones were formed:
  Radical Socialist party
  Progressive party
  Catalan Left
  Catalan Action

1933: Division of both the Radical Socialists and Federal Republicans into three parties each creates four more parties.

1934: Division of the Radicals in two adds yet another party.

Though the Azaña ministry survived the president's first attempt to find an alternative government in June 1933, it was further weakened by criticism from the most moderate sector of Azaña's own Republican Action party. Another major blow was struck by the first elections to the Tribunal of Constitutional Guarantees, the body that was to serve as Republican supreme court. The Tribunal was chosen by municipal councillors, the bar associations, and the national Academy of Jurisprudence; the majority of those elected represented moderate liberal and moderate conservative opinion. This was interpreted as a repudiation of the Azaña regime by the local government leaders of Spain.

Azaña subsequently won a vote of confidence by 146 to 3, but his victory was compromised by the fact that only one-third of the Cortes deputies cast their ballots. Since Azaña could not rally a true majority, the president of the Republic exercised his constitutional prerogative of withdrawing confidence and forcing the cabinet's resignation. Lerroux was authorized to form a new ministry, but his cabinet could not win support from other parties and was weaker than its predecessor. When the Cortes reopened, the left combined with the conservative minority to bring down the Lerroux government, though it lacked the votes to form a successor. Splintering of the middle-class left had broken up the only bloc with enough deputies to govern, and Alcalá Zamora had little alternative to scheduling general elections for November 1933.

The breakup of the leftist coalition profoundly disappointed the Socialists. So long as there remained any possibility of keeping the Azaña ministry in power, the majority still supported the policy of collaboration, yet this support became more qualified after the Azaña government first began to totter. Of the major Socialist leaders, only Besteiro had persisted in his opposition to continued participation, warning again and again that the Republican left coalition would not lead to direct solution of the country's problems. In a speech on the 50th anniversary of the death of Marx in March 1933, he had explained:

A government that pays unemployment relief as in England or enacts the fruitful social legislation that we have in Spain thanks to a Socialist minister of labor can govern through a socialist policy, but restricts itself to a purely reformist socialism. If socialism takes that course solely and exclusively, it will not benefit the new masses of proletarians being formed day by day through the fulfillment on a grand scale of the laws established by Marx. Those new proletarians can never be content with reformist socialism. The danger appears if socialism does not hold to Marxist principles, and prematurely accepts the responsibilities of government. Reformism then irremediably isolates itself from the masses, whose intelligence is not yet awake, but who have a revolutionary spirit that we ought to cultivate by attracting to our ranks as a guarantee of their triumph and ours.[10]

Besteiro did not mean that a revolutionary socialist dictatorship should be established to do what the Republic could not, for he denied that Spain's civic culture or economy were sufficiently developed to support a genuinely socialist regime, whether democratic or dictatorial. In a speech to UGT miners at Mieres on July 2, 1933, Besteiro said flatly that "the country is not economically or socially prepared for a Socialist government," and that in such circumstances he must oppose "the dictatorship of the proletariat," which would only result in futile bloodshed. He had earlier emphasized that socialism could not take charge until it controlled "all the means of power of bourgeois society through the decided, energetic and continuous penetration of the proletariat. Only when these are completely dominated does it become possible to change all the structure of social life from top to bottom."[11] The Socialists should retire to creative opposition, continue the education and organization of the working classes, and avoid being compromised by the limitations of left Republican government.

Besteiro's chief opponent was not the reformist social democrat, Prieto, but the labor minister, Largo Caballero, who was president of the party's executive commission. Largo deprecated Besteiro, currently head of the UGT national committee, as an impractical theoretician and a vain intellectual. He greatly overestimated the capabilities of the Spanish Socialist movement and, once he had tasted power in government, was loath to give it up. Heretofore Largo had never advocated tactics of violent revolution; a disciple of Iglesias, he had devoted his life to slow, practical, constructive trade unionism. He had been a member of the Institute of Social Reform from 1904 until its demise, and

10. Gabriel Mario de Coca, *Anti-Caballero* (Madrid, 1936), 79.
11. *Ibid.*, 81.

had taken some part in almost every piece of social legislation passed in Spain during the twentieth century. In the subsequent crises of 1934 through 1936, he shrank from direct, conclusive revolutionary action to establish a Socialist regime, and in 1933 he did not really think that the problem would arise. In a big rally at Madrid on July 23, he said that "We are going to conquer power within the Constitution and under the laws of the state." This did not mean that Largo was a reformist social democrat like his other chief rival, the Socialist Minister of Public Works, Indalecio Prieto. Largo was a convinced, if vague-minded, Marxist and he looked down upon Prieto as an unscrupulous, opportunistic politician who, he later claimed, "had never really been a Socialist." In his July 23 speech Largo reminded his Socialist audience that Marx had categorically declared that a dictatorship of the proletariat was inevitable in consolidating a socialist society and hence that even though it would probably be possible to win control of the government by parliamentary means, the standards of liberal democracy would not suffice to complete the path to socialism. He said that the dictatorship of the proletariat ought to be achieved and exercised with as little violence as possible, but that would depend upon the degree of resistance encountered.

Socialist leaders found it disgusting that the agrarian reform was still not being carried out in 1933, but had been persistently deferred by the Republican left in favor of anticlerical legislation, army reform, and even balancing the budget. The left Republican government showed no interest in legislation to provide unemployment compensation. The number of jobless was rising and social unrest among the southern peasantry was increasing sharply. By 1933 the number of UGT wildcat strikes grew along with the rate of barn burnings and other disorders in the southern countryside. After all the changes, propaganda, and agitation of the past two years, it was not surprising that hundreds of thousands of workers were gripped by excitement and gave vent to shrill demands. Altogether, strike activity nearly doubled in 1933.

Strikes and labor unrest were no longer the work of the CNT

TABLE 5.1. *Spanish   Strike   Statistics,   1930–33*

	Number of strikes	Workers on strike	Number of days lost
1930	402	247,460	3,745,360
1931	734	236,177	3,843,260
1932	681	269,104	3,589,473
1933	1,200	420,000	5,100,000

SOURCE: Spanish Ministry of Labor.

or the Communists alone. By the summer of 1933 the Socialists changed their previously strong stand on behalf of public order, and called for repeal of the stringent Law for the Defense of the Republic, since it was now being invoked against UGT members.

It became fashionable among the Socialist Youth and sectors of the UGT to talk of the immediacy of the "revolution," though there was little clear agreement about what this meant. A series of position speeches were given before the Socialist Youth Summer School at Torrelodones in August. Besteiro's restatement of what he considered the "orthodox Marxist" position was coldly received. Prieto was more discreet, but warned there were limits to what Spanish socialism could achieve in the present political and economic situation of Europe, which would probably make an all-out Socialist regime at the present time impossible. Prieto did his best to point out how fallacious were the comparisons being drawn between Russia in 1917 and Spain in 1933. In Russia nearly all institutions had collapsed prior to the Bolshevik coup; in Spain the Church and the Army remained, the government was intact, and the middle classes were stronger than in eastern Europe.

When Largo's turn came on August 11, he shifted the emphases from his earlier speech in Madrid and told the impatient young people what they wanted to hear. Largo referred to a letter from Engels to Kautsky in 1875 which stressed that a democratic republic was the specific political form that would lead to the dictatorship of the proletariat, and on these grounds justified the Marxist orthodoxy of participating in a left Republican government. "I myself have always had the reputation of being conservative and reformist, but people have gotten this mixed up." He defended the Socialist policy of electing as many deputies and city councilmen as possible to expand the power base of socialism, but stressed that "today I am convinced that it is impossible to carry out [ultimate] Socialist tasks within bourgeois democracy." Parliamentary democracy would only bring the Socialist movement part way; when the time to install a completely Socialist regime came, the party should not be bound by constitutional restrictions.

Let us suppose that the movement of attempting the installation of our regime arrives. There are those, not only outside our ranks but within them as well, who fear the need to establish a dictatorship. If this is the case, what would our situation be? For we cannot renounce our goal nor can we tolerate any act that might impede the achievement of our aim. . . .

In the critique that Marx made of the Gotha program, among other things he said this: "There is a period of revolutionary transition between capitalist and communist society, of transformation from one to the other. A phase of political transition corresponds to this, and during that period the state cannot be anything but the dictatorship of the proletariat."

Referring to communism, he said that he did not agree with Soviet foreign policy but was fully in accord with Russian Communist domestic policy.[12]

This speech roused great enthusiasm among young Socialists, who in August 1933 first raised the cry of "Long live Largo Caballero! Long live the Spanish Lenin!" His unofficial remarks were said to be more radical than the published version of his speech, and *El Socialista* added on August 16 that there had been much confusion and wishful thinking about the real nature and aims of Spanish Socialists. The editorial stressed that the party had not stayed out of the Comintern because the party was revisionist but because it was more genuinely Marxist than the Bolsheviks.

This permits us to do what the Third International does not allow. That is, to participate in a government with the Republicans and still recognize the transitory revolutionary dictatorship of the proletariat as the ineluctable postulate of scientific socialism.

What did the bourgeois newspapers suppose? Undoubtedly they supposed us to be inoffensive social democrats, full of pseudodemocratic

12. *El Socialista,* Aug. 13, 1933.

prejudices, and so foolish that, if it were necessary to prevent a fascist dictatorship, we would merely ask for new elections. What a shock it will be to our enemies when they realize that all Spanish Socialists are united, that we have no evolutionists, that we all want to leave the government and that if Besteiro doesn't like the violence of a proletarian dictatorship—and no one is happy about such violence—he would like even less to see the working class movement destroyed!

Some Socialists may be more, some less, frightened by the dictatorship of the proletariat—for it also frightened Lenin—but that is a draught one swallows willingly because of its purpose: the building of socialism, the emancipation of society from all injustice.

Socialist leaders had originally expected that the coalition left government would remain unified, fulfill its regular parliamentary term, and in the process complete so sweeping a program of social reform that it would build the power for a general Socialist victory at the polls, making it possible to establish a Socialist-dominated government peacefully. But the disunity of the middle-class left and the hostile reaction of much of the electorate to the government's program had cut short the life of the constituent assembly by at least a year or two. Though broad labor legislation had been passed, only a mere beginning had been made on agrarian reform. Most Socialist leaders felt by the fall of 1933 that their votes had been used by the Republican left to concentrate on the goals of middle-class radicalism, while postponing the deepest Socialist aims. After 1932 the membership of the Socialist party had ceased to expand, and it had begun to lose supporters to the small but now growing Communist party. The CNT had used every opportunity to radicalize and proselytize among the workers, and the Socialists were experiencing difficulty holding their most militant supporters in line.

They were also keenly aware of events abroad, especially in central Europe. Reformist social democracy had proven impotent to stop Hitler's triumph in Germany, while the refusal of the more militant Austrian Socialist party to cooperate with conservatives in parliamentary government had helped to create a situation in which the continuation of liberal democracy was impossible. Spanish Socialists were sympathetic to Austro-Marxism, whose position equidistant between Bolshevism and social democracy had paralleled their party's earlier stand. The conclusion drawn by many from events in central Europe was that social democratic reformism had led to the destruction of German socialism, and that the Austrian party's mistake was not in rejecting social democratic collaboration, but in failing to adopt a forthright revolutionary posture.

Ignoring the implications of the Spanish electoral law (which they had helped to write) that favored broad coalitions, the Socialist leaders rejected an alliance with the Republican left and ran an entirely independent ticket. The Socialists were correct in calculating that their electoral appeal was greater than that of the middle-class left, but erroneously reasoned that a broad leftward shift had occurred among the lower classes that would enable militant, independent socialism to win a major victory, if not outright government control, by itself. Socialist propaganda in the electoral campaign spoke frequently of the menace of a "fascist" reaction, referring primarily to the new clerical coalition, the Spanish Confederation of Autonomous Rightists (CEDA), which bore considerable resemblance to the Austrian Christian Social party. The CEDA's main goal was constitutional reform to protect Spanish Catholicism. Its clerical appeal gave it the ready-made support of a significant minority of the electorate, so that the CEDA stood as the spearhead of reaction. Moreover, the Socialists were also aware of the tiny fascist party, the Falange, that was organized by a handful of enthusiasts in October.

The CEDA was committed to the alteration of part of the structure of constitutional government in Spain. During the campaign, its leader, José María Gil Robles, did not hesitate to say that if parliament failed to preserve the rights of religion and traditional values, the forces of conservatism would not hesitate to go beyond parliament.

The Socialist position paralleled this exactly, warning that if the election ended in a conservative victory that imperiled the recent gains of the workers, parliamentary forms would not be respected. Largo declared in a speech at Salamanca on November 15:

I say to you that if we win on the 19th, we shall make the capitalists change their minds. But if we lose, it seems to me that we will enter a new period in which electoral activity will not be enough. It will be necessary to do something more powerful. Anything but renounce our ideals! There will be no justice so long as socialism does not triumph. Only when we can hoist the red flag of the revolution on the official buildings and towers of Spain will there be justice.[13]

The UGT provided a good deal of money for the campaign—though not so much as the CEDA collected. Socialist propaganda was insistent and direct: a vote for moderate liberals or conservatives meant the return of hunger and tyranny. The Socialists promised better living conditions, the maintenance of popular liberties save for the "exploiting class," and ultimately an egalitarian utopia.

The CEDA, on the other hand, benefited from the extension of the vote to women for the first time in Spanish history—a measure of democratic honesty by the preceding leftist government that contributed to the left's undoing. The middle-class clerical vote alone was worth about 25 percent of the general electorate. Allied in many provinces with the Radicals, the CEDA emerged from the election with the largest representation of any party in parliament—115. The Radicals, who capitalized on the reaction among the moderate sections of the middle classes, were not far behind with 102 deputies. The Socialists drew more votes than the Radicals but, without electoral allies, their representation was cut in half by the voting system, and they returned only 60 deputies. Azaña's faction was reduced to only 10; had it not been for last-minute assistance by the Socialists, Azaña himself might have lost his seat. The Radical Socialists, split in three, lost most of all, and disappeared as an organized political force. Altogether, the conservative parties had approximately 185 seats, the moderate liberals of the center about 150, and the left groups less than 100. Nearly all parties conceded that the balloting had been administered fairly and honestly.

13. Eduardo Comín Colomer, *Historia del Partido Comunista de España* (Madrid, 1965), I, 593–94.

SIX *The Left in Catalonia,*

1931-1934

ASIDE FROM THE CLERICAL ISSUE, the most controversial of the new Republican reforms was the granting of regional autonomy to Catalonia. In most modernizing countries the regions that have exhibited centrifugal tendencies have been backward, rural, and preindustrial. In Spain the opposite occurred: the most socially and economically advanced regions—Catalonia and the Basque provinces—generated centrifugal ambitions because of concrete regional cultural and economic differences, and because the structure of most of the rest of the country was developing less rapidly. Attachment to Carlist regionalism may be seen as a stage in the development of twentieth-century regional nationalism, but nationalism as a completely self-conscious, organized force did not emerge until after the social interests that sustained Carlism were well on the decline and modernization was in full swing. Moreover, Catalan and Basque nationalism were to a significant degree based upon the urban, middle-class elements that had resisted Carlism, though this was less the case in the Basque provinces than in Catalonia. Basque nationalism developed after that of Catalonia and was influenced by the latter, but remained more homogeneous, Catholic, culturally conservative, and in general more identifiably post-Carlist than did Catalan nationalism. It was represented by two parties: the moderate, middle-class, ultra-Catholic Basque National party (PNV), and the small, socially radical Basque National Action group (ANV), always overshadowed by the larger body. Unlike the Catalanist parties, Basque nationalists were never able to draw an absolute majority of the vote in the Basque provinces. There were various reasons for the wider support gained by regionalism in Catalonia. Catalan was the common tongue of most inhabitants of Catalonia, whereas the archaic Basque language was dying out and was used only by a minority of Basques. A large proportion of the Catalan upper classes supported Catalanism, but most wealthy Basques had little interest in regionalism and looked politically and economically to Madrid. Finally, many Basque workers voted for an organized proletarian political party (the Socialists), while the working classes in Catalonia, dominated by apolitical anarchosyndicalism, had no party of their own to vote for and often gave their ballots to the more radical Catalanist candidates.

The sense of regional consciousness that developed in late nineteenth-century Catalonia was, like all modern nationalist mystiques, the work of the intelligentsia. It began with the Catalan cultural renaissance of the second half of the century and only gradually, in conjunction with Catalan provincialism and federalism, became explicitly political. In the early twentieth century it assumed solid political form in the Lliga Regionalista, the party of the Catalan middle classes, which largely dominated Catalan politics from 1907 to 1919. As mentioned earlier, the Lliga was a "modern" political party, with regular membership, permanent organization, and a precise, practical program. A "Mancomunitat," or provincial federation, of the four Catalan provinces was established in 1913. It provided for pooling of provincial administrative activities but did not altogether transcend the existing structure of Spanish local government. In its efforts to press for genuine regional autonomy, the Lliga was hampered by the splintering off of left Catalanist factions that variously demanded more advanced social programs, absolute autonomy, and/or no compromise with the central government. The Lliga had nevertheless maneuvered the Cortes to the point of initiating discussion on a regional autonomy statute when the acceleration of social conflict brought declaration of martial law and temporary cloture of the Cortes in the spring of 1919.

The Lliga and moderate Catalanists never came that close to their goals again. Class struggle was the shoal on which they foundered. As the rule of violence in Barcelona became fixed, middle-class opinion looked more and more to the central government and to military assistance. The polarization of Catalan capitalism and the working-class movement left a vacuum which was eventually to be filled by new manifestations of left Catalanism that appealed to the lower middle classes and the peasantry. A new group called Catalan Action was organized by intellectuals and professional men in 1922, and was supported by the well-organized Barcelona white-collar union, CADCI. During the Primo de Rivera dictatorship one of the founders of Catalan Action, Francesc Macià, kept alive the banner of Catalanism through an extremist conspiratorial organization, Estat Català (the Catalan State), which had its own antigovernment terrorist section, the "Black Flag."

Macià, who emerged as the undisputed leader of left Catalanism, was not an unemployed intellectual like many of his colleagues. He came from an aristocratic line of large landowners in Lérida—one of the few latifundist families in Catalonia—and had been a professional army officer before his Catalanism forced him to resign the commission. Nearly seventy years old, this tall, lean, white-bearded, fiery-eyed cavalier altogether failed to embody the vaunted Catalan petit-bourgeois *seny* (common sense) but looked the spitting image of the romantic Castilian visionary Don Quijote. He was able to take advantage of the political gyrations that occurred in Catalonia, as in much of the rest of Spain, during the late 1920's. Most of the middle classes turned against the monarchy and seemed to seek a more liberal government that would bring civil liberty and regional autonomy. Macià and his associates occupied government offices in Barcelona even before the Republic was established in Madrid and proclaimed the "Catalan Republic of the Iberian Federation." He drew the various factions of the Catalan lower middle class together in a loose federation called the Esquerra Catalana (Catalan left) that routed the Lliga and swept the 1931 elections. The Esquerra leaders backed down from their first melodramatic proclamation and cooperated with left Republican leaders in the Spanish government who promised to draft a Catalan autonomy statute. This met stiff opposition from both conservatives and Socialists; the latter feared that regional autonomy might mean the tyranny of the Catalan middle classes over the workers. The outcome of the autonomy issue, like that of agrarian reform, was settled by the defeat of the abortive rightist revolt of 1932 that strengthened the hand of the left. The autonomy statute of September 1932 created an autonomous regional government called the Generalitat (after the executive body of medieval Catalonia) with jurisdiction over regional justice, police, public works, and much of the educational system and civil administration. Macià was elected the first president without opposition, and the following year the Catalan Pilsudski passed away peacefully of old age with his revolutionary vision accomplished. Thus far he is the only Spanish statesman of the twentieth century to have died a success.

TABLE 6.1. *Catalonia's Percentage of Total Spanish Resources, Production and Consumption, 1931–32*

Territory	6.4	Agrarian production	13
Population	12.1	Banking assets	19.5
Railway mileage	9.1	Savings accounts	34.4
Roads	8.3	Property taxes	11.5
Corporate capital	28.7	Industrial taxes	26
Electric power	31.2	Automobiles	22.2

SOURCE: Jaume Alzina, *L'Economía de la Catalunya autònoma* (Barcelona, 1933), 105.

A major goal of the Esquerra was to appease the hostility of the working-class movement and draw it into collaboration. The Esquerra did not have altogether clear-cut economic aims, but Article 1 of its official program expressed the need to "socialize riches in the interests of the collectivity," without specifying exactly what that meant. Macià tried to appeal to anarchosyndicalist workers, but his own ideas did not go beyond middle-class nationalist radicalism. In talks to Barcelona laborers, he stressed that the real way to social justice was through education, and that the reform of education in Catalonia was one of the Generalitat's primary goals. The Esquerra was supported by the white-collar CADCI and a rural affiliate, the Unió de Rabassaires, of upward-striving renters and sharecroppers. It had no organized blue-collar proletarian backing.

Macià's successor as head of the Esquerra and president of the Generalitat was Lluis Companys, a debonair, weak-chinned politician with a talent for maneuver and strong sympathy for the lower classes. Companys had been associated with CNT leaders in earlier years and had served as defense lawyer for *cenetistas* charged with terrorism. Though not a social revolutionary, Companys believed in broad reforms, especially for pro-Catalanist peasants, and he had been one of the chief organizers of the latter's Rabassaire syndicate. One of his major ambitions was to draw the CNT into constructive trade union reformism in an autonomous, democratic, socially progressive Catalonia. A supple politician, he was never above indulging in a strong dose of demagogy for those sectors of the working classes whom he judged susceptible.

Barcelona's first chief of police under the Republic did a great deal to clean up the local security forces and no effort was made to hamper expansion of the CNT. The return of complete liberty in April 1931 produced the same results as the liberalization policy of 1922–23: an outburst of anarchist vengeance against former militants of the Sindicatos Libres in the greater Barcelona area. Within less than a month 19 anti-CNT workers were killed, but there were no prosecutions and apparently not even any arrests. It was up to the CNT's *Solidaridad Obrera* to publish an editorial on April 22, 1931, entitled "It's Time to Stop," calling on CNT and FAI organizational committees to declare "that they are absolutely opposed to a return to individual *atentados,* a procedure that is completely inefficient in the material order and in the moral order renders abhorrent those who resort to such tactics."

In May 1931, Companys, as the first Republican civil governor of Barcelona province, ordered destruction of district police records, wiping clean the slates of innocent workers, anarchist murderers, and common criminals alike. This was not merely a political concession to the CNT but also a genuine expression of the ideological Jacobinism of the Republican left, for whom the new regime brought the "Year One" and the beginning of all authentic government.

The effort toward approximation between left Catalanism and the CNT was completely frustrated by the predominance of the FAI, the recently organized anarchist federation, within the syndicalist movement. During the summer of 1931 local CNT unions showed willingness to cooperate with government authorities in the arbitration of labor disputes, but revolutionary anarchosyndicalists exerted growing pressure to eradicate the spirit of compromise. On September 1, 30 anti-FAI syndicalist leaders released the so-called *Treintista* Manifesto (Manifesto of the Thirty). They warned that "a simplistic revolution will lead to a Republican fascism," provoking an authoritarian reaction among the middle classes. *Faístas* condemned the *treintista* dissidents as traitors and reformists, but in fact they were more sober revolutionaries who realized that there could be no democratic syndicalist revolution until the syndicates were sufficiently numerous, educated, and disciplined to supplant the existing system. Reliance on direct action alone would simply conjure up a second, more vindictive Primo de Rivera. By September the FAI had gained control of the main Barcelona syndicates and provoked a series of large-scale strikes and disorders. *Faístas* took over *Solidaridad Obrera* in the following month, and made it the main source of inflammatory revolutionary agitation in Spain during the next three years.

By the close of 1931 the CNT had officially expanded to at least 800,000 members—some leaders claimed more than a million—regaining its peak strength of 1919-20. Peasant support from Andalusia was proportionately less important than in earlier years; the great majority of the CNT's members were workers in Catalonia and the Levant, and in scattered urban and industrial areas in Aragon, central Spain, Asturias, and Galicia. After the first elections, which as usual were boycotted by anarchosyndicalists, *Solidaridad Obrera* declared that "there can be no peace, not even a minute's truce, between the constituent Cortes and the CNT." The new regime was labeled "a Republic administered by hangmen and assassins." While the Socialists collaborated with Republican parliamentarianism, anarchosyndicalists saw an historic opportunity to rally the entire working class in a great revolutionary thrust. Local sections of the CNT remained free to initiate strikes whenever they pleased. Largo Caballero's arbitration commissions were mostly ignored, and disputes broke out in nearly every area where the CNT had any strength. This agitation first culminated in the anarchist and Communist insurrection at Seville in June 1931, which required army units and the use of artillery, and then in the general strike at Barcelona in September. During November and December there were brief local general strikes in eight cities in widely scattered parts of Spain.

Anarchosyndicalism relied on spontaneity, and the FAI rushed recklessly from one local disorder to another. In anarchist ideology, the state and society were so rotten that they could be expected to collapse at any time. Within a period of twenty-three months there were three attempts at revolutionary insurrection—the *tres ochos* of January 8, 1932, of January 8, 1933, and of December 8, 1933. The first attempt occurred in the industrial Llobregat valley west of Barcelona, involving mainly textile workers' and miners' syndicates. The second was centered in Barcelona, but was accompanied by disorders in Madrid, Valencia, Cádiz, and Seville. The third focused on Aragonese towns, supported by outbursts in Madrid, Valencia, La Coruña, Cádiz, and Seville. None of these local insurrections was well organized, and each was quelled without too much difficulty, though in the main centers the Army had to be called out to assist the police. In none were as many as 100 people killed. In between the main revolts, there were numerous local acts—bombings, riotings, church burnings, brawls, and shootings, As one pro-

treintista leader later wrote, "It will be hard to equal the narrow fanaticism of the Spanish anarchomystics in their course from September, 1911 to July, 1936." [1]

The utopia to be achieved by this unalleviated anarchy was officially defined in the following terms:

There is only one regime that can give the workers liberty, well-being and happiness: it is Libertarian Communism.

Libertarian Communism is the organization of society without a State and without private property.

It is unnecessary to invent anything or to create any new social organization to achieve it.

The centers of organization around which the economic life of tomorrow will be coordinated exist in present-day society: they are the syndicate and the free municipality.

Workers in factories and other enterprizes . . . group together spontaneously in the syndicates.

With the same spontaneity the inhabitants of the same locality join together in the municipality, an assembly known from the origins of mankind. In the municipality they have an open road to the solution, on a local basis, of all the problems of communal living.

These two organizations, federative and democratic, will have sovereignty over their own decisions, without being subjected to the tutelage of any higher organs.

Nonetheless they will be led to confederate for the purpose of common economic activities and, by forming federations of industry, to set up organs of liaison and communication.

In this way the syndicate and the municipality will take collective possession of everything that now belongs to the sphere of private property; they will regulate . . . economic life in every locality, although they will have men in charge of their own actions: that is to say, liberty.

Libertarian Communism thus makes compatible the satisfaction of economic necessities and respect for our aspirations to liberty.

Because of the love of liberty the libertarians repudiate the communism of the convent, the barracks, the ant-hill or the herd as in Russia.

Under Libertarian Communism, egoism is unknown; it is replaced by the broadest social love. [2]

1. Horacio M. Prieto, *El anarquismo español en la lucha política* (Paris, 1946), 3.
2. *Boletín de Información C.N.T.-A.I.T.-F.A.I.*, no. 193, Feb. 27, 1934, in John Brademas, "Revolution and Social Revolution: The Anarcho-Syndicalist Movement in Spain, 1930–1937" (Oxford University Ph.D. Dissertation, 1956), 343.

Two years of feverish agitation did not bring "libertarian communism" any nearer realization, for anarchist domination and what Gerald Brenan has called "playing at revolution" steadily weakened the CNT. During 1932 the organization's size and strength declined, though at first this seemed only to redouble the anarchist paroxysms. Febrile extremism was by no means acceptable to all the local CNT syndicates, and strife among the top syndical leaders was intense. For example, the CNT's national committee had refused to endorse the plan of the movement's FAI-controlled revolutionary council ("national defense committee") to collect special dues for the formation of five or six large regional paramilitary units to support the January 1932 revolt. Some of the larger and more moderate syndicates resented the FAI's use of smaller, more easily manipulated syndicates to carry extremist policies, and demanded proportionate representation at syndical congresses. Personal animosities re-enforced differences over policy and tactics. Several of the *treintista* leaders were expelled from the confederation during the course of 1932 and by the end of that year were organizing a new Libertarian Syndicalist Federation (FSL) on principles of syndical democracy and more prudent, politically calculated revolution. Dissident moderate syndicates in Sabadell (near Barcelona) were formally expelled from the CNT in April 1933, and as a result another splinter group of CNT Opposition Syndicates was formed, carrying the majority of CNT members in Valencia with it.

Angel Pestaña and a handful of other antianarchist syndicalists chose a different tack and organized a tiny Spanish Syndicalist party. Pestaña was denounced as a traitor and protofascist, though he tried to make it clear that he still espoused the basic principles of revolutionary syndicalism. The Syndicalist party was not conceived, as some have said, in the image of the British Labour party, but rather to achieve democratic political representation for revolutionary syndicalism so that the revolution might be brought about in a coherent, rational, democratic manner.

Constant provocations brought increasingly severe repression of the Confederation. Even the left Catalanist leaders lost patience during the course of 1932. After the January 1933 insurrection, imprisoned CNT leaders in Barcelona were savagely beaten by the police. Many local headquarters were closed, moderate workers were frightened away, and during the winter of 1933 it was estimated that at least 9,000 *cenetistas* were in jail throughout the country as a whole. By 1933 the CNT had gained membership in several regions such as Madrid that were usually considered UGT strongholds, and had set up a dozen or so rural cooperatives in scattered provinces of the north and southwest, but its spring regional conference in Catalonia showed a membership there of only 209,000—less than in 1920. The split in the Confederation and competition from other groups prevented the CNT from regaining a near-monopoly of Catalan labor organization and by the end of 1933 the syndicalist movement was in at least a partial decline, losing members in several of its strongholds. The doctrine of the permanent apolitical insurrection, isolated from all other leftist groups, was a complete failure as a revolutionary tactic.

If revolutionary anarchosyndicalism resulted only in frustration for the CNT, the movement still remained the principal force of organized labor in Catalonia, and thwarted the efforts of Marxist or Catalanist worker groups to build a strong following in the region. A separate Socialist Union of Catalonia (USC) had been organized in 1923 by a handful of Catalanist social democrats who split off from the Spanish Socialist party because the latter did not concede the right of Catalan autonomy. The USC was in its early years a moderate reformist Catalanist worker group and enjoyed scant support. A radical offshoot of Estat Català, the Catalan Proletarian party of Gabriel Alomar did little better though associated with the white-collar CADCI.

Slightly more important was the Worker-Peasant Bloc (BOC) organized by the young intellectual Joaquín Maurín and a handful of other dissidents in the winter of 1931 as an outgrowth of the Catalan-Balearic Federation of the Spanish Communist party. Andrés Nin's Trotskyist Communist Left was also centered in Barcelona but had even fewer supporters than the BOC. To counter the schism of the entire Communist movement in Catalonia, the Comintern in 1932 founded a separate new

Communist party of Catalonia (PCC) headed by Ramón Casane-
llas, murderer of the prime minister Dato and sometime hero to
Spanish extremists. The PCC failed to build as large a following
as even the small BOC, which boasted only 3,000 members in
1933.

A sharp-eyed journalist reported that

> The masses were more willing to listen to any tubercular intellec-
> tual of the FAI than to hear the intelligent, impassioned words of
> Andrés Nin or Joaquín Maurín. For the masses, these were not the
> true shepherds. . . .
> When Maurín said, "We must have so and so put in jail . . . ,"
> he was not allowed to go further but interrupted by cries of "No more
> jails!" "We want to get rid of jails!" And if he explained, "I meant that
> we must send usurers and hangmen to jail . . . " the response was
> "Dictator!" "No more, no more!" "Down with Russia!" [3]

The failure to achieve agreement with the working-class
movement was a major setback for the left Catalanist regime,
but other problems followed. They centered mainly around the
issues of economic decline, the scope of regional autonomy, the
comeback of the moderates in the 1933 elections, and the frustration of agrarian reform in Catalonia. Between 1931 and 1933,
the region's number one industry, textiles, enjoyed a period of
great expansion despite the international depression. It had
normally depended upon the domestic Spanish market for
85 to 90 percent of its sales, and a key factor in this boom was
the increase in domestic purchasing power achieved by the
Spanish government's Socialist-administered labor arbitration.
After the postwar depression of 1920 only about 100,000 workers
were employed in the Catalan textile industry; by mid-1932
this figure had doubled, easing for labor the strain that depression had brought to other industries. Yet the textile demand
was seriously overestimated and shrank considerably during the
first half of 1933, while the small foreign market declined further.
Moreover, the prosperity of 1932 accelerated the introduction
of automatic equipment, which accounted for 15 percent of
plant machinery by mid-1933. The combination of these factors
reduced textile employment by one-third in 1933, though the

3. Francisco Madrid, *Film de la República comunista libertaria* (Madrid-
Barcelona, 1932), 156, 160.

market had improved somewhat by the end of the year. In general, after 1932 the Catalan economy, like Spanish industry as a whole, was in a state of sluggish depression. Though even in Catalonia the resulting industrial unemployment was not so severe as in some of the major industrial countries, it contributed to mounting social tension.

The antileftist reaction in the national elections of 1933 was also reflected in Catalonia, where the refusal of the CNT to give its votes to the Esquerra enabled the moderate Lliga to win a narrow victory, with a margin of 5 percent in the popular vote. After a moderate liberal government was formed in Madrid, the Catalan regime stood alone as the last bastion of left Republican power in Spain—"the last bulwark of the Republic," according to a speech of Azaña's a few days after the elections.

The Esquerra turned the tables on the Lliga in the Catalan municipal elections of January 1934, winning a majority of the region's city council seats, and it continued to hold firm control of the Generalitat. The Lliga protested electoral fraud, arbitrary Esquerra use of the Catalan police, and the formation of paramilitary groups under Esquerra sponsorship. Its major demand, however, was the introduction of proportional representation in regional Catalan elections so as to deprive the Esquerra of its disproportionate majority in the Generalitat. When Companys refused to concede this, the Lliga leaders rejected further cooperation. They adopted the classic Spanish opposition ploy of *retraimiento* (withdrawal) and abandoned the Generalitat completely in February 1934.

The Esquerra hailed the municipal elections as the first sign of a reversal of the conservative trend of 1933, and prepared to make the most of it. During the first half of 1934 the Generalitat passed a large amount of new legislation to improve public health regulations, encourage cooperatives, establish rural credit facilities, expand educational facilities, and revise the application of the limited share of local taxes that were assigned to the regional government.

Because of the animosity of the CNT and the industrial depression, it was not easy to improve the situation of the industrial workers. In fact, little was attempted, and the Lliga's proposal for a system of workmen's compensation insurance was ignored. The Esquerra leaders chose instead to concentrate on reforms for the lower-middle strata of the peasantry who, organized in the Unió de Rabassaires, had, in contrast to the industrial workers, voted strongly Catalanist.

The agrarian problem was much less severe in Catalonia than in southern Spain. Large estates were almost nonexistent, save for a few in Lérida province (one of them belonging to the Macià family). So-called "large landowners" in Catalonia averaged only 40–50 hectares each, or the equivalent of an ordinary family farm or less in the United States. Due to intensive care and use of fertilizers, farm productivity in Catalonia was well above the Spanish average. The proportion of outright land ownership was not so high as in several other parts of northern Spain, but most rural families held small farms on reasonably stable terms of renting or sharing. There was little genuine sharecropping; long-term renting or a more secure form of "associate sharing" (*parcería asociada*) prevailed. Nevertheless, the profit margin for most rental farms was low and the agricultural market, particularly for wines, was severely depressed. Rental conditions discouraged maximal investment and optimal rationalization of the terms of production. Contracts for the Rabassaire vineyard cultivators had been under dispute for several generations. Though Catalan landowners could scarcely have been said to have "exploited" severely their renters and sharecroppers, the latter were under severe pressure by the early 1930's. Landlords' profits rarely exceeded 3 percent, yet terms of divided dominion proved an obstacle to peasants and handicapped their planning and production.

From the very beginning of the Republic the provincial governments in Catalonia had encouraged suits for revision of unfair rental contracts. During the first year of the new regime, however, less than 3,500 petitions were filed, though the Rabassaire organization had more than 21,000 members. In May 1932 the Esquerra obtained approval of law for all four provinces authorizing peasant cultivators to withhold up to 50 percent of the rent or owners' share of profits from the moment they presented a petition for revision of contracts. Soon nearly 30,000 suits had been filed, the bulk of them in Barcelona province where agitation was strongest. Between 1932 and 1934 a sizable number of these suits were either dropped or settled by minor concessions on the part of the owner.[4]

A great deal of confusion already existed in agrarian contracts when the Generalitat finally proposed to complete the social transformation of the Catalan peasantry by a sweeping new Law of Cultivation Contracts that was approved on April 12, 1934. This established the right of all peasant farmers to buy any land that they had cultivated continuously for at least 18 years. Those who had held contracts to farm the same piece of land for six years in succession were guaranteed the right to renew the same contract annually at the end of that term. The right of owners to expel any tenant who failed to pay his rent or cultivate the land properly, or in the event that the owner wanted to cultivate the land personally, was explicitly recognized. Terms and disagreements would be adjudicated by arbitration tribunals.

This was obviously not a revolutionary measure, but it set off a storm of controversy among the landowners and their political allies. In addition to opposing forced transfer of ownership, they feared after the experiences of 1931–33 that the Esquerra-dominated tribunals would discriminate in setting prices. Resistance was led by the Lliga, which decided to take a strong stand for fear that rural property owners would swing to rightist parties.

The Catalan law was in fact designed to complete the embourgeoisement of the most upward-striving sector of the peasantry, and did almost nothing to assist the most disadvantaged element, the minority of landless laborers. Socially, the issue might be described as a struggle of the rural upper-middle and middle-middle classes of Catalonia against the lower-middle class. Most Rabassaires and sharecroppers already possessed at least some capital of their own, and the law did nothing to change

---

4. Five hundred of 741 requests in Lérida-Cervera, 780 of 1,317 in Tarragona-Tortosa, 1,036 of 1,451 at San Feliu de Llobregat, according to J. de Camps i Arboix, "La Questió agraria a Catalunya," *Quaderns* (June 1945), 6–13.

the existing division of land exploitation, for all peasants given the right to buy or to achieve more secure contracts were already farming individual plots. Moreover, the Esquerra did not seem to have any proposals for technical improvement of Catalan agriculture aside from expanded rural credit. Their goal was simply an independent lower-middle class Catalanist peasantry.

Opponents of the measure called it unconstitutional, since Article 15 of the autonomy statute reserved to the central government the right to alter contractual obligations by law. It was the Esquerra's position that the law was covered by Article 12 which gave the Generalitat jurisdiction over agrarian policy in Catalonia. The controversy seemed to trap the Republican constitution in contradiction, and the case was referred to the authorized branch of government, the Tribunal of Constitutional Guarantees. On June 8, the Tribunal voted by 13 votes to 7 that the legislation was unconstitutional.

This decision was galling to the Esquerra, and was all the more ironic because Article 15 had been written in primarily by the Socialists to prevent middle-class Catalanists from domineering over the working classes. Extreme Catalanists were already very dissatisfied with the way that autonomy was working out, for the Generalitat still did not have full control of regional education and held only very limited power over regional taxation and commerce. To them, the Tribunal's decision was the last straw, and marked the beginning of an all-out assault on Catalan autonomy. On June 12, the Esquerra's delegation walked out of the Madrid Cortes, and left Republican leaders from other parts of Spain also denounced the Tribunal's verdict. Though the constitutional legality of the whole process of referral and annulment was unquestionable, the Generalitat proceeded to pass the cultivation law for the second time, showing that it would not abide by the Tribunal's decision.[5]

5. The response of the Catalanist and Republican left to the first test of the constitution they had so recently finished writing brought hostile and sarcastic remarks not merely from conservatives but from moderate liberals as well. *El Sol* editorialized on June 27: "Sr. Azaña answered Sr. Cambó, 'I wouldn't have let the law come to a vote [in the Tribunal]; I would have intervened before it was acted upon.' Of more fertile genius, Sr. Maura, for his part, would have sought to have Catalonia desist by negotiations 'between the two

Companys made a series of speeches in Catalonia that summer saying that Catalans would fight rather than submit to tyrannical control over their affairs. In fact, Companys personally hoped to negotiate a satisfactory solution to the impasse, and private conversations were begun with the president of the Republic and other officials. At the same time, Companys feared that he would be outflanked by Catalanist radicals and maintained an intransigent tone publicly, though published versions of his speeches were sometimes watered down so as not to alarm opinion in other regions. Under heavy pressure from militants to show that the Generalitat would not surrender, he shuffled his cabinet, bringing in Dr. Josep Dencàs of the separatist Estat Català group as Catalan Minister of the Interior. Then he appointed the reckless twenty-six-year-old Estat Català militia chief, Miquel Badia, to the post of Chief of Security, or police boss of Catalonia.

The Estat Català had originally been a group of youthful activists organized by Macià in 1922, and incorporated into the

---

governments.' Anything, or rather, everything except the use of the means established precisely in order to resolve conflicts of legislative jurisdiction. Because that is, in substance, the question: that the law foresees the conflict, provides a juridical channel to which it should go, a procedure for substantiation, a means of resolution, and it is precisely those who have written the law who do not want it to be employed and would have preferred any sort of prelegal, postlegal or illegal expedients, whether the 'negotiations' praised by Sr. Maura or the 'interpositions' of Sr. Azaña. Furthermore, the referral to proper jurisdiction, if it has any aim, is properly that of transforming any political conflict between the two parliaments or governments into a legal plea, an interpretation of law free from passion and rancor; in sum, to make aseptic political disputes between the central power and the autonomous region by raising them to a different level, less subject to exacerbation, so that what might be a grave illness is reduced to a slight rash. But all the zeal of the inventors of so judicious and prudent a method of vaccination has been, on the contrary, to infect the conflict with politics, inflame it and aggravate it to an extreme. No more could have been done against the letter, spirit or finality of the Republican legislation that they themselves made.

" . . . There is no way in which two governments can subsist if there is not a superior organism with jurisdiction over conflicts. For that function the Tribunal of Constitutional Guarantees was instituted. If as soon as it pronounces a decision adverse to one party the latter counteracts it, there is no longer coordination between the state and the region, but full independence. . . . And this destruction of the state is supported by its very authors [the Republican left]."

Esquerra federation in 1931. It was the main faction of youthful militancy within the Catalanist left. Held in balance with somewhat more moderate forces so long as Macià lived, after his death it aspired to dominate the entire Esquerra and espoused outright separatism from the Spanish state. Badia, head of the Estat Català's militia, the Escamots, was a former terrorist who had spent most of his adult life (1925–31) in prison for participating in an attempt on the life of Alfonso XIII. He was strictly an apostle of direct action, with no ideological or political sophistication, but his leadership exerted a strong attraction on restless lower-middle-class youth who were fascinated by the rhetoric and the poses of ultranationalism and violence. The young physician Dencàs provided the main political and ideological leadership of Estat Català, such as it was. He had no clear program, but seized upon the notion of combining nationalism and some form of corporative syndicalism under a strong nationalist state. In a loose sense, the Estat Català leaders might be considered "fascists" of a sort. The group was particularly strong in Barcelona, where it was said to control 62 of the 75 neighborhood Esquerra centers. By mid-1934 it exercised predominant influence in the Esquerra which, with between 60,000 and 70,000 regular members in its local centers, was one of the largest organized political forces in Spain.

Under Badia the Catalan police began a sharp crackdown on the CNT, considered by many Catalanists a thoroughly divisive and subversive movement. The police were not above applying force, though in lesser amounts, against other political sectors, and even in several instances pressured the nominally independent court system. Arrest of a public prosecutor led to a scandal in September that forced Badia to resign as police chief, but he still remained in charge of paramilitary activities.

Dencàs later wrote that from the time he took office as Catalan Minister of the Interior he served as chairman of a secret Revolutionary Committee composed of representatives of all the left Catalan factions [6] to prepare for armed resistance

6. Esquerra Republicana de Catalunya, Estat Català, Acció Catalana, Partit Nacionalista Republicà de Catalunya, Unió Socialista de Catalunya, Partit Nacionalista Català, Unió Democràtica de Catalunya, Nosaltres Sols (the Catalan words for *sinn fein*—"ourselves alone"), and Palestra. Josep Dencàs, *El 6 d'octubre des del Palau de Governació* (Barcelona, 1935), 42.

against the central government. The weird world of Barcelona politics approached another crisis as this fascistoid brand of nationalist radicalism, while repressing revolutionary syndicalism with one hand, armed itself with the other for revolt against a moderate government in Madrid that would soon be accused of fostering "Spanish fascism."

SEVEN *The Revolutionary*

Insurrection of 1934

AFTER THE ELECTIONS OF 1933 all sectors of the left were faced with a completely new political situation, for they had lost parliamentary power in a new Cortes, composed mainly of moderate liberals and conservatives. This ought logically to have led to a moderate conservative government in which the country's largest political party, the CEDA, participated, yet the limited victory of the CEDA created a serious problem. Though the new party and its leaders restricted their activities to the sphere of parliamentarianism, the CEDA did not categorically endorse the existing Republic system and was unwilling to be labeled "Republican." It had received support from monarchists in 1933, and though most genuine monarchists left the party in 1934 and 1935, the CEDA leadership espoused an "accidentalist" doctrine of government forms, declaring that whether a regime was Republican or monarchist was much less important than its legislative and moral content. The CEDA's minimum program called for constitutional revision to protect the rights and interests of the Catholic Church. Though it had never taken any concrete action that exceeded legal bounds, vague threats in the electoral campaign about building a "new state' and not shrinking from violence fed the suspicions of those who questioned the CEDA's intentions. There was little doubt about the commitment of the CEDA's main leader, Gil Robles, to legal tactics, but some uncertainty as to whether he represented the entire party. It should be pointed out that in the Spanish climate of 1933–34 it was almost impossible for a Catholic party to declare itself 100 percent "Republican," since the Republican left harped on the theme that only left Republicanism was "true Republicanism," that even moderate Republican liberals were not full-fledged Republicans, and from the beginning of the regime had made Republicanism synonymous with anti-Catholicism.

To all the left, Republican or revolutionary, the situation was clear-cut. As the largest conservative group, the CEDA represented the spearhead of reaction and was moving in the same direction as the Fatherland Front in Austria, whose leader Dollfuss had closed parliament and was ruling by decree. The parliamentarianism of the CEDA was explained as a Trojan-horse device to enable clericals to gain control of the government, after which they were supposedly going to establish a dictatorship and destroy the working-class movements. Within a few days after the election Socialist spokesmen warned that if the clericals were allowed to form a cabinet the Socialists would respond with revolutionary insurrection. Leaders of the middle-class left said that a CEDA government would be the end of the Republic and affirmed that they would have nothing to do with such a regime. In so saying, they increased the chasm and the CEDA continued to refuse to endorse "Republicanism" categorically.

The president of the Republic, Alcalá Zamora, was troubled by the CEDA's refusal to commit itself to the existing regime. Though he shared the Catholic goal of constitutional reform, he was hostile to the CEDA leaders and feared the reaction of the left if a government reflecting the composition of the new parliament were formed. Instead, he nominated a minority Radical cabinet led by Lerroux, which he hoped would be moderate enough to gain the voting support of the conservatives, but not so conservative as to provoke the left. The administration of the Radical government was in some ways more liberal and democratic than was that of its left Republican predecessor. No effort was made to rule by decree as the left had for a period of time in 1931 and, unlike the left in 1931 and in 1936, the Radical ministry did not annul the results of any elections unfavorable to it. Nonetheless, in order to be tolerated by the conservative bloc, it had to make concessions. Anticlerical laws were not enforced and Catholic educational activity was continued as usual. Even the subsidy to the Church was maintained, though at a reduced rate. The new Minister of Labor did almost as much to favor employers in the arbitration committees as Largo Caballero had done to favor the workers; the law that established *términos municipales* requiring employment of local workers was annulled. The new Lerroux ministry was an inherently unstable minority government, and the CEDA leaders made it clear that they would soon be demanding greater influence over legislation. One result was a government amnesty for the rightist rebels of 1932. This infuriated the left and convinced them that the Radical government was simply playing into the hands of the right. Though the cabinet had to be reorganized, it managed to stay in power through the summer of 1934.

During the early months of 1934 the idea of armed revolt gained ground steadily, particularly among the Socialist Youth, radical intellectuals, and the more extreme sectors of the UGT. Direct action was encouraged by the constant disorders of the anarchists, and by the Communists, who had combated the constitutional Republic from the beginning and called for violent revolutionary insurrection. But it was encouraged most of all by the tension in the Socialist party, whose policy from 1931 to 1933 had been frustrated by the disunity of the Republican left and then by the party's own decision to try to capitalize on discontent by going it alone in the general elections. Youthful militants and disgruntled leaders wanted to make up all the ground that had been lost in one fell swoop, and yet the goal of an outright revolutionary revolt was too radical for most influential spokesmen to espouse openly. It would have contradicted the policy pursued throughout the party's history, and not even the most radical seriously claimed that the Socialist party was strong enough to seize power by itself in a coup d'état. But collaborationism and reformism were equally discredited, and the stock of the maximalists rose in most sections of the party and in much of the UGT. Proponents of direct action became increasingly insistent, and demanded at the very least an active policy that would regain the initiative. This meant widespread strikes and preparation for paramilitary action.

Economic conditions contributed to the radicalization of the working classes, though not in such a simple, clear-cut way as might be thought. As far as industrial production was concerned, the worst year was 1933. All major industries increased their output in 1934, and most continued their expansion during 1935. Most skilled workers were probably better off in 1934–35 than they had been in 1932–33. Gross unemployment rates continued to rise, however, due to two main factors: worsened conditions for agricultural laborers and the return of unemployed Spanish laborers from abroad. Between 1931 and 1934 nearly 75,000 workers returned to the country, while emigration dropped off.

Improving economic conditions in certain sectors did not bring more harmonious labor relations, however, for the UGT was increasingly motivated by ideological rather than economic considerations. During 1933 there had been three times as many strikes as in 1930. The pressure in Catalonia and most other CNT-dominated areas did ease during 1934, and some of the better paid sections of the UGT (Vizcayan metallurgists, for example) were quieter than in 1930, but discontent mounted among the most disadvantaged and also among certain unions most influenced by purely political motivation, such as UGT clerk syndicates.

As usual, distress weighed most heavily upon the landless peasants. The Lerroux government continued the agrarian reform, and indeed settled proportionately more families on new land each month than had Azaña's ministry, but it refused to extend social legislation. The ending of *términos municipales* together with new chairmen for *jurados mixtos* brought lower wages for

TABLE 7.1. *Spanish Industrial Production, 1931–35*
(in millions of tons)

	Coal	Pyrites	Lead	Tin	Iron	Steel
1931	6.53	3.13	.15	.24	468.8	655.8
1932	6.27	2.12	.13	.11	295.1	537.7
1933	5.42	2.26	.11	.27	331.5	527.3
1934	5.34	2.09	.09	.33	357.8	588.9
1935	6.33	2.18	.08	.43	344.2	637.2

SOURCE: Jaime Vicens Vives et al., *Les mouvements ouvriers en temps de dé-*
pression économique (1929–1939) (Paris, 1960).

laborers. The effects of administrative changes were compounded
by the trade decline, bad weather conditions in certain provinces,
withdrawal of marginal land from cultivation, the surpluses produced in 1932, and general political and economic uncertainty.
Rural workers suffered disproportionately from unemployment;
among Spanish labor as a whole, the unemployment rate rarely
rose above 10 percent, but among the million landless farm-
workers, the figure in 1934 was nearly 40 percent. The situation
was most severe in the latifundist provinces of the south and
southwest, and was reflected in severe unrest. In 1931 there had
been only 85 recorded agricultural strikes; in 1932 there were 198,
involving 91,000 laborers and 810,000 working days. In 1933 this
had increased to 450 rural strikes involving 241,000 strikers and
2,057,000 working days. The number killed in rural disputes had
risen from 9 in 1931 to at least 26 in 1933.

TABLE 7.2. *Unemployed Workers in Spain,*
July 1933–July 1936

	Total unemployed	Number of agrarian workers unemployed	Agrarian workers' percentage of total unemployed
1933 (July–Dec.)	593,627	382,965	64.5
1934	667,263	409,617	61.4
1935	696,989	434,654	62.4
1936 (Jan.–July)	796,341	522,079	65.6

SOURCE: Edward Malefakis, "Land Tenure, Agrarian Reform and Peasant
Revolution in Twentieth Century Spain" (Columbia University Ph.D. disserta-
tation, 1966), 378.

Soon after the Cortes elections the militants moved to take over the UGT and especially its largest but weakest and poorest federation, the agrarian FNTT. They submitted the following motion to the UGT's national committee:

In view of the present political situation, the plenum agrees upon the immediate and urgent organization, together with the Socialist Party, of a movement of national revolutionary character to conquer political power for the working class, accepting the collaboration of all those forces that want to contribute to the movement and can be relied upon for our interests and aims. The time to begin the movement will be decided upon, in so far as possible, by the plenums of the General Union and the Socialist Party; if that is impossible, by the respective executive or national committees of both organizations.[1]

This was rejected by a vote of 28 to 16. Instead the national committee released the text of a joint accord made between itself and the executive committee of the party on November 25, which declared that the working-class movements must be ready to "rise up vigorously" if a government that would infringe constitutional liberties came to power.

The party newspaper, *El Socialista,* was completely in the hands of the militant revolutionaries. When the clerical *El Debate* asked for peace and harmony, *El Socialista* replied on January 3, 1934, "Harmony? No! Class war! Hatred to the death of the criminal bourgeoisie!" Daily it published lists of UGT syndicates which it claimed supported a revolutionary orientation and demanded that the UGT's national committee change its policy. *El Socialista* particularly incited local syndicates of the FNTT to build pressure against that union's national committee through letters and petitions. This tactic succeeded, forcing the resignation of the moderate Lucio Martínez, founder of the FNTT, who was replaced by an advocate of revolutionary strikes. During January the extremists took over a number of other key unions and were able to change the composition of the UGT's national committee.

A major target was the committee's president, Julián Besteiro, who had continually to defend himself from charges of "reformism." Besteiro's position was that he was not a reformist,

1. *Boletín de la Unión General de Trabajadores,* no. 61 (Jan. 1934).

since he believed that only a complete revolutionary transformation of society would suffice, but that revolution was a highly complicated process for which simplist extremism was inadequate. He warned against thoughtless adventures that would needlessly cost Spanish workers their recent gains. In a May Day radio speech the previous year, he stressed,

> Now it cannot be said in Spain as did Marx at the end of the "Communist Manifesto" that the proletariat has nothing to lose but its chains. Now it has things to lose: all the political and economic gains that it has won in its struggle against the bourgeoisie—the eight-hour day, mixed arbitration committees, retirement pay, and so on.[2]

Before the end of January the pressure became so intense that Besteiro felt he had no alternative save to resign the presidency of the national committee, and the extremists soon completed their takeover of the UGT leadership.

The new national committee paid no attention to Besteiro's argument that the workers were not yet educated for the tasks they must assume in a revolutionary society. It immediately announced:

> Though it may seem strange, there is no lack of workers, and even of workers who call themselves socialists and revolutionaries, who resolutely affirm that the social revolution, the act of force that will topple bourgeois society and free the proletariat from the yoke that oppresses it, cannot take effect until all or nearly all the workers are educated and want to carry out their emancipation.
>
> In our duty as members of a revolutionary party, we must combat such an idea, which, if spread through the proletarian masses, would make the reign of the bourgeoisie little less than eternal.
>
> The education of all the working class cannot precede the revolution, but must follow it.[3]

The extremism of Largo Caballero and other UGT leaders was further encouraged by the influence of radical young Socialist intellectuals, chief of whom were two brothers-in-law, Luis Araquistain and Julio Alvarez del Vayo. An active role for intellectuals was rather new in the Socialist party, and had a destructive effect. The case of Vayo is clear, for he was largely a tool of the Communists, but that of Araquistain is more

2. Comín Colomer, *Partido Comunista*, II, 460–61.
3. *Boletín de la Unión General de Trabajadores*, no. 62 (Feb. 1934).

complicated. Araquistain had great intellectual drive and a disconcerting facility for changing tack abruptly. During 1931–32 he had seemed to endorse social democratic reformism, but this mood was ended by the breakdown of the Azaña government. He termed the 1933 elections plebiscitary in nature and the prelude to revolution. In a speech of October 29, 1933, Araquistain declared: "The dilemma is thus: a frankly bourgeois dictatorship or a frankly Socialist dictatorship," and endorsed Largo's insistence on all power for the Socialist party.

Though disturbed by the victory of "reaction," Araquistain was intelligent and honest enough to admit that there was no real danger of "fascism" in Spain. In an article in the April 1934 issue of the American journal *Foreign Affairs*, he noted that the ingredients for fascism were lacking in his country. There were no large numbers of unemployed veterans or of university youth without a future, no huge proportion of unemployed, no strong sense of nationalism or imperialism, and no genuine fascist leaders of importance. Yet this optimistic forecast seemed only to spur his revolutionary agitation, for it meant that there would be less formidable opposition to a Socialist victory.

In the spring of 1934 he founded a new journal, *Leviatán* (Leviathan), and his editorial in the first issue on May Day declared:

> The Republic is an accident. We must return to Marx and Engels, not with our lips, but with our brains and willpower. Almost all of us were deceived and the time has come to admit it. Revolutionary socialism has not failed, but the distortion of it has. Marx and Engels were right about everything in their theory of history and of the state and in their plan of action. Let us not trust in parliamentary democracy even if sometimes socialism wins a majority; if violence is not used, capitalism will defeat socialism on other fronts with its formidable economic weapons.

The revolutionary Socialists were no longer interested in alliance with the middle-class left. The attitude of the middle-class left toward the Socialists was somewhat more ambiguous. When Azaña learned of the trend among Socialist activists he was taken aback. According to a memo written three years later, he expressed himself in the following terms to a Socialist moderate on January 2: "The mistake of provoking an armed insurrection will not be reparable and could place both the Republic and Spain itself in peril of destruction. The country will not support an insurrection because four-fifths of it is not Socialist." [4] On the other hand, leaders of the Republican left did nothing to restrain the extremists. Since they condemned all conservatives as "non-Republican," they believed the latter had no right to participate in Spanish politics. Hence leftist opposition need not be restricted to constitutional means alone. Azaña told a large left Republican meeting on April 16, "Now they tell us that we must respect the letter of the Constitution. But above the Constitution is the Republic and even higher above it stands the Revolution." [5] What Azaña meant by "revolution" was clearly not at all the sort of thing intended by militant Socialists, yet Azaña was willing to play on this ambiguity. In the same speech, he urged the renewal of the Socialist–left Republican alliance, a constant goal throughout 1934 and 1935. There is no evidence that Azaña wanted to foment a violent revolutionary insurrection in 1934, but his words and deeds were calculated to keep the left stirred up and encourage extraparliamentary pressure to nullify the authority of the Cortes.

The first steps to form a broad alliance of revolutionary forces had been taken in Barcelona a year earlier. Hitler's accession to power at the end of January 1933 had shown what might happen when the left was disunited. Only a few weeks after the Nazi triumph, Joaquín Maurín and representatives of the BOC met with leaders of the Socialist Union of Catalonia to discuss an antifascist alliance. This took the shape of an Antifascist Worker Alliance (Alianza Obrera Antifascista) that was also joined by the Catalan section of the Socialist party, the Catalan section of the UGT, the *treintista* dissidents from the CNT, the Unió de Rabassaires, and Nin's Communist Left. The Alliance had three goals: to defend the gains of the working class; to defeat fascism; and to prepare for the revolution that would introduce a federal socialist republic in Spain. This was strictly a confed-

4. Joaquín Arrarás, *Historia de la segunda República española* (Madrid, 1958), II, 300.
5. *El Sol* (Madrid), April 17, 1934.

eral alliance that left each member organization free to carry on its separate activity and propaganda, but a regional committee was established to coordinate joint endeavors. The Alliance seemed at first defensive in conception but soon took on a more offensive spirit. Electoral defeat of the parliamentary left made the Socialists more receptive to extension of the Alliance beyond Catalonia. At the beginning of 1934 Maurín visited Largo Caballero in Madrid and roused strong support. In February Largo talked with Alliance leaders in Barcelona, while announcing publicly that the only possible outcome of the present situation would be "either a rightist dictatorship or a worker dictatorship." Expansion of the Alliance to other areas was agreed upon, though formation of the Worker Alliance in the Madrid region was not announced until May 6. Its aim was to prepare for "the fight against fascism in all its forms and the preparation of the working-class movement for the establishment of the federal socialist republic." A year later Maurín explained that

the Worker Alliance is not a soviet, since its characteristics are different, but it carries out the functions of the soviet, whose place it advantageously fills given the features of Spanish worker organization. What the soviet was for the Russian revolution, the Worker Alliance is for the Spanish revolution.[6]

While the Socialists grew more radical, the CNT was sagging. A six-week general strike in Zaragoza in March-April 1934 had been its last major effort. For the first time, the CNT's strategy had become defensive rather than offensive, for that strike, which also ended mostly in failure, had been designed simply to win the release of some of the several thousand *cenetistas* still in jail from the insurrection of the previous December. In every region save Asturias the CNT clung to its apolitical isolation and would have nothing to do with the Worker Alliance. The Confederation was losing members, and Pestaña wrote in the first number of *Leviatán:*

The areas where the CNT has preserved the greatest influence are Zaragoza, Logroño and part of Logroño province, Andalusia, excluding Huelva, and one or two other towns. In the Levant its influence is

6. Joaquín Maurín, *Revolución y contrarrevolución en España* (Paris, 1965), 119.

quite scattered. There is not a single town where its former influence remains completely intact, save for an isolated village or two. It has been lost altogether in Castile. Galicia is doubtful, though not Asturias, for if the CNT has lost ground in Gijón, it has held fast in La Felguera and other towns. But what influence it once had in Bilbao has been reduced to the minimum, as in Guipúzcoa and Navarre. In Catalonia the influence of the CNT as a class organization is nil, but it still receives attention out of fear rather than respect. In Catalonia and especially in Barcelona the elements that belong to the CNT impose themselves on the working class by force.

During the winter and spring of 1934 the initiative in social disputes passed from the CNT to the UGT, and particularly to the latter's most radical federation, the FNTT. The mouthpiece of the FNTT, *El Obrero de la Tierra*, announced on February 3, "We Declare Ourselves for the Revolution!" It hammered away on the theme that only a direct, sweeping revolution would solve the rural problem, praising the Stalinist collectivization program and demanding the expropriation of all land save small private family farms in order to build a system of collectives in Spain.

Though the plight of the landless southern peasants was extreme and undeniable, the picture of a Spanish countryside seething on the verge of irresistible revolution was greatly exaggerated. Only in parts of the south were landless peasants a numerical majority. Edward Malefakis' class analysis of rural Spain in the 1930's estimated that in the northern and middle provinces the composition was as follows:

Upper and upper-middle-class owners	18–19%
Moderate lower-middle-class	40–42%
Permanent hired hands	5– 6%

This added up to a total of 63 to 67 percent of the population more or less identified with the existing order of things. In the southern third of the country that proportion was much lower:

Upper and upper-middle-class owners	15–16%
Moderate lower-middle-class	16–17%
(including $\frac{4}{5}$ of family owners and $\frac{1}{3}$ of family tenants)	
Permanent hired hands	7–10%
(assuming only $\frac{3}{4}$ of the total of 10% to be antirevolutionary)	

In the south, only some 38 to 43 percent of the population might be considered stable, and it was here that agitation became concentrated.

The minimum program of the FNTT stipulated that rural employment be carried on only by *turno riguroso* (hiring in each area only those workers inscribed in proper order on the local labor list), that harvest machinery be outlawed to increase employment, and that special supervisory committees of farm workers be established in each district to oversee fulfillment of contracts. The response of the Radical government was fairly conciliatory, but in some rural areas UGT and CNT workers were blacklisted by employers. Farm wages declined to some extent, though apparently not so much as the left charged.

When the government refused to give in to the demands, the FNTT called an agrarian general strike that lasted from June 5 to June 20 in some areas. The strike began in 1,563 municipal districts and spread through most parts of Spain, but was most effective in the latifundist regions. Half the villages in the provinces of Ciudad Real, Córdoba, and Málaga were affected, and one-fourth of those in Badajoz, Huelva, and Jaén. In the province of Seville the strike was supported by the CNT and lasted longer there than anywhere else. The contest was conducted with restraint by both sides and martial law was not declared. A total of 13 people were killed, most of them not in confrontations with authority but in fights between strikers and nonstrikers. Destruction of property did occur, especially in Seville province. The principal exercise of authority by the government was to arrest strikers on the slightest excuse of infringing the law; this resulted in 7,000 detentions during a period of two weeks. Hundreds of prisoners were temporarily shipped to jails several hundred miles distant, but most were released before the end of July.

The whole effort resulted in fiasco for the FNTT. Support was widespread, but not so complete as was hoped. Resources did not permit the strike to continue long enough to be effective, and it did not provoke disorders in other sectors of society. Instead of building morale and enthusiasm for a revolutionary test with landowners, the strike nearly wrecked the FNTT. Many peasants dropped out, some syndicate headquarters were closed down, and the Federation was gravely weakened in those areas where it had been strongest.

The first Socialist plunge into extremism in 1934 thus collapsed, but had no sobering effect on the incendiaries. They blamed the failure of the strike on the "reactionary" nature of the government, its use of the police, and the failure of the FNTT to coordinate its effort with other revolutionary groups. During the summer of 1934 the climate of Spanish socialism became even more febrile.

The agrarian strike marked the start of concrete preparation by the Socialists for insurrection. On June 6 the party's executive commission sent instructions to local sections to organize for direct action. All able-bodied male members of the Socialist Youth were to assemble themselves in a paramilitary militia that was later to be expanded to include members of the regular party and the UGT. A secret three-man revolutionary committee, composed of Largo, Enrique de Francisco, and Anastasio de García, was set up in Madrid to direct operations. Efforts were to be made to accumulate weapons and concoct bombs, but the revolutionary committee proved indecisive, and the Socialist militia remained largely in the planning stage. Money was spent on arms; one cache of 600 weapons was discovered by Madrid police in June and another 50 pistols in the home of a Socialist Cortes deputy, but systematic preparation was lacking.

The most active elements were *grupos de choque* (shock units) organized by the Socialist Youth in Madrid and a few other areas. They had begun to launch attacks on Falangists and conservatives in the autumn of 1933 and by mid-1934 Falangist gunmen were replying in kind.[7] Street incidents multiplied in Madrid during the summer of 1934 without any distinct plan or purpose. The Minister of the Interior, Rafael Salazar Alonso (subsequently murdered by the left in 1936), was alarmed by the number of teenagers participating in political street battles. Late in August he promulgated a decree forbidding anyone under 16 to join a political organization and requiring that anyone under 23 have his parents' consent. By that time the police had arrested 367 leftist minors and 103 rightist minors in Madrid alone. At least a dozen minors had been killed so far that year

7. There is a detailed discussion of these incidents in my *Falange* (Stanford, 1961), 51–58.

in fights in Madrid, seven of them rightist and four leftist.[8]

Years later, in a speech in Mexico, Indalecio Prieto recalled that Socialist affairs had been conducted with great confusion during the spring and summer of 1934:

The Socialist Youth had been given a free hand so that they might engage with absolute irresponsibility in all kinds of disorders. Though motivated by frenzied enthusiasm, this hindered achievement of the ultimate goal. No one placed restrictions on the outrageous acts of the Socialist Youth who, without paying attention to anyone else, provoked general strikes in Madrid without realizing that they were frustrating the ultimate revolutionary general strike which was to be the key to the whole movement, since a great city cannot be subjected by such efforts. Furthermore, certain deeds committed by members of the Socialist Youth that prudence requires me to remain silent about met with no reproach nor restraint nor any calling to account. . . .[9]

The summer was filled with strike activity, and the government took a conciliatory attitude in helping to settle certain key disputes. The Radical Minister of Labor, for example, awarded striking metallurgists and construction workers in Madrid a major victory by pushing through a reduction of the work week to 44 hours accompanied by an 8 percent wage boost, one of the biggest achievements of any trade union in the world during 1934. Minor victories did not, however, have a moderating effect on the revolutionary sectors of the Socialists. Intensification of the Catalan constitutional conflict increased the possibility of gaining left Catalanist support for the "antifascist," "federal socialist" movement planned by the Worker Alliance. In an interview published in *El Sol* on July 10, even Julián Besteiro agreed that the left would be justified in a posture of rebellion were the Catalan agrarian legislation not permitted to stand. Contacts were initiated between the Worker Alliance and the secret Catalanist "defense committee" in Barcelona.

The real axis of the Alliance was the Socialist party, but the Socialist leaders proved reluctant to relinquish their party's independence to a nationally organized Alliance. Despite the

8. Further statistics are given in Salazar Alonso's *Bajo el signo de la revolución* (Madrid, 1935).

9. Quoted in Andrés Saborit, *Julián Besteiro* (Toulouse, 1962), 346.

initial agreement, the Socialists dragged their feet in efforts to organize the Alliance in most areas. The small revolutionary parties centered in Catalonia feared that the Socialists would merely use the Alliance to increase their own leverage while refusing to bind themselves to a democratic national movement that would transcend their party cadres. In July a conference of the Libertarian Syndicalist Federation of CNT dissidents, who had become strong supporters of the Alliance, demanded that the Socialist party commit itself to a united, coordinated national Alliance within 60 days or else withdraw from the regional Alliances. This had little effect; Socialist policy remained ambiguous.

MEANWHILE, a major effort was made to bring the Spanish Communist party into the regional alliances. When the Republic began, the Communist party had no more than 800 regular members, flanked by 15,000 workers in Communist-dominated unions.[10] During the early years of the new regime it had continued the Comintern-dictated tactic of isolationist revolutionary extremism, working for the direct overthrow of the Republic, which was to be replaced by a "worker-peasant" dictatorship. The Comintern had not denied the need to complete the "bourgeois democratic revolution" in Spain, but held that this was being quickly accomplished and that there was no need to assist it. All the social reforms of 1931–32 were combated as reactionary bribes and the Socialist party denounced as "the champion of reaction in the offensive of bourgeois and agrarian counterrevolution against the working classes." The Achilles heel of the Azaña administration was repeatedly struck with calls for "all land to the peasants"—across-the-board expropriation. A separate Communist trade union organization, the General Confederation of Unified Labor (CGTU), was established in June 1932, claiming 280,000 members, but probably having no more than one-third that number. Another purge of the party leadership was then

10. These are the figures given by Dolores Ibarruri in a speech at Moscow in May 1934, in the stenographic report of the XVII meeting of the All-Soviet Communist party, in L. V. Ponomareva, *Rabochee dvizhenie v Ispanii v gody revoliutsii 1931–1934* (Moscow, 1965), 78.

carried out to eliminate the idea that the party should collaborate with the Republican left even temporarily. Two Comintern agents, the Hungarian Ernö Gerö and the Argentine Vittorio Codovila, were sent to reorganize the party's cadres as effective conspiratorial cells. Henceforth a greater effort was made to penetrate the CNT and especially the UGT. Communist agitators had helped to provoke at least a dozen violent strikes in 1931 and 1932, and their activities were redoubled. After losing the entire Catalan section of the party, the Comintern came out strongly for Spanish regionalism. A separate Communist party of Catalonia (PCC) was founded in 1932 and from that time forward the party program called for full autonomy to the extent of outright independence for Catalonia, Galicia, and the Basque provinces. The Communist vote rose from 300,000 in 1931 to 400,000 in 1933, and party membership stood at some 20,000 in 1934. Despite numerical weakness, the Communists took steps to create their own paramilitary force. Dolores Ibarruri, the grey eminence of the party, has written that

> With its own forces and the aid of some military chiefs, the Communist Party formed the Antifascist Workers' and Peasants' Militia (MAOC) in 1933 in nearly every province of Spain. . . . Their immediate superior was Pedro Checa, the party's secretary of organization.[11]

Communist propaganda was active and well financed. To what extent this contributed to the radicalization of Spanish socialism is a moot point; the Spanish left had already shown the capacity to work itself into a frenzy without foreign assistance.

The Communists had persistently called on the Spanish Socialists to join a "United Front," though on terms that would have involved reorganization of the two parties under Communist hegemony. The discussion of Socialist-Communist unity was taken up seriously by both parties for the first time in a series of party press editorials during late December 1933 and January 1934. The Socialists were interested only in a federation of the two parties in which the much larger Socialist organization would be dominant, while the Communists proposed the organization of an entirely new united Marxist front from the bottom up. The Communist proposal was to bypass the existing Socialist

11. Dolores Ibarruri, *They Shall Not Pass* (New York, 1966), 207.

organization through the formation of new local groups in which the Communists would have much greater influence. On May 16, 1934, the Communist organ, *Mundo Obrero,* also called for the development of a united antifascist militia. In the formation of paramilitary units the Communists were proportionately much more advanced than the Socialists.

Revolutionary Socialists insisted that there was no reason for the Communists not to join the Worker Alliance, since it was devoted to the same goal that the Communists had been preaching. Segundo Serrano Poncela of the Socialist Youth wrote in *El Socialista* on July 29, 1934,

> The Worker Alliance has no abstract or partial objectives. It is not organized to win political triumphs within bourgeois democracy. It is in essence the insurrectional preparation for the conquest of power. . . .
>
> The Worker Alliance groups are the tool of insurrection and the organ of power. Despite radical differences from the Russian soviets, they have the same spinal column as the latter. The Communists demand above all the organization of soviets to prepare for the insurrectional conquest and retention of proletarian power. That is precisely what the Alliance groups seek.

He asserted that the main difference between the situation in Russia in 1917 and that of Spain in 1934 was the absence of large organized proletarian groups in Russia, which had made it necessary to form entirely new revolutionary councils, the soviets. This was said not to be necessary in Spain because of the existence of a large organized Socialist party and trade union system.

For three years Communist spokesmen had been urging the rest of the left to join their party in immediate revolution. Formation of the Worker Alliance at first caused them to back down, for local Communist cells stood little chance of dominating Worker Alliance federations in most districts. Communist spokesmen defended the party's reluctance by pointing out fundamental weaknesses in the existing Alliances: poor organization, lack of unity, failure to prepare for coordinated strike activity, lack of attention to the peasants, and not least of all the Socialists' own reluctance to complete the national formation of Worker Alliances. The Communist leaders began to temporize, and suggested cooperation for more limited ends.

On August 31 the executive committee of the Socialist Youth released a statement complaining that

> The Communist Youth propose unity of action for small, partial battles, for political and economic improvements. They avoid the problem of organizing the struggle for power. We, on the other hand, consider the latter essential, and therefore have unalterably insisted that the Communist organizations enter the Worker Alliance for the concrete objective of organizing the insurrection.
>
> In our judgment, the phase of small, partial battles has been completed. . . . There only remains the final battle, for which unity of action is indispensable.

Communist policy was changing in 1934, for by that time the Russian leaders were beginning to realize that central European fascism was a more formidable foe than they had supposed. The Communist policy of isolationist maximalism had merely facilitated the triumph of Nazism in Germany, weakening social democrats and moderates and driving frightened middle-class people into the arms of the Nazis. A continuation of such policies would strengthen conservatism in west European countries and encourage more militant anticommunism, while abetting the expansion of the fascist powers. French Communist leaders had begun to suggest a Popular Front federation with other forces of the left. In Spain the latter seemed more militant and potentially stronger than in France, but the Spanish Communist party was in 1934 weaker than its French counterpart. Should it stand aside from the Worker Alliance, it would be irremediably isolated and lose the influence on the extreme left that it had acquired during the past three years. On September 12 the central committee of the party, after receiving instructions from the Comintern, agreed to enter the Worker Alliance, so long as it was understood that there would be free deliberation on the future activities of the Alliance. The party secretary, the ex-*cenetista* José Díaz, warned that while the ultimate goal was to strengthen proletarian power for the revolution, it would be a grave mistake to ignore immediate, temporary objectives. Sponsors of a joint assembly of Socialist and Communist Youth in Madrid on September 14 claimed that 80,000 sympathizers attended.

There was actually broad diversity of opinion within the Alliance, and many segments did not share the reckless emphasis on all-out revolution of the Socialist Youth. For example, the young leader of the Madrid sector of the Trotskyist Communist Left, G. Munis, published a pamphlet, *Qué son las Alianzas Obreras,* in September, criticizing the overly "optimistic" thesis of the Socialist Youth that "the ascendant process of the revolution is following its course." He denied that Spain was in the same situation as Russia in 1917. The country was not a ripe plum about to fall into the hands of the revolutionaries, for the forces of Spanish conservatism were still strong. Munis emphasized that the immediate goal of the Alliance should be to achieve the complete unity of all working-class groups and organize a unified paramilitary force, but the notion of an insurrection might be premature. Like the Socialist moderates and the Republican left, Munis suggested that the most practical immediate goal in national politics should be to force dissolution of the Cortes and new general elections, which would permit the left to begin to take over power peacefully.

For his part, Indalecio Prieto, the head of the social democratic sector of the Socialist party, went along with the plans of the extremists for insurrection in the event that the CEDA was allowed to form a government. He even served as a member of a small program committee of the Socialist leadership to outline the concrete goals of the revolutionary movement. The resultant program called for the nationalization of all the land, dissolution of all religious orders and confiscation of their property, dissolution of the Army and the Civil Guard, purge of government employees, and the organization of workers' committees to supervise industry.

Mounting opposition from left and right made it evident that the days of the Radical government were numbered. When it collapsed, there would be two possible alternatives: formation of a coalition government of Radicals and *cedistas,* or the calling of new elections. The prerogative of the president to call new elections before a parliament's natural term of expiration was limited by the constitution to two times during a presidential term, and the action was subject to review by the new parliament. Since a workable majority was readily at hand, it appeared that the president would have little constitutional alternative to permitting the CEDA to form part of the next ministry. On October 1 the Cortes reconvened and the CEDA brought down the government. After several days of consultation, Lerroux was authorized to form a new ministry containing three representatives of the CEDA. Four Republican leaders, Azaña, Felipe Sánchez Román (head of the most moderate of the small left Republican groups), Diego Martínez Barrio (leader of the most liberal part of the Radicals, who had earlier played a key role in weakening the Azaña government), and Miguel Maura all dispatched virtually identical notes to the president condemning the action and announcing that they broke off all association with the "existing institutions" of the country. This *pronunciamiento* of the middle-class left and liberals was designed to place pressure on Alcalá Zamora to withdraw confidence from Lerroux and call new elections. Its promulgators evidently expected support from a Socialist general strike.

With even middle-class liberals unwilling to tolerate the functioning of parliamentary democracy under the constitution, the extremists swung into action. On October 4 the revolutionary committee of the Socialists in Madrid sent word to the local sections of the party to launch the insurrection, and the Worker Alliance mobilized other forces in Barcelona. But in most provinces the Socialists had not made concrete plans, and the result was confusion and inaction. The FNTT was too weak to organize a general strike, and there were few disturbances in the south. In Madrid a general strike began on October 5, but the only signs of "insurrection" were sporadic sniping attacks on police and government buildings by the *grupos de choque* of the Socialist and Communist militia, nominally unified on October 3. Though the capital was paralyzed for several days and the Army had to be deployed, the revolt in Madrid was a complete failure. For all their talk, the Madrid Socialists lacked the preparation and desire to go through with a real insurrection. The same was true in most of the rest of central and northern Spain. UGT militia were effectively organized in part of the Basque mining and industrial region; several opponents were shot, but the revolt there came to nothing for lack of support. The only exceptions were in Catalonia and Asturias.

The revolt in Barcelona had two foci: the Worker Alliance and the Generalitat. It caught Companys and the more moderate Esquerra leaders almost by surprise, for they had nearly completed negotiations with the preceding Radical administration in Madrid over an effective compromise formula for ratifying their agrarian reform legislation. The Lliga had ended its boycott, returning to the Catalan regional parliament on September 29. However, formation of the new moderate-conservative government in Madrid convinced the Esquerra leaders that the Generalitat should resort to a direct show of force. Though Dencàs' "defense committee" was supposed to prepare the paramilitary forces of left Catalanism, it accomplished little, in part because of the reluctance of Companys, who would not permit government money to be used for arms. Dencàs had disarmed the regional Somatén, a middle-class nonparty militia of moderates who were antiproletarian and frequently lukewarm in their Catalanism, but the weapons collected were few in number and not effectively distributed among the Catalanist militia. Badia had carried out a "reorganization" of the Catalan police to remove moderates and conservatives, but did not entirely complete the task.

Late in September, Azaña came to Barcelona, apparently to reach some understanding with the Catalanist left. Earlier there was talk of declaring an alternative left Republican government in Barcelona and calling for new elections, as had been tried once under the old regime in 1917. But there is no evidence that Azaña wanted to participate in an armed revolt; events subsequently trapped him in Barcelona.

The Worker Alliance never reached concrete agreement with the Generalitat due to the reluctance of Companys and the aversion of Dencàs and Badia to cooperating with proletarian revolutionaries. According to CNT spokesmen later, the Worker Alliance groups represented only 15 percent of the organized workers in Catalonia, a figure that appears to be approximately correct. But the Worker Alliance was making plans to seize the initiative, while the CNT seemed played out. The FAI-CNT would cooperate neither with the Generalitat, which they considered an agent of reaction, nor with the Worker Alliance, which they considered an instrument of tyranny and political perversion.

The armed manpower at the Generalitat's disposal in Barcelona was not especially large for a city of 1 million. There were some 3,000 Assault Guards under the authority of the Generalitat, and about 400 members of the Mossos d'Escuadra, the Generalitat's special constabulary, in the capital. Badia had about 3,400 armed youths in his Exèrcit Català d'Escamots, the bulk of them in the capital and the remainder organized among the Rabassaire groups of Barcelona province. When the time came, the Worker Alliance could mobilize only 800 militia in the capital.

On October 5 the Worker Alliance declared a general strike in Barcelona. This proved effective in a large part, though not all, of the city. The CNT officially refused to support it, but many local *cenetistas* did, making it the first non-anarchosyndicalist organized general strike in Barcelona's history. The strike and acts of violence associated with it, such as church-burning, proved even more effective in some provincial towns, such as Badalona, Granollers, Palafrugell, and notably Lérida, where the BOC had proportionately its greatest support.

Leaders of the Worker Alliance urged the Catalanists to join them in revolt against the "pro-fascist" government in Madrid. Companys would not give the word, while the general strike made Dencàs nervous. On October 6 he tried to make the Worker Alliance stop requisitioning automobiles and guns. Detachments of Escamots were sent to protect important buildings from being seized by workers. The confusion was heightened by intermittent anarchist sniping attacks on Catalan police.

While conflicting news arrived from Madrid and elsewhere, the excitement grew and extremists urged Companys to declare the complete freedom of Catalonia from the central government. He refused all day long until finally, after seeing no sign that the government in Madrid would resign or make concessions, he gave in and at 7:00 P.M. on October 6 proclaimed over the radio the existence of a "Catalan State within the Spanish Federal Republic." The Catalanist *pronunciamiento* was, in military parlance, a *cuartelazo* (barracks revolt) for after the declaration the Catalanist leaders did nothing but hole up in the government building of the Generalitat and the Interior Ministry a few blocks away. A small detachment of no more than 1,500 troops from the local army garrison captured both buildings by morning. All the leaders were arrested save Dencàs, Badia, and a few intimates who escaped by means of a previously prepared tunnel dug through the Interior Ministry basement into a large outlet of the Barcelona sewer system. This ignominious exit and the obvious care taken to prepare it ahead of time gave rise to much mirth. Order was soon restored in Barcelona and in the rest of Catalonia. Some 46 people were killed in the capital, a lesser number in the provincial towns.

The only thorough revolutionary insurrection occurred in Asturias, the only region where all the revolutionary groups joined the Worker Alliance. Asturias is a province of small farms, large-scale mining, and heavy industry. Though a modern labor force took shape later in Asturias than in Catalonia, it developed a militant social consciousness second to no other region. This was in part because of the character of Asturian industrial society, concentrated to a high degree in large-scale mining and metallurgical enterprises, in distinct contrast to the small-shop structure of Catalan industry. Immigrant workers were drawn mainly from nearby regions; the rate of literacy and level of cultural development were apparently slightly higher than among Catalan workers, and the ethos somewhat less individualistic. At the time of the 1917 general strike the Asturian miners had sustained their walkout with greater tenacity than any other group of workers in Spain. During the early years of the Primo de Rivera regime Austurian UGT syndicates had shown great moderation in cooperating with management, but a reaction against this set in, with new labor disorders beginning in 1927. The strike rate had risen steadily since the start of the Republic, and in 1932 Asturias surpassed Barcelona province as the site of greatest labor discontent. During that year there had been 94 strikes in Asturias (42 of which lasted more than five days), compared with 66 walkouts in Barcelona province.

Asturian labor had built the strongest position to be found

in any industrial region of Spain. Most of the disputes since 1930 had resulted in general or partial victories for the workers. The Asturian miners were the best-paid sector of Spanish labor and enjoyed a well-developed system of fringe benefits, but many grievances remained. Asturian mines were poorly equipped compared with those of the rest of western Europe, and the accident rate was very high. In the face of steep production costs, Asturian entrepreneurs eagerly looked for marginal economies, sometimes at the workers' expense. Moreover, the decline in the coal and steel market after 1931 had resulted in serious unemployment in the province, especially by 1933. The militancy of the miners—the central core of the Asturian labor force—was heightened by the fact that approximately 60 percent of them were under 30 years of age (and 20 percent of them under 21). The wages of apprentice miners were much less than the average, they were the first to be laid off, and they derived least advantage from the system of fringe benefits.

By 1934 the total labor force in Asturias numbered at least 110,000, 50,000 in the mining basin and 60,000 among the other towns in the province. At least 70,000 of the workers were members of trade unions, resulting in a greater proportion of organized workers in Asturias than in any other province of Spain. (At the peak of labor organization of Barcelona province during 1920 and 1931, the proportion had been about the same—60 to 70 percent—but this had declined a bit in Barcelona by 1934). The largest force was the UGT, which had nearly 40,000 members, including 22,000 in its militant Asturian Miners' Syndicate. The CNT had less than 25,000 followers, concentrated especially in the coastal towns, and was comparatively weak in the mining basin. The Asturian sector had always been one of the most active and radical parts of the Socialist trade union movement, and had not fully cooperated with the social-democratic reformist trend of 1931–32. By 1934 its members were suffering the consequences of the depression and the partial exhaustion of the rather thin coal and iron resources of the region. Some of the local Socialist consumer cooperatives had gone bankrupt, partially due to lack of funds, partially due to poor management. The Asturian UGT was inflamed, united, and determined to assert worker control over industrial society.

Socialist alliance with the CNT was possible in Asturias because the Asturias-León-Palencia federation the CNT had not fallen under control of the FAI. Living in a more highly developed and concentrated industrial area, Asturian anarchosyndicalists were less attracted to simplistic notions of apolitical "spontaneous revolution." When the Socialists and Communists began to set up local "united front" committees in several parts of Asturias at the beginning of 1934, CNT leaders joined with them in a few towns. On March 28, 1934, representatives of the UGT and CNT in Asturias signed a pact of alliance for revolutionary trade union activity and opposition to further association with "bourgeois parties." Later, on September 15, regional CNT delegates voted 21 to 16 to participate in the Worker Alliance that had been formed in Asturias by the Socialists and a handful of local followers of the BOC.

The other main revolutionary force in Asturias was the Asturian Communist Federation, which claimed 3,000 members in 1934, or about 15 percent of the total Communist party following in Spain. Communist trade unions purported to have 8,000 members, including 6,000 in the Communists' United Syndicate of Asturian Miners.[12] Asturian Communists were particularly successful in their propaganda activities, which reached far beyond the party membership and helped keep worker emotions at fever pitch. Several Communist front organizations were active, and Asturian anarchosyndicalists were among the members of the local chapter of the Society of Friends of the USSR. The provincial Communist Youth group was particularly zealous, and was characterized by the national leadership as the strongest in Spain. As elsewhere, the Asturian Communists had concentrated on building their own revolutionary "united front." The revolutionary committee of the nominally multiparty Worker Alliance in Asturias was at first composed exclusively of Socialists; the two Communist representatives did not enter it until October 4.

12. These and most of the preceding statistics on Asturias are drawn from E. Teper, "Asturiiskii proletariat v borbe za edinstvo (1933–1934 gg.)," in *Problemy rabochego dvizheniya v Ispanii* (Moscow, 1960), 135–200.

The orders sent out by the Socialist committee in Madrid mentioned specifically only a "general strike," which was declared in Asturias on October 5. The workers' organizations had kept the towns and roads of the province in intermittent disorder since mid-September, and what followed during the next two weeks was the most intensive, destructive proletarian insurrection in the history of western Europe to that date. The heart of the revolt was Mieres, in the center of the mining district southeast of the provincial capital, Oviedo. It was occupied by armed worker militia at dawn on the fifth. Police officers and outposts were attacked all over southern Asturias, and the revolutionaries moved into Oviedo on the following day. Soon most of the province, except for the center of Oviedo, defended by the local army garrison, was in their hands. The rebels showed great courage in assaults on police and army posts; miners were especially effective in their use of dynamite sticks. One of the leaders later wrote that "forty per cent of our combat achievements were due to the use of dynamite." [13]

At least 30,000 workers, possibly more, participated in the armed revolt. The size of the revolutionary militia was limited only by the number of weapons available. The joint Socialist-Communist militia leadership prior to the rising had acquired only 1,700 rifles and 4,000 pistols and shotguns (one revolutionary source said that in Madrid there had been only 665 rifles, including 20 machine guns),[14] but the official inventory of the arsenals and arms factories occupied at Oviedo and Trubia listed 25,000 rifles and shotguns and nearly 500 automatic weapons.[15] Against the 30,000 or more armed workers, there were 1,500 soldiers and 1,200 armed policemen in the province. Within less than forty-eight hours the revolt was completely out of control, and the government had to summon from Morocco elite shock forces of the Legion and Moorish Regulares that were well trained in irregular warfare.

A revolutionary regime was declared in most of the towns occupied by the rebels. The nature of this regime depended on

13. Manuel Grossi, *La insurrección de Asturias* (Barcelona, 1935), 63.
14. Manuel Benavides, *La revolución fué así* (Barcelona, 1935), 50-52.
15. Spanish government, *La revolución de octubre en España* (Madrid, 1935).

the predominant political complexion of the workers in each district. In the town of Sama the municipal revolutionary committee declared the existence of the "dictatorship of the proletariat" and the formation of a "red army." The anti-Marxist anarchosyndicalists protested this imposition of Marxist forms on what was supposed to be a spontaneous joint effort and the Sama committee later withdrew the proclamations. Lack of representation on the provincial revolutionary committee placed the CNT at a disadvantage, and its representatives eventually joined on October 11.

By that time sizable army reinforcements had been moved in from three sides and the rebel zone was shrinking. On October 12 the Socialist miners' leader, Ramón González Peña, and his comrades realized that the revolt was receiving no support elsewhere and would soon collapse. When they proposed to negotiate a cessation of hostilities, the two Communist representatives withdrew and a separate Communist committee was formed to continue the struggle. Less than forty-eight hours were needed, however, to show the hopelessness of the isolated rebellion. The Communists then rejoined the Socialists to negotiate a surrender.

By the time most of the region had been pacified (October 18), approximately 900 of the revolutionaries had been killed. The police and Army suffered approximately 300 fatalities, and at least 40 civilian conservatives were murdered, including 29 priests. Some of the rebels, though evidently many fewer than was charged, were shot out of hand when captured. In addition to the fighting, there had been enormous wanton destruction of property. Besides burning churches, the revolutionaries devoted much energy to blowing up many other buildings that symbolized the presence of their class enemy. There had been nothing like the Asturian revolt in Spanish history, or in that of the rest of western Europe since the Paris Commune.

EIGHT *Formation of the*

Popular Front

A FTER THE INSURRECTION in Asturias, the Spanish government
faced the extraordinarily difficult task of trying to put
back together the pieces of the body politic. The prime
minister, Lerroux, had the advantage of being one of the few
experienced politicians in the country to hold a position of
leadership. He had a reputation for opportunism and financial
corruption, but his very practicality had taught him that the
only way a government could function successfully within a
liberal representative system was by conciliating a broad cross-
section of opinion. This required moderation and compromise;
the entry of conservatives into the cabinet should only bring
a shift in emphasis, not lead to the complete annulment of liberal
policy. Lerroux did not at first intend to go any farther right
than was necessary. As soon as the Asturian revolt had been
controlled, outspokenly militarist army commanders were transferred to other regions and the censorship was lifted. Neither
the Socialist party, the UGT, the Rabassaires, nor the other main
leftist groups that participated in the rebellion were banned by
law, though approximately 20,000 of their militants, mainly from

Asturias, were arrested. Soon after the revolt, a young Radical deputy who wanted to have the leftist groups outlawed was rebuked by Lerroux in these terms: "You're very young, Pérez Madrigal. Let me tell you something: from now on we must be the defenders and rehabilitators of Socialism in defeat." [1] Lerroux knew perfectly well that in a liberal democratic system the middle-class parties could not immediately fill the void temporarily left by the Socialists, and that the only way a democratic Republic could function in the future would be through the Socialists' renewed cooperation with Republican reformism.

Yet Lerroux' hands were tied by his CEDA allies and, in turn, Gil Robles and the moderate leaders of the CEDA were under heavy pressure from sectarian conservatives and military leaders. The latter encouraged police brutality against captive leftists, especially in the Asturian jails, and a militant campaign for death sentences for all the leaders and those guilty of criminal deeds. Lerroux and the moderates, with the support of the president, blocked this; none of the revolutionary leaders were shot, and only four of the rank and file. But police brutality and tortures in the first weeks after the insurrection was defeated subsequently gave rise to an enormous leftist propaganda campaign that exaggerated its extent and further inflamed feelings. The determination to pin a share of the blame directly on Azaña, who had been arrested in Barcelona at the time of the revolt, also backfired. He had eventually to be released and was made to appear an innocent martyr of conservative vengeance. It has been argued that the handling of the repression was not moderate and generous enough to conciliate the left—if indeed such a thing were possible—and that it was not sufficiently firm and thoroughgoing to repress them effectively.

In Catalonia the autonomy statute was suspended. Under a law of December 18, 1934, the authority of the Generalitat was temporarily replaced by that of a governor-general appointed from Madrid. Public order, justice, and education were taken out of the hands of regional administration. Even the small ultraliberal National Republican party of Sánchez Román agreed with moderates and conservatives that the exercise of Catalan

1. Joaquín Pérez Madrigal, *Memorias de un converso* (Madrid, 1952), 158.

autonomy had gone too far. Sánchez Román, one of the most respected lawyers in Spain, recommended the passage of a new statute curtailing Catalan autonomy, at least in the sphere of public order. But disorder in Barcelona was not ended even after the revolt; martial law had temporarily to be reimposed because of local incidents, mainly due to the CNT.

Catalan liberals of the Lliga, as other sectors of the liberal minority, saw the danger that arose not merely from the left, but also from the sectarian reaction of the conservatives to leftist demands, constitutional or revolutionary. At the close of the Lliga congress in March 1935, the party's leader Cambó admonished the Spanish right to avoid

a new declaration of war that merely reflects the change in parliamentary strength of the belligerents. For if the latter occurs, just as the policy of Azaña provoked the reaction of the right, the policy of the right would provoke an irresistible resurgence of the extreme left. . . .

Nothing is being done in Spain to achieve a pacification of feeling, to achieve at least an armistice that would permit cooperation. . . . A work of sabotage is going on which by blowing up bridges endeavors to make relations between different ideologies irreconcilable.

. . . There is the danger that just as Sr. Azaña in announcing the death of Spanish Catholicism gave it the impetus to regain vigor once more, so his accusers, in attempting his political destruction through judicial persecution, may make him the popular idol of Spain.[2]

Cambó's speech repeated the warning voiced by Miguel Maura when the latter addressed the conservative deputies in the Cortes soon after the insurrection:

Mark my words: the course that you are presently following brings to mind the bitter days of the constituent Cortes, when only passion, hatred and rancor were breathed. That provoked the reaction which you represent; let not your present conduct spark another reaction, for, should that occur, it will leave standing nothing of that which is common to both of us.[3]

Disputes over punishment of revolutionary leaders and those guilty of major crimes provoked several changes of cabinet, and it proved difficult for the president, Alcalá Zamora, to prevent the CEDA from gaining the government representation

2. Lliga Catalana, *Dos anys d'actuació* (Barcelona, 1935), 303–05.
3. Speech of Nov. 16, 1934, quoted by Maura in *El Sol,* June 20, 1936.

to which that party's electoral strength had entitled it. Another reorganization of the cabinet on May 6, 1935, gave the CEDA 5 of the 13 seats in the government; it was frequently referred to as the "Lerroux–Gil Robles ministry," with the CEDA chief holding the key post of Minister of War.

A legislative study project was soon introduced to prepare for the CEDA's main goal—constitutional revision. The party's minimum aspiration was to restore full civil rights to the Catholic Church. In addition, provision was made for consideration of curbing the scope of Catalan autonomy, and amending some of the technical and procedural aspects of the constitution. Nevertheless, the government was in no hurry to press constitutional reform to a final conclusion. The domination of moderates and conservatives in the present parliament, which still had more than two years to run, seemed assured. Current law stipulated that after the constitution had been in effect four years (that is, after December 9, 1935), amendments might be passed by a simple majority vote of the Cortes, whereas a two-thirds margin was required prior to that date. Furthermore, as a check on the amendment process, it was required that after successful passage of a constitutional amendment, the amending Cortes be dissolved. The parliament resulting from the elections that followed would then review the preceding amendments. For all these reasons, the CEDA-Radical ministry was in no hurry to complete the process of amendment before 1936.

The Lerroux–Gil Robles government moved more rapidly to protect conservative interests. Its ability to do so was enhanced by the fact that the insurrection had eliminated much of the Socialist parliamentary representation, giving the moderate-conservative majority disproportionate influence. On July 25, 1935, a law for the reform of the agrarian reform was passed. The confiscation of *grandes'* estates and the singling out of "neighboring lands" near villages for more immediate expropriation were repealed. Moreover, terms of computation were greatly changed and the classification of lands in the 1932 inventory was dropped. Owners of large properties were henceforth allowed to sell, give to their children, or otherwise alter the status of excess land that might be liable to expropriation.

Each case was to be judged on an individual basis, if necessary to be adjudicated by local courts and compensated for at full market value. This gave opportunity for endless delay and special local political influence. The maximum budget of the Institute of Agrarian Reform was limited to 50 million pesetas per year, which would permit the settlement of no more than two to three thousand families annually. No previously expropriated land was returned and no peasants who had already been officially settled were evicted, but the balance of power in the countryside had clearly swung in the other direction. Landowners dominated local government and rural labor tribunals. The wages of laborers dropped; in parts of the south farm rents were raised and some renters were expelled. Peasants who had been temporarily settled on an emergency basis were particularly hard hit. Thus the reform program, which had continued to go forward under Lerroux in 1934, was largely if not completely frustrated by the CEDA-Radical coalition of 1935. Lacking organization or leadership, disgruntled peasants carried out only 15 agrarian strikes in all Spain during the latter year, but in much of the south there was a sense of absolute desperation.

In education, the government followed a prudent course. Leftist charges, frequently repeated in later years, that the education budget was reduced are untrue. The budget was actually increased slightly, but the rate of expansion originally projected by the Republican left was slowed.[4] It should be kept

4. This was recognized even by wartime Republican propaganda literature. The official 1937 *Política del Frente Popular en Instrucción Pública* stated that the budget for primary education had increased by the following annual increments:

	Pesetas		Pesetas
1931	14,314,090	1934	20,371,035
1932	57,290,745	1935	9,000,000
1933	43,637,411	1936	3,496,474

In 1933 the Republic had devoted only 6.5 percent of the national budget to education, a lower proportion than in Portugal or any other country in Europe save Albania or Bulgaria. The figure was noteworthy only because of even lower proportionate expenditures under the monarchy. For that matter, the Catalan Generalitat, quick to deride Madrid in this regard, devoted only 8.1 percent of its budget to education and culture. See Jaume Alzina, *Els pressupostos de les corporacions públiques* (Barcelona, 1936).

in mind that so long as Catholic schools were not closed the education gap could still be narrowed without spending as much money as the left Republicans had calculated.

There was no new social legislation, and the unemployment rate increased. The government's only direct response to the economic depression was the beginning of a renewed public works program whose short-term effects were slight. The cabinet members could not agree on fiscal policy, for the moderate Minister of Finance, Joaquín Chapaprieta, proposed drastic budget reductions in many categories combined with tax increases. By September 1935 opposition to various aspects of both policies made it impossible to hold the existing Lerroux–Gil Robles ministry together.

Intragovernmental dissidence enabled Alcalá Zamora to intervene directly in the conduct of executive affairs once more. Though no ministry could govern without a parliamentary majority, the president had the right to bestow or withhold his confidence from cabinet reorganizations as he saw fit. According to his personal interpretation of the constitution, the lack of an upper chamber in the Spanish legislature conferred wide discretionary powers upon the president, who was not necessarily obliged to bestow confidence on the parliamentary leaders who might enjoy the greatest parliamentary voting support. Thus he had constantly refused Gil Robles the opportunity to form a ministry of his own, had encouraged the splitting of the Radical party, and engaged in various intrigues to divide the CEDA and weaken its support. In September 1935 he proscribed Lerroux as well, and appointed the Finance Minister Joaquín Chapaprieta, member of a tiny independent moderate liberal group, to reconstitute the coalition of moderates and conservatives. Throughout 1935 the government was frustrated both by its own disunity and the determined refusal of the president to permit a fully representative government to function.

Lerroux remained in the Chapaprieta government as foreign minister. One month later, in October, Alcalá Zamora publicly released information facilitated by the left concerning the acceptance of bribes by several Radical party figures for attempting to arrange the introduction of a new gambling device, *"Straperlo,"* in San Sebastián. The resultant inquiry exonerated Lerroux personally, but brought his final resignation from the cabinet. The Radicals had a long history of financial irregularities, and the *"Straperlo"* affair, together with a subsequent scandal involving a shipping contract, completely destroyed what was left of the Radicals' reputation with neutral opinion. Though these financial incidents were of slight importance in themselves, they received enormous publicity in the extremist press (both right and left) and had a considerable impact on the public mind. The common term for a black market deal in vernacular Spanish ever since has been *straperlo*.

Thus Spanish conservatives were unable to capitalize on the defeat of the insurrection, and the conditions that developed were propitious to the revival and reunification of the left. Though beaten and momentarily impotent, the cadres of the leftist parties remained intact. Resurgence could scarcely be expected, however, if the disunity that had characterized leftist activity in 1933 and 1934 persisted. Even the Socialists were only a small minority. The moderate conservative coalition governing Spain in 1935 could be defeated only through a unified effort of the left.

This proposition was at first accepted only by the more moderate opposition leaders. In April an agreement was signed between the officials of Azaña's Republican Left party, Sánchez Román's National Republican party, and Diego Martínez Barrio's Republican Union party (the most liberal segment of the Radicals which had split off from the latter during 1934) to work together to re-establish a government based on the original left Republican principles of 1931. Sánchez Román, Martínez Barrio, and Indalecio Prieto published articles in Prieto's *El Liberal* (Bilbao) discussing the need for a general leftist alliance. Prieto, who had prudently fled the country on the eve of the insurrection, wanted to extend this to include the working class groups, and the leaders of the middle-class left were looking in the same direction, for under the electoral system their minority had not the slightest hope for victory by itself. Azaña set the tone by an intransigent speech made at Bilbao in July calling for an absolute victory of the left in new elections, rejecting compromise of any sort with the moderate conservative government then in power. Alternation of liberal and conservative governments as under the constitutional monarchy was categorically condemned; only complete victory for the left and the elimination of conservative influence would suffice.

Prieto did his best to facilitate reconciliation of the Socialists and the Republican left by circulating a manifesto in March 1935 that explained the October insurrection as a sacrifice by the working-class movement to defend the Republican constitution, the same defense made by some of the Asturian revolutionary leaders in their pleas in court. Prieto recognized that many young Socialists were highly agitated and said that the party's main duty in the near future would be to "educate and channel the youth groups."

Prieto's cooperative social democratic policy within Republican legality was rejected by other spokesmen, for the radicalization of Spanish socialism was accelerated by the insurrection. One of the clearest expressions of Socialist maximalism was a small book called *Octubre: segunda etapa* (October: the Second Phase), written by Carlos Hernández Zancajo on behalf of the executive committee of the Socialist Youth federation. Its purpose was to press for the "Bolshevization of the Socialist Party," which according to Zancajo meant its "revolutionary purification."

In spite of whatever errors Spanish Socialism may have committed—and one errs only if one is willing to fight—no one can detect in it the characteristics of European social democracy. Our party has always advocated revolutionary violence and has employed it on various occasions, most recently in October. It has not given indication of sharing the petit bourgeois pacifism of the Second International, which entrusted all anti-militarist activity to the League of Nations. It has maintained its revolutionary principles and, facing the possibilities of victory that the present situation offers the working class, has fervently propagated the slogan of the dictatorship of the proletariat and the Worker Alliance against the bourgeoisie.

Zancajo said that the opportunity for revolution was all the greater because "the employer class lacks organization," and opposed a "Popular Bloc" with the Republican left against moderates and conservatives because association with the middle-class left compromised Socialist principles and was said to be unnecessary for victory. He concluded with the following string of slogans:

For the bolshevisation of the Spanish Party!
(Expulsion of the reformists. Elimination of centrists from positions of command. Abandonment of the Second International.)

For the transformation of the party's structure
toward greater centralization and the formation
of a clandestine apparatus!

For the political unification of the Spanish proletariat
in the Socialist Party!

For anti-militarist propaganda!

For the unification of the trade-union movement!
(Entry of all the small autonomous groups into the UGT, and alliance of the latter with the CNT.)

For the defeat of the bourgeoisie and the triumph
of the revolution in the form of the dictatorship
of the proletariat!

For the reconstruction of the international working class
movement on the basis of the Russian revolution!

To combat the wave of Bolshevization, the small circle of veteran moderates around Julián Besteiro founded a biweekly, *Democracia,* in mid-June 1935. Besteiro and his close associates no longer held any important positions within the party, but felt they must make an effort to save the movement before it was too late. *Democracia* was fiercely attacked by Araquistain's journal, *Leviatán,* forcing Besteiro to deny yet again that he was either a "reformist" or a "Kautskyist." He insisted that true Marxist revolutionism would avoid the maximalists' misreading of Spanish society and politics. The Spain of 1935 was not the Russia of 1917. The middle classes were still comparatively strong whereas the working class movement had not had enough preparation to enable it to carry out a revolution. To expect events in Spain to follow the same course as in Russia would at the present time be suicidal. Besteiro wrote,

My position is that the dictatorship of the proletariat, in its full meaning as an authoritarian government, was an ineluctable necessity in Russia and that the Bolsheviks did well in facing that situation, together with the grave burdens which it imposed. The choice was between socialist dictatorship or anarchy, and the result was not in doubt. But by the same token I have judged that the attempt to gain the same results in European nations was doomed to failure and would produce severe disturbance.

Besteiro deemed it futile and counter-productive to attempt violent revolution in a situation that still permitted orderly political and social evolution. Given the nature of conditions in Spain, the extraproletarian elements that had either assisted or tolerated Bolshevism in Russia would turn against premature revolutionary maximalism and bring down the working class movement in cataclysm.

The repeated denial by Besteiro and also by Prieto that Spain in 1935 was in the same situation as Russia in 1917 was entirely correct, and with the benefit of historical perspective might be carried further. Special wartime conditions made possible the Communist triumph in Russia; uniquely disturbed conditions also existed in 1919 in Hungary, another country less modernized than Spain, but there Communist revolution failed completely. The Spanish middle classes were stronger than those of Russia or Hungary, and the cultural crisis was not so profound in Spain as in Russia. The Spanish intelligentsia was not so thoroughly alienated and was captive to the mystique of revolution in a lesser proportion. The revolutionary myth was capable of assuming a messianic religious quality among its devotees in Spain similar to the religious frenzies of earlier times but could not quite achieve the same total weight as in Russian society. Pronouncements of doctrinaire anticlericals to the contrary, Spain had by no means altogether "ceased to be Catholic." Social transformation and cultural relativism and immanentism had not deprived traditional religion of its meaning for a very large minority of the population. But in 1935–36 the revolutionaries in nearly all parties, mesmerized by their own propaganda, could not appreciate these facts.

Most Socialists who enthusiastically espoused "Bolshevization" were not crypto-Communists, but Spanish revolutionaries who wanted to make of their party an authoritarian revolutionary instrument as effective as Russian Bolshevism. The Socialist maximalists had extraordinarily naïve and uncritical notions about affiliating with the Comintern and cooperating with the Communist party, and when they spoke of union with the latter they conceived of it as the eventual absorption of the Communists by the Socialist party.

The Spanish Communist party and its agents within the Socialist organizations did everything possible to encourage this trend. The year 1935 marked the real beginning of the rise of Spanish communism. The party increased approximately 50 percent in membership, while the Socialist membership remained approximately the same. Both the militant youth and middle-class opportunists attracted to the wave of the future were being drawn more to the Communists than to the Socialists. Communist propaganda, always active, increased greatly in volume. By mid-1935 the Communists claimed to be publishing 42 newspapers and bulletins in Spain, some legally, others clandestinely. One of the most effective Comintern agencies was the relief organization, International Red Aid, which provided assistance to the impoverished families of many of the 15,000 to 20,000 militants in jail—something that the Spanish government did not do—and won much sympathy for communism among the families of Socialists and even among some *cenetistas*. Of more than 600 revolutionaries smuggled out of Spain for further training in Russia and France, only one-third were regular Communists, one-third were Socialists, and one-third members of other leftist groups.

The wave of Bolshevization, whatever many of its proponents intended, accelerated Communist penetration of the Spanish Socialist party. While Prieto remained in exile, the Socialist deputy Carlos Lamoneda, who had been a member of the Communist party from 1921 to 1933, served as secretary for the group of Socialist deputies that remained in the Cortes. He and another leading crypto-Communist, Alvarez del Vayo, dominated relations between the parliamentary representation and the party at large. When requests came in from local sections for guest speakers at rallies, they frequently selected them from the most inflammatory and pro-Communist deputies. Equally important was the secretary of the Socialist Youth, Santiago Carrillo, a pro-Communist fellow traveler who was helping to steer the Socialist Youth organization along a course that would converge with the route of the Spanish Communist party.

In May 1935 the Communist leadership launched a special manifesto "To All Socialist, Communist, Anarchist and Syndicalist Workers of Spain; To All The Workers of Spain, Catalonia, the Basque Country and Morocco." It complained that "the leadership of the Socialist Party has never seriously planned the problem of organizing and preparing the masses for insurrection because it was afraid of declaring a plebeian revolution and planned a coup d'état only to impress the bourgeois parties." The only solution, it said, was to form a new "Worker and Peasant Alliance" of all true worker and peasant groups for the "transformation of the democratic bourgeois revolution into the socialist revolution." Thirteen specific goals were announced:

1. Confiscation without compensation of all lands of the large landowners, the Church, and the government (local and national), to be given to the workers for individual or collective cultivation, "according to their own decision."

2. Cancellation of all debts and services owed by the peasants.

3. Provision to the peasants of all necessary machinery, credit, and technical assistance.

4. "Radical improvement" of the living and working conditions of farm laborers.

5. Confiscation and nationalization of major industries, finance, transportation, and communications.

6. Drastic improvement of the working conditions of the proletariat, including full employment, higher salaries, and the seven-hour day (and a six-hour day for those in difficult or dangerous jobs).

7. Free welfare insurance for sickness, accidents, unemployment, old age, and maternity for all workers.

8. Recognition of the complete autonomy of Catalonia, the Basque country, and Galicia, even to the extent of their establishing independent states.

9. Immediate and unconditional liberation of northern Morocco and all other Spanish colonial territories.

10. "Radical reduction of taxes on small businessmen and smallholders." Annulment of their debts to financial institu-

tions and big business.

11. Dissolution of all the armed forces, and the arming of the workers and the peasants. Purge of all "enemies of the people" in government employment.

12. Creation of a worker-peasant Red Guard, with the election of officers. Purge of "all counter-revolutionary officers."

13. "Proletarian solidarity of all the oppressed of the earth and fraternal alliance with the USSR."

The seventh congress of the Comintern met in Moscow from July 25 to August 20, 1935, and endorsed the formation of popular fronts allying Communists, other leftists, and democratic middle-class liberals as well, in countries where broader unity was needed to defeat fascism or beat back the forces of conservatism. Formation of a Popular Front was in no way to limit the independent organizational activity or ultimate goals of the Communist party. Adoption of the tactic did not originally envisage official alliances with middle-class parties, but only electoral and other kinds of cooperation with individual elements from such groups. Initially it did not plan to extend Communist support to liberal parliamentary governments, but was only intended to broaden the base of Communist strength while upholding the eventual aim of the dictatorship of the proletariat. Before the end of 1935, however, the Comintern decided to enter into temporary political alliances with middle-class liberal parties in both France and Spain.

Meanwhile, the Communists pursued the more direct goal of working unity and ultimate fusion of Socialist and Communist parties in a united revolutionary party, an end sought for years in most countries where a larger organized Socialist party existed. The first ploy attempted in Spain was a Communist proposal in September for fusion of the UGT and the much smaller CGTU. It suggested that in those regions where the UGT syndicates were larger, CGTU workers simply enter the UGT syndicates, but that in districts where CGTU groups were approximately equal to or larger than their UGT counterparts, fusion conferences be held attended by delegates chosen according to the size of the respective groups. The militant UGT leadership rejected this proposal, in large part because it did not believe the CGTU syndicates were equal in size to the UGT in any single district of Spain. It also pointed out that the suggestion of proportional representation created a factional subgroup in the revolutionary organization, contrary to "true Leninism."

On October 23 the Communist central committee sent a letter to the Socialist executive committee proposing syndical uniy and the formation of a united Marxist party on the Leninist-Stalinist organizational basis of "democratic centralism." The Socialist militants gave signs of being impressed by the degree of autonomy nominally granted individual Communist parties by the recent Comintern congress. Given their numerical inferiority, the Communists were willing to make concessions, and on November 20 terms of fusion between the UGT and CGTU were agreed upon. In most areas the CGTU membership was simply to join the local UGT syndicates. In those few regions where Communist unions had been organized in a trade not represented by a similar UGT syndicate, the CGTU affiliate would be accepted as the local UGT union representing that craft. The fusion got under way at Seville on December 11.

A fusion of smaller independent revolutionary parties was carried out in Barcelona during September when Andrés Nin agreed to merge his Communist Left with the Worker-Peasant Bloc (BOC) led by Joaquín Maurín. The new party was called the Worker Party of Marxist Unification (POUM) and by the end of the year numbered approximately 7,000 affiliates. Its main base was in Catalonia (especially Barcelona and Lérida) but there were also nuclei in Madrid, Asturias, Galicia, Extremadura, and the Valencia region. The POUM was organized on the basis of practical revolutionary activity that would include parliamentary participation, at least temporarily, and cooperation with the leftist sectors of the regionalist movements. In largely agreeing to the participationist policy of the POUM, Nin was forced to renounce doctrinaire Trotskyism. A few members of the former Communist Left in Madrid and Barcelona refused to accept POUM tactics and retained their own minuscule Trotskyist organization, which they called "The Bolshevist-Leninist Section."

This consolidation of independent anti-Stalinist Marxism in Catalonia was countered by a new attempt to draw together the pro-Stalinist elements. Before the end of the year the Catalan Communist party succeeded in establishing a "liaison committee" to coordinate its efforts with those of the Catalan section of the Socialist party, the Unió Socialista de Catalunya, and the Partit Català Proletari. The latter had originated as essentially reformist parties of "social Catalanism," led by intellectuals and suported by white-collar employees. After October 1934 they veered sharply to the left, and considered Stalinist communism a natural ally in carrying out the "Catalan revolution."

While the extreme left in Catalonia was regrouping, leaders of the Esquerra attempted to maintain as much as possible of the unity and breadth of the middle-class Catalanist left. Despite pressure from moderates, an official statement of the Esquerra in mid-1935 defended the Estat Català group as an integral part of the Federation. Meanwhile, the new leaders of Estat Català in 1935 moved distinctly to the left, hoping to expand their social appeal.

There was a great deal of switching back and forth between the extremist parties and the moderate groups as well. Impatient Socialists joined the Communists, and impatient Communists joined the Trotskyists or the POUM. Just as liberals left the Radicals for being too conservative, monarchists left the CEDA for being too liberal. While the Socialist Youth were trying to prepare their colleagues for direct action, some CNT leaders were endeavoring to moderate anarchosyndicalism.

Meanwhile, the division between the radical majority and the moderate minority within the Socialist movement deepened. With Largo Caballero and many of his chief associates still in prison, Prieto and the moderates temporarily controlled the party's executive commission. They tried to quiet the loud Socialist Youth leadership by asserting that most local youth groups did not support them. This charge was easily countered by public messages of support for the extremists from two of the most important provincial youth groups (Asturias and Badajoz).

To provide a regular outlet for the revolutionary sector of the party, a new biweekly, *Claridad,* was begun in July. Serving as the mouthpiece of Largo Caballero, it helped to increase the temperature in the party further. Largo wrote in *Claridad* on

November 23,

It would seem impossible that there are "socialists" who fear the concept "bolshevization." The sense that the young people give it is simply the purification of the party, the reaffirmation of its Marxist ideology and its organic reconstruction, with the objective of making it an efficient instrument of combat.

And on the question of unification with the Communist party,

Let us make every effort on our part to see that trade union and political unification, which is so necessary, not be frustrated. . . . We must collaborate with those elements of the Second International that are willing to work for unification with the Third International, a need which is making itself felt. If that becomes impossible, the time will have arrived to make a final decision about remaining in the Second International. But first it is important to know whether the Second International adopts a position of solidarity with the political conduct of the Spanish Socialist Party.

Like the younger Bolshevizers, Largo demanded greater centralization of control in the party, and party authority over the parliamentary delegation, where the "centrists" might otherwise regain strength. Regarding the Socialists' program, he wrote,

We must include in the minimal program the nationalization of banking and of the land. . . . Concerning our maximal program, it should be understood that holding political power does not simply mean putting a Socialist government in Madrid. Holding political power means control over all the resources of the State. For that task it is indispensable that a Socialist government create its own instruments and this, whether we like it or not, is the dictatorship of the proletariat.

On December 10 a full meeting of the national committee of the Socialist party was held, with an agenda that listed the main questions facing the party: extension of the Worker Alliance into a genuinely national federation, formation of a Popular Front with the Communists and/or the middle-class left, amnesty for thousands of militants still in prison, and so forth. After the meeting opened, however, the moderates ignored these fundamental questions to begin a tactical maneuver against the power of Largo Caballero. They repeated the same proposition that had temporarily provoked Largo's resignation as president of the party on the eve of the insurrection. It was a seemingly innocuous proposal: in response to earlier charges of Largo complaining about the indiscipline and conservatism of many of the Socialist deputies in the Cortes, the moderates moved that the party's executive commission be made responsible for directing the parliamentary delegation. In principle, Largo, as president of the executive commission, was all in favor of this, but owing to a technicality in party statutes, such a delegation of authority was illegal unless authorized by a general party congress. Largo Caballero's compulsive legalism in matters referring to the party organization made it impossible for him to accept an arrangement prohibited by statute, especially when he realized that it was a resolution aimed at discrediting him in the eyes of associates. A year earlier Largo had briefly resigned rather than tolerate this same infringement. The old trade unionist gave further proof that he could never be the "Spanish Lenin." Trapped in his obsessive party legalism, he refused to accept the increased power that he had been demanding for months and in a fit of rage resigned the presidency. The vote had been seven to five with two abstentions, giving the moderates only a plurality. Three other committee members, all supporters of Largo, were still in prison, but after he resigned they followed suit, turning the plurality of the moderates into a majority on both the executive commission and the national committee as a whole. The committee announced that a special intraparty election would be held in mid-January to fill the vacancy in the party presidency created by Largo's precipitous resignation. The candidate of the moderates was Ramón González Peña, chastened head of the Asturian miners, who now bitterly repented having been pushed by the Bolshevizers into the insurrection of the previous year.

Claridad replied on December 21 by repeating the maximalist program and calling for a

Purge of the Party   Purge of the Union   Purge of the Youth.

Largo declared in the issue of December 23 that even if his position and leadership were upheld by a party referendum, he would never again serve with the same national committee that had proceeded in such dishonest fashion. He demanded the resignation or ouster of all the moderates. For their part, leaders of the Socialist Youth strongly denounced the maneuver of the moderates and insisted that despite all the criticism about the indiscipline of the Socialist Youth, they—the Bolshevizers—had never transgressed orders of the national committee or the statutes of the party.

Claridad demanded that instead of a referendum on the presidency, elections be held for the vacancies on the executive commission in accord with Article 50 of the PSOE statutes which declared that in the event of resignations new elections were to "take place immediately." Though a total of six resignations had occurred by January 1936, the national committee refused to use the elections for the purpose of filling vacancies on either the national committee or the executive commission. *Claridad* then took the position that the national committee had so abused its power as to lose its mandate, and instructed all of Largo's supporters throughout Spain to cast votes for names to an entirely new national committee. A chorus of demands rose from Youth groups and provincial sections that the entire national committee resign so that new elections could be held. This was ignored.

According to *Claridad,* approximately 75 percent of those who cast ballots among the local party sections in mid-January voted for Largo Caballero and an entirely new pro-Largo national committee. This report appears to be correct, but the votes of most of Largo's supporters were nullified by the national committee on the grounds that many ballots were not cast by regular party members but by new elements, sometimes Communists, brought in illegally by Largo's supporters and that, moreover, most of them had not voted on the question submitted by the national committee but on a different issue of their own choosing. Ramón González Peña was declared the newly elected president and further intraparty voting was then postponed until some unspecified date following the impending national parliamentary elections.

Meanwhile the left was provided its great opportunity for resurgence by the president of the Republic, who had decided to dissolve the parliament and hold new elections. The occasion for Alcalá Zamora's intervention was the breakup of the Chapaprieta moderate-conservative government over financial policy. There had been 13 cabinet crises in twenty-five months, though some of these had been due in large part to the president's own constant intervention in parliamentary affairs. During the 1934–35 biennium little had been accomplished, but political hostilities had been enormously exacerbated and all the leftist leaders, from Azaña to the Communists, were demanding new elections as soon as possible. The financial scandals involving Radical politicians had greatly discredited Lerroux' party in the opinion of most of the public, leaving Gil Robles' group as the only strong party in the Cortes. Alcalá Zamora feared that a CEDA government might precipitate the end of the existing Republican system, while a continuation of the moderate-conservative coalition would only increase the tendency toward polarization. The new prime minister appointed on December 15, Manuel Portela Valladares, was a moderate liberal who did not even hold a seat in parliament but was a personal crony of the president's. His extraparliamentary ministry was organized in order to find an alternative to the Radical-CEDA coalition by forming a new political alliance of moderate liberals associated with the president that could either win a majority or gain the balance of power in new elections. The Cortes was then closed sine die to facilitate these maneuvers. The constitution, however, stipulated that parliament could be shut down for no more than 15 consecutive days during the latter part of the calendar year, and after the first of January outraged cries were heard from a wide variety of opinion. Consequently a presidential decree released on January 7, 1936, scheduled general elections for February 16. It argued that consultation of public opinion was justified because of the extraordinary events of 1934 and changes in political opinion that had subsequently occurred. It further indicated that this decision was fully constitutional since it was the first regular dissolution of the Cortes carried out during Alcalá Zamora's term—the Cortes of 1931–33 having been a constituent assembly, not a regular parliament—whereas the constitution permitted the president if necessary to dissolve parliament twice during his term in office.

Alcalá Zamora completely misread the political dynamics of the country and expected that Spanish opinion would register a healthy reaction against the excesses of the left and the sterility and selfishness of the right by returning a majority for the moderate liberal center. In fact, the elections gave the left their great opportunity. During the week that followed rapid consultations were held between the leaders of the middle-class left and the Marxist parties, resulting in an agreement to form a broad electoral alliance of the left that would adopt the Communist-proposed title of the "Popular Front." The minimal program to which all the participating parties pledged themselves included the following main points:

1. Complete amnesty for the insurrectionists of 1934, and for all those accused of politiciosocial crimes since 1933, but prosecution of all those guilty of "acts of violence" in repressing political crimes.

2. Reappointment of all workers and public employees dismissed for political reasons and full compensation for all losses suffered by them.

3. Reform of the Tribunal of Constitutional Guarantees to remove conservative influence; reform of the court system to establish its independence, promulgate social justice, and increase its speed and efficiency.

4. Restoration of the authority of all sections of the Republican constitution; reform of the Cortes and its committee structure; passage of organic legislation to guarantee the functioning of provincial and municipal government; reform of the law of public order to achieve greater safeguards for individual rights.

5. Continuation of the agrarian reform; lower rents and greater security for smallholders; reduction of taxes and interest rates for smallholders; increased technical assistance for smallholders.

6. Protection of small producers and small shopkeepers; reform of industrial taxes and tariffs; encouragement of production; extension of public works.

7. Subjection of the functioning of the Bank of Spain to the public interest; regulation and improvement of the functioning of banks and savings institutions.

8. Restoration of all the social legislation of 1931–33; in-

creased wages; a broad public housing program; expanded education on all levels.[5]

This was mostly a social democratic reformist program. Contrary to many assertions, it did go beyond the original left Republican position in some respects, but steered clear of the anticlerical obsession that had exhausted so much energy in the past. It established agreement on a set of minimal principles for an electoral coalition, and did not constitute a plan for coalition government. It was understood that after a Popular Front victory the next government should be formed by the middle-class left alone, though the other members of the electoral coalition would support that government with their votes in parliament at least until it had carried through the minimal program espoused in the electoral agreement. Altogether the Popular Front was composed of Azaña's Republican Left, the Esquerra, Martínez Barrio's Republican Union, the Socialists and the UGT, the Communist party, the POUM, and the small pro-Stalinist leftist groups in Catalonia. The fulcrum of the pact was the Socialist party. The Bolshevizing elements had earlier foresworn any further association with the middle-class left, but Largo Caballero and his associates were persuaded to join the Popular Front by two factors: its limitation to a purely electoral alliance, omitting any obligation of political collaboration afterward, and recognition of the fact that in their current state of weakness the revolutionaries needed assistance to obtain the release of the 15,000 or more [6] militants in jail.

Only one sector of the middle-class left abstained—Sánchez Román's National Republican party. This group had included the word "National" in its title to show it was a Republican progressivist party that hoped to avoid extremist sectarianism and

5. This synopsis is drawn from the original Popular Front program published in *El Socialista*, Jan. 16, 1936.
6. Joaquín Arrarás, *Compendio de la historia de la segunda República española* (Madrid, 1965), 374, cites the official statistics of Spain's penal population as of February 15, 1936, as 34,526. Since the normal average was around 20,000, this would indicate an excess of some 15,000 revolutionaries was currently being held. The figure ordinarily cited by leftist propagandists in 1935–36 was 30,000.

attract support from all classes. Sánchez Román completely dis-associated himself from the October insurrection. He had already recognized that the extension of Catalan autonomy went too far, and he knew that it would be suicidal to encourage the revolutionary left further. He had urged the unity of the middle-class left in order to build support for a responsible liberal reformist government. Sánchez Román agreed with most points of the Popular Front program, but insisted that the Communist party be excluded. Furthermore, he urged that the Socialists give up their plans for extralegal paramilitary forces and stressed the importance of recognizing the authority of the constitutional Republican government. He feared that the Popular Front would merely serve as a vehicle to rebuild the power of the revolutionaries.

Azaña preferred to overlook this obvious danger. He saw the radicalization of Spanish socialism as a transitory phenomenon, a temporary response to "reactionary government" in Madrid, ignoring the fact that "Bolshevization" had begun while Azaña was still premier. Moreover, he knew that the middle-class left could not build a majority without the Socialists, whose support had always formed a fundamental part of his political plans.

Martínez Barrio, who emerged as Azaña's chief collaborator among the Republican left, had recently warned that the revolutionary left should not think that they could use the Popular Front as a Kerenskyist Trojan horse. More frequently, however, he stressed that there need be no reason why the democratic working-class movements could not collaborate with a free Republican government. In a normal situation, even an all-Socialist ministry "would not have to do more, nor less, than the program carried out by their counterparts in Belgium and England." [7] The problem was that the Spanish Socialists were not the "counterparts" (*congéneres*) of the Belgian Socialists or the British Labourites. Some years later, after his fears had been realized, he lamented.

Sánchez Román, Azaña and I expressed ourselves with such clarity that all Spanish society could have understood our position, and most

7. Diego Martínez Barrio, *Orígenes del Frente Popular Español* (Buenos Aires, 1943), 25.

especially the political and working-class groups to the left of us. Azaña particularly distinguished himself by the precision with which he spoke. . . . If the trade union movements or the Socialist and Communist parties disagreed with our point of view, why didn't they make it clear? Why did they agree to a pact whose fundamental aim was the consolidation of the Republican regime established in 1931 and of its constitutional charter?

Certain Socialists and all the Communists were suffering from the mirage of the Russian revolution of 1917, and handed us the dismal role of Kerensky. According to them, our mission was limited to smoothing their road to power, since the possibilities of the democratic revolution in the history of the Republic had been exhausted.[8]

This is a good example of the confusion of the leaders of the middle-class left, a confusion not assuaged by the passage of time. It is doubtful that Azaña ever "distinguished himself by the precision with which he spoke" about his opposition to the goals of the revolutionary left in 1936, though he did make clear his determination to avoid any compromise with conservatives. Nor was the Popular Front limited to "consolidation of the Republican regime." But, most important, the revolutionaries did not hide the fact that they would not long be satisfied with the Popular Front program. This was repeated *ad infinitum,* but was persistently ignored by the middle-class left because it contradicted the latter's subjective rationalization of the position they had chosen to adopt. The leaders of the middle-class left were perfectly willing to run the risk of playing into the hands of the revolutionaries so long as they could achieve a decisive defeat of the moderate liberals and conservatives.

Largo Caballero addressed the first big Socialist meeting of the campaign in Madrid on January 12. He explained that the revolutionary Socialists had made an electoral agreement with the middle-class left in order to obtain an amnesty for all their imprisoned comrades, but emphasized that this did not mean they were going to accept a parliamentary Republic in place of the revolution for which they were working. Ten days later, the "Spanish Lenin," as he was known to the revolutionaries, addressed a joint Socialist-Communist rally, and during the course of the meeting the Communist central committeeman

8. *Ibid.,* 60–61.

Jesús Hernández gave a report on the progress being made toward a united *partido único:*

We have always intended to forge a united party that has nothing to do either directly or indirectly with the bourgeoisie; a party that adopts as its standard the armed insurrection for the conquest of power and the establishment of the dictatorship of the proletariat; a party that, in case of war, will have nothing to do with the bourgeoisie; that ought not and will not lend it aid; a party that, guided by the norms of democratic centralism, achieves a single will, unanimous decision in all its efforts. We are on the way to achieving such a party.[9]

At another joint mass meeting on February 11, the Communist party secretary, José Díaz, emphasized again that the goal of the Popular Front was to complete the "democratic bourgeois revolution" as quickly as possible, "and then, through the dictatorship of the proletariat, achieve the establishment of socialism." As at all the electoral meetings of the revolutionaries, he hailed the October insurrection,

which had the virtue of showing the proletariat of the world how the enemy can be conquered, for which there is only one effective, indispensable way—when the enemy vacillates and the proletariat is organized in a broad, united front, to strike the decisive blow through the organized struggle of the masses, through insurrection.[10]

The propaganda of the Popular Front groups was especially effective in arousing the sympathy of lower-middle-class people for the families of those who had suffered in the repression of 1934–35. Spanish people, like those in most western countries, have a certain amount of natural sympathy for the oppressed, and this was skillfully enlisted in winning votes. By contrast, the moderate liberals became increasingly isolated. There was no possibility of their cooperating with the middle-class left, and the conservatives, after the frustrations of the last two years, were much less sympathetic than in 1933. The sterility of Radical coalition rule and the financial scandals of Lerroux' associates alienated many who had voted for the Radicals in the previous contests. Moderate liberals protested the danger of political polarization between left and right, and specifically

9. *Mundo Obrero,* Jan. 23, 1936.
10. *Ibid.,* Feb. 12, 1936.

warned of the futility of another Azaña government that would have inevitably to give in to the revolutionaries, but some elements of the lower middle classes paid them little heed. Conservatives made the same dire prophecies, but had more confidence in a victory of their own. They raised a good deal of money and stressed Catholic sentiment for all they were worth, hoping for a clear-cut victory that would enable them to form an all-conservative government led by Gil Robles.

Both extremes recognized the plebiscitary character of the election, the conservatives tacitly, the revolutionaries explicitly. José Díaz published an article in *Mundo Obrero* on February 3 that declared, "Our struggle in Spain does not bear any similarity to 'normal elections' in countries such as England, the United States, Switzerland and so on." After the election, he said, the original Popular Front program must be fulfilled as soon as possible so that new goals could be met: "The expropriation without indemnity of the lands of the large landowners and the Church. . . . The complete liberty of the Catalan, Basque and Galician peoples. . . . The dissolution of monarchist and fascist organizations." [11] Conversely, many conservatives understood that a definitive conservative victory would bring sweeping constitutional amendment, introducing a more limited corporative Republic, perhaps similar to that of neighboring Portugal (which so assiduously avoided involvement in Spanish problems).

Yet the situation was not so radically defined in the minds of most voters as it was in the minds of militants. Evidence of all the diversity of opinion among the Spanish public at that time leads one to the conclusion that the majority of those who cast their ballots for the conservative National Front on February 16, 1936, were not voting for an authoritarian regime but for the defense of religion and of property, and that the majority of those who opted for the Popular Front were not supporting violent revolution but endorsing individual freedom and social reform.

The first electoral reports on the night of February 16 were somewhat contradictory but in general they seemed to

11. In Communist terminology this meant any conservative group, such as the CEDA or the Agrarians.

indicate a trend that would lead to victory for the left. By the following day disturbances had broken out in many towns and riots by leftist inmates occurred in a number of prisons. At Zaragoza there seemed a danger that the anarchosyndicalists would take over the town altogether; the Director General of Security hurried up from Madrid to restore order. The Portela Valladares government had been placed under severe strain for several days prior to the election, and the prime minister was soon at his wit's end. When urged by army generals and rightist leaders to declare a state of martial law that might lead to annulment of the elections, he found that Alcalá Zamora would not authorize such a move. A less drastic "state of alarm" was declared in the hope that this would be mild enough not to provoke another leftist insurrection. Portela's nerves snapped almost completely and he pleaded with the president to accept his resignation, even though according to the constitution the care-taker ministry entrusted with elections was supposed to remain in office until legal registration of the electoral results had been completed. Because of Portela's desperate haste to shed responsibility, a new cabinet consisting exclusively of left Repub-licans under Azaña was sworn in on the evening of February 19. Azaña indicated that he found it awkward to receive power in such precipitous and technically improper fashion, but no other solution seemed possible.

The failure of the neutral ministry to remain in office long enough to verify the electoral results cast some uncertainty over the exact outcome. In several provinces, moderate provincial governors also hastily resigned their posts and local authority was turned over to left Republican officials before the count had been completed. The degree of electoral participation was about 70 percent—one of the highest in Spanish history. Absten-tion exceeded 40 percent only in three relatively conservative provinces—Burgos, Guadalajara, and Teruel—which felt less threatened than did most of the country, and in Málaga, which was one of the most backward districts. The Popular Front triumphed in nearly all the large urban and industrial areas and in all the coastal provinces save Santander, Vizcaya, and Guipúzcoa. It won in the working class districts, in most regions of extremely poor or landless peasants, and in the most ignorant, illiterate provinces. The conservatives won in most of the areas with high literacy rates and a large Catholic lower middle class of smallholders (Navarre, all of León, most of Castile, half of Aragon). In Catalonia and the Levant, however, regions with a large middle class voted for the left, in the former instance partly on behalf of regional autonomy, and in the latter for left Republican progressivism. The center won only the two Basque provinces of Vizcaya and Guipúzcoa and the Castilian province of Soria, and split the Galician province of Lugo with the left.

In the first round of the voting, the left won altogether slightly more than 200 seats out of the total of 473 that made up the Cortes. This plurality was not due to an equivalent lead in the popular vote, for in the total balloting for the first round the popular vote for left and right was approximately equal.[12] Under the complicated list voting system, however, the decisive factor was not proportionate cumulative vote, but the concentration of ballots province by province. Popular Front votes were combined much more effectively for majority lists in the larger districts. The second round runoff contests were held at the end of the month under leftist supervision and considerable pressure from the leftist street mob. In the runoffs the Popular Front increased its plurality further, though the constitutional legality of the administration of the vote was dubious.

When the credentials committee of the new Cortes met in mid-March, it proceeded to reduce the center and rightist representation even further. Two seats were taken away from the right in Orense province and given to the left, four rightist deputies elected in Burgos and Santander were disqualified on technical grounds and their seats given to the left, and the results in Cuenca and Granada provinces, where 11 conservative and 3 center deputies had been chosen, were annulled because, after many rightist votes had been disqualified, no group had the minimum 40 percent required. The Socialist president of the

12. Under the Republican voting regulations, it was almost possible to compute exact popular vote totals—save for individual candidates in each province—because of the provision for split-list and partial-list voting, which was used extensively in 1936 by middle-class voters to choose between parts of rival lists.

credentials committee, Prieto, finally resigned that post to protest the fraudulence of these maneuvers. When completed, they left approximately 4,700,00 votes credited to the Popular Front and less than 4,000,000 for the right. As finally constituted, the new Cortes was composed of 271 deputies from the left, 137 from the right, and 40 from the center, with new elections to be held for 14 seats. The representation by party was as follows:

Popular front		Center		Right	
Republican left*	117	Portela group	14	CEDA	86
Socialists	90	Basque Nat'lists	9	Agrarians	13
Esquerra	38	Radicals	6	Lliga†	13
Communists	16	Progressives	6	Renovación Española	11
Syndicalist party	2	Maura group	3	Carlists	8
POUM	1	Liberal Democrats	1	Independent monarchists	3
Independent left	7	Federalists	1	Independent conservatives	3
TOTALS	*271*		*40*		*137*

* Also including Martínez Barrio's Republican Union party.
† The Lliga was a moderate liberal party of the center but, with electoral pragmatism, had joined the conservative alliance to benefit from the latter's voting strength.

The Popular Front had won a decisive victory and dominated the new parliament. Though the conservatives polled at least a half-million more votes than in 1933, this did not offset the increased strength of a united left for which even anarchosyndicalists had gone out to vote. By contrast, the overwhelming polarity of opinion isolated the moderate liberals of the center, who were nearly wiped out. Alcalá Zamora's gamble had completely failed.

AFTER RESUMING OFFICE, Azaña announced that he would carry out the Popular Front program as rapidly as possible. The Cortes was not scheduled to convene for nearly a month, but pressure was so great from the revolutionary parties for an immediate amnesty of the 15,000 imprisoned insurrectionists that Azaña felt he could not wait for full congressional approval of his first measures. Though the constitution stipulated that political amnesties could only be voted by a regular parliamentary majority, such niceties were no longer observed. On February 21 the Permanent Commission of the Cortes, representing all major parties, granted approval of a complete amnesty for the insurrectionists, some of whom had already been freed in mass jailbreaks. Several days later similar approval was given for the restoration of Catalan autonomy under the 1932 statute. A government decree reestablished labor tribunals with the same prolabor majority they had under the previous Azaña administration. Another order restored local officials and functionaries dismissed because of complicity in the insurrection and established commissions to rule on claims by workers who had been fired for allegedly political reasons. Those whose claims were upheld were to be rehired by their old employers and compenstated for wages lost in the interim, though this might constitute a crushing burden to small businessmen.

The Communist party had achieved noticeable political influence for the first time and immediately established itself as the most active member of the Popular Front, constantly pressing for further goals. The party's over-all strategy was summarized in *Mundo Obrero* on February 18, two days after the election:

> We shall follow the path of completing the bourgeois democratic revolution until it brings us to a situation in which the proletariat and the peasantry themselves assume the responsibility of making the people of Spain as happy and free as are the Soviet people, through the victorious achievement of socialism, through the dictatorship of the proletariat.

The left Republican government was to be encouraged to a swift completion of the Popular Front program, then to further measures outlined by the Communists during the electoral campaign; these included expropriation of land on a large scale without compensation and the outlawing of the rightist parties. After the conservatives had been eliminated and the revolutionary left had expanded, the Republican left, according to a *Mundo Obrero* editorial of February 24, would have to give way to a "Worker-Peasant government." The latter concept in Communist planning represented the transitional phase from parliamentary democracy to socialist dictatorship. Communist leaders emphasized that the change could only be carried out by stages, and chided the revolutionary Socialists about premature talk of the "dictatorship of the proletariat." [1]

The Spanish Communist party emerged from the elections with 21 deputies (16 representing the party itself and 5 from the pro-Stalinist Catalan Marxist parties) and possibly 30,000 regular members. It is still asserted in historical studies that the

1. In a joint Communist-Socialist meeting shortly before the elections, José Díaz had stressed that a "Worker-Peasant government does not mean either the dictatorship of the proletariat or the construction of socialism," according to *El Socialista,* Feb. 12, 1936, in Pozharskaya, 128.

Spanish Communist party was too small in the winter and spring of 1936 to be taken seriously. If Spain had in 1936 been a modern western country under normal political conditions, a Communist party of that size would have held comparatively little importance. Proportionate to the total population, however, the Communist party of Spain was larger at the beginning of 1936 than was the Bolshevik group in Russia at the start of 1917. Spain was entering a phase of political disintegration, with political opinion increasingly polarized and the established moderate and conservative parties nearly impotent. There were two mass revolutionary movements in the country, but neither knew exactly what it wanted and how to get it. Only the Communist party had the nerve and discipline of an effective revolutionary group. In such a climate it flourished and began to expand even more rapidly than before. Within five months its membership increased threefold. To achieve a position of predominance, however, the indispensable preconditions were continued deterioration of political and social conditions, complete Bolshevization of the Socialist party, and its fusion with the smaller Communist organization.

As soon as the elections were over, Largo Caballero's supporters demanded that the Socialist national committee hold new elections to choose more representative leaders. Prieto suggested that a congress be convened in Asturias, where the Socialist miners were disgusted with Largo Caballero and the Madrid maximalists for having failed to support them effectively in the insurrection. On March 8 new elections were held for the executive commission of the Madrid section of the party. After Largo and his followers won by a margin of three to one, Largo insisted that any party congress must be held in the national capital, where he was assured of strong support.

On March 12 *Claridad* published the text of a long letter from the central committee of the Communist party to the executive commission of the Socialist party, dated March 4. It proposed the creation of joint Socialist-Communist Worker-Peasant Alliance groups on all levels from the local to the national. The proposed twelve-point program was almost identical to the thirteen-point program announced in the party's 1935 manifesto, save that the earlier point ten, urging financial support of small property owners, was dropped, and a new concluding goal was added. This announced the ultimate aim as formation of a "Worker-Peasant Government" based on the Worker-Peasant Alliance, with the Alliance committees playing the same role in Spain as the soviets in Russia.

The letter proposed that the Worker-Peasant Alliance prepare for the establishment of a united party on the following conditions:

Complete independence vis-à-vis the bourgeoisie and a complete break of the social democratic bloc with the bourgeoisie; prior achievement of unity of action; recognition of the need for the revolutionary overthrow of the domination of the bourgeoisie and the installation of the dictatorship of the proletariat in the form of Soviets; renunciation of support for the national bourgeoisie in the event of an imperialist war; construction of the unified party on the basis of democratic centralism, assuring unity of will and of action, tempered by the experience of the Russian Bolshevists.

The Socialist executive commission made no immediate reply, but on the following day (March 5) the *caballerista* executive commission of the UGT proposed to the executives of the Socialist party and Socialist Youth that a joint committee be formed of two representatives of each of the working-class parties of the Popular Front to unite energies for the execution of the Popular Front program. Two weeks later, the *caballerista* leadership of the Madrid section of the Socialist party announced that it would ask the next party congress to grant priority to achieving a united party with the Communists.

That same month the Socialist moderate Gabriel Mario de Coca finished writing a brief book criticizing the "bolshevization of the party." He concluded with these words:

I close my work with an impression of Bolshevist victory in every sector of the party. The Socialist parliamentary minority in the Cortes will be impregnated with a strong Leninist tone. Prieto will have few deputies on his side while Besteiro will be completely isolated as a Marxist dissenter. . . .
The outlook that all this leaves for the future of the working class and of the nation could not be more pessimistic. The Bolshevist centipede dominates the proletariat's horizon and Marxist analysis indicates that it is on its way to another of its resouding victories. So that if in

October 1934 it only achieved a short-lived Gil Robles government accompanied by the suspension of the constitution and the most horrible, sterile shedding of working class blood, it can now be expected to complete its definitive work in the future [cataclysm].[2]

This prophecy, absolutely accurate, was repeated many times by men of varying background; it had little effect.

The Communists and revolutionary Socialists built strong pressure against the government to follow up its amnesty of the insurrectionists by punishing those who had repressed the insurrection. Dolores Ibarruri (La Pasionaria), the most influential member of the Spanish Communist central committee, exhorted in a speech of March 1,

We live in a revolutionary situation and cannot be delayed by legal obstacles, of which we have had too many since April 14 [1931]. The people impose their own legality and on February 16 asked for the execution of their murderers. The Republic must satisfy the needs of the people. If it does not, the people will throw it out and impose their will.[3]

The government made a symbolic concession on March 11 when it ordered the arrest of General López de Ochoa, the commander of the army forces that had pacified Asturias. It took another step five days later, ordering the arrest of the national leaders of the small (20,000-man) fascist party, Falange Española, and the closure of its main headquarters. Henceforth the Falange became in effect an illegal party as more and more headquarters were shut down and an increasing number of party members were arrested throughout the spring. The government's explanation was that the Falangists had been guilty of terrorist acts. That was entirely true, but if such deeds merited the closing of the party, the Socialist party, Communist party, POUM, and CNT ought also to have been closed down. In addition to engaging in intermittent terrorism, they had attempted armed rebellion against the constitutional Republic, something that the Falange had not yet done. But the Azaña administration was making little effort to carry on impartial

2. *Anti-Caballero: Crítica marxista de la bolchevización del Partido Socialista* (Madrid, 1936), 207, 211.
3. *Mundo Obrero,* March 2, 1936.

government. Its only policy seems to have been more and more concessions to the left to win the revolutionaries' support so it could stay in office as long as possible. After proscription of the Falange, violence and disorders continued to increase. The official line of the government and the leftist parties was that nearly all the violence was either due to the Falangists or was a response to "provocations" by them.

The government was rapidly outflanked by the revolutionaries in the acceleration of agrarian reform. Responding to heavy pressure, the newly reenergized Institute of Agrarian Reform decreed on March 20 that the principle of "social utility" (under terms of which a law passed by the moderates in 1935 had provided that in special circumstances land might be expropriated without compensation) would be extended to all categories of land, and particularly to land in townships where "property is heavily concentrated" or "a high proportion of the population consists of poor peasants." The Socialist FNTT did not wait for this measure to be put into effect. It had reorganized its following in the southwest, and on the night of March 25 carried out a well-planned occupation of large properties by peasants in Badajoz province. *The New York Times* correspondent reported that 60,000 peasants in 263 villages participated. Though this mass action was technically illegal, the government quickly decided it was better to legitimize the takeover ex post facto, even though not all the property involved belonged to large holders. According to a recent study, the following amount of land was redistributed during the next months:

March	249,616 hectares	
April	150,000 "	(approximate)
May	46,391 "	(statistical averages for May and June)
June	46,391 "	
July 1–17	40,000 "	
July 18	23,000 "	announced

By April the government had largely gained control of the land transfers, whose volume declined during May as the spring plowing neared completion. On June 2 the Cortes passed new legislation reversing the eviction of tenant farmers that had

taken place during 1935, and on June 11 the original Agrarian
Reform bill of 1932 was restored, including the 1935 "social
utility" clause, but dropping the 1932 provision that had been
prejudicial to medium-sized properties.

Nevertheless, the degree of effervescence in the southern
countryside only increased as the spring advanced. From May 1
to July 18 there were at least 196 peasant strikes and one of
them, organized by the CNT in Málaga province early in
June, claimed to have the support of 100,000 peasants. As the
summer advanced, nearing the start of a new agricultural season,
it seemed that the pressure for occupation would be greater than
ever.

In the southwest the larger landowners had in many cases
deserted their properties after the elections. The medium and
small owners had little alternative, however, but to stay on, so
that it was the rural middle classes, not the latifundists, who bore
the brunt of the harassment, violence, and property destruction
which wracked much of southern and central Spain during the
spring and early summer. In Extremadura the Socialist Youth
set up "civic guard" militia groups that were given official police
authorization in towns with Socialist mayors. These activists
made many arbitrary arrests and sometimes beat up landowners and conservatives. Though there were comparatively
few political murders in the rural areas of southern and central
Spain, the wave of anarchy, regularized only to the extent that
the revolutionaries were actually beginning to take over local
authority in some areas, had the rural middle classes in a state
of absolute panic.

And yet much of the Socialist- and anarchist-dominated
peasantry had little notion of a thoroughgoing social revolution.
All that most of them wanted was either higher wages or a
reasonable amount of land of their own to work on easy terms.
As Julián Besteiro warned in the Cortes and as an agrarian
expert warned in the pages of *El Sol* (July 15 and 17), the real
effect of all the strikes and rural harassment in southwest Spain
was not to effect a positive revolution in terms of ownership and
production but to divert as much as possible of the short-run
profits to the poorer peasants and laborers. Mechanization was

thwarted and small and medium holders were being ruined without any real attempt to lay the basis for a more efficient and equitable rural economy. The economic consequences of the agrarian prerevolution in the south were primarily destructive.

After the acceleration of the agrarian reform, the next major move of the left was the deposition of the moderate president of the Republic, Alcalá Zamora. Both left and right were disgusted with him, the left because he had refused to support the Azaña government in 1933, the right because he had blocked the formation of further moderate conservative coalition ministries at the end of 1935. Alcalá Zamora conceived the function of the presidency in a Republic with a unicameral legislature as that of a moderating authority that must exercise direct initiative to keep the government from diverging too sharply toward either extreme. His continuation in office, restricted though his prerogatives were, was the last remaining guarantee of moderation with the Republican system. For that reason the left was determined to be rid of him. The excuse used was Article 81 of the constitution, which stipulated that the action of a president who dissolved the Cortes twice during his term of office would be reviewed by the new Cortes chosen in the second election to determine whether or not he had properly fulfilled his functions in accordance with the popular will. There could be no question from the Popular Front point of view of the need to dissolve the previous Cortes; without new elections the left would never have had the majority with which to depose the president. Throughout 1935 spokesmen of all the leftist groups reiterated that their major request of the president was dissolution of the Cortes. As Azaña had said in a speech of October 20, 1935,

Calling new elections is the immediate goal of the Republican Left. Our abstention from any kind of government coalition that might be formed before calling new elections is total and irrevocable. . . . The left has only one recommendation: new elections.

After their constant petition had been granted, they then argued that Alcalá Zamora was still culpable for not having dissolved the preceding Cortes earlier. Despite the dubious applicability of Article 81, it was the only tactic that could be invoked, for the section on impeachment—Article 82—required a two-thirds majority of parliament, and the left was not sure it could muster that. On April 7, with the right abstaining, the left voted the deposition of the president of the Republic.

When special elections for presidential electors (*compromisarios*) were held on April 26, there was massive middle-class abstention. The choice of the leftist candidate, Azaña, seemed inevitable, for the center and right were demoralized and even more disunited than before. Only a little more than one-third of the registered electorate voted, and the Permanent Commission lowered quorum requirements below the customary 40 percent in order to register a valid contest.

All the while activity of the Communists and revolutionary Socialists increased. By April the Communist party claimed 50,000 members and by May 60,000, a figure nominally equal to that of the Socialists (which officially stood at 60,000 at the end of June, though the actual Socialist membership was probably larger than the moderate-controlled executive commission was willing to admit, most of the new Socialist members being *caballeristas*). During the spring of 1936 Spain was inundated with Communist propaganda, and its self-assured demagogy about constituting the "wave of the future" attracted not merely working-class militants but other thousands of self-selected middle-class elitists who wanted to be part of the vanguard of tomorrow.

According to the central committeeman Hernández, the chief Comintern adviser in Spain, Artur Stepanov, outlined Communist plans in the following terms: "There is no doubt that Spain is undergoing the same historical process begun in Russia in February 1917. The party must learn to apply the tactic of the Bolsheviks: a brief transitory phase and then the soviets!" [4] This rise in Comintern expectations paralleled exactly the exited interpretations of the Socialist intellectuals, the most articulate of whom was Araquistain.[5]

4. Jesús Hernández, *La Grande trahison* (Paris, 1953), 12–13. ,
5. The most coherent statement of the Spanish Socialists' fascination with a comparison between their situation and that of Russia was made in a lecture

Delegations were sent to Moscow by both the Communist and Socialist Youth groups to arrange their fusion under the blessing of the Comintern. Organization of the United Socialist Youth (JSU) [6] was announced on April 1. The JSU's 41,200 members [7] made it the largest political youth movement in the country. Though some of the local groups of the Socialist Youth did not recognize the fusion, the non-Communist leadership of the Madrid section was deposed. In Catalonia the liaison committee of the small pro-Stalinist Marxist parties of that region continued to function. Plans were made for a Communist-dominated United Socialist party of Catalonia, which could bypass the POUM and challenge the CNT for leadership of the revolutionary left in Catalonia.

The Popular Front Cortes reconvened for its second session on April 15. This was the most disorderly assembly in the history of Spanish parliamentarianism. As the Socialist historian Ramos Oliveira observed,

---

by Luis Araquistain on February 8 entitled "Historical Parallel Between the Russian and Spanish Revolutions." He denied the validity of Besteiro's explanation that it was the wartime disintegration of established institutions that had permitted Bolshevism to triumph in Russia. Furthermore, he denied the validity of Besteiro's emphasis, similar to that of the Mensheviks, that Spain would not be ready for socialism until it had completed the full series of phases of social and economic development prescribed by Marx. According to Araquistain, "history, like biology, is full of leaps." In Russia and Spain, the relative backwardness of society made it all the more susceptible to revolution. Conditions in prerevolutionary Russia and contemporary Spain were said to be analogous. The working class movement was strong, the resistance of middle-class and conservative groups was weak. The Republican upsurge of 1930–31 was "Spain's 1905." The Spanish Republic had built "a weak state," whose institutions could not resist revolutionaries. "These objective, undeniable facts lead me to think that Spain may very well be the second country where the proletarian revolution triumphs and becomes consolidated. Nor am I particularly worried about the danger of counterrevolutionary intervention from abroad. Neighboring great powers are fully occupied with their own problems. . . . And finally, the USSR would not permit other European states to intervene directly in the internal affairs of a Socialist Spain." He concluded that "the historical dilemma is fascism or socialism, and only violence will decide the issue," but since what passed for "fascism" in Spain was weak, socialism would win. *Claridad*, Feb. 13, 1936.

6. Socialist moderates dubbed the Juventud Socialista Unificada the "Juventud Socialista URSSificada," making a pun on the Spanish letters for USSR.

7. According to a JSU memo of July 1937. (Bolloten Collection, Hoover Institution.) Cf. Santiago Carrillo, *En marcha hacia la victoria* (Valencia, 1937).

Each session was in continuous tumult, and since nearly all the representatives of the nation went about armed, a catastrophe could have been feared at any meeting. In view of the frequency with which firearms were displayed or made reference to, the insulting precaution of frisking the legislators on their entry had to be adopted.[8]

An attempt was made to shout down the more prominent conservative spokesmen whenever they took the floor. Socialist and Communist deputies vied with each other in hurling threats at Gil Robles and at Calvo Sotelo, the monarchist leader. The president of the assembly made feeble attempts to restore decorum.

At the beginning of the new session Gil Robles and Calvo Sotelo warned that the explosion of violent strikes, street brawls, *atentados,* barn burnings, and church burnings that the government did little or nothing to restrain was bringing the country near a state of de facto civil war. Gil Robles declared that the government should not think that the middle classes would bend their necks meekly before the axes of the revolutionaries.

On May 10 Azaña was formally elected president of the Republic. There was speculation that he might be succeeded as prime minister by Indalecio Prieto, who would form a stable moderate Socialist—left Republican cabinet. Meanwhile, negotiations were also carried on by one of the most liberal of the CEDA leaders, Giménez Fernández, with Prieto and other comparatively moderate elements about the possibility of forming a broad national coalition government extending from moderate conservatives to the moderate Socialists, in which the CEDA would not actually participate but which it would support with its votes. Some such realignment was the only constructive, legal means of holding the revolutionaries in check, but all efforts came to naught. Hopes for a moderate coalition cabinet led by Prieto were dashed by a caucus of most of the Socialist Cortes deputies on May 12. It voted 49 to 19 against participating in any sort of government coalition, even with the middle-class left.

Prieto later claimed that Azaña showed no real interest in the formation of such a ministry. Whether or not that was really the case, the new president ended by appointing a "domestic

8. *Historia de España* (Mexico City, 1952), III, 244. According to an official announcement 270,000 new gun licenses were taken out in Spain within a period of less than thirty-six months between mid-1933 and mid-1936.

cabinet," led by one of his most trusted and aggressive supporters, Casares Quiroga. It is clear that by this time Azaña was profoundly depressed—indeed almost benumbed—by the hopeless political situation into which he had maneuvered himself. His reaction was one of personal withdrawal, leaving the administration of affairs in the hands of his new prime minister. Casares Quiroga had the reputation of being the "hardest" of Azaña's lieutenants, but he suffered from tuberculosis and was not a truly energetic leader. His reputation for toughness was based mainly on his speeches, which were usually aggressive and provocative. Casares Quiroga would admit of no danger to the left, but instead blamed all difficulties on the right. Under his leadership the government of the Republican left followed a consistent policy of appeasing the revolutionary left and antagonizing the right, thus consummating the political polarization of Spain.

On May 5, approximately one week before becoming prime minister, Casares Quiroga responded serenely to complaints about the collapse of public order:

Calm, señor Calvo Sotelo! What worries me at present is the right, for . . . the social revolution does not worry me at all. In a difficult moment the other day I did not find those men [the revolutionary leaders] and the masses whom they represent wielding a knife to stab me in the back; I found on certain occasions some excesses, but loyalty nonetheless, and in difficult moments I found the support of leaders, of public opinion and of a working class that enabled us to conjure the peril. But yourselves—not yourselves: rather those on your flank, who, separating themselves from you, rush toward violence, which you claim to condemn but which at times you seem to encourage—these are the people who are making every effort to subvert the Spanish state, or rebel against it, or create an atmosphere of perpetual disquiet, which is much worse than an armed rebellion.[9]

To the Popular Front denunciations of a "fascist" danger forming on the right, Calvo Sotelo replied accurately,

Fascism, here and elsewhere, is not an original postulate, but an antithesis, not an action, but a reaction. In England, where there is no Communism, there is scarcely any fascism. In Spain, where Communism is a reality—and even when you utter words of almost Panglossian optimism to show your lack of concern for the social danger, I am fully

9. "Diario de las Sesiones de las Cortes," in José Pla, *Historia de la segunda República española* (Barcelona, 1940), IV, 428.

convinced that secretly you think otherwise—since in Spain Communism advances, whether you desire it or not, within the government and expands by force, fascism—not as a specific organized force, which is least significant—but as an uncoerced, indefinable sentiment of national defense, which many do not know how to define or organize, will con-continue to grow until the social danger disappears.[10]

Indalecio Prieto himself warned in a speech at Cuenca on May 2,

A country can survive a revolution, which is ended one way or another. What a country cannot survive is the constant attrition of public disorder without any immediate revolutionary goal; what a nation cannot survive is the waste of public power and economic strength in a constant state of uneasiness, of anxiety and worry. Naïve souls may say that this uneasiness, this anxiety, this worry, is only suffered by the upper classes. In my judgment that is incorrect. The working class itself will soon suffer from the pernicious effects of this uneasiness, this anxiety, this worry, because of the disarray and possible collapse of the economy, because though we aspire to transform the economic structure, we cannot escape the consequences of that structure so long as it does exist. . . .

Let it not be said, to the discredit of democracy, that sterile disorder is only possible when there is a democratic government in power, because then such disorder would mean that only democracy permits excesses and that only the lash of dictatorship is capable of restraining them. . . . If disorder and excess are turned into a permanent system, one does not achieve socialism, nor does one consolidate a democratic republic—which I think is to our advantage—nor does one achieve communism. You achieve a completely desperate anarchy that is not even advocated by anarchist ideology. You achieve economic disorder that can ruin the country.[11]

The program of the revolutionaries for achieving public order was simple: to arm the left and outlaw the right. On April 2 *Claridad* headlined: THE PEOPLE'S MILITIA. THEY MUST BE ORGANIZED IN EVERY VILLAGE OF SPAIN. One week later the Communist press demanded that the government officially shut down all the rightist parties and newspapers as "fascist" and "counterrevolutionary."

On April 18 a public meeting of the Madrid section of the Socialist party was held. The *caballerista* majority de-

10. *Ibid.*, 429–30.
11. *Ibid.*, 437–38.

manded the calling of a new party congress to ratify the dominance of the revolutionaries, and the exertion of greater pressure on the Azaña government to complete the Popular Front program so that they could move on to a Socialist Republic under the dictatorship of the proletariat. The elderly Besteiro rose once more to challenge the "bolshevizing" trend, and asked if they were proposing the dictatorship of the Spanish proletariat or the dictatorship of the Spanish Socialist party. He asserted that the revolutionaries were transforming the formerly democratic Spanish Socialist party into a Russian-style Communist party; to face the issue squarely, a vote on that question should be taken among all party members. As so often in the past, Besteiro told the militants unpleasant truths which they refused to hear. He suggested that the forces opposed to the Popular Front were stronger than the revolutionaries cared to admit, and that the analogies drawn with Russia were as false as ever. There the established system had been totally exhausted by an enormous world war, permitting the Bolshevists to build through the use of force and terror an artificial majority. By no stretch of the imagination, he went on, could it be claimed that the Spanish Marxist parties in 1936 had a majority of the population behind them. Nor did Spanish socialism have the kind of leaders who could impose a terrorist dictatorship even if they wanted to.

> In Russia there were revolutionary redeemers because there existed revolutionaries trained in the hard, cruel struggle of persecution and emigration. Those men had the fiber and determination of violent revolutionaries. But regarding yourselves, comrades—do you think that you are equal to that? [12]

These harsh realities were greeted by the crowd with loud protests, jeers, and threats.

The only political position more advanced than that of the Communists and revolutionary Socialists was the stand taken by the POUM, which held that the electoral victory opened a phase of permanent revolution in which the revolutionary forces should proceed as quickly as possible. For the POUM, the Azaña administration existed only to be superseded

12. *Claridad,* Apr. 20, 1936.

immediately. Its organ, *La Batalla,* on April 10 denounced the parliamentary support being given Azaña by the rest of the left: "This fundamentally false position of the working-class parties in supporting the bourgeois government, when the moment is extremely propitious for revolutionary action, will be of disastrous consequences." In a speech at Gijón, Maurín said on April 19 that a union of all the proletarian forces could rally 4 million workers and conquer power directly. He urged a united revolutionary front so "that Spain could become the second country to brandish the lighted red torch of a soviet regime." [13]

This proposal was too precipitous even for the Communists, who continued to urge support of the Popular Front at least until its legislative program had been completed. Moreover, the Communists were determined to isolate the POUM, whose leaders remained staunchly anti-Stalinist and opposed to Comintern control. On April 24, *Mundo Obrero* denounced "The renegade Maurín, enemy of the Popular Front."

Meanwhile, the Communists continued to work for the same policy—a union of all the revolutionary forces—but excluding the POUM. From the middle of April they stepped up requests for syndical unity between the UGT and the CNT. The latter, relatively quiescent in 1934–35, had entered a new phase of expansion since the beginning of 1936. The fact that many local CNT leaders had urged their followers to vote for the Popular Front in the recent election also encouraged the hope that the anarchosyndicalists might finally be enticed out of their apoliticism.

The national congress of the CNT met in Zaragoza, headquarters of the FAI as well as of the syndicalist Confederation, on May 10. The delegates represented 988 Sindicatos Unicos totaling 560,000 workers. Of these the largest concentration was still Catalonia, followed by Andalusia-Extremadura with approximately 120,000, and the Levant with more than 50,000. As the spokesmen at the congress related, it was very hard to determine the exact membership of the Confederation due to its "revolutionary, combative character." The total following of the CNT must have been at least 50 percent greater than the total

13. *ABC,* Apr. 21, 1936.

represented, amounting to some 800,000 to 900,000, and was in a period of rapid growth.[14] Moreover, the syndicalist movement was partially reunited at this congress with the return of most of the separate Libertarian Syndicalist Federation, which was disbanded.

In response to Largo Caballero's gesture toward revolutionary syndical unity, 884 syndicates voted in favor of a "Revolutionary Alliance" with the UGT, while only 12 were opposed, but this was based on the proviso that the UGT follow Largo's line renouncing any collaboration with the middle-class left or the existing Republican system and move directly toward the total destruction of the existing politicoeconomic order. If such a program were to be adopted at the next UGT congress, it was agreed that a liaison committee be named to negotiate an alliance between the syndical movements which would then be submitted to a binding referendum by both groups. The classic revolutionary program of Spanish anarchosyndicalism was explicitly reaffirmed, stressing the collectivization of industry, expropriation without indemnity of all landed property larger than 50 hectares, and the restructuring of the country on the basis of a confederation of autonomous communes. The official report also denounced Azaña as "the leader of socializing radi-

14. It might be noted that the revolutionary old guard of the CNT had a low opinion of the tone and commitment of the new influx into the organization. A spokesman for the Barcelona Textile Syndicate lamented that revolution would actually be harder in the spring of 1936 than in the spring of 1931, when political institutions lay in shambles. A delegate from the Sagunto dockworkers complained:

> Since 1934 the organization has changed radically. The anarchist blood that used to flow through its veins has diminished greatly. Unless a salutary reaction occurs, the CNT is moving rapidly toward the most castrating, enervating reformism. The CNT of today is not the same as in 1932 and 1933, in essence or in revolutionary vitality. The virus of politics has wrought great damage. It suffers from the obsession of gaining more and more members without stopping to consider the harm this causes its internal structure. It has completely forgotten the ideological formation of its members and only seeks to incorporate them numerically. . . .
> Let us carry out a thorough, conscientious campaign of libertarian education.

El Congreso confederal de Zaragoza (Mayo, 1936) (Toulouse, 1955), 145–46.

calism, the most cynical and coldly cruel politician known to Spain," and Companys as "a cheap politician who once lived off his flattery of anarchism and subsequently persecuted it passionately."

Concurrent with this "transcendent event," as Largo termed the Zaragoza congress, important sectors of the Catalanist left were moving toward the revolutionaries. On May 14–15, an assembly in Barcelona representing 50,000 members of the Unió de Rabassaires approved a five-point program calling for: (a) expropriation without indemnity of "private property"; (b) collective ownership of land, with profits therefrom to be received by those who worked it; (c) formation of compact family cultivation units; (d) establishment of cooperatives where needed; (e) syndical organization of all farmers and farm workers. This program, affirming both family farms and collectivization, was contradictory. The general tone of the meetings left little doubt that rank-and-file Rabassaires adhered strongly to the institution of private family farms, but the leaders were strongly influenced by allies among the small Marxist parties in Catalonia and, amid the hysteria of those weeks, pushed through a much more radical, if vague and contradictory, line. The Rabassaires then voted to separate from the governing Esquerra federation in order to carry out their program in association with the Catalan socialist groups. At exactly the same time the small, formerly reformist Unió Socialista de Catalunya rejected future collaboration with the Generalitat and announced plans to join the Comintern. The new leaders of Estat Català had already repudiated the "rightist" line of Dencàs, who was drummed out of the party that same month in order to facilitate closer approximation to the Catalan revolutionary left.

While the revolutionaries went on from strength to strength, nonpolitical and Catholic syndicates languished. At the end of 1935, the Free Syndicates, the National Confederation of Catholic Syndicates, and a Spanish Federation of Workers, recently organized by the Jesuit priest Jesús Ballesta, came together in a United National Labor Front, claiming 276,389 members—no more than 15 to 20 percent of organized labor in Spain. The

UNLF found its organizational efforts stymied in 1936; in June the Madrid headquarters were closed by the government on the grounds of alleged "provocations."

On May 19 the new prime minister, Casares Quiroga, declared the government to be in a state of war against the Falange and all supporters of "fascism." Conservative spokesmen protested the incorrectness of a constitutional government declaring war on fascist extremists while maintaining a political alliance with violent leftist revolutionary associations.

In view of the attitude of Casares Quiroga and further deterioration in the political situation during the days that followed, Sánchez Román and his National Republican associates urged that a change in policy be adopted before it was too late. The National Republican party approved the following motion on May 25:

At the present time, the PNR, its authority increased by having foreseen the difficulties that the Popular Front would face and enjoying the freedom of movement provided by its absence from the government, has the responsibility of uniting other Republicans in an understanding of the seriousness of the political situation, recognizing the failure of the so-called Popular Front in its present form and the need to take measures to save the country and the Republic.

Political agreement should be based on the following measures:

Immediate execution of the program of defense of the Republican state [perhaps referring to the stringent security law passed by the first Azaña government], vigorously reestablishing the principle of authority together with a program of social reform and economic development agreed upon by the Republican Left, Republican Union and National Republican Parties.

Fulfillment of the reforms benefitting the working class that were included in the Popular Front electoral program.

Necessary measures must be taken to prevent those social and political forces that are actually most interested in the execution of this program from being the greatest obstacle to its accomplishment.

The following steps should be taken:

a) Severe repression of incitement to revolutionary violence.

b) General disarmament [of political militias].

c) Dissolution of all political, professional, economic or religious organizations whose activity gravely threatens the independence, constitutional unity, democratic-republican form or security of the Spanish Republic.

d) Prohibition of uniformed or paramilitary societies.

e) A law establishing the legal responsibility of leaders of political organizations for the crimes provoked by the latter's propaganda.

f) Prosecution of local government authorities for the infractions of law which they may commit in exercising their functions. Where circumstance requires, mayors may be relieved of supervision of public order and this function transferred to other authorities.

g) The rules of parliament will be reformed to improve the structure and functioning of parliamentary committees, so that with the assistance of technical agencies new legislation can be completed more quickly.

Señor Sánchez Román will present our request to the leaders of the Republican Union and Republican Left Parties. Once an agreement has been reached, the Socialist Party will be publicly invited to participate in a new government in order to carry out this program.

Should the Socialists refuse to collaborate, the [left] Republicans will urge the President to form a government of representatives of all the Republican forces [presumably referring to the center parties] willing to support the program approved by the left Republican parties. A team of Republican ministers recognized for their authority, competence and prestige will be appointed. They will govern above the level of party politics, rejecting any kind of demagogic appeal.

If the government does not receive parliamentary support, Cortes sessions will be suspended in conformity with constitutional statutes.

Alternatively, parliament might be presented with a bill authorizing the government to legislate by decree, under the powers granted by Article 61 of the constitution, regarding concrete matters that demand urgent attention.[15]

The formation of a government endowed with decree powers to restore order was suggested by various moderate and conservative spokesmen. The most widely publicized proposal came in a series of six articles by Miguel Maura in *El Sol* between June 18 and 27. Maura declared that the Republican left had been performing a national service in channeling the onslaught of the revolutionaries, but that in recent months its leadership had completely collapsed. He said that his fear was not so much that Spain might fall under a Communist-type dictatorship—for which Spanish conditions were hardly suited —as that the country would soon disintegrate in unprecedented anarchy.

15. García Venero, *Internacionales*, III, 106–08. García Venero says that he has seen the original document and has "no doubt of its authenticity."

Peaceful citizens, whatever their political sympathies, now believe that the laws are a dead letter and that public insults, assaults, arson, property destruction, homicide and attacks on the armed forces have ceased to count in the penal code when committed by those in red and blue shirts [the JSU] or under the starred emblem of the hammer and sickle. The clenched fist [the Communist salute] has become safe conduct for the worst excesses.

A reaction against this was inevitable and gives cause for concern in taking a form that is called "fascism," . . . though of authentic Italian fascism it has only the name and a few doctrinal postulates of which the majority of its affiliates are ignorant.

Today the Republic is no more—though I would like to believe unconsciously—than the tool of the violent, revolutionary sector of the working classes, which, shielded by the liberal democratic system and the blindness of certain leaders of the Republican parties, is preparing in minute detail an assault on the government and the extermination of capitalist and middle-class society. . . . They tell us this themselves in their newspapers and public meetings.

. . . We Republicans who made the greatest personal sacrifice to collaborate with the regime are called "fascists."

. . . If the Republic is to be this, it is inexorably condemned to swift extinction at the hands of those who claim to be its defenders, or what is more probable, at the hands of a reaction from the opposite direction.

Maura called for a multiparty, coalition "national Republican dictatorship" to save the country, but added, "I do not harbor the slightest hope that my reasoning could convince those who currently bear responsibility for government."

There is no indication that these appeals from former associates, men of proven liberal principles, had any effect on the president. In 1933 Azaña had said he did not fear seeing the Republic "fail" so much as seeing it "corrupted." To avoid corruption through compromise, Azaña presided over the progressive disintegration of the regime. He was willing to risk the destruction of his country rather than infringe his principles.

The scope of Communist activity steadily increased. Great attention was given to paramilitary work. By June the militia organization (MAOC) had 2,000 organized members in the Madrid district, and was given the goal of expanding into "a mass organization of semimilitary character" as "the organiza-

tional basis for the future worker-peasant Red Army." [16] Parallel
to the MAOC was the "Antimilitarist section" of the party, led
by the Russian-trained Galician Communist, Enrique Líster,
who had undergone a year or more of preparation at the
Frunze Academy. Simply put, the task of Líster's bureau was the
subversion of the Spanish Army. It set up Communist cells in
as many military detachments as possible, and was particularly
successful among noncommissioned officers in the Madrid garrison. Another semisecret military organization manipulated by
the party was the Republican Antifascist Military Union
(UMRA), first organized by leftist army officers in 1934 to combat
the union of conservative nationalists within the Army (UME).
The UMRA's chief organizer was a Communist officer on the
General Staff, Capt. Eleuterio Díaz Tendero. Such groups were
further complemented by Communist infiltration into the security
forces in Madrid and certain other cities where conditions
were propitious. Unofficial contacts were established between
the security forces and the Communist and Socialist militia in
some areas, and police officers played a role in training the latter.

After the Comintern agent Vittorio Vidali (Carlos Contreras)
arrived in Spain in May to assume supervision of paramilitary
activities, Communist terrorist squads were separated from the
regular MAOC groups in order not to compromise the latter.
Terrorist deeds were directed primarily against Falangists under
terms of the urban guerrilla civil war that was under way, and
an effort was made to avoid killing policemen in order not to
antagonize the middle-class left.

The Socialist militia was much less well organized; in fact,
in most areas regular Socialist paramilitary forces did not exist
save on paper. A major exception was the Socialist-Communist
stronghold, Madrid, where the main Socialist militia unit, *La
Motorizada,* had its own transportation facilities and several
thousand organized volunteers. In addition, the Socialists had
expanded their *grupos de choque* in Madrid and other key
centers. These, in turn, were becoming honeycombed with

16. *Material de discusión para el Congreso Provincial del Partido Comunista
que se celebrará en Madrid, durante los días 20, 21 y 22 de junio de 1936.*

Communists so that it became increasingly difficult to distinguish Socialist squad members from the MAOC.

The strike wave initiated by Spanish labor had international repercussions by May, when a big maritime strike tied up Spanish shipping in a number of foreign ports. By early June the dockers and crewmen had won a total victory with a large wage increase, a reduction in hours, and massive fringe benefits. Terms of the new contract required such an increase in manpower to get the work done that there were neither enough new crewmen nor enough space in the crewmen's quarters of Spanish merchant ships to hold them, leaving many ships idle in port and Spanish commerce facing catastrophic loss. Indalecio Prieto had earlier warned in a major speech that though Spain could survive a revolution, what the country could not survive was prolongation of merely negative anarchy and disorder, which destroyed national institutions and ruined the economy. On May 25 he warned that because of their economic absurdity the terms of the impending seamen's settlement would provoke "a crisis infinitely greater" than the preceding exploitation of dockers and crewmen.[17]

Prieto was, as usual, denounced as a "social fascist" and the strike wave spread. The total number of strikes reported in the liberal newspaper El Sol increased to 139 during the month of June, and to 145 during the first seventeen days of July. These figures are far from complete, since most strikes did not draw mention, but they serve to indicate the trend. On June 9 the newspaper calculated that 1 million workmen were out on strike.

The CNT's Solidaridad Obrera tried to mitigate the rash of local strikes by urging workers not to waste their energy on walkouts with merely economic goals so as to save their strength for the final revolutionary general strike. But regional CNT groups could not resist the temptation to go the Socialists one better in syndical extremism, outflanking the UGT by making impossible demands that employers could not match. Adopting a position even more extreme than the Socialists, the CNT

17. El Sol, May 26, 1936. This data was first brought out in a seminar paper at UCLA by Mr. C. Sheldon Thorne.

seized the initiative and began to expand membership more rapidly than its rivals. This revolutionary competition, however, soon degenerated into gunfights between the unions with dead and wounded on both sides.

In Barcelona, the terms demanded by hotel workers would have wrecked the hotel industry. When owners offered to cede part of their property to workers as shares in return for a more cooperative settlement, the CNT refused. In similar revolutionary local strikes, the Valencia street car company and the Andalusian Railway Company were forced into dissolution, their services taken over by the government. Less spectacularly, hundreds of small businessmen were being ruined. After the contractors' association gave in to exorbitant demands of striking CNT construction workers in Seville, the secretary of the CNT national committee, Horacio Prieto, urged his comrades to moderate demands before desperate employers, who were now willing to concede anything that was reasonable, were pushed into the arms of a protofascist reaction. His warnings, like those of Indalecio Prieto among the Socialists, were ignored.

Unemployment continued to increase (insofar as unemployed workers could be distinguished from strikers), production began to decline once more, tax receipts dropped, and more capital left the country. It became increasingly difficult to fund the debt and float government bonds. The balance of payments was running so strongly against Spain in June as to threaten the value of the peseta. Spanish business leaders pleaded with the government to try to do something to stabilize the economy and reach some sort of agreement with the revolutionary trade unions. On June 7 *La Veu de Catalunya* published a "Manifesto" signed by 126 employers' associations. It expressed willingness to accept most of the Popular Front's economic program, but urged the government to take immediate measures to control economic anarchy, suggesting a temporary end to wage increases, reform of the labor tribunals to achieve fair arbitration, and a national "Labor Conference" to try to straighten things out. Resolutions of the extraordinary assembly of the national Chambers of Commerce and Industry in Madrid, as reported in *El Sol* on June 26 and July 5, expressed the same attitude. These urgent pleas were, as usual, ignored by the Azaña regime.

On June 16 Gil Robles rose again to protest in the Cortes, emphasizing that the present government had met no parliamentary opposition whatever to any of its measures, had been able to have everything its own way, fully dominated the legislature, yet was completely unable or unwilling to maintain order in the country. The state of alarm had been prolonged since February 17, but to no avail. The government imposed censorship on moderate and conservative newspapers to prevent them from reporting the full dimensions of the problem, while doing nothing to curb incendiary outbursts of the revolutionary press.

The only available police figures on political violence in Spain between February 17 and July 17, 1936, show the following:[18]

	Killed	Injured
February 17–29	13	58
March	53	210
April	52	109
May	43	124
June	29	11
July 1–17	25	25
	215	537

Insofar as these figures have any validity, they indicate that there may have been a decline in violence during June, though the rate shot up again during the first half of July. The statistics for injured mean little, for the majority of those slightly injured in street affrays were probably never reported in official figures.

Política, the organ of Azaña's party, admitted that there had been a significant increase in politically motivated strikes, but excused them as the inevitable response to fascist provocation. Even the Communist *Mundo Obrero* began to warn that the strike wave was getting out of hand and condemned indiscriminate CNT agitation. Within a few more days, however, the joint UGT-CNT strike of construction workers in Madrid pulled 85,000 off the job; when the UGT reached a settlement, the

18. Comín Colomer, *Partido Comunista,* III, 681–749.

CNT kept the strike going and attacked UGT members returning to work.

Violence spread almost blindly. Street warfare between gunmen of the extreme left and extreme right was paralleled by a series of lethal shootings between the CNT and the Marxist groups. Strife between the two factions of the Socialist party also flared into the open. During a Socialist meeting at Ecija in the south on May 31, shots were fired by revolutionaries at Indalecio Prieto and other moderate leaders.

Prieto and his associates clung desperately to their control of the party executive in the hope that they could ride out the storm, and the next party congress was postponed until October to provide a cooling-off period. Communist fellow travelers urged the revolutionaries to split the party and fuse with the Communists, but Largo still had too much sense of Socialist loyalty and legality to do such a thing. Since the date of the congress had been postponed, the executive commission conceded the holding of new elections on June 28 to elect a regular president and vice-president in place of the current interim leadership. This solved nothing, for the same disagreements immediately reappeared. The moderates on the national committee refused to recognize the membership rolls of all the *caballerista*-dominated local sections. Moreover, *Claridad* demanded that an entire new executive commission be elected. According to the moderates' count, 10,993 valid votes were cast for González Peña and only 2,876 valid votes were admitted for Largo Caballero.[19]

The revolutionary Socialists cried gross fraud. In view of the heavy majorities they were drawing in most local sections, they seemed to have reason to doubt the accuracy of the executive commission's report. *Claridad* claimed that the latter was undermining the party's strength and making it look ridiculous by having it appear that there were only 23,000 Socialists in Spain sufficiently concerned about Socialist affairs to cast their votes. Moreover, charged *Claridad,* the executive commission

19. *El Socialista,* July 1, 1936. The commission also reported that even if all invalid votes were counted, the total would rise to 12,088 for González Peña and 10,318 for Largo Caballero.

manipulated membership lists at will and arbitrarily struck
out many names, including whole sections of the party that had
been unable to pay their dues during the repression of 1934–35.
On July 2 *Claridad* insisted that nearly 22,000 votes had been
cast for Largo, and published a long list of totals from the
local sections in different parts of the country. Moreover, it
protested accounts in the moderate press of the recent provincial
Socialist congress in Jaén, where, according to *Claridad,* the
moderate line had once more been rejected and the revolutionary
platform, including the building of a broad Worker-Peasant
Alliance and a unified Socialist-Communist party, had carried
by 1,438 votes to 523.

The executive commission's report gave the membership
of the party as less than 60,000, which if correct would have
indicated a decline of at least 20 percent since 1932. The Communist party was claiming nearly 100,000 members. Largo declared that if the executive commission was so confident of its
statistics it should call a general congress immediately to resolve
the major issues. *Claridad* suggested that a special investigative
commission, selected half by the executive commission and half
by the *caballerista*-dominated Madrid section of the party, be
chosen to scrutinize the electoral results. The executive commission decided to have none of that.

During the second week of July, Largo Caballero was in
London to represent the UGT at the international trade union
congress. There, once more, he struck down the line assiduously
cultivated by Socialist moderates and left Republicans which
tried to present the 1934 insurrection as merely an effort to
"save the Republican constitution." Largo stressed that the insurrection had been strictly a "class movement." [20] On July 10
another Andalusian provincial Socialist congress, this time at
Cádiz, supported the radical position by a vote of 88 to 2.[21]

Meanwhile, on July 1 the Communist delegation in the
Cortes submitted to other Popular Front factions a legislative
proposal to require the arrest of everyone in any position of
responsibility at the time of the Asturian repression from Ler-

20. *Claridad,* July 10, 1936.
21. *Ibid.,* July 13, 1936.

roux on down, subjecting them to plenary prosecution and confiscation of property.[22] This measure was unconstitutional and was not supported by most of the middle-class left. It was an attempt to implement the announced Communist tactic of using the Popular Front majority to eliminate the conservatives, after which the collapse of the Republican middle-class left could be easily accomplished. On July 9 the Communists won a pledge from the other Popular Front groups to delay the normal summer closure of the Cortes until the question of "responsibilities" for the Asturian repression had been settled.[23]

After a special caucus of the Popular Front deputies and visits by the Socialist executive commission to the prime minister on July 9 and 10, there was renewed speculation about a change in government. Though no precise information was available, rumors suggested that despite Communist encouragement the revolutionaries had lost control of the Socialist Cortes delegation, which might be willing to support a more moderate and broadly based ministry. In an interview with an Argentine reporter on July 11, Calvo Sotelo, who had become the strongest spokesman for the parliamentary opposition, opined that despite the increase in strikes he believed there was less danger of another leftist insurrection than there had been in February.

The rumors and conversations of July 10 and 11 proved a brief lull before the final storm. Calvo Sotelo and key leaders of the CEDA had already been informed that a military revolt against the Azaña regime was imminent and had pledged support. Conversely, the Communists and revolutionary Socialists would do all they could to oppose formation of a moderate coalition ministry.

The last word was spoken by the terrorists. With one exception early in March, both sides had restricted their targets to the opposition's rank and file or low-echelon leaders. The murder of Calvo Sotelo in the early hours of July 13 by a hetero-

22. *Claridad*, July 3, 1936.
23. *Mundo Obrero*, July 10, 1936. It should be noted that at no time between February and July 1936 did the government or the leftist parties present concrete evidence substantiating the vociferous charges of extreme ruthlessness in the police repression in Asturias during 1934 and 1935, of which so much propaganda capital was made.

geneous squad of off-duty police officers and leftist terrorists broke this unwritten rule. It was an assassination without precedent, for never before in the history of a western European parliamentary government had a coleader of the parliamentary opposition been murdered by a group composed mainly of members of the official state security forces.

Since the elections, a number of ultraleft-wing police officers who had participated in the 1934 insurrection had been restored to their commands, even though previously convicted by the courts. Alcalá Zamora had refused to permit right-wing army officers purged for their complicity in the 1932 revolt to be reinstated, but the Popular Front regime felt no such scruples concerning revolutionary leftists in the police, some of whom were leaders of the UMRA. The Undersecretary of the Interior, Bibiano Ossorio Tafall, a member of Casares Quiroga's Galicianist left, was assiduously courted by the Communists and emerged as a leading crypto-Communist during the Civil War. He apparently gave active support to left-wing extremists in the police and may have encouraged their association with the Marxist paramilitary units.[24] One UMRA militant, the retired Engineers officer Carlos Faraudo, who helped train Socialist militia, had been murdered by Falangist gunmen on a Madrid streetcorner on May 9. Another, an Assault Guard lieutenant, José del Castillo, was killed near his home on July 12 when on his way to night duty. There is some evidence that leftist police officers conferred that evening with the Minister of the Interior, a bland, middle-aged incompetent of the Catalanist left, Juan Moles, to demand measures against the conservative leaders.[25] At any rate, within a few hours of Castillo's death, a special detachment set out from Assault Guard barracks, led not by an Assault Guard officer but by a Communist Civil Guard captain, Fernando Condés, who had earlier been condemned to life imprisonment for his part in the 1934 insurrection. Calvo Sotelo was hauled out of his apartment in the middle of the night, carried off in an Assault

24. Ossorio Tafall's role was first pointed out to me by one of the principal leaders of the Galicianist left.

25. The Communist Manuel Benavides wrote in *La Publicitat* (Barcelona) on December 1, 1937, that Moles had "authorized house searches" of leading conservatives. This is not, however, corroborated by other evidence.

Guard troop truck, shot in the back of the head, and dumped in a suburban cemetery. The triggerman in the murder was a leftist gunman, Victoriano Cuenca (onetime bodyguard of the Cuban dictator Machado), who had been provided with an Assault Guard identification card by leftist officers.[26]

Within forty-eight hours both Calvo Sotelo and Castillo were buried in Madrid. Prieto drew the following image of the funeral processions in an article entitled, "Today's Spain Reflected in the Cemetery":

> After burying José del Castillo, the workers walk downhill toward Madrid with their jackets over their arms. When they pass in front of the arcade of the General Cemetery, they brush against a barrier of Civil Guards on horseback, who look like an extension of the wall that ends there. Behind the mounted guards file groups of fascists escorting the corpse of Calvo Sotelo. There is an exchange of wrathful stares. This perfectly symbolizes the Spain of today.[27]

On the afternoon of July 13, the Communist party presented the other Popular Front parties with a draft of proposed legislation that it planned to submit to the Cortes on the following day. It read:

> Article 1. All organizations of fascist or reactionary character, such as Falange Española, Renovación Española, CEDA, Derecha Regional Valenciana, and those whose characteristics are related to these, will be dissolved, and all properties of these organizations and their leaders will be confiscated. . . .
> Article 2. All persons known for their fascist, reactionary and anti-Republican activities will be jailed and prosecuted.
> Article 3. The government will confiscate the newspapers *El Debate, Ya, Informaciones, ABC* and all the reactionary press of the provinces.[28]

There was no opportunity to present this proposal, for reopening of the Cortes was postponed for eight days to avoid parliamentary debate of the murder. Several members of the assassination squad were placed under arrest, but no attempt was made to detain Condés, Cuenca, or several other leftist officers implicated.[29] The government did shut down the head-

---

26. These details were brought out by the subsequent judicial investigation by the Nationalist regime.
27. *El Liberal,* July 15, 1936.
28. *Mundo Obrero,* July 13, 1936.
29. Cf. Indalecio Prieto, *Cartas a un escultor* (Buenos Aires, 1961), 39–41.

quarters of the two monarchist parties in Madrid and suspended two leading conservative newspapers.[30] On the day after the murder, Azaña's *Politica* made a verbal appeal for "discipline" in support of the all-out struggle being waged between "so-called fascism" and a government determined to "extirpate the last residues of feudalism." This lame terminology, ill suited to Spanish political realities in mid-1936, reflected the inability of the middle-class left to come to grips with the breakdown of constitutional government. It has sometimes been observed that fewer Spanish governments are overthrown than commit suicide.

30. The Madrid headquarters of the CNT, which had been provoking severe labor disturbance and was also strongly opposed to the Marxist parties, was also closed.

T E N   *The Political Revolution*

of 1936

O F THE SPANISH revolutionary groups, only the Communists had a fairly definite plan in 1935 and 1936 for the revolutionary conquest of power, and even they seem to have lacked a specific timetable. This was almost inevitably the case, for despite the rapid Communist expansion in membership and influence, the Spanish Communist party still remained a comparatively small force that could achieve little by direct independent action. The Socialists, hopelessly divided, did not develop a precise program for revolution even within the maximalist wing of the party. Largo's only clearly invoked goal was to wait until the left Republican government collapsed. The CNT was also divided, despite the Zaragoza unity congress. The Barcelona leaders and the national committee secretary, Horacio Prieto, recommended restraint, whereas CNT chiefs in other areas plunged ahead with strikes, evidently intending to push worker agitation helter-skelter into the breakdown of the economy. Only the POUM, with its minuscule forces, would have moved directly into a revolutionary government. Thus the revolution that finally occurred after July 19, 1936, was precipitated by the initiative of the counterrevolutionaries and was a response to the rebellion of portions of the Army.

The paralysis of the Spanish middle classes during the months that preceded the explosion was impressive. Mesmerized by the increasing disruption of the economy and the withering away of the Republican state, divided among their numerous political factions, the middle classes and their erstwhile leaders seemed helpless to offer an alternative, or even a strong reaction. After July 13 many expected a cataclysm, but beyond that conservative leaders could agree on only one thing: Whatever was to be done would have to be done by the Army.

It has been conjectured that the revolutionaries were actually hoping to provoke the Army to revolt so as to force it into an indefensible role in which its antileftist elements might be destroyed, leaving the middle classes without protection and opening the way to a leftist takeover. But this interpretation gives people such as Largo Caballero credit for a Machiavellianism of which they had never shown themselves capable, and which Largo Caballero implicitly denied in a statement in *Claridad* on July 7. The Socialist maximalists did not want to precipitate events so long as these continued to work in their favor, nor were the Communist leaders more foolhardy.

The murder of Calvo Sotelo and the other disorders of the first half of July do not appear to have been a planned provocation of the Army per se but simply a continuation of the prerevolutionary assault on public order and the country's polity and economy. Their intent was more to destroy the existing system than to replace it with something concrete. Indalecio Prieto continued to offer his pessimistic warnings, lamenting that "only one thing is clear: we are going to deserve a catastrophe because of our stupidity." [1] His last futile remonstrance, published in *El Liberal* (Bilbao) on July 17, was afterward seized on by wartime Nationalist propaganda, for he observed that

The citizens of a civilized country have a right to peace and it is the government's duty to see that they have it. For some time—why try

1. Julián Zugazagoitia, *Historia de la guerra de España* (Buenos Aires, 1940), 9.

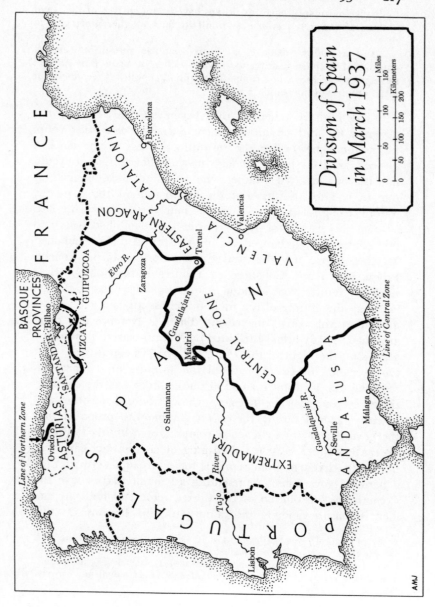

Division of Spain in March 1937

to deceive ourselves?—Spanish citizens have been deprived of that right because of the state's failure to fulfill its duty of guaranteeing it to them. . . .

Just as history manages to justify popular revolutions, it can approve of military insurrections, when either of them puts an end to regimes which are not compatible with the political, economic or social progress of the people. . . .

The military rebellion that began on July 17 was not designed to head off an imminent Socialist-Communist coup, for no one knew when the revolutionary left might make a direct assault on power, though many believed that it would not be long delayed. Rather, the rebellion was designed to put an end to disorder and the destruction of the economy, restore strong government, and eliminate the power of the left.

On the evening of July 18, after the revolt had begun to take shape, Azaña changed his course abruptly. He summoned Martínez Barrio, now the Speaker of the Cortes, Sánchez Román, Prieto, and Largo Caballero to a hurried consultation. Ever since his return from London, Largo Caballero had been demanding the arming of the trade unions as a guarantee against a counterrevolutionary movement. There is evidence that some arms had already been distributed by Madrid officials to workers' groups on the night of the 18th,[2] but Azaña's consultants, with the exception of Largo, opposed the "arming of the people," realizing that it meant the end of public order and the constitutional system. Sánchez Román, whose advice had been persistently ignored during the past eight months, proposed that the government try to reach a compromise with the military, on the basis of a ceasefire, disarming of civilian auxiliaries on both sides, freedom from reprisals for both sides, formation of a national government representing all major parties save the Communists, dissolution of the Cortes, reform of local government to ensure fair administration, and new elections. On this

2. *Ahora* (Madrid), Aug. 1, 1936, in Comín Colomer, *Partido Comunista,* III, 758–61; César Falcón, *Madrid* (Madrid, 1938), 58, 60; and the testimony of General Castelló, Republican Minister of War, July-August 1936, in Maximiano García Venero, *El General Fanjul: Madrid en el alzamiento nacional* (Madrid, 1967), 285–86.

basis, a new cabinet was hastily formed by Martínez Barrio on the night of July 18–19.[3]

General Mola, the leader of the army rèvolt, rejected the political compromise offered to him early on the morning of July 19. As head of the conspiracy, he was determined to eliminate all the leftist parties and refuse any further risk of the sort involved in liberal democracy. He believed that the obligations assumed in preparing the revolt precluded an opportunistic change of course to accept a compromise with the moderate left. In so doing, Mola may have kept faith with his colleagues but he betrayed the interests of most of his fellow countrymen. After Martínez Barrio failed in his effort at conciliation, liberal democracy was finished in Spain for the next generation. If the rebellion were successful, it would install military dictatorship. If the rebellion were crushed, it would be succeeded by an extraconstitutional leftist regime.

This dilemma developed not merely because of the revolt itself, but because the left Republican leaders soon sank into almost absolute paralysis. During the days of July 17 to 19 scarcely half the Spanish Army followed the conspirators into rebellion, while most of the Navy, Air Force, and police remained loyal. If Azaña had made a determined effort to uphold the Republican constitution prior to July 17, the revolt probably would not have occurred. If he and his colleagues had made a determined, all-out effort to preserve the integrity of the state after July 17, it need not be assumed that such an attempt would have been doomed to failure. In Madrid, for example, there were nearly as many armed police as soldiers; the former were better trained and probably in better condition. Only two regiments in the capital joined the military rebellion, and it is not impossible that the situation might have been controlled without turning the revolutionaries loose. In his last conversation with Azaña on the night of July 18–19, Miguel Maura had called for absolute concentration of authority in the hands of the Republican gov-

3. This is based on the account given by Ramón Feced, Minister of Agriculture in the short-lived Martínez Barrio government, to García Venero, in *El General Fanjul* (Madrid, 1967), 287–90.

ernment, but that required a courage and audacity that Azaña altogether lacked. Azaña believed that in a crisis the revolutionaries would not obey the orders of the government without being granted duality of power. Large-scale, violent street demonstrations against the Martínez Barrio cabinet in Madrid on July 19 reinforced this impression. Very possibly Azaña's belief was correct, but the fact remains that he refused to test it.

The second government formed on July 19 was an all-left Republican ministry headed by a rather obscure middle-class left professor, José Giral. It proceeded immediately to the arming of "the people," meaning of course not the people but the organized leftist groups. It was only after this point that the number of army units in active rebellion passed the proportion of 50 percent, and the lines of civil war were drawn.

Perhaps the best analogy in earlier European history to what happened in Spain in 1936 and 1937 was the situation in Hungary in 1918 and 1919. The analogy is quite imperfect, for the developments in central Europe were largely conditioned by foreign affairs, whereas those in Spain were mainly, though not exclusively, the product of domestic events. The military collapse of Austria-Hungary brought the defeat of the old order and the establishment of a quasi-revolutionary "middle class radical" government in Hungary that might be compared with the Azaña–Casares Quiroga ministry. The Versailles decree on the Hungarian peace settlement undercut the authority of the Károlyi regime as the military *pronunciamiento* in Spain undermined that of Azaña. Both regimes of the middle-class left then quasi voluntarily gave way to Socialist-Communist governments. The Communists became the main driving force in both Spain and Hungary, but their numerical and organizational weakness compared with the larger, established trade union movements made it impossible for them to extend their control completely in either country. In both situations, foreign assistance to the counterrevolutionaries helped finally to decide the issue. The Red Terror was followed in both countries by a White Terror which probably exceeded it in scope. Not too much can be made of this analogy because of dissimilarities of great importance in the two situations, yet it may be worth mentioning as a reminder that what happened in the Spanish Civil War was not so unprecedented as has sometimes been claimed.

Though the Giral government sat in Madrid for the next six weeks, its authority was to a large degree ignored by the revolutionary parties in the capital. In most other regions that did not fall to the insurgents, it was ignored almost altogether. In each district of the nominally Republican zone, power fell into the hands of the largest of the leftist forces or a loose coalition thereof. In Catalonia, this process resulted in a curious dualism between the de jure authority of the Generalitat and the de facto power of the CNT. In Asturias the same coalition that generated the 1934 insurrection took over. A similar revolutionary junta was formed in Santander. The Giral ministry dispatched a special commission to administer the Valencia district, but that had to give way by the end of July to a "Popular Executive Committee" representing the leftist parties. Other juntas took over the capitals and provinces of most of south central and southeastern Spain. Only in the two Basque provinces of Vizcaya and Guipúzcoa did a nonleftist group, the Basque Nationalist (PNV), gain dominance, in collaboration with left Basque nationalists (PANV) and the three main revolutionary movements. Though the PNV had received less than one-third of the votes cast in the three Basque provinces (including Álava) in the February elections, a statute of regional autonomy similar to that of Catalonia was hastily ratified in Madrid on October 1, after the Giral government had given way to a Popular Front cabinet. Under wartime conditions, Basque autonomy became virtual independence. Thus by the late summer of 1936 "Republican" Spain had broken up into a series of autonomous regional groupings somewhat reminiscent of the situation that obtained during the War of Independence against Napoleon or the cantonalism of the First Republic in 1874. The parliamentary constitutional system, already passing into abeyance, came to a final and abrupt end after mid-July. Carlos Rama has aptly called its successor the "Revolutionary Republican Confederation of 1936–37."

Much has sometimes been made of the fact that the most "modern" and industrialized sectors of Spain were taken over by the revolutionaries. It might be equally emphasized that most of the more literate sectors of the country, where property was more widely distributed and society largely lower middle class in ethos, in Old Castile and León, joined the military Nationalists. In Zaragoza, the headquarters of the FAI-CNT, revolutionary anarchosyndicalism fell prey to its own carelessness and poor organization, succumbing to a united force of garrison troops and local police. A general strike was strangled soon after it began. In Seville the Army enjoyed audacious leadership and the Communist-anarchist rivalry left the revolutionaries divided and ineffective in their moment of crisis. A few hundred troops held control of the center of the city until reinforcements arrived. In Extremadura and western Andalusia, two major foci of revolutionary activity under the Republic, the CNT and UGT were unable to mobilize themselves for all-out struggle. The rural middle and upper classes formed militia of their own to assist the military, and the revolutionaries in southwest Spain soon collapsed, in part the victims of their own destruction of social discipline and cooperation.

All the revolutionary movements expanded their membership greatly during the early months of the Civil War. Among the organized parties, the Communists made the largest gains, for they adjusted most rapidly and uniformly to the new situation. The Socialist party and the FAI registered a more moderate rate of increase. The Socialists remained divided and their position was somewhat ambiguous. The FAI was highly elitist and sectarian, and it also began to waver between political compromise and revolutionary intransigence.

Both the mass trade union movements increased greatly, and each claimed 2 million members by the end of 1936. Of the two, the CNT proportionately gained more, capitalizing on the upsurge of enthusiasm among the lower classes in the leftist zone. As the movement of spontaneous revolution, it mushroomed through eastern Spain and in some of the central provinces. By contrast, the UGT benefited rather more from the influx of frightened middle-class people seeking syndical affiliation to save them from the Red Terror, yet it lost much of the FNTT peasant membership in the southwestern provinces occupied by the insurgent Nationalists and encountered difficulty in competing with the popular revolutionary demagogy of the CNT. The divided, uncertain leadership of the Socialists handicapped them in trying to rival the CNT in spontaneous proletarian identification, and did not prevent sizable portions of the UGT from falling under Communist influence in the months that followed. Thus the CNT and to a much lesser extent the POUM emerged as the principal spontaneous, independent expressions of revolution in Spain during the first year of the Civil War.

After the defeat of the small, scattered units of military rebels in Catalonia, the CNT was able to arm 40,000 of its members in that region and become the predominant force in northeastern Spain. Nonetheless, it was not this alone that made the CNT ipso facto masters of Catalonia, but rather that the left Catalanist leaders in the Generalitat chose to avoid direct confrontation. They were apparently urged to stand up to the anarchists by the heads of the pro-Stalinist Marxist groups in Catalonia, who officially formed the Unified Socialist party of Catalonia (PSUC) on July 25. In Catalonia, as in Madrid, there were numerous loyal police units, as well as regiments of loyal troops, on whom the left Republican leadership might have relied. But a confrontation with the CNT in Catalonia amid a broadening Civil War throughout Spain would have been a difficult and bloody undertaking. In view of the renewed leftward tendencies in the Esquerra and many years association with the revolutionaries, Companys preferred a compromise in the hope of defeating the right and then of domesticating the CNT without bloodshed.

On July 22 Companys embarked on an explicit system of revolutionary dualism that had little parallel in modern Europe. The existing regional government was flanked by creation of a Central Committee of Anti-Fascist Militia charged with directing the military effort against the rebels in the northeast, but also given authority over most of the domestic responsibilities of the Generalitat. The membership of the "Central Committee" and most of its subcommittees was chosen in approximately equal proportions from the CNT, the FAI, the UGT, the Catalanist left, and the small revolutionary parties. In their moment of triumph Catalan anarchosyndicalists gave Catalan Marxism over-representation, apparently in the hope that this would encourage the Popular Front parties to give the CNT equal representation in the Popular Front juntas formed in Socialist- and Communist-dominated areas. The CNT did, however, veto PSUC participation in the first nominal wartime ministry of the Generalitat that was set up at the beginning of August. Like the government sitting impotently in Madrid, it was composed exclusively of the Republican left. Subsequently, CNT leaders explained that they assented to nominal continuation of the Generalitat's ministry not because they doubted the capacity of the CNT to take over full authority, but because of the pressure of the war and especially because of the need not to frighten foreign opinion further. In turn, the *Butlleti de la Generalitat* recognized that real power rested with the Anti-Fascist Committee, and announced that " a revolutionary order has been established, which all the member organizations of the Committee have bound themselves to support." Horacio Prieto was later even more explicit when he wrote that "We went straight to a dictatorship; even the Bolsheviks themselves, in their first historical opportunity, were not so quick to establish absolute power in [the areas which they controlled in] Russia." [4]

The first phase of the Spanish revolution was not political reconstruction, social change, or even concerted military action against the insurgents, but the "Red Terror," which raged almost without control during the first months of the Civil War. In the Nationalist zone there appeared a torrent of literature about this, continuing in diminished volume down to the present. Much of the writing was hyperbolic, but the reality was grim enough. The military rising of July 17–20 opened a valve of destructive fury among the revolutionary groups which surprised and horrified some of the latter's own leaders. Such murderous zeal reflected many years of agitation, for without protracted incitement to the slaughter of their fellows the working class organizations could hardly have carried out so awesome a pogrom of the middle classes and opposition workers. There was also the immediate incentive of fear. The military

4. *El anarquismo español en la lucha política* (Paris, 1946), 7.

revolt marked the ultimate crisis. Should the counterrevolutionaries win this round, the result would be final, and the revolutionaries were eager to eliminate their "class enemies" while
there was time. During the Civil War, Nationalists talked of
half a million people slaughtered by the terror in the leftist
zone. By 1939 a more responsible commentator had scaled this
down to the approximate figure of 100,000. More careful statistics
released in the 1960's at the National Sanctuary in Valladolid
indicate a total of about 61,000 violent deaths.

The Red Terror began with the slaughter of many of the
officers captured when the insurgent Montaña infantry barracks in Madrid was overwhelmed by armed leftists and police
on July 20. This massacre was widely publicized, and helped
set the tone for executions conducted with equal ferocity by
revolutionaries and insurgent Nationalists. Reports, customarily
exaggerated, of the killings behind enemy lines stimulated firing
squads on both sides. There is no valid way of determining who
exacted the greater toll. Though the Red Terror may have
taken more lives than the Nationalist repression while the
war lasted,[5] the victors were subsequently able to complete the
task at their leisure.

It has frequently been said that the real differences between
the Red Terror of the left and the White Terror of the Nationalists was that the former was spontaneous, unorganized,
and mostly brought to an end within six months or so, whereas
the Nationalists' purge was quickly institutionalized and was
later accelerated rather than restrained. Regarding the character
of the Nationalists' repression, this observation is largely if not
entirely correct, but it is somewhat misleading concerning the
Red Terror. The latter was not a product of blind, spontaneous
mob fury. Nearly all the work of the Red Terror was carried
on by small groups from the revolutionary parties, who specifically constituted themselves for this task, in most cases with
the approval and sometimes at the initiative of superiors in their

5. Hugh Thomas, author of the most impartial general history of the
Civil War, calculated the number of executions by the Nationalists at
40,000. *The Spanish Civil War* (New York, 1961), 631. In the second edition
of this book four years later, Thomas decided to raise his estimate to
50,000.

organization. Nor were all the murder squads mere offshoots of the revolutionary organizations; in Madrid, for example, some of them were organized as regular police units under the left-Republican-directed Ministry of the Interior during July-August 1936.

The number of shootings was highest in Madrid, Catalonia, Valencia, Málaga, and certain rural districts of south-central Spain. The squads that did the killing largely reflected in their membership the dominant revolutionary forces in each area. The Communists later tried to blame most of the killings on the "uncontrollables" of the FAI-CNT and the "fascist provocateurs" of the POUM, but this was an oversimplification. In general the Terror was directed against the middle and upper classes and whoever was identified with conservative organizations. The most intensely persecuted group, however, was the clergy, of whom at least 6,832 (including 283 nuns) were executed during the Civil War.[6] Moreover, in anarchist areas, a great deal of energy was expended in vengeance on antileftist workers.[7]

Amid its relative impotence, the left Republican ministry of July-September 1936 did almost nothing to try to halt the Terror. It probably could have accomplished little in any event, but it scarcely even tried moral suasion. Azaña was said to have wrung his hands in private, but he lacked the courage to do anything in public. In Madrid, where loyal police units were still at hand, they were almost never used to shield the victims of the Terror. In Barcelona, Companys did not even try to protect his own Minister of Public Order, an ex-army captain named Escofet, who spoke out against the Terror and was consequently forced by the FAI to flee to France. Even in the orderly territory of the autonomous Basque government the Red Terror was not completely avoided. In addition to sporadic killings by revolutionaries in the early weeks, Communists joined anarchists in the massacre of prisoners in three jails in Vizcaya and Guipúzcoa.

The first to protest were the most conscientious leaders of

6. Antonio Montero Moreno, *Historia de la persecucíon religiosa en España 1936–1939* (Madrid, 1961), is the authoritative study.

7. The subsequent investigation in Tarragona, for example, is said to have identified 60 percent of the victims there as workers. José María Fontana, *Los catalanes en la guerra de España* (Madrid, 1956), 88.

the revolutionaries themselves. On July 30 *Solidaridad Obrera* issued the following anouncement from the Catalan federation of the CNT:

> . . . We declare coolly, with terrible serenity and the unalterable intention of doing what we say, that if all these acts which are spreading terror through Barcelona are not stopped, WE WILL PROCEED TO SHOOT EVERY INDIVIDUAL who is proved to have committed acts against human rights. . . . For the honor of the people of Barcelona, for the dignity of the CNT and of the FAI, these excesses must be stopped.

And it repeated on the following day:

> For Revolutionary Honor!
> THE TRIUMPHANT REVOLUTION REQUIRES THAT
> THE PURGE CARRIED ON BY ANTIFASCIST
> FORCES BE HUMANIZED!
> In agreement with the directives of our higher committees, who always work in understanding with the members of the CNT and of the FAI, we must work intensively to curb the acts of vandalism committed by certain elements in the antifascist ranks.

By far the most outspoken protest on either side was made by the veteran CNT writer and ex-*treintista* Juan Peiró, in a series of articles printed in *Llibertat* (Mataró) during the late summer of 1936 and soon afterward published with further commentary in a little book entitled *Perill a la reraguarda* (Danger in the Rear Guard). He deeply resented the accusations made by the Communists that the CNT and POUM were responsible for crime and disorder in Catalonia:

> . . . I declare with full responsibility that all the anti-fascist groups, beginning with Estat Català and ending with the POUM, and including the Esquerra and the PSUC, have contributed a proportion of thieves and assassins equal to that of the CNT and the FAI. There is at least one group whose disgusting misdeeds greatly exceed those of the CNT and the FAI. What has happened, dear reader, is that each group has used the same tactic: to "operate" in the district where its own syndical or political organization is sparsely represented so as to throw the moral responsibility for its misdeeds on the members of the organization preponderant in that area.
>
> I never denied the fatal, ineluctable fact that revolutions involve the shedding of blood. On the contrary, I have always recognized that the more profound the revolution is, the greater the bloodshed. Revolu-

tions that have been carried out without bloodshed are not revolutions. . . .

But in a popular revolution bloodshed must not be allowed to exceed the limits set by individual conscience or the true requirements of the revolution. There has never been a revolution which . . . does not seek the support and collaboration of the popular classes whose interests coincide with the revolution, yet no one could demonstrate an historical example in which terrorism, systematic murder for its own sake, killing without regard to right or wrong, though it may respond to murders by the enemy, have been or ever could be the tactic required to win the consciences of those whose support the revolution needs. The French Revolution itself, so prodigal in shedding innocent blood, after a few years fell into the hands of a self-seeker, Napoleon, who had the soul of a tyrant. . . .

When a people sinks into the degradation inevitably produced by scorning human life, such a people for long loses its sense of spiritual value and human dignity. It is no longer a people which can cherish the greatest of all values: freedom. . . .

Catalonia and Spain have fallen into this degradation. Human beings have been consumed in the same way that the weaker animals in the jungle are devoured. For some time there has been no law here save that of the stronger. Men have killed for the sheer sake of killing, because they could kill with impunity. Amid this tempest, men have been killed—not because they were fascists, or enemies of the people, or foes of our revolution or any such thing—but capriciously, for the satisfaction of those who wanted to watch men die. Many who have been killed were shot because of personal vengeance or old scores which have been settled in these circumstances of lawlessness and impunity.

A people in rebellion have been infiltrated by amoral elements who rob and murder by profession and by instinct. And even after the people in rebellion have been controlled, the others—the amoral—have continued robbing and murdering to the dishonor of the revolution and the mockery of those risking their life at the battlefront.

Many of those who have carried out expropriations have had no other interest than to seize other people's money and goods for themselves. Such individuals are not revolutionaries but thieves. If all those who, to the common shame, call themselves revolutionaries had their homes searched for stolen goods, there would not be enough room in the prisons to hold them.

Peiró later added,

For the sole fact of being wealthy capitalists or simply lower middle class people, hundreds of men who have had nothing to do with fascism or the military revolt that is filling our country with blood have been shot. Many of these have been murdered after having been forced to hand over large amounts of money—money which has not gone to the support of the revolution or the war but simply to satisfy the greed of individuals much worse than the capitalists whom they so vilely and cowardly murdered. . . .

If I wanted to be precise I could cite a list of concrete incidents in which the unfortunate ones lined up against the wall after being "taken for a ride" have had nothing more fascist about them than the hatred of those who held a grudge against them. Personal vengeance has motivated the shooting of many, themselves as much the victims of reaction and capitalism as anyone else. Due to political rivalry, many men of the [moderate] left have been slain, and others shot by mistake simply because in time past under economic pressure they were forced by their employers or the local political boss to vote as the latter wanted.

In the Barcelona district, and especially in Lérida, the shedding of blood has been so arbitrary, systematic and excessive, that the Anti-fascist committees of certain towns have had to purge their colleagues on the committees of neighboring towns. And how many district committees in Catalonia have had to order the shooting of "revolutionaries" who seized the opportunity to steal and then frequently to murder so that their robberies would not be discovered? . . .

In Mataró, for example, everyone knows that in a village only a few kilometers outside town one of the leaders of the local Anti-fascist committee burned all the old furniture in his home to make room for sumptuous new furnishings which he had stolen. This "revolutionary," who boasts of having "liquidated" God and the Virgin Mary, has carried out his "own revolution" to provide himself with furnishings fit for a king, fine clothes, art objects and a fantastic collection of jewelry. Everyone who knows about this shameful, scandalous example associates it with the revolution, and wonders if to fall into such shame it is necessary to carry out a revolution so long as that revolution has no other goal than to prevent the triumph of the thieves and assassins in the ranks of fascism.

Here Peiró put his finger on the primary rationalization for the men of conscience in the Popular Front: that no matter how great were the crimes in the Popular Front zone, the revolution must be supported in order to defeat the "fascism" championed by the Nationalists. The crimes in the enemy zone were said to be much worse because they were encouraged and condoned by the military regime in Salamanca, whereas the revolutionary parties were supposedly bringing the disorders under control.

Protests similar to those of the more conscientious anarchists were repeated by Madrid Socialists, first in *El Socialista* on August 3 and then most forcefully and dramatically by Indalecio Prieto in a radio address on August 10. By mid-August a series of "control patrols" had been formed in many parts of the leftist zone to try to regulate the activist squads and, as Peiró wrote, a number of better disciplined local Antifascist committees in Catalonia took upon themselves the task of restraining their counterparts.

To provide an orderly channel for the purge of Nationalists and their sympathizers, "revolutionary courts" were formed during the month of August in most districts. At Barcelona a CNT delegation from the Anti-Fascist Militia Committee had already taken over the Generalitat's Ministry of Justice. The revolutionary court system as ratified by the nominal authorities in Madrid and Barcelona during August provided for emergency tribunals composed of three professional jurists assisted by a panel of representatives of the Popular Front parties and the CNT. According to the government decree of August 23, the purpose of the revolutionary courts was to incorporate the "people" into the juridical process so that they could become "an efficacious auxiliary to the resolutions of the jurists." To save time, reports and testimony need not be heard if such information would "not alter the nature of the crime or the responsibility of the criminal," and it was stipulated that only one certified judge need be present to validate decisions. Verdicts were to be rendered within five days of the hearing and were unappealable. The system was slow in going into effect, and the work of the murder squads continued in some districts unabated. Some of the major mass killings occurred in November and December 1936, particularly at Madrid and Santander. By the beginning of 1937, however, the period of revolutionary dualism in police activities was coming to a close, and repression was more and more taken over by reconstituted state forces. During 1937 the revolutionary courts became institutionalized. Lawyers were provided for the defense, and proceedings were not altogether arbitrary, with sentences rarely in excess of 5 to 10 years' imprisonment.

As far as the war effort was concerned, the most significant thing about the Red Terror was not its cruelty but its ineffectiveness. During the early period, especially, local revolutionary patrols in most cases acted independently and often at random. Since they did not form part of a centrally organized police system, they lacked precise information regarding enemy activists and were often motivated by rumor or whim. The fixation on priest-killing was a prime example of the irrationality of the terror in the leftist zone, for it does not appear that any but a tiny number of clerics were engaged in fifth-column or espionage activities. As it turned out, the Red Terror seems to have incited almost as much resistance among the middle classes and opposition workers as it crushed. The purge in the Nationalist zone was more calculated and effective, directed primarily though not exclusively at leftist leaders and hard-core activists. It, too, failed to eliminate active opposition in the rear guard, but brought such resistance within more narrow limits. The repression in the leftist zone only became relatively efficient in 1937 and 1938, when systematic police administration was installed, primarily though not exclusively under Communist leadership.

The chaotic events of the summer of 1936 revealed that there was only one united and effective political organization in the leftist zone—the Communist party. The anarchosyndicalists dissipated their strength in multiple uncoordinated ventures and saw no clear solution to the revolutionary dualism that had developed, and the Socialists remained split between the extremists awaiting the final collapse of Republican government and moderates who wished to sustain it. The Communist party controlled the largest youth movement in Spain and already possessed paramilitary cadres which enabled it to assume from the start a commanding place in military affairs, especially in the central zone. The Comintern advisers were keenly aware of the decisive significance of military power, and the party's energy was devoted disproportionately, though not exclusively, to the fighting front.

The Communist political line shifted drastically. After July 17 there was no more talk about preparing for a "worker-peasant" dictatorship. Party spokesmen called for total loyalty to the Popular Front and the union of all the left to defend Republican legality. Many official statements declared that the war was purely defensive, and was not at all being fought with immediate revolutionary change in mind. Ibarruri wrote in *Mundo Obrero* on July 30 that in defending the "Republic," the left projected no radical new goals but was merely defending the "bourgeois democratic revolution" that the French had carried out in 1789. The party organ reiterated on August 9 that

> It is absolutely false that the present workers' movement has as its goal the establishment of a proletarian dictatorship after the revolution has ended. . . . We Communists are motivated exclusively by the desire to defend the democratic Republic established on April 14, 1931.

The Communist change of line was dictated primarily by two factors: the need not to frighten the democratic constitutional regimes of western Europe, whose support would probably be needed against the Nationalists; and the need to conciliate at least temporarily the lower middle classes within Spain and avoid driving them into the arms of the counterrevolutionaries. During the first weeks, however, the Communists altogether lacked the strength and influence to channel the mass explosion of revolutionary enthusiasm that burst out in many parts of leftist Spain. All they could do was to work with the middle-class left and use their influence among the revolutionary Socialists to moderate the latter.

It was not the Communists but the Socialists, the CNT, and the POUM who were the principal standard bearers of revolution. On August 1 *Claridad* called for a revolutionary regime in place of the remaining shell of Republican government, declaring that "As a result of the military rebellion, we are in the midst of a profound revolutionary process," and adding that "it is necessary that all instruments of the state, and especially the army, also be revolutionary." And on August 22: "The people are no longer fighting for the Spain of July 16, which was still a Spain socially dominated by the traditional castes, but for a Spain from which those castes are definitely eliminated. The most powerful support for the war lies in the total uprooting of fascism, economically and in every other way. That is revolution." *Claridad* termed it a "social war more than a civil war."

Both Largo Caballero and the FAI-CNT leaders insisted upon de facto control of military and much of economic affairs by the worker militia and the syndicates. They acquiesced in the continuation of revolutionary dualism, side by side with the nearly impotent left Republican government, only until the Nationalists had been crushed. Largo held to the orthodox Marxist position of waiting for the inevitable collapse of the middle-class left government, which would then be replaced by a Socialist regime.

But revolutionary dualism left the leaders of the revolutionary Socialists and anarchosyndicalists in an ambiguous situation. The revolutionary explosion provided their great historic opportunity, yet the fact that it came at the beginning of a civil war against an increasingly vigorous adversary soon supported by Germany and Italy placed the revolution in considerable jeopardy. Even the CNT leaders admitted that complete displacement of the Republican government would further disrupt what was already a chaotic military struggle, prejudice the leftist cause in vital relations with other countries and very likely provoke internecine strife. The Socialist attitude became increasingly sober after mid-August, following the swift and easy Nationalist conquest of Socialist Extremadura. As the small elite forces of the insurgents moved nearer Madrid, the need for an all-out effort by the left was urgent. In the capital conversations began between representatives of the UGT and CNT, leading to rumors that a "National Revolutionary Junta" under Largo Caballero would soon replace what was left of the Republican regime.

It is impossible to judge the accuracy of these rumors. Such a change would have been a disaster from the Communist viewpoint, prejudicing military development and shortcircuiting the Communists politically. Communist influence was greatly strengthened during August by the consolidation of the non-intervention policy vis-à-vis Spain on the part of France and Britain, and the reestablishment of full diplomatic relations with the Soviet Union by the Madrid government. Marcel

Rosenberg, the first Soviet ambassador ever received in the Spanish capital, arrived on August 24 and, as the representative of the only great power actively supporting the leftist cause, enjoyed enormous prestige and influence. Every effort was bent to encourage the formation of a strong and united Popular Front Republican government, one that would represent and lead all the major leftist parties yet still preserve the façade of Republican legality and keep the regime within the nominal sphere of the western constitutional democracies. Such a ministry could be presented to the western world as merely the Spanish equivalent of Léon Blum's French Popular Front government. Even if it did not bring England and France to change their position, it might make further German and Italian assistance to the insurgents too awkward to continue. If worst came to worst, a Popular Front Republican government would at least in the eyes of western opinion provide a more acceptable recipient of covert Russian aid than would an all-out revolutionary regime. Formation of such a ministry might thus turn the international situation to the Spanish left's advantage; it would assist the Non-Intervention Committee in localizing the conflict, restricting it to dimensions that the left could more easily dominate.

On September 4 Largo Caballero replaced Giral as head of a new Popular Front Republican cabinet. It was composed of 5 Socialists (2 revolutionaries, 3 moderates), 4 left Republicans (including 1 Catalanist), 2 Communists, 1 Communist agent who was officially Socialist (the foreign minister, Alvarez del Vayo), and 1 Basque Nationalist. The CNT refused to participate but agreed provisionally to cooperate with the new government, naming one delegate to represent it in the functioning of each government ministry. Both the memoirs of the ex-Communist central committeeman Hernández and the official Spanish Communist history of the Civil War agree that Communist participation was insisted upon by Largo himself. According to Hernández, the party leaders had never planned governmental participation before the formation of a "worker-peasant" regime, and the central committee only accepted Largo's invitation after receiving explicit instructions from Moscow. This marked the first time that the Communists formed part of a coalition government in any country (save perhaps the Béla Kun regime), and also the first time that they collaborated with Christian leaders (since the Basque Nationalists were strongly Catholic). This was but one of the first of several major features by which the Popular Front governments of wartime Spain anticipated the coalition regimes and "People's Democracies" that emerged from the wreck of the Second World War in Europe.

It was announced that the Largo Caballero government had been formed in order to win the war. Its official program went only slightly beyond that of the preceding left Republican cabinet: further emergency social and economic reforms, exaction of revolutionary justice and temporary administration of private property in the public interest, but no sweeping economic or institutional changes save for the recognition of the "people's courts." No attempt was made to convene the Cortes and the constitution was in almost universal abeyance, but the Communist propaganda machine hailed the Largo Caballero government as "a continuation of the previous government." Though this line had to be modified for domestic use within the leftist zone, it was consistently pumped by the international Communist propaganda apparatus throughout the western world. The masquerade of a violent, terrorist system of revolutionary dualism as a "democratic constitutional Republic" constituted what has been aptly termed the "grand camouflage" of the Spanish Civil War.[8]

8. Burnett Bolloten, *The Grand Camouflage* (New York, 1961).

ELEVEN *The Social and*

Economic Revolution

A T THE VERY OUTBREAK OF hostilities, the workers' militia and syndical groups began to requisition whatever they thought useful for their purposes. In some areas the syndicates also seized de facto control of those sectors of the economy in which they were most involved. The Giral government recognized that the needs of civil war required the control of economic resources, and on July 25 named a "Supervisory Committee" to oversee military requisitioning and control of key sectors of industry by military or syndical agencies. Due to the fragmentation of authority in the leftist zone, the Committee had little power beyond the greater Madrid district. In this central zone, where the nominal government remained and where the key military struggle was focused, attention was more rapidly absorbed by military affairs than in other sectors of leftist territory. The CNT was much weaker there than in the east, and the UGT showed less interest in syndical economic control. According to the best estimate, about 30 percent of Madrid industry was brought under government or military supervision on behalf of the war effort. The rest limped along as well as it could under the purge of ownership and management, disruption of supply, market and labor conditions, and de facto control by those workers who remained on the job. The formation of Largo Caballero's Popular Front ministry brought little change in this situation. Its economic program was aimed at expediency and posited no sweeping structural changes in industry for the time being. Similarly, in the provinces of central and south central Spain where the UGT was fairly strong, there was little pressure for direct economic revolution so long as the fighting raged.

In the autonomous Basque territory the degree of revolutionary change in economic production ranged from very slight to nil. Basque industry functioned in a more nearly normal fashion than did that of any other part of the leftist zone, though it was soon hampered by supply shortages. Relatively stable productivity enabled the Basques to provide the revolutionary juntas to the west in Santander and Asturias with some 70 million pesetas of food and goods, both domestic and imported, plus foreign exchange to facilitate other purchases. Though such assistance was accepted, the anarchists and Socialists in the neighboring juntas frequently referred deprecatingly to the Basques as "counterrevolutionaries." [1]

The Republican left, like all factions save the Communists and the POUM, was divided on the issue of social revolution. The more moderate wanted to restrict all revolutionary change to the minimum, whereas the more radical and/or flexible, such as Companys and the Catalanist left, wanted to adjust to sweeping social and economic changes, legalizing them and channeling them in directions compatible with the eventual revival of the constitutional Republican state. Azaña was appalled by the revolution and aghast at the Red Terror; since so many of the *tremendismos* in his own speeches were emitted for rhetorical effect, he had apparently believed the same was true of revolutionary propaganda. The reality was shattering, and the resulting moral annihilation of the leadership of the middle-class left was as debilitating as the latter's numerical weakness. As he later

1. "Informe" on the situation in the Basque country during the war prepared by President José Antonio de Aguirre for the Republican government-in-exile, Oct. 15, 1950. (Bolloten Collection, Hoover Institution.)

wrote in *La velada en Benicarló,* Azaña doubted that the Republican left had the strength to resist revolutionary changes, but even if so, he lacked the will to attempt it for fear of "unleashing a second civil war."

Some of his lieutenants went much farther to accommodate themselves to the revolutionaries. In a speech at Castellón in January 1937, Fernando Valera, one of the most active young Castilian leaders of the middle-class left, stressed that the latter's task was to "humanize the revolution." More specifically, he called for the extension of regional autonomy to Valencia and later to other areas, the establishment of autonomous communes, the formation of agrarian cooperatives, and in general the creation of a mixed but mostly free economy, partly private, partly collectivized, that would carry on both war and "humane revolution" at the same time.[2] This coincided almost exactly with the new minimum short-term Popular Front program of the Communists as developed in the latter part of 1936.

The main economic concern of the inland, rural provinces that made up most of the leftist zone was agriculture. During the first weeks of the Civil War much of the land held by large owners, and many medium properties as well, were seized de facto by the UGT and CNT (and in Lérida by the POUM syndicates). In many cases the soil was worked on much the same terms as before, save that ultimate control no longer rested in the hands of the landlord. Hundreds of agrarian collectives were also formed on an ad hoc basis, especially in the eastern provinces, whereas prior to the Civil War there had been only a few dozen in all of Spain. In several regions where both the CNT and UGT had a following, the two syndical organizations cooperated, though normally de facto seizures or the formation of collectives or cooperatives in a given area was the exclusive work of the single strongest local movement.

The channeling of the agrarian revolution was one of the most vital problems facing the Popular Front regime, for two reasons: on the one hand, the majority of lower-middle-class peasants had to be conciliated sufficiently to avoid driving them

2. Fernando Valero, *Sentido revolucionario de la República española* (Castellón, 1937).

into the arms of "fascism"; on the other, the demands of the landless and radicalized minority had to be met sufficiently to maintain their enthusiasm for the leftist cause. The only revolutionary party to grasp the full significance of this was the Communists. As early as July 27 *Mundo Obrero* denounced the violent, forced collectivizations carried on by the CNT in the northeast, but acknowledged that legal agrarian reform must be greatly accelerated. The Giral ministry took timid steps in August to legalize the seizure of property "abandoned" by its owners and another measure provided for acquisition of legal title by long-term renters. When the Largo Caballero government was formed, the Communists saw to it that one of the three posts given them was the Ministry of Agriculture, which went to a central committeeman, Vicente Uribe. Since the August decree was intended only to provide ex post facto legalization of confiscations that had already occurred, Uribe issued a new decree on October 7 expropriating the lands of all those associated with the Nationalist movement, whatever their previous status. At the beginning of 1937 one of the top young Communist troubleshooters, Enrique Castro Delgado, was made head of the Institute of Agrarian Reform. By the spring of that year the Institute had officially ratified the transfer of ownership of approximately 25 percent of the arable land in the southeastern and south central provinces of Spain.

The work of the Institute was largely restricted to the main part of the leftist zone and had little effect in the northern and northeastern provinces, which were almost entirely autonomous during the first ten months of the Civil War. In the central and southeastern provinces, however, it followed a slowly progressive policy of expropriation which ultimately reached the following totals, according to an IAR report of August 8, 1938,[3] as shown at top of next page.

---

3. This report is included in the collection of papers by the IAR official, Miguel Vidal, entitled "El Campo español," Bolloten Collection. The totals are complete figures for all expropriations in these provinces since the passage of the original agrarian reform legislation in 1932.

An earlier announcement of the IAR in March 1938 declared that a total of 5,692,202 hectares had been attached or expropriated but this figure very possibly includes totals for the Catalan provinces as well, where the agrarian reform was rather less intense.

Province	Total land expropriated in hectares	Confiscated for political reasons	Expropriated for reasons of "social utility"	Occupied directly by peasants under provisional title
Albacete	481,256	450,000	28,256	3,000
Alicante	106,604	——	95,788	10,816
Almería	135,425	126,912	8,513	——
Badajoz	500,000	——	500,000	——
Ciudad Real	1,086,925	258,049	726,876	102,000
Córdoba	323,093	199,138	39,175	84,780
Cuenca	435,467	199,347	232,970	3,150
Granada	531,836	——	12,400	519,436
Guadalajara	84,522	18,073	58,649	7,800
Jaén	855,655	394,886	3,156	457,613
Madrid	185,866	7,716	165,705	12,445
Murcia	260,060	147,885	60,875	51,300
Toledo	289,362	233,224	56,138	——
Valencia	147,141	127,172	19,969	——
TOTALS	5,423,212	2,162,402	2,008,470	1,252,340

By mid-1938 the total confiscations amounted to slightly more than one-third of the arable land in the provinces affected. As a program of forced expropriation not regulated by representative govenment, the Spanish land confiscations ranked second only to the Stalinist collectivization effected a few years earlier in the Soviet Union. During the original Russian Revolution and Civil War of 1917–21 perhaps only 25 percent of the arable land in Russia changed hands. During the early 1920's land reforms of an equal or greater extent were carried out in some of the smaller east European countries, but each of those had been administered by a representative constitutional government chosen by fairly broad parliamentary suffrage.

The IAR refused to recognize many of the anarchosyndicalist collectives formed in northeastern Spain without any effort at legitimization. As of mid-1938, the number of agrarian collectives legally recognized by the IAR was only 2,213, identified in the table at the top of the next page.

The IAR report of August 8, 1938, qualified the condition of collectives in the provinces of Madrid, Toledo, and Valencia "good"; in Alicante, Almería, Badajoz, and Ciudad Real "difficult"; and generally "bad" in Córdoba, Cuenca, Albacete, Gra-

Province	Number of collectives	UGT	CNT	Mixed	Total extent in hectares	Number of families
Albacete	238	210	15	13	92,000	3,550
Alicante	37	23	8	6	22,800	2,270
Almería	37	18	4	15	29,237	2,099
Badajoz	23	17	—	6	350,000	2,650
Ciudad Real	181	112	45	24	1,002,615	33,200
Córdoba	148	—	—	148	141,000	8,602
Cuenca	102	37	5	60	135,179	4,820
Granada	33	—	—	33	45,000	20,000
Guadalajara	205	198	7	—	63,400	2,700
Jaén	760	—	—	760	685,000	33,000
Murcia	122	53	59	10	78,000	4,920
Madrid	76	56	15	5	59,500	5,411
Toledo	100	77	23	—	170,400	9,700
Valencia	151	22	103	26	54,844	21,900
TOTALS	2,213	823	284	1,106	2,928,975	156,822

nada, Guadalajara, and Murcia. Agrarian collectivization under wartime conditions in Spain was not very successful.

A total of more than 300,000 peasant farmers received land in one form or another:

Province	Average			Total hectareage owned by latter	Total hectareage received by latter	Resulting average size holdings of peasant recipients who already owned land
	Number of peasants receiving land	Number of hectares received by each	Number of recipients who already owned land			
Albacete	40,000	12	20,000	250,000	100,000	18
Alicante	15,374	7	1,500	3,500	5,800	6
Almería	8,940	15	852	13,500	1,500	16
Badajoz	3,540	140	500	15,000	70,000	125
Ciudad Real	44,827	24	unknown	unknown	unknown	24
Córdoba	12,097	16.5	1,300	2,000	21,450	18
Cuenca	23,665	19	20,000	230,000	140,000	19
Granada	35,000	20	unknown	unknown	unknown	20
Guadalajara	3,859	20	1,500	8,000	22,000	20
Jaén	45,000	20	4,000	6,000	75,000	21
Madrid	25,000	8	12,000	50,000	57,000	11
Murcia	16,275	16	984	1,000	15,500	16
Toledo	16,400	17	6,700	25,000	26,800	8
Valencia	26,800	6	18,000	65,000	43,200	6
	316,777	17	87,336	669,000	578,250	14

Though statistics are mostly unavailable for the northern provinces held by the Popular Front, economic changes were carried out on a broader scale in Catalonia, eastern Aragon, and Asturias than in the main zone. In Asturias control of nearly all mining and industrial operations was seized by syndical councils during the first days of the Civil War. There was considerable friction between the CNT and the UGT, the former pressing for direct collectivization. The CNT seems to have expanded its following almost exclusively among the working class, while professional personnel and lower-middle-class people seeking shelter gravitated toward the UGT.

The syndicates did not attempt full-scale collectivization and reorganization of Asturian mining and heavy industry under wartime conditions. After the first two months, the local factory councils were taken under the nominal supervision of the Labor Committee of the Provincial Junta. Lack of supplies and technical assistance reduced production, but there was a certain amount of reconversion to war matériel. Factories and mines functioned much as before, save that control and profits were in the hands of the councils. The structure of industry was scarcely altered, and formal ownership did not officially change hands.

The only major industry fully collectivized was the fishing industry of Gijón. By the autumn of 1936 nearly all the fishing operations off the Asturian coast had been organized under a CNT collective, with individual shares assigned by an industrial council. The fishing collective seems in practice to have functioned as a producers' and marketers' cooperative, since most of the fishermen previously had worked on an individual or family basis. It is significant that the only de jure collectivization was carried out in the most thoroughly lower-middle-class industry of the region.

One major drawback to revolutionary change was the sizable degree of foreign capital invested in Asturian industry. The Socialists were particularly aware of the diplomatic and military complications that might arise from confiscation of foreign properties amid full-scale civil war. Hence de jure collectivization never developed in the major Asturian industries.

The Spanish social and economic revolution of 1936 reached

its peak in Catalonia and eastern Aragon. The CNT militia columns hastily sent into eastern Aragon from industrial Catalonia in late July and early August did little fighting against the weak Nationalist forces in Aragon, but devoted themselves to establishing the revolution. The former Zaragoza Communist leader José Duque, probably not without bias, described the situation in Aragon during the first months of the war:

> Aragon was at the mercy of semi-military columns, composed for the most part of men who had spent their whole lives casting invective, not merely against militarism in general, but also against any principle of authority, discipline or organization. The columns were formed without any effort at control or selectivity, and two types of men predominated in them: the anarchist militant whose intentions were honorable but who was fanatical to the point of frenzy in his ideological convictions, which led him to commit mad political deeds; such men were consequently incapable of understanding the situation created in the country by the military rebellion and lacked the faintest idea of how to organize the struggle against a trained army. Drunk with enthusiasm after winning the street battles in Barcelona, they thought there was nothing more to fear and refused to concern themselves with military problems, intent only on correcting Kropotkin's blueprint. The second type consisted of the provocateurs, the adventurers found in all revolutionary disturbances, denizens of the Barcelona underworld who had left their dens on smelling booty, all the detritus of Barcelona, its most representative *lumpen*. The result of the collaboration of both these types was necessarily what Aragon came to represent in that period: the region where there existed neither restraint nor measure in committing any kind of crime or satisfying any sort of ambition.[4]

FAI spokesmen announced that rural Aragon had become the "Spanish Ukraine" and that they would not be defeated by Marxist militarism as had Nestor Makhno fifteen years earlier. The more responsible CNT leaders remained in Catalonia or helped organize columns for the assistance of Madrid, while the Catalanist leaders urged the recruitment of the most violent and irresponsible anarchists for Aragon. The result was a kind of inverse selection of some of the most extreme elements. Nor was the situation much improved by formation of a central anarchist Council of Aragon in September.

4. José Duque, "La situacion de Aragón al comienzo de la guerra" (Bolloten Collection.)

CNT spokesmen claimed that within six months 70 percent of the peasantry in eastern Aragon had been organized into some 450 collectives. This was probably an exaggeration. The leftist-occupied sector of Aragon comprised slightly more than half that region and had a population of nearly 450,000. "Seventy per cent of the peasantry" in that area would have amounted to at least a quarter million people, whereas the first regional agrarian congress of the CNT held at Caspe in February 1937 only claimed to represent 275 collectives with approximately 140,000 members. This is a much more credible figure and, even at that, the agrarian revolution went farther in eastern Aragon than anywhere else in Spain. Though Aragon was not a latifundist region, it does seem that many of the poorer peasants welcomed the anarchist columns, and resentment only became widespread after several months of terrorism. Even then, a sizable minority of the Aragonese peasants apparently remained loyal to the anarchist-inspired collectives.

Nearly all the agrarian collectives in Aragon were imposed with a greater or lesser degree of force, but there was no attempt to establish unifomity in their structure or operation. Conditions varied greatly from village to village. Some functioned like co-operatives rather than true collectives, some paid regular wages to their members, some used ordinary money, others fashioned their own legal tender, and some tried to avoid money altogether by distributing all their products directly or allocating consumption certificates. In general, there appears to have been comparatively little pressure against smallholders—and sometimes little against medium holders—who were willing to join co-operatives. In the most dry or barren districts, where conditions made collective cultivation difficult, private holders were sometimes left completely alone. But others who resisted were shot outright.

In Catalonia there was less change in the agrarian structure than in eastern Aragon or several other regions, but in Catalan industrial centers the Spanish revolution of 1936–37 found its fullest expression. This was due primarily to four factors: the long preparation of a mass revolutionary movement represented primarily though not exclusively by the CNT; the autonomous status of Catalonia under the nominal Republican regime; the fact that Catalonia was untouched by direct military pressures during the first half of the war; and the willingness of the influential left Republican minority, which held the reins of legitimate authority, to collaborate with a process of social and economic revolution. During the first few weeks of the conflict most of the industrial establishments in Catalonia were taken over either directly or indirectly by the workers. Borkenau estimated that whereas 30 percent of the establishments in the Madrid area were *intervenidos,* or brought under worker control, 70 percent of the factories in Barcelona and 50 percent of those in the Valencia region were seized outright by the trade unions or revolutionary committees. The Barcelona bourgeoisie disappeared almost overnight as an economic class and many of its members were liquidated physically as well. According to an undated report of the CNT's Sindicato Unico of textile workers:

Of the total number of bourgeois owners [of textile plants in Catalonia] who used to operate some 20,000 units, . . . 10 percent have remained in their factories as simple workers as a result of collectivization, about 40 percent have been eliminated from the social sphere [presumably murdered or imprisoned], and about 50 percent are in hiding or have fled abroad.[5]

The quasi-official acceptance of revolutionary dualism by a CNT regional plenum on July 22 meant that for the time being no effort would be made to go beyond de facto worker control to carry out a full program of libertarian communism. Companys, for his part, responded with pragmatic acceptance of existing conditions. Though he later described the situation as "a revolution with all the psychological characteristics of revolutions: collective neurosis, excess, imprecise desires, mysticism, cruelty, panic and so forth," [6] Companys accepted some of the economic changes completely and was willing to bargain concerning others. As the leader of most of the Catalan lower middle class, he felt that the government could ratify sweeping adjustments in favor of the lower classes against the upper bour-

5. Quoted in Agustín Souchy and Paul Folgare, *Colectivizaciones* (Barcelona, 1937), 59.
6. In an essay of May 1937 that was suppressed by the censor. (Bolloten Collection.)

geoisie, so long as the main interests of small property holders were preserved. Syndical control of most of the Catalan economy was thus legally exercised through the control and supply sections of the Anti-Fascist Militia Committee, which served for two months as de facto regional government. Most industrial establishments appear to have gotten back to work, at least to some extent, by the eighth or ninth day of the conflict (July 27–28), yet conditions remained highly disturbed. Lines of authority were uncertain, supply and distribution disrupted, many workers absent serving in the militia, and those on the job finding it difficult to settle down and work the same as before.

The Generalitat tried to help regularize the situation by recognizing an official Worker Control Committee for each factory, and on August 6 decreed that it would name a delegate to sit on each committee and assist in management. The delegates named were usually workers from the factories involved and did little to protect legal government interests, but the very fact of their acceptance by the control committees constituted nominal recognition of the continuing dualism and maintained a vestige of the Generalitat's authority. A later decree of August 21 went considerably further by declaring that elections to the control committee in each establishment would be supervised by the Generalitat. This, however, seems largely to have been a dead letter.

One significant sphere in which the Generalitat was generally successful was the protection of foreign property interests. Even the CNT leaders were impressed by arguments concerning the damage that might be done the leftist cause abroad by hasty confiscation of foreign capital. An accord was soon worked out with the British consulate in Barcelona protecting 87 British-owned plants in that area.

Specific decrees regulating working and social conditions were also promulgated. To meet the demands of the CNT and the latter's chief revolutionary competitor, the POUM,[7] the

7. On July 24, 1936, the central committee of the POUM announced a new minimal program:
   1) Thirty-six-hour work week.
   2) Ten percent salary increase for all earning less than 500 pesetas per month [practically the entire labor force].

Generalitat declared a general 10 percent wage increase and reduced the normal working day to 7 hours. Apartment rents were also lowered by decree.

The Generalitat made few efforts of its own to requisition *(incautar)* industrial facilities, in part because there was little that had not been taken over by the syndicates. It did, however, take measures to supervise or control *(intervenir)* key establishments related to war production and various factories that became the object of intersyndical rivalry or whose direction was too difficult for the syndicates. Nearly all these direct *intervenciones* were made at the request of the factory committees themselves, and reached a total of 435 factories controlled by the government as of October 1936. Of these, 360 were located in Barcelona and the remainder in the smaller industrial towns.

The Generalitat also created on August 7 a War Industries Commission composed of members of the several ministries and committees connected with war production. By mid-September the Commission had taken control of 24 factories in the greater Barcelona area. By the autumn of 1937 it supervised 500 factories and more than 50,000 workers.

Yet the Generalitat had almost no control over the Catalan border with France or shipping facilities, which were dominated by the CNT for most of the first year of the Civil War. The CNT set up dozens of export cooperatives and agencies, mainly for the sale of raw materials from CNT-dominated producers in Catalonia and the Levant. The foreign credit accruing from exports was, however, entirely insufficient to provide imports needed for Catalan industry.

---

3) Twenty-five percent rent reduction.
4) Back pay for days on strike.
5) Full unemployment compensation.
6) Control of production by shop committees.
7) Division of large land holdings, and abolition of farm rent and sharecropping.
8) Revision of the Catalan statute to permit sweeping social progress.
9) Immediate purge of the police and military, with officers henceforth to be elected by the rank and file.
10) Maintenance of workers' militia.
11) Summary prosecution of all leaders of the rebellion.

G. Munis, *Jalones de derrota* (Mexico City, 1947), 254.

Neither the CNT nor the POUM was willing to renounce further changes until the military struggle was over. The initial transformation under revolutionary dualism was regarded as merely the first step in a continuous process which was to lead to libertarian communism according to the anarchosyndicalists, and to the dictatorship of the proletariat according to the POUM-ists. Andrés Nin of the POUM wrote that what happened in Spain constituted "a proletarian revolution more profound than the Russian revolution itself," [8] arguing that the relative speed with which production resumed after the explosion of July 19–21 revealed the strength and maturity of the Catalan proletariat. Revolutionary dualism did not mean an equal partnership, for the workers were already predominant. At the beginning of August, Nin insisted that

> The government does not exist. We are collaborating with them, but they can do no more than sanction whatever is done by the masses. Our present tactics are to fortify our position by successive advances such as the seizure of utilities, industries, and land, obtaining higher wages, shorter hours, and so on.[9]

Some of the anarchists were eager to press on toward complete collectivization of industry. They denied that this would hamper the war effort, on the grounds that a collectivist economy led by the syndicates would be more productive in any event. On August 27 the CNT bulletin exhorted,

> All workers of all industries should proceed immediately to take over enterprizes and collectivize them. This should be done as quickly as possible; then they should at once name a workers' council which will manage the industry with the advice of those technical experts that may be needed.

Whereas the anarchists seemed willing to ignore the political issue while pressing for economic revolution, the POUM insisted that the two should go together. In a speech at Barcelona on September 7, Nin declared that "in Catalonia we can say that the dictatorship of the proletariat already exists" [10] because of the de facto rule of the revolutionary committees. He launched

8. *Les problèmes de la révolution espagnole* (Paris, 1939), in Pierre Broué and Emile Témime, *La Révolution et la guerre d'Espagne* (Paris, 1961), 131.
9. *The Times*, Aug. 3, 1936.
10. *La Batalla* (Barcelona), Sept. 8, 1936.

the slogan "Down with the bourgeois ministers," demanding an end to dualism by transferring all power to the representatives of the revolutionary groups.

The most radical element of all was the POUM youth movement (Iberian Communist Youth—JCI) with headquarters in Barcelona and Lérida, and small offshoots in Madrid and Asturias. The JCI central committee called for the formation of special "Spanish Soviets" composed of all the revolutionary parties to complete the process in a fashion similar to what these naïve hotheads thought had occurred in Russia. That was too much even for the POUM leaders, who argued this was unnecessary because of the much greater degree of organizational strength of the Spanish worker groups compared with those of Russia in 1917. All that was needed in Spain was to put full power in the hands of representatives of the existing revolutionary organizations.

A meeting of CNT national representatives in mid-September endorsed a proposal for revolutionary political reorganization that came close to the POUM position. Instead of a Popular Front government of all leftist parties, it proposed that the "anti-fascist" struggle be led by a National Defense Council representing all the syndical and leftist organizations (the suggested composition was 5 seats for the CNT, 5 for the Marxist groups, and 4 for the Republican left). This would eliminate the vestiges of the "bourgeois Republic" yet still permit collaboration with the middle-class left, since "the fight against fascism is above anything else." [11] The National Defense Council would give up the Popular Front government's pretense of maintaining the old administrative system and would officially recognize regional and local autonomy. Creation of national workers' militia would replace efforts to form a new hierarchically structured Republican Army. The popular tribunals that had been authorized in the month preceding would completely supersede remaining vestiges of the old court system. The Bank of Spain, all properties of the Church, and major industry would be immediately expropriated. The economy would be controlled by the syndicates, coordinated by federated industrial and national

11. José Peirats, *La C.N.T. en la revolución española* (Toulouse, 1951), I, 215.

economic councils. The revolutionary leadership of Spain was then to call an "International Conference of Anti-fascists" to encourage political and economic cooperation between Spain and other countries with leftist or progressive liberal governments.

All Popular Front parties save the POUM were opposed to this proposal, and the CNT was not united behind it. The surge of CNT membership, together with the vast increase in the movement's social and economic power, was transforming anarchosyndicalist attitudes. In Catalonia there had developed a new kind of mass property-owning (or at least property-controlling) syndicalism operating in dualistic collaboration with the regional government. The revolutionary committees could not entirely dispense with this collaboration no matter what the extreme left desired. The Catalan revolutionary committees and syndical councils lacked financial resources; only the Generalitat had the legitimacy and the connections to help finance the syndically controlled economy. At the end of August it had seized the resources of the Bank of Spain in Catalonia to provide credit for the regional economy after the Madrid government had refused its requests.

Companys' goal was to use the proprietary instincts of the new syndicalism and the recognized need for cooperation behind the military effort to bring all the revolutionary organizations into the regular Catalan government. By the end of August the Central Committee of Anti-Fascist Militia agreed to function under the nominal authority of the Generalitat's Defense Councillor, while the services of its various economic subcommittees were being increasingly synchronized, as far as nominal authority was conerned, with the respective administrative sectors of the Generalitat. It was not far from this synchronization of dualism to the unification of the process under complete coalition government. That step was taken on September 24 by a congress of 500 delegates of the CNT Regional Federation of Catalonia. The long debate in the anarchosyndicalist movement between politicism and apoliticism was for the first time clearly resolved in favor of the former. For the sake of antifascist war and syndicalist revolution, the congress voted to participate in the Generalitat cabinet. Two days later Companys formed under his own leadership a new ministry in which the Esquerra retained the posts of Finance, Culture, and Security. The FAI-CNT took those of Defense, Economics, Supply, and Public Health. The Rabassaires retained that of Agriculture and a councillor without portfolio was named to represent Acció Catalana. The Stalinist PSUC was given Public Works and Labor, and the POUM's Andrés Nin became Councillor of Justice. This ended revolutionary dualism on the top political level and brought dissolution of the Central Anti-fascist Committee, though many of the local committees continued for some time.

Two days later a new national conference of the CNT assembled in a worried atmosphere. The largest sector of the Confederation had plunged into official collaboration, and all the replies from other organizations to the proposal of September 17 had been negative. The alternatives to full-scale collaboration with the Popular Front regime were disappearing, and unless an almost impossible change occurred in the Civil War, it seemed only a matter of time before the CNT would come to terms with the Largo Caballero government.

In the autumn of 1936 the CNT was coparticipant in a struggle that did not conform to the revolutionary conditions postulated by anarchosyndicalist doctrine. The CNT had not become the movement of the majority of Spanish workers, but only of their largest single minority sector. It was in no position to dominate the economy unilaterally but had to cooperate with other institutions to sustain its own economic interests. The need for credit, raw materials, and technical assistance for its own expropriated industries propelled it toward complete collaboration. Property-owning syndicates assumed a more moderate, proprietary role than anarchist purists demanded, and were less inclined to endanger their interests by insisting on doctrinaire positions. The consolidation of any sort of revolution depended upon military victory, and no matter how much governmental participation contradicted revolutionary apoliticism, there was general consensus that political participation to protect the CNT's goals and interests was more prudent than military collaboration without any voice in the executive. Apparently the CNT leaders originally bargained for six cabinet seats in Largo

Caballero's government on the grounds that their movement had the largest following in the leftist zone. When the anarchosyndicalists finally entered Largo Caballero's Popular Front government in November 1936, their representation was limited to two regular ministries—Justice and Health—and the division of a third—Commerce—into two separate portfolios for Commerce and Industry.[12]

The most immediate task of the new coalition government in Catalonia was to regularize the revolution. Juan Fàbregas, the CNT economist and writer who was the Generalitat's new Councillor of Economics, set about to legalize the collectivization of industry. The way was paved by a UGT-CNT pact signed on October 22, which agreed to respect the decisions of the new Generalitat ministry and accepted government direction of war industry. The pact stipulated collectivization of large industry, municipalization of major housing units and of large and medium landholdings, and unified syndical supervision of economic production.

The Generalitat's Collectivization Decree of October 24 declared immediate collectivization of all industrial concerns that were either owned by adherents of the insurgent Nationalists or employed 100 workers or more. Plants employing between 50 and 100 workers might be collectivized if this were requested by three-quarters of the employees of any given enterprise. Smaller factories could be collectivized only with the owners' consent. Only the owners of small properties and foreign investors would be indemnified. Each collectivized plant was to be directed by a council chosen by the workers and renewed every two years. The Generalitat would have a representative on each council and reserved the right to ratify the appointment of council chairmen in the larger collectives. Completely foreign-owned firms were handled differently under separate councils supervised by

12. García Venero has conjectured that yet another reason motivating the CNT's entry into the national government was the fear that the leftist forces were on the verge of decisive defeat in central Spain and that, if this occurred, the CNT would be in a strong position with a voice in the government and an unweakened popular base in the east to negotiate an end to the struggle favorable to syndicalist interests. But there is no concrete evidence to support this hypothesis.

the government. The individual collectives would be coordinated by "General Councils of Industry" for eight different categories of industrial production, plus two more for commerce and finance. Worker control committees would legally supervise production in small noncollectivized concerns, and the Industrial Councils were authorized to form "industrial concentrations" (agrupaments industrials) synchronizing private and collectivized plants when necessary to harmonize production. This law made it possible to set up a hundred or so concentrations during the next year in which small private producers were squeezed out.[13] The Collectivization Decree was intended to lay the groundwork for a mixed but largely collectivist economy in which production would be controlled by the syndicates, and distribution and consumption would be channeled through cooperatives.

The syndicates had already taken some measures to rationalize specific sectors of the economy, eliminating inefficient small shops and middlemen in certain areas of commerce, in baking, in some kinds of artisan products, and even in sectors of the textile and metallurgical industry. This rationalization was partially planned, but for the most part seems to have been a by-product of the elimination of the middle classes and benefited only a small sector of the economy. There was also at least some opinion in the anarchosyndicalist movement that recognized the crucial importance of technological modernization, though very little could be done under wartime conditions.

Other changes by the Generalitat in the autumn of 1936 redistricted and reorganized local government, granting broad autonomy for local affairs and dividing municipal representation on the approximate ratio of 3:3:2 for the CNT, the middle-class left, and the Communists, with a lesser proportion for the POUM.

13. In his study of the wartime Catalan economy, Josep Ma. Bricall has identified the following number of agrupaments by sector, not counting others which were not properly legitimized:
Construction, 48 (one of which accounted for 30,000 workers)
Food and Agriculture, 19
Textiles, 8
Metallurgy, 7
Chemicals, 7
Transport, 3
Graphic Arts, 2

The building industry, most of housing, public utilities, and local communications facilities were municipalized. Plans were drawn for a broad increase in local educational facilities; during the next two years public school attendance in some towns was reported to have increased by as much as 60 percent, but this figure does not take into account the total destruction of Catholic education.

The economic decrees of October 1936 did not actually inaugurate changes so much as they legitimized existing ones. The syndically controlled industrial economy continued to function much as before, save that wartime difficulties presented an increasingly grave handicap to production. The greater degree of order and harmony that the new legislation sought was only partially attained. Fàbregas had to organize new commissariats within the Generalitat's Council of Economy to replace the revolutionary committees and, as he later admitted, the Junta of Syndical Economic Control that he appointed to regulate the worker control committees was never able to exercise its authority effectively.

Fàbregas wrote in the spring of 1937:

It must be recognized that the state of tension and overexcitement that the outbreak of the struggle produced in the feelings of the people seriously depleted the working capacity of all our industrial centers. These psychological effects, combined with the legal reorganization, have since July 19 reduced to a dangerous degree the capacity and productivity of labor, increasing the costs of production so much that if this is not corrected rapidly and energetically we will be facing a dead-end street. For these reasons we must readjust the established work norms and increase the length of the working day.[14]

In another memoir he was more specific, emphasizing that

Certain groups of workers have ignored the letter and spirit of the collectivization decree, carrying out collectivizations without any economic or scientific basis. . . .

The lack of social spirit among certain sectors of the workers has resulted in a pronounced utilitarian, egocentric zeal, so that some collectives have been considered the exclusive property of their members rather than something held in usufruct. . . .

Contrary to the terms of the decree, nearly all the collectivized

14. *Els factors econòmics de la revolució* (Barcelona, 1937), 38.

enterprises have taken charge of the assets only, being unwilling to take responsibility for liabilities, which has produced an imbalance in financing the enterprises. . . .

The state of tension and overexcitement engendered by the subversion has become chronic. This has produced a situation of social indiscipline, resulting in a lamentable decline of productive capacity and labor output. . . .

The reigning social indiscipline means that everyone does whatever he pleases, ignoring the guidelines and decisions of the Council and the Junta, capriciously interpreting the collectivization decree and violating both its letter and spirit, making it difficult for these organizations to direct the new social and economic life of Catalonia.[15]

Fàbregas underlined the failure to develop General Councils of Industry to supervise each branch of collectives, as well as the lack of a general credit office to regulate the distribution of profits. He also pointed out the inevitably deleterious consequences for production of losing the bulk of the national market under conditions of civil war.

Evidence of difficulties in the syndically controlled economy soon came in abundance. The Republican government's Minister of Industry reported that by January 1937 he had received petitions asking for state intervention in no less than 11,000 enterprises in various parts of the leftist zone that were in need of economic assistance.[16] Horacio Prieto has written that the syndicates and collectives were concentrating on their individual affairs rather than cooperating with each other or with the regulatory agencies. "We would not be telling the truth if we said that in the majority of cases they were guided by morality and competence." [17] The lack of cooperation was noted by CNT committees and leaders on both the provincial and national levels. A CNT commission in Barcelona reported in July 1937 that

Reckless concern to collectivize everything, especially the enterprizes that hold monetary reserves, has revealed a utilitarian and petit-bourgeois sprit in the masses. . . . While considering each collective as private property, and not as mere usufruct, the interests of other

15. *Vuitanta dies en el govern de la Generalitat* (Barcelona, 1937), 84–85.
16. Juan Peiró, *De la fábrica de vidrio de Mataró al Ministerio de Industria* (Valencia, 1937).
17. *El anarquismo español en la lucha política*, 8.

collectives have been ignored. . . . Collectivized enterprizes have worried only about their own liabilities, producing an imbalance in the finances of other enterprizes.[18]

The POUM's *La Batalla* called this "syndical capitalism."

New financial arrangements for workers in Catalonia revealed great concern for security, a need deeply felt in a society that had provided almost nothing in the way of insurance and pensions for the lower classes. Broad new arrangements were worked out for illness and accident insurance, family allowances, and pensions. Basic wage increases in Catalan industry during the second half of 1936 went considerably beyond the 10 percent authorized by the regional government, and probably came closer to 30 to 35 percent, though at least half the increased purchasing power was eliminated by inflation. There was apparently less interest in trying to establish an adjusted general family wage instead of individual salaries among the industrial syndicates than among the agrarian collectives in Aragon. Moreover, even in syndically controlled industry the wages of female workers continued to lag distinctly behind those of men in comparable jobs.

It should be pointed out that the failure to achieve greater cooperation and coordination among collectives and syndically controlled enterprises was not due merely to the "utilitarian," "petit-bourgeois" spirit that CNT and POUM purists complained of. Wartime economic pressures and lack of technical skills also hindered cooperation. Another factor of some importance was the old anarchist belief in full autonomy. Workers in some Catalan enterprises had little to say to foreign correspondents about higher wages or better housing. They seemed more interested in personal equality and dignity and in achieving subgroup autonomy for their round of activities in place of the automatic pressures and drive for broad integration of a fully organized industrial society.

Wartime shortages, the loss of markets, and lack of raw materials, together with the disruptive effect of the collectivizations and worker control, made it impossible for Catalan industry

18. Quoted by Juan Andrade, "L'Intervention des syndicats dans la révolution espagnole," *Confrontation Internationale* (Sept.-Oct. 1949), 43–48, in Broué and Témime, *La Révolutión et la guerre d'Espagne* (Paris, 1961), 145.

TABLE 11.1 *Catalan Industrial Production, 1936–38*

	1936	1937	1938
January	100	70	60
February	98	58	60
March	97	66	60
April	94	69	41
May	95	65	30
June	98	68	32
July	82	71	37
August	64	68	31
September	73	66	33
October	69	60	
November	63	53	
December	69	58	

SOURCE: Unpublished dissertation by Josep Ma. Bricall on the wartime Catalan economy and the Generalitat (University of Barcelona, 1968).

to regain prewar levels of output. Production declined steadily. A downturn in November 1936 reflected the exhaustion of prewar stocks of materials, and there was an even more severe slump in February 1937, at the time of the first major effort to convert to large-scale military production. In 1938, as the fighting moved directly into Catalonia, the decline was very steep.

The severe wartime and revolutionary economic maladjustment made it impossible not merely to reduce unemployment but to keep it from rising. There is no way to render the statistics in Table 2 in terms of exact percentages of the total Catalan

TABLE 11.2. *Unemployment in Catalonia, 1936–37*

	1936	1937
January	55,288	91,416
February	58,925	79,641
March	54,386	79,565
April	68,497	79,802
May	75,259	84,685
June	72,782	79,404
July	60,219	76,115
August	55,630	81,048
September	51,547	80,701
October	58,577	79,771
November	80,231	77,107
December	86,905	

SOURCE: Bricall.

labor force. Before the war, the latter numbered approximately 600,000, but it is impossible to determine whether the large number of wartime refugees provided enough potential workers to compensate for those in military service. It might roughly be hypothesized that the wartime unemployment rate ranged from 10 to 15 percent, with higher proportions in certain industries such as textiles, construction, and shipping. There is no way to measure the degree of underemployment, but it was apparently also considerable.

Prices in Barcelona increased greatly, as indicated in Table 3. This was only partly due to wage increases. Lowered production, shortage of credit, and the addition of 700,000 refugees to the Catalan population by the spring of 1937 all added to the pressure. Banks and financial institutions were operated under the supervision of the Generalitat and in the desperate search for credit most safety-deposit boxes were forced open. Yet private financial resources as such were not confiscated, and most banks continued to earn money on their capital. The Generalitat resorted to large-scale regional credit emissions, adding further to the inflation, and even issued its own regional money, though this was not well received by most of the populace.

The problem of agricultural ownership and production in Catalonia was handled on much more conservative terms than

TABLE 11.3. *General Index of Wholesale Prices in Barcelona, 1936–38 (1913 = 100)*

	1936	1937	1938
January	168.8	223.7	434.4
February	168.2	244.4	457.7
March	167.2	266.5	524.5
April	169.1	294.3	530.1
May	170.6	297.6	547.9
June	171.9	303.7	551.6
July	174.7	315.8	554.2
August	178.9	322.7	554.2
September	183.1	342.7	556.9
October	194.4	358.8	562.3
November	202.9	375.4	564.4
December	209.6	389.1	564.7

SOURCE: Bricall.

was that of industry. The CNT's great strength lay in the industrial areas, whereas the lower-middle-class peasantry was an important source of support for the Catalanist left. The moderate position of the Esquerra and the Unió de Rabassaires was also supported by the PSUC and the Catalan UGT to avoid alienating the Catalan peasantry in the manner that the anarchists had antagonized much of the Aragonese. A Generalitat decree of August 6 repromulgated the Rabassaire legislation of 1934. This measure did not actually go so far as a decree at approximately the same time by the shortlived Giral government in Madrid that gave renters and sharecroppers in other parts of Republican territory the opportunity to buy any land that they had farmed successively for six years. A second Catalan decree of mid-August placed a moratorium on all mortgages and reduced the maximum legal interest rate to 4 percent. Collectivization regulations as subsequently extended to agriculture permitted expropriation only of land that the families of owners were unable to work. Given the relatively scant CNT membership in the countryside, there was little pressure for the formation of collective units. The ideal of politically left-wing renters and sharecroppers in Catalonia, as in Andalusia, was the family farm, no matter what the more radical leaders of the Unió de Rabassaires might say. This desire was in part satisfied by a Generalitat decree of January 5, 1937, that granted formal legal usufruct of all land to those who had cultivated it as of July 18, 1936. The Republican decree of October 1936 that confiscated the lands of Nationalist supporters was not officially extended to Catalonia until July 14, 1937. Nearly all the changes effected by these measures reinforced the tendency toward individual family-size cultivation units. According to the official bulletin of the Generalitat, only 55 legally recognized agrarian collectives were formed in Catalonia during 1936, 24 of them by the CNT.[19]

Approximately 80 percent of the peasant cultivators of Catalonia were already members of peasant syndicates of one persuasion or another before the Civil War began. The politically moderate syndicates of small and medium holders were not

19. The political affiliation of the others was:
    Rabassaires 5, FESAC 5, UGT 1, "Municipal" 1, Mixed 19.

recognized by the revolutionary forces, however, and at the end of August the Generalitat promulgated a decree requiring obligatory organization of all the Catalan peasantry in an official Catalan peasants' union (FESAC). This could not be set up under revolutionary dualism and was not fully organized until mid-1937 or later, but it eventually made possible a degree of control over the peasantry and regulation of agrarian production, prices, and financial assistance. The FESAC was controlled by the Rabassaire leadership and was strongly supported by the PSUC. It helped keep the great majority of the peasantry beyond CNT influence. By and large, the peasantry remained a stable, moderate force throughout the revolution and civil war in Catalonia, maintaining a reasonably high rate of food production—in contrast to the industrial decline. Efforts of the FESAC to regulate food prices enjoyed no more than moderate success, however, for as scarcity grew worse peasants tended to hold back part of their crops and push prices higher.

Commentators on the Popular Front zone have frequently remarked that despite revolutionary changes in political and economic affairs there was no drastic upheaval in social mores and behavior even among the leftist working classes. This observation seems to be broadly accurate, with the possible exception of the Catalan towns and certain other urban centers where the social revolution was most profound, at least during 1936–37. Changes were immediately noticeable in dress, where elimination of formal wear, including the use of neckties, was for several months more severe and thoroughgoing than in the Soviet Union. Until the winter of 1937 even more functional apparel, such as military uniforms, was frowned upon. In Barcelona and other centers there was also a relaxation of sexual mores, but the unrestrained libertinism of the Russian Revolution was not seen in Spain. The coalition revolutionary government of the Generalitat went further than any other executive in the leftist zone in the liberalization of marriage and divorce laws. Very liberal facilities for legal abortion were also arranged in Barcelona and some of the larger Catalan towns.

One of the major revolutionary changes that the extreme left wanted to effect was in justice and the penal system. Their ministers—Nin in Catalonia and García Oliver in the central government—held the official ministries of justice, and on January 25, 1937, a total amnesty was promulgated for all crimes committed prior to the beginning of the revolution. This primarily affected inmates in the Basque territory, for elsewhere most prewar criminals had been informally released, but for the first time the amnesty was made official. Four months later the system of people's courts was extended to cover common as well as political crimes. The norm of justice was explained by Nin as the power of "members of the jury to decide exclusively according to their revolutionary consciences." [20] García Oliver explained in Valencia on January 31, 1937:

Justice must be warm, must be living; it cannot be shut up within the boundaries of a profession. We do not necessarily scorn books and formal procedures but we know for a certainty that there were too many lawyers.

Justice ought not to doubt whether or not it is in the right; it should possess an inflexibility superior to circumstances. Justice should be more than popular; it should be primitive.

. . . Justice is so subtle that all that is needed to interpret it is one's heart.[21]

20. H. E. Kaminski, *Ceux de Barcelone* (Paris, 1937), 137.
21. Juan de Castilla, *La Justicia revolucionaria en España* (Buenos Aires, 1937), 13–14.

TWELVE *International Response*

S AVE FOR ITS COLONIAL INVOLVEMENT in Morocco, Spain was
inactive in foreign affairs during the early twentieth century.
Though the country's geographical location gave it a certain
strategic importance, Spain had avoided entanglement in the
prelude, development, and aftermath of the First World War.
The Primo de Rivera regime was no more—and almost less—
ambitious than the constitutional monarchy, but it did take one
new initiative, signing a ten-year treaty of friendship with Fascist
Italy in 1926. The Spanish dictator felt a common interest with
his Italian counterpart, and the 1926 treaty carried a secret
clause promising Italy a military base in the Balearics in the
event that country should be involved in war with France.

Both the Socialist party and the CNT had always been
strongly internationalist and anti-imperialist, and, with the Republican left, had led opposition to establishment of the small
Spanish Protectorate in northern Morocco. When the Republican
regime came to power, it renounced any ambitions in foreign
policy other than maintenance of the status quo and firm support
for the League of Nations. During their five years of rule, the
Republican leaders, both left and right, eschewed any sort of
diplomatic initiative or individual understandings with other
countries. The Republic retreated into virtual isolation and
could scarcely be said to have had a clearly articulated foreign

policy, for its support of the status quo and the League was not accompanied by any assessment of the forces in international affairs or a practical calculation of Spain's potential relationship to the great powers. The treaty with Italy was not denounced but simply ignored; most Republican leaders seemed ignorant of its secret clause. At the time of a visit by the French foreign minister to Madrid in 1932 there was speculation about some form of defensive alliance between the two democratic republics, but Azaña showed no interest in any sort of diplomatic understanding with France. Moreover, when Azaña returned to power in 1936, his superior "realism," in reality a serious lack of foresight, cancelled plans of the last regular cabinet of 1935 to support sanctions against the Italian aggression in Ethiopia.

Among other powers there had been scant reaction either to the establishment of the Republic or its subsequent turmoils. Mussolini was, of course, opposed to the Republic from the start because its political structure and goals ran counter to those of Fascist Italy and because the rapid growth of militant leftism might create a "Red menace" in the west Mediterranean. Republican Spain also offered asylum for a number of antifascist exiles. Conversely, Spanish monarchist conspirators negotiated with the Italian regime between 1932 and 1934 for assistance in their efforts to overthrow the Republic in favor of a vaguely defined monarchist corporative state. Between 1934 and 1936 a few small detachments of Carlist volunteers were provided with training facilities in Italian territory. Yet there is no evidence of any sort of active Italian intervention within Spain prior to the beginning of the Civil War. Mussolini had little faith in the ability of the Spanish right to overthrow the existing regime, and is even said to have put out discreet feelers concerning the possibility of a Republican renewal of the Primo de Rivera treaty when it expired in 1936. If such efforts were indeed made, they were completely ignored in Madrid.

The neighboring corporative and authoritarian Portuguese Republic of Dr. Salazar was also hostile, but was acutely aware of its weak position as much the smaller Iberian power. It was more afraid of leftist intervention in Portugal than it was ambitious to assist efforts to overthrow the Republic in Spain and consequently followed a very correct policy. Spanish rightist conspirators were allowed to operate on Portuguese soil, but no assistance was offered and their activities were restricted. Conversely, elements of the Spanish left helped opponents of the Portuguese regime plotting in Spain in 1932, though these initiatives were ultimately quashed by the Spanish government itself. During the 1930's the lack of interest felt by most Spaniards for affairs in Portugal was overwhelming.

The only power that actively intervened in political machinations within Spain prior to 1936 was the Soviet Union, through the worldwide Comintern network of revolutionary subversion. It is now understood that by the 1930's Stalin had little faith in the possibility of provoking armed revolution in western countries, and referred to the Comintern as a *lavochka* (gyp joint). Yet this has sometimes been overemphasized; under Stalin the Comintern never renounced revolutionary subversion, and only began to de-emphasize it to some degree after adopting the Popular Front tactic in 1935. As has been seen, Comintern activity in Spain increased after the Asturian insurrection, for Spain seemed to be one of the few countries in which a sizable expansion of Communist influence was possible at relatively small cost.

Nevertheless, the Russian government was probably also taken by surprise when the Civil War and revolution suddenly broke out in full fury. Its initial response was limited. A Politburo meeting was held on July 21, but Stalin apparently decided to wait and see how the situation developed before becoming involved in any major way. There is some evidence that a handful of Red Air Force planes and their pilots were shipped out of Odessa on July 23,[1] apparently arriving in eastern Spain around the first of August, but nothing more was done directly during the first 40 days of the war. A Comintern meeting in Prague on July 26 decided to raise an international Communist volunteer force to fight for the leftist cause—the beginning of the famous "International Brigades"—but to what extent they would receive

1. According to the memoirs of one of the flyers, Achmed Amba, *I Was Stalin's Bodyguard* (London, 1952), 27–28. Cf. Clara Campoamor: "In August it was announced that a quantity of Russian planes had been brought to Madrid." *La Révolution espagnole vue par una républicaine* (Paris, 1937), 174. This is also mentioned by Col. José Gomá, *La Guerra en el aire* (Barcelona, 1958), 63–64.

direct Russian military assistance was not decided. Meanwhile, similar decisions to send limited detachments of planes, plus a shipment of ammunition, to the opposing Nationalist forces were made by Hitler on July 26 and by Mussolini on July 27. Spanish Nationalist representatives emphasized to German and Italian officials the danger of leftist revolution in Spain, an argument well attuned to fascist and Nazi ideology and one taken particularly seriously by Mussolini. Equally or more important, however, was the opportunity for both central European dictators to extend their influence into southwestern Europe, turning France's flank. This aid enabled the Nationalists to move their best units from Morocco and gave them a real chance for victory, but aside from these first shipments neither Hitler nor Mussolini originally had any intention of making a major commitment of men and matériel. During August 1936, Hitler refused further requests for assistance to the Nationalists until it could be seen how significant were their chances for victory. This paralleled the attitude of Stalin vis-à-vis the Spanish left.

The Giral government made its first direct request for arms to France, not merely because of the latter's geographical proximity and the presence in office of a recently elected French Popular Front regime (needless to say, more moderate and more broadly based than its Spanish counterpart), but also because under the arms contracts that Azaña had negotiated several years earlier French factories were to be the official suppliers of certain categories of weapons to the Spanish armed forces. The French response was positive, though it is not clear how soon French planes actually began to arrive in the Republican zone. Whereas Nationalist historians have claimed that the first French warplanes landed on July 25, the only direct documentary study indicates that they did not cross the Pyrenees until approximately August 4. A total of 38 French warplanes had been sent by August 9, and 56 more followed between that date and October 14.[2] They were

2. According to data in the archives of the French border prefects cited in D. W. Pike, *Conjecture, Propaganda, and Deceit and the Spanish Civil War* (Stanford, Calif., 1968), 44–46, 48, 233.

Nationalist historians, such as Gomá, 142, and Col. Juan Priego López, "La Intervención Extranjera," *Ejército*, no. 195 (Apr. 1956), I, 3–10, give different dates and figures. They refer to captured documents of the People's Army but fail to cite specific sources.

accompanied by a rather ineffective private group of mercenary aviators led by the esthete André Malraux.[3]

As is well known, the initial French policy of assistance to the Republican leftist coalition soon gave way to a position of nominal nonintervention of any kind. The first French proposal to this effect was made on July 25 before either Germany or Italy had lent assistance to the rebels, and was designed to avoid the possibility of any subsequent confrontation between the Great Powers that might arise should the western democracies and the fascist states find each other supplying opposing sides. Contrary to what has sometimes been said, the British government did not originate the nonintervention proposal, but press opinion in both Britain and Belgium generally favored it, and after the first of August the French government officially adopted this program. Yet it did not adhere to absolute nonintervention, and allowed a small trickle of arms to continue. Luis Araquistain, the Republican ambassador to France in 1936 and 1937, wrote that even after the nonintervention principle had been theoretically adopted by the great powers, "France did not cease to aid the Spanish Republic, but due to the small amount of matériel available and its antiquated quality, . . . such aid turned out to be insignificant. . . ."[4]

Much of the pressure that might have been brought to bear against the nonintervention policy by clear proof of German and Italian military assistance was counterbalanced by alarm over the extent of the revolution in the leftist zone. British and French economic interests were threatened, and to the British government a leftist pro-Communist dictatorship was no more desirable—perhaps less so—than a right-wing, pro-German Nationalist dictatorship, at least in the international climate of 1936–37. French opinion was more evenly divided, but sharp conflict within it and the fact that the Spanish revolution went far beyond the immediate goals of the French Socialist party made this an agonizing problem for Léon Blum as premier in 1936–37.

The British Labour party, which supported nonintervention

3. Cf. the remarks of the Republican Air Force commander-in-chief, Gen. Ignacio Hidalgo de Cisneros, *Mis memorias* (Paris, 1964), II, 324–25.
4. "Las grandes potencias y la guerra de España," *Cuadernos*, no. 23.

in 1936, changed its stance in 1937 to favor permitting the Republican regime to purchase British arms, and by 1939, after the failure of British and French appeasement, Blum bitterly repented not having continued major military assistance to the Spanish left. This was not so much because of support for the revolution as regret at not having blocked German and Italian policy.

If the course of the revolution helped to inhibit the policy of the western democracies, the attitude of the western democracies also served to inhibit the extent of the revolution. The international climate was much less favorable for thoroughgoing leftist revolution in 1936 than in 1917. The fascist regimes of Germany and Italy were entering their aggressive phase, the powerful Socialist parties of central Europe had been crushed, the French left was not so united as it seemed, the Portuguese republic had gone under a decade earlier and even the Soviet Union was entering a quasi-Thermidorian period under Stalin. Perhaps the major factor in inducing Largo Caballero to form the Popular Front government of September 1936 was that a more radical solution to the political dilemma of the revolutionaries would have alienated western opinion. For their part, CNT leaders have said that one of the main considerations in their acceptance of revolutionary dualism was the need to avoid alienating opinion in the liberal countries. Pressures from Britain and France were also important in encouraging the moderate policy of the Basque government and enabling the latter to keep the extreme left under control.

On August 23 the Soviet Union signed the Anglo-French nonintervention agreement. This was a logical extension of the policy of nominal collective security and rapprochement with the western democracies that Stalin had followed for the past year. Since Russian military matériel did not arrive in Spain in large quantities until after the first of October, it has frequently been assumed that Stalin was not planning major intervention at the time that he adhered to the international agreement, and only reversed his policy after proof that Germany and Italy were not willing to abide by this arrangement. It is not possible at present to date exactly Stalin's decision to intervene, but the available evidence indicates that it was taken at almost precisely the same time that the Soviet Union signed the nonintervention agreement. Three days later (August 26), a high-ranking NKVD officer, Alexander Orlov, was appointed chief security officer for the Russian effort in Spain, with the official post of adviser to the Republican government on intelligence, counterintelligence, and guerrilla warfare.[5]

Stalin's main concern, of course, was not with collective security but with maximalizing Soviet power. He had no confidence in political or military agreements with western countries unless these were immediately implemented by concrete action, and it was clear almost from the start that Britain and France had little stomach for direct enforcement of the nonintervention agreement. On the other hand, a Nationalist victory in Spain would strengthen the fascist powers and weaken the Soviet Union's position, lessening the prospects for western support of Communist policy.

There is no evidence that Stalin proposed to set up a full-fledged Communist regime in Spain. Even if that had been possible, such a naked display of Soviet imperialism would have thoroughly alienated Britain and France, and drawn even greater military opposition from Germany and Italy. According to the Red Army intelligence officer Walter Krivitsky, Stalin's idea was more simply to "include Spain in the sphere of the Kremlin's influence." "Without public intervention, but by adroit use of his position as the source of military supplies, Stalin believed it possible to create in Spain a regime controlled by him."[6] A compromise leftist Republican regime, revolutionary enough to hold the domestic support necessary for victory in Spain, but moderate enough to win approval from the western democracies, featuring only one or two official Communist cabinet members, but with Communists controlling the key sources of power, would create the optimum situation for the Soviet Union in southwestern

5. According to the answers written by Orlov on April 1, 1968, in response to a questionnaire submitted by the author. (Hereafter cited as "Orlov mss.")

Orlov observes, "My reasoned impression is that Stalin vacillated till the middle of August and that he committed himself to supply Republican Spain with aircraft, tanks, Soviet airmen and tankists by, or on, August 26, 1936."

6. Walter Krivitsky, *In Stalin's Secret Service* (New York, 1939), 76, 80–81.

Europe. It might encourage France to join firmly in collective security with the Soviet Union, and, even if not, could generate significant leverage against the fascist powers.

Stalin apparently also had a secondary purpose, and that was to retain the support of friends abroad whose loyalty to the Soviet Union was beginning to be tested by the massive purges that Stalin had begun at home. Assistance to the leftist cause in Spain would refurbish the image of the Soviet Union as the world's principal champion of leftist progressivism.[7]

Even after the decision had been made, risks and expenses were kept to a minimum. It soon proved possible to ensure payment for war matériel by transferring most of the Bank of Spain's gold reserve to Russia, for the rapid advance of the insurgent forces on Madrid raised anxiety among the Popular Front government leaders about protecting their financial resources. According to Orlov, who arrived in Spain on September 9, Azaña signed a directive on September 13 authorizing Largo Caballero's Socialist Minister of Finance, Juan Negrín, to move the gold reserve from Madrid "to the place which in his opinion offers the best security."

Whatever the legality of the decree, it surely did not contemplate shipment of the treasure outside the country. But as the military situation deteriorated, Negrín, in desperation, stretched his authority. With the knowledge of only the President and the Prime Minister, he sounded out our Soviet trade attaché about storing the gold in Russia. The envoy cabled Moscow, and Stalin leaped at the opportunity.[8]

Orlov was placed in charge of supervising the operation. Negrín had apparently already moved the reserve to Cartagena on the

7. On August 3, a "responsible Soviet official" in Moscow told the United States' chargé, Loy Henderson, that "Soviet leaders" believed "that if the Soviet Union is to continue to maintain hegemony over the international revolutionary movement it must not hesitate in periods of crisis to assume the leadership of that movement." *Foreign Relations of the United States* (Washington, D.C., 1938), II, 461.
8. Alexander Orlov, "Now Stalin Relieved Spain of $600,000,000," *Reader's Digest* (Nov. 1966), 37–50. According to Orlov, Azaña's original authorization stipulated that "in due time" the decision would be submitted to the rump Popular Front Cortes for ex post facto ratification. However, it scarcely need be said that the affair was never mentioned by the leftist leaders until after the war was over.

southeast coast, whence some 650 tons, approximately three-quarters of the total Spanish gold reserve, were shipped to the Soviet Union between October 22 and October 25, 1936.[9]

Small quantities of Soviet arms, accompanied by Red Army advisors, seem to have reached the Republican zone during September, but the first major shipments did not come until the month of October.[10] This counterbalanced and perhaps slightly exceeded earlier German and Italian support for the insurgents. Moreover, the Soviet government provided further assistance in buying arms from other countries through NKVD-controlled purchasing agencies supplied with Republican funds. The Soviet bid, was, however, quickly matched by the Germans and then raised even higher by the Italians. On October 31 the German government decided to send an entire air corps of nearly one hundred combat planes, the first units of which arrived at Seville on November 6. During December Mussolini began to move in detachments of ground troops, raising the stakes beyond Stalin's willingness to compete.

Two of the murkiest points of Civil War diplomacy concern possible efforts by the Largo Caballero government to exploit concessions in Morocco in return for increased foreign support, and the terms of an apparent effort in the spring of 1937 to reach a settlement among the four western powers that would force the Soviet Union from Spain. Prior to the Civil War, all the revolutionary parties had stood for the independence, or at least the full autonomy, of Spanish Morocco. Only a few weeks were needed to show the vital importance of Morocco to Franco's Nationalists as a base of operations and as a source of many thousands of highly combative native mercenaries. The Popular Front regime could have attempted to alter the status quo in Morocco to its advantage by two different policies. One was to

9. Orlov, "How Stalin Relieved Spain" "N.K.V.D. Chief Yezhov quoted to a friend of mine Stalin's gleeful words: 'They will never see their gold again, just as they do not see their own ears!' "
10. Since sizable quantities of Russian planes and tanks were not committed on the Madrid front until the last days of October, it has commonly been assumed that they did not arrive at the Spanish coast until mid-October. Orlov, however, declares that a shipment of 40 tanks, 30 fighter planes, 80 tank crewmen and "a large supply" of munitions arrived at Cartagena "during the first week of October." (Orlov mss.)

have tried to incite a revolutionary outbreak of the native independence movement in Spanish Morocco to subvert Franco's
rear and shift the balance of power. The other was to use the
Spanish protectorate, or portions thereof, as a pawn in negotiations with the major powers of western Europe to achieve an
end to the war on terms favorable to the Popular Front. Of the
leftist parties, only the POUM came out publicly for a revolutionary independence policy, for such a course would have probably completed the alienation of the west European powers from
the leftist regime. It has sometimes been claimed that the Communists were especially influential in encouraging the Largo
government to pursue a moderate policy on the Moroccan issue.
Their official history of the Civil War denies this, claiming that
it was Largo Caballero and Prieto who refused to make a major
effort to incite native rebellion.[11] Conversely, there is evidence
from regular diplomatic sources that Republican officials hinted
at concessions to Britain and France in northwest Africa in return
for support in the war, but this was spurned.

The Moroccan question may also have been associated with
extremely obscure maneuvers by Largo's ambassador in Paris,
Luis Araquistain, and representatives of the four major west European powers during the winter and spring of 1937. After the real
nature of Soviet policy and the success it was achieving within
the leftist zone had become apparent, these negotiations were
initiated by Largo Caballero and Araquistain to seek an end to
the war on terms favorable to all concerned and rid Spain of
Russian influence. According to two subsequent reports written
by Araquistain,[12] the soundings were carried out by the Spanish

11. *Guerra y revolución en España* (Moscow, 1966), I, 223. This Communist
account claims that the only direct initiative was the sending of Largo's
trusted subordinate Carlos Baráibar to the French zone of Morocco, where he
wasted a lot of money in futile efforts to bribe native leaders in the Spanish
zone to rebel. It is supported to some extent by scattered and skeptical remarks
on such efforts penned by Azaña in his memoirs for 1937. (*Obras completas*,
IV.)

12. Copies of Araquistain's reports to the Republican government are said
to be among his papers in the possession of his son Ramón, who refuses to
allow scholars to consult them. The account above is based upon a manuscript
by Julián Gorkín (who has himself read the papers), "Russia y España ayer
y hoy: II. ¿Pudo terminar la guerra en 1939?" It was confirmed in general
terms by Ramón Araquistain in Geneva, Sept. 24–25, 1967. Cf. Gorkín, *España*,

ambassador and by a French diplomat of maximum confidence. Principal contacts for the major powers mere Dino Grandi, the Italian ambassador in London, Hjalmar Schacht, Léon Blum, and Anthony Eden. The idea was to settle the war on terms largely favorable to the Spanish left but also guaranteeing the economic and imperial interests of the four major western powers, and on this basis gaining their united support to the complete exclusion of the Soviet Union. The principal Italian concern was said to be cession of a naval base on Menorca; Schacht spoke of mining and other economic concessions to Germany, possibly including interests or territory in Spanish Morocco. Blum is said to have found all this quite distasteful, but was willing to make concessions in order to achieve German and Italian withdrawal from Spain. The British leaders, Baldwin and Hoare, were most strongly opposed. According to Araquistain, Communist agents learned of the negotiations, probably through the Republican Foreign Minister, Alvarez del Vayo, who, as noted, was a crypto-Communist (and also Araquistain's brother-in-law). The accounts of both Araquistain and the former Communist central committeeman Jesús Hernández agree that Soviet concern to throttle a potential diplomatic realignment was a major factor in the overthrow of Largo Caballero.

Of the three European dictators who intervened in the Civil War, only Mussolini was willing to commit a sizable proportion of his military resources. The frustration of his expeditionary force at Guadalajara in March 1937 compromised Italian prestige but reinforced the complex combination of ideological sympathy and expansionist ambition that involved him so heavily on the Nationalist side. Hitler's relationship was more detached. The German dictator soon realized that this war provided a great opportunity to exploit his old ploy of militant anticommunism—so effective in the domestic stuggle to win over portions

---

primer ensayo de democracia popular (Buenos Aires, 1961), 67, which also refers to Largo Caballero's account in the latter's "Memorias." (These unpublished memoirs by Largo are not to be confused with the series of letters edited by the veteran Socialist Enrique de Francisco and published under Largo's name with the title *Mis recuerdos*.) Luis Araquistain referred vaguely to such negotiations in his "La intervención de Rusia en la guerra española," *Cuadernos*, no. 24, 55–65.

of the German middle and upper classes—and so neutralize much
of Europe while he pursued German aggrandizement. In October
1936, when the German-Italian axis was officially established,
Hitler is said to have told the Italian foreign minister:

> We must go over to the attack. And the tactical field on which we
> must execute the maneuvre is that of anti-Bolshevism. In fact many
> countries which are suspicious of Italo-German friendship for fear of
> Pan-Germanism or of Italian Imperialism and would join the opposite
> camp, will be brought to group themselves with us if they see in Italo-
> German unity the barrier against the Bolshevik menace at home and
> abroad.[13]

Hitler grasped that a long struggle in Spain might assist Germany's aggressive plans in central Europe by helping to divert
western attention while focusing hostility against the Communists and their allies and possibly tying down a portion of
the Soviet Union's strength. He apparently first told military
advisors on December 13, 1936, that an early end to the Spanish
struggle was not necessarily desirable from Germany's point of
view.[14] In April 1938, when he had completed *Anschluss* with
Austria and was preparing to concentrate his full energies against
Czechoslovakia, Hitler suggested that there was little more to be
gained from continued involvement in Spain. He spoke momentarily of reaching an understanding with Mussolini that
would leave Italy a free hand in prosecuting its own interests in
the Spanish conflict.

For its part, the Soviet Union began to de-escalate in mid-
1937, at the very time that the Communists had achieved political
and military hegemony in the Republican zone. The decline in
Russian military involvement, like its rise, was not so much
prompted by the situation in Spain itself as by the broader cal-
culations of the Soviet government. The outbreak of Japanese
aggression in the Far East posed a grave potential threat to
Soviet security on the other side of the world. Furthermore, after
one year of struggle to build for Russia a stronger relationship
with the western powers, no results had been achieved. Yet Stalin

13. Malcolm Muggeridge, ed., *Ciano's Diplomatic Papers* (London, 1948), 57.
14. According to the interrogation of Gen. Walter Warlimont by the United
States Army, Sept. 9, 1945, in Albert C. Horton, "Germany and the Spanish
Civil War, 1936–1939" (Columbia University dissertation, 1966), 106–09.

did not write off the Spanish enterprise altogether, for it was costing the Soviet Union very little, while a clear victory for Franco would only strengthen the position of Russia's enemies. A major effort to win a leftist triumph would be too expensive and run the risk of direct conflict with Germany, but continuation of the struggle at a lower rate of Soviet assistance would allow Stalin to retain his Spanish gambit at minimal risk. According to Orlov, instructions were sent in the summer of 1937 that Soviet policy would no longer be to provide the large-scale assistance calculated to secure an all-out victory, but to extend the struggle on a long-term basis, keeping the leftist forces in the field as long as possible and so denying complete victory to the Nationalists.

The Spanish struggle came to be of extraordinary importance to many people throughout Europe and in America as well, not because of the issues that were at stake in Spain but because of what they were interpreted to mean in terms of the political and social experience of people in other countries. The conflict was not seen as a contest between revolution and counterrevolution in Spain, but as a struggle between "fascism" and "democracy." Just as Spaniards themselves had contributed to the breakdown of their own political system by false analogies to other countries, the Spanish situation was likened to that of Germany and Austria in 1932–34, whereas a better comparison might have been Hungary in 1919. Acceptance of this notion by most leftists and liberals throughout the western world represented in part a triumph of Communist propaganda, but it was more than that. Leftists and ultraliberals abroad needed little persuasion to judge Spanish affairs by their own standards. Not merely did the Civil War seem to represent the antithesis to the capitulation of the central European middle classes to fascism, but the revolution also stood for the antithesis of western political liberalism's failure to cope with economic depression and social crisis. Elsewhere there seemed to be confusion, muddling, and surrender; in Spain there appeared to be positive commitment and direct action based on nominal principles of "democratic solidarity." A great many people in the western world vicariously enjoyed a morality play in which they recast the roles to suit themselves. The Spanish Popular Front was seen as the exact antithesis of parliamentary politicians submitting to Hitler, of capitalist entrepreneurs unable to provide employment, of Conservative party spokesmen who encouraged the workers' psychology of social alienation. It was not viewed as the murder of priests, the cancellation of constitutional government, or the expropriation of modest property owners.

In Britain and France, especially, hundreds of thousands of people came to feel an intense degree of psychoemotional solidarity with the struggle of the Spanish left. It divided public opinion in these two countries to a greater degree than anything in England since the Great Reform Bill or in France since the Dreyfus Affair. In the United States public opinion polls showed a strong majority in favor of what was known as the "Republican" or "loyalist" cause, though the great bulk of American opinion was opposed to any direct American intervention.

In the Soviet Union, until about mid-1937, there was popular concern as well. The Spanish revolution was the only major event in Europe since the establishment of the Communist dictatorship that could be presented as a mass effort to achieve goals approximately similar to those of the new Russian society. Though of course sparked by the Communist propaganda apparatus, the interest and enthusiasm of Russian people seems to have been genuine, as judged from the observations of western visitors to the Soviet Union at that time.

Leftist political exiles from central and east central Europe were attracted en masse to the Spanish struggle. They provided many volunteers for the International Brigades and included in their ranks a large proportion of the younger and middle-aged Communist leaders in those countries. After 1945, Communist veterans of the Spanish Civil War were liberally distributed throughout the elite ranks of the new east central European leadership.

During the Second World War and after, the Spanish contest was frequently called the "prelude to" or "opening round of" the broader European conflict. This is not entirely accurate. The factors that produced the blowup in Spain were hardly similar to those that brought the Nazi-Soviet Pact and the

German-Russian invasion of Poland. The prelude to world war was Munich, not Madrid, and the neutrality of Franco was a demonstration of that. The defeat of the Spanish revolution did not necessarily menace British and French security, but German domination of central and east central Europe certainly did.

Developments attending the course of the Civil War nevertheless did contribute significantly to the situation in which the world war began. The British and French position on nonintervention was not merely inimical to the chances for victory of the Spanish left but encouraged Hitler to believe that the western powers would be reluctant to oppose German action when it was not directly aimed against their vital interests. But in the latter connection the crucial issue was Czechoslovakia in 1938; by comparison the fate of the Spanish left was secondary.

In fact, it may be questioned whether or not the Second World War could ever have developed as it did had not the Soviet Union soon reversed the policy that it had followed during the Spanish conflict. Events in Spain indicated by 1939 that non-Communist Spanish leftists seemed almost to prefer Franco to continued Communist tutelage, and this accentuated Communist isolation. The Second World War was not begun by the alignment of forces that struggled in Spain, but started only after the Soviet Union, the only existing regime of the revolutionary left, made a pact with the most extreme antileftist government to occupy east central Europe. This momentarily reversed the relationship of forces that had existed in the Spanish war, which was a struggle to the death between the left and right.

THIRTEEN *Internal Politics of the*

Spanish People's Republic

COMMUNIST DOMESTIC POLICY during the Spanish Civil War was to maximalize the party's influence within the leftist zone and channel the revolution so as to make it more compatible with foreign opinion and prosecution of the war. In the first weeks the party had emerged as the most vigorous and cohesive supporter of government authority, and the principal champion of centralized military and economic direction to overcome the disorganization resulting from revolutionry dualism. Communist propaganda influence was greatly enhanced by the scope of the international Comintern network, which had a much more formidable propaganda apparatus than was available to the nominal Republican government. Furthermore, Communist appointees were placed in control of state censorship within the leftist zone soon after the conflict began. Though the Communists never established a monopoly of information and proselytization, they achieved a general hegemony.

The effort to mask revolutionary extremism and proclaim the defense of a middle-class Republic, though propagated abroad by the Communist and Republican propaganda networks, was too negative to be effective within the leftist zone. The Communist line on the Civil War was consequently adjusted to three different levels of propaganda: on the international plane, the conflict was defined as one between parliamentary democracy and militaristic fascism; within the leftist zone in general, it was increasingly referred to as a popular national Republican war of independence against fascist imperialism; in certain areas—particularly in anarchist regions—it was called a people's revolutionary struggle aaginst the international forces of counterrevolution. Since the end of the Civil War, professional historians in the Soviet Union have customarily defined it as the Spanish "national" or "people's" "revolutionary war."

Five months passed before the first complete Communist wartime program was published in a manifesto from the central committee of the party.[1] The eight-point proposal of December 1936 bore some similarity to Lenin's program of "War Communism" at the start of the Russian Civil War:

1. Complete power for the central government.

2. A regular organized army based on universal service.

3. "Iron discipline" in the rearguard.

4. Nationalization of the "principal branches" (cf. "commanding heights") of industry and nationalization of all war industry.

5. Formulation of a Popular Front government Council of Industrial and Economic Coordination with complete power over the economy.

6. "Workers' control" over industry (meaning workers' advisory councils under state control).

7. Increased agrarian production and greater rewards for the peasantry.

8. Coordination of agriculture and industry.

The central committee replied to charges that the Communists were "sacrificing the revolution":

The accusations made against us from time to time saying that we sacrifice the interests of the revolution in order to win the war are not only perfidious but also puerile. The struggle to win the war is insep-

1. *Las ocho condiciones de la victoria* (Dec. 18, 1936).

arably united to the development of the revolution. If we do not win the war the revolution will be frustrated. This idea must penetrate deeply among the masses if we do not want to cripple the effort to win the war. We fight to create a better society in which the repetition of such criminal and monstrous deeds as this military rebellion will be impossible. But all the deluded and irresponsible who try to carry out programs of "socialism" or "libertarian communism" in their own separate provinces or towns must be made to understand that all these efforts will come tumbling down like card castles if the fascists are not annihilated. . . .

Our party—a consistently, responsibly revolutionary party, that does not gamble with the interests of the working masses, but labors unceasingly to unite the masses in the struggle—does not want to sacrifice the masses uselessly, does not want to carry out premature revolutionary efforts at the expense of the workers, but to create the conditions necessary for their triumph.

The tactical position that was worked out by the Comintern leadership for Spanish domestic politics defined the wartime leftist regime as a "popular" or "people's" "Republic," giving a new meaning to a term that had frequently been used by the middle-class left since 1931 to refer vaguely to the Republic as representing the interests of the majority of the citizenry. The first concrete expression of the doctrine of the People's Republic as applied to the situation in the leftist zone was provided by Díaz in a speech before the party's central committee at the beginning of March 1937:

We are fighting for a democratic and parliamentary Republic of a new type with profound social meaning. The struggle being waged in Spain does not have the goal of establishing a democratic Republic such as that of France or any other capitalist country. No, the Republic for which we are fighting is different. We are fighting to destroy the foundations of reaction and fascism, without the destruction of which no true political democracy can exist.[2]

But he went on to explain that in the new Spanish People's Republic, those foundations had already been destroyed, for large land holdings had been expropriated and the power of the traditional armed forces, the oligarchy, and the Church had been eliminated. The popular revolutionary forces must be careful

2. José Díaz, *Tres años de lucha* (Barcelona, 1939), 390.

not to divorce themselves from the "democratic classes" (referring mainly to the middle-class left and the regionalists) whose assistance would be needed to win the war. Hence the importance of limiting the social and economic revolution to an intermediate stage while emphasizing unity, discipline, and government power to defeat "fascism." Thus the Communists provided, at least temporarily, what Burnett Bolloten has called "hope for the middle classes."

It is not surprising that some of the most moderate and best-trained elements in the leftist zone joined the Communist party, as did many careerists and opportunists who wanted to be on the side of what was emerging as the most effective force. But many of the new members of the party also came from the ordinary working classes and the peasantry. Moreover, many thousands of them were not mere opportunists for, whatever judgment is made of Spanish Communists during the Civil War, it must be recognized that they were second to none in determination and heroism. Their casualty rate was in fact the highest of any political group.

By June 1937 the Spanish Communist party claimed a total membership of 387,000, including 22,000 in Vizcaya and 64,000 in Catalonia. Díaz announced that membership was drawn from the following social groups:[3]

87,660 industrial workers	15,485 middle-class people
62,250 agricultural workers	7,045 professional people
76,700 peasant proprietors	

The incompleteness of this class breakdown may reflect the degree of exaggeration that possibly existed in the Communist statistics, but there is no doubt that the increase in membership was very great. The most important center of strength was Madrid, where by 1938 the party claimed 63,000 members, somewhere between 5 and 10 percent of the city's shrunken wartime population. Statistics for the JSU were even higher; a memo of July 1937

3. José Díaz, *Por la unidad, hacia la victoria* (Valencia, 1937), and "Las lecciones de la guerra del pueblo español," *Nuestra Bandera*, 2 (July 1940), 9–25. Cf. Francisco Anton, *Madrid, orgullo de la España anti-fascista* (Valencia, 1937).

reported the JSU membership was

April 1, 1936	41,210	May, 1937	300,156
July 18, 1936	150,368	July, 1937	400,000 [4] approx.

The JSU subsequently claimed half a million in 1938,[5] but it should be pointed out that a sizable statistical overlap existed between the party affiliates and the youth movement, many militants holding dual membership. Communist influence in the UGT also continued to increase, though Largo Caballero still dominated the UGT's executive commission, on which the Communists had in the meantime failed to place a single representative.

Communist-front organizations flourished. They included the Union of Girls, Antifascist Women, The Militia of Culture, The Friends of the Soviet Union, The Union of Young Mothers, The Alliance of Antifascist Intellectuals, and above all, International Red Relief, which by February 1937 claimed 353,000 affiliates in the Popular Front zone. Proselytization among women, the young, and cultural circles was especially pronounced.

Socialist party membership doubled during the first year of the war. In speeches of mid-1937 several Socialist leaders referred vaguely to figures of 160,000, but this did not equal the meteoric rise of the Communists. The FAI quadrupled its membership to 154,000 by the end of 1937[6] but also lost ground to the Communists. The Anarchist Youth (FIJL) expanded its following considerably, growing from 30,000 in mid-1936 to three or possibly four times that in 1937,[7] but it was still a distant second

---

4. This memo, a copy of which is in the Bolloten Collection, listed the number of formally constituted JSU cells as follows:

70,080 among peasants	28,021 among workers
29,021 among women	14,213 among students

Cf. Santiago Carrillo, *Las tareas de la juventud española* (Madrid, 1937), and in *Frente Rojo* (Valencia), April 2, 1937.

5. Felipe M. Arconada, "En el V aniversario de la creación de las J. S. U. de España," *Nuestra Brandera*, II:4 (April 1941), 44–58.

6. Diego Abad de Santillán, *Por qué perdimos la guerra* (Buenos Aires, 1940), 296–98.

7. A total of 120,000 was claimed by the *Memoria del pleno peninsular de regionales, celebrado los días 21, 22 y 23 de febrero* (Barcelona, 1937). However,

to the JSU. The POUM had less than 10,000 members before the Civil War began and remained comparatively small. Its syndical federation claimed 60,000 members in July 1936, but even a substantial increase would have left it exiguous in proportion to the two mass trade union movements. The paucity of the POUM's following was the more fateful since this was the only other group that could rival the Communists in unity and organization.

The Communist emphasis on discipline, government authority, and economic moderation had the paradoxical result of making the Communists natural allies of the middle-class left and regionalist moderates. In the province of Vizcaya the Basque Communist party became a trusted collaborator of the Basque Nationalist government. Some of the local facilities and presses of the CNT were confiscated and turned over to the Communists. The Basque Communist leaders carried their Basquism so far that theirs was the only section of the otherwise well-disciplined and virtually totalitarian Communist apparatus to escape the reins of central control. In later years Spanish Communist leaders had harsh words for the reluctance of Basque Communists to co-operate with the central command.

In the important and productive district of Valencia, the Communists moved resolutely to protect the moderate, Catholic landowning peasantry from the ravages of the CNT and the revolutionary Socialists. Both the FAI and the CNT were comparatively well organized in the smaller towns around Valencia. They claimed to have organized as many as 340 agrarian collectives in the greater Valencia region—probably an exaggeration—which the CNT historian Peirats asserts were the best-organized CNT collectives in Spain. But the majority of the peasants in the Valencia region, where property was reasonably well distributed, ranged from moderately liberal to conservative in their political attitudes. In mid-October 1936 the Communist party in Valencia moved to set up an entirely new Provincial Peasant Federa-

---

José Peirats, *La C.N.T. en la revolución española* (Toulouse, 1951,) II, 74, gives a total of 82,221—excluding the north—broken down as follows:

Catalonia	34,156	Levant	8,200
Central Spain	18,469	Andalusia	7,400
Aragon	12,089	Extremadura	1,907

tion (FPC). It was designed to protect the interests of the lower middle-class peasantry and was justified by its secretary, Julio Mateu, on the grounds that as of July 1936 in the province of Valencia, the number of smallholders and renters and their families numbered 198,719, whereas the number of laborers and their families numbered 119,535. Hence the "kulaks" and "middle peasants" heavily outnumbered the "poor peasants." Altogether, 55.8 percent of the Valencian peasants were said to work land belonging to them or their family; the moderate social forces were so strong that they could not be ignored. By early 1937 the FPC claimed 50,000 members.[8]

The greatest regional political triumph of Spanish communism was scored in the key revolutionary region, Catalonia, where the four small pro-Stalinist Marxist parties (Partit Comunista de Catalunya, Unió Socialista de Catalunya, Partit Català Proletari, and the Catalan section of the Socialist party) were officially merged on July 23, 1936, as the Partit Socialist Unificat de Catalunya (PSUC). This was the first Socialist-Communist *partido único* ever formed in Europe, and was a product, not as in eastern Europe after 1945, of Red Army occupation, but of the febrile revolutionary climate of Catalonia.[9] It advertised itself as the *partit ùnic bolxevic revolucionari de Catalunya* (sole revolutionary Bolshevist party of Catalonia) and quickly began to make a major impact in Spain's most incendiary region where Marxism had always been weak. The PSUC stood somewhat to the left of the Communist party proper because of the need to compete with the CNT and POUM, but it immediately joined the Comintern and came under direct Muscovite control, its personal Comintern tutor being the Hungarian Ernö Gerö.

The policy of the PSUC was partly based on organized revolutionary Catalanism, insofar as this was compatible with the military effort, but above all it stressed Popular Front unity and government authority to prosecute the war. From the very

8. Julio Mateu, *Qué es la Federación Provincial Campesina* (Valencia, 1936); *Por qué se constutuyó la Federación Provincial Campesina* (Valencia, 1937); *La Obra de la Federación Campesina* (Valencia, 1937).
9. Little attention has been paid in historical study to the formation of the PSUC. There is a rather superficial account by L. V. Ponomareva, "Katalonskii proletariat v borbe za edinstvo. Obrazovanie Obedinennoi Sotsialisticheskoi Partii Katalonii," in *Ispanskii narod protiv fashizma* (Moscow, 1963), 258–321.

beginning it assisted most of the Generalitat's efforts to protect the lower middle classes and encouraged Companys to take a more determined stand against CNT excesses than the wily Catalanist was willing to. The PSUC also dominated the Catalan sector of the UGT, which gained membership as rapidly as did the CNT, though starting from a lower level. The Catalan UGT became the refuge of white-collar employees and moderates seeking protection from the CNT. As the vehicle of lower-middle-class syndicalism, it incorporated government employees, the Catalan students' union, and a new 18,000-member union of petty manufacturers, shopkeepers, and artisans (GEPCI). In addition it soon won over some of the Opposition Syndicates of the CNT which, despite the Zaragoza unity congress, had never officially returned to the parent organization. The Opposition Syndicates had originally broken with the CNT on the issues of politicism and organized revolution; many of them ultimately found Catalan communism more to their way of thinking than all-out anarchosyndicalism. Some CNT spokesmen claimed that by the last months of 1936 the CNT's membership in Catalonia had expanded to the unlikely figure of 600,000, a figure equivalent to virtually the entire prewar Catalan proletariat. The Catalan UGT claimed 350,000 by September 1936 and nearly 550,000 by November 1937. This was probably also an exaggeration, but there is no doubt that the PSUC and the UGT gained much ground on the CNT in Catalonia. For the first time, Catalan anarchism had a formidable revolutionary rival. By June 1937 the PSUC announced a total of 64,000 affiliates,[10] of whom it was asserted 62 percent were industrial workers, 20 percent peasants, 16 percent white-collar employees, and 2 percent from the lower middle class. By mid-1938 the PSUC claimed to have a membership of approximately 90,000.

10. The figure is variously given as 54,000 and 64,000; perhaps neither statistic need be taken too seriously. The PSUC leaders further claimed that 25 percent of their membership was from Barcelona, and that by mid-1937 cells had been organized in 685 of the 1,068 towns of Catalonia. More of the new members were said to have come from the CNT than from any other single group. Luis Cabo Giorla, *Cataluña ha dado un ejemplo de unidad* (Barcelona, 1937); Miguel Valdés, *El Partido Socialista Unificado de Cataluña, partido único revolucionario bolchevique de Cataluña* (Barcelona, 1937).

The PSUC's mission was to build Communist strength in Catalonia while channeling the revolution and helping to restore order so that Catalan resources might be mobilized for the war effort. The bitterness of other Popular Front leaders about the excesses of revolutionary regionalism in Catalonia was well expressed in Azaña's biting commentary:

The Generalitat acted in rebellion against the government . . . , moving toward de facto separation. . . . It legislates that over which it has no authority, it administers things that do not belong to it.

In many of their assaults against the state the Catalanists use the FAI as a shield . . . [and] then protest that the state does not come to their aid when they fall prisoners to the CNT.

The regular government of Catalonia exists in name only. The representatives of the syndical groups in the government stand for little or nothing; their comrades neither obey them nor fulfill the agreements painfully worked out in the council.

. . . After eight months of war, no useful armed force has been organized in Catalonia, though the Catalans opposed having been organized and commanded by the government of the Republic. Now that everyone has begun to clamor for an army, they will have the advantages of having burned the mobilization records, of having made bonfires with equipment, of having let the FAI take over the barracks and chase away recruits. The newspapers, and even the leaders of the Generalitat, speak daily of the revolution and of winning the war. They talk about how Catalonia is intervening in this not as a province but as a nation. As a neutral nation, some observe. They talk about the war in Iberia. Iberia? What's that? An ancient country in the Caucasus. . . . Since the war is in Iberia it can be taken calmly. In this situation, if we win, the result will be that the state will owe money to Catalonia. Catalan affairs, more than any others during the Republic, excited the hostility of Army officers against the Republic. During the war, the plague of anarchism was unleashed from Catalonia. Catalonia has greatly weakened the resistance against the rebels and the military strength of the Republic.[11]

The Catalanists were as usual divided between several tendencies which conflicted with each other even among the various subsectors of the Esquerra. Though the majority of the left Catalanists favored fundamental social changes, they also supported Companys' efforts to channel the revolution. Though they accepted the need to support the central war effort, they refused to surrender any significant measure of regional auton-

11. *La velada en Benicarló* (Barcelona, 1939), 101–04.

omy for that purpose. Though most Catalanists feared the strength and ultimate aims of the CNT as the major obstacle to their goals in the region, they hesitated to oppose the anarcho-syndicalists directly not merely because of doubt as to the outcome but also because many feared that direct conflict between the two main federative forces would play into the hands of the central government.

The subversive side of regionalism was revealed in a maneuver first exposed by *Solidaridad Obrera* on November 27. During that autumn, when it appeared that Madrid would inevitably fall to the insurgents, a series of murky negotiations were carried on by the Estat Català sector of the Catalanist left and certain elements of the CNT. It appears that some of the latter, fearing the war was already lost, looked toward a "national syndicalist" arrangement with Franco's Nationalists that might preserve part of the recent social and economic changes. Key Estat Català leaders had earlier been in contact with Mussolini; through middle-class Catalan refugees in Paris they carried on secret negotiations for French support of an autonomous Catalonia that would apparently accept Franco's victory in the rest of Spain. One of the principal figures in the Estat Català scheme was Andreu Reverter, Councillor of Security in the Generalitat, who had been appointed to that post in September as a concession to the extremists in his group. Moreover, it appeared that Juan Casanoves, the acting president of the Generalitat, was also implicated. After the scandal broke, approximately 100 people were arrested. Soon afterward Reverter was secretly executed on a charge of gross financial corruption (which very possibly was also true) to save face for Catalanism. Casanoves was permitted to flee to France.

In most questions, Catalan communism was able to cooperate effectively with the Generalitat throughout the autumn and winter of 1936 to try to restore government authority. At the beginning of October regular police organization was reestablished. Soon afterward local revolutionary committees were ordered dissolved and the formation of ordinary municipal coalition govenments under the Generalitat was decreed. At the end of October all militia forces in Catalonia were declared subject

to regular military discipline. A series of decrees were issued
during November in a futile attempt to collect the tens of
thousands of weapons held by the CNT and POUM. On November 16 Companys closed down 3,000 positions in revolutionary courts and local government held by the extreme left, and
on December 4 command of the small force of Catalan security
guards was transferred directly to the president of the Generalitat
to ensure authority and discipline. Yet this course was filled with
conflict: the exteme left greatly resented the elimination of the
organs of revolutionary dualism, the Generalitat was itself willing to go only part way toward the consolidation and centralization of authority and would not relinquish any of its own powers
to the central government, and the Catalan Communists were
ultimately determined not merely to subdue the extreme left
but to circumscribe the Generalitat as well.

The Generalitat logically considered that its most immediate
domestic problem was how to cope with the great popular support of the CNT, but the Catalan Communists, following the
obsessive dictates of Stalinism, concentrated their fire on the
POUM. POUM leaders did not oppose collaboration with the
Communists on equal and independent terms, but were alarmed
by the sharp increase in Communist influence and the leverage
provided by Russian military assistance. Having more experience
with revolutionary movements than the Socialists or the leaders
of the middle-class left, they did not share the latter's attitude of
pas d'ennemis à gauche and held no illusions concerning the
purpose or extent of Stalin's commitment to the Spanish left.

The Communists denounced the POUM as "Trotskyists"
and counter-revolutionary provocateurs. Though some of the
individual POUM leaders might have been considered "Trotskyists," the organization had clearly dissociated itself from
Trotskyism. Even before he joined with the BOC in forming
the POUM in 1935, Andrés Nin had rejected Trotsky's instructions to merge his Communist Left with the Spanish Socialist
party as a ploy in Trotsky's tactic of trying to revolutionize the
Second International. Consequently, as mentioned in Chapter 8,
the ultra-Trotskyist sector of the Communist Left refused to
participate in the POUM and formed a separate Bolshevist-

Leninist Section in Madrid and Barcelona, which remained independent during the revolution. For his part, Trotsky was at first unimpressed by the Spanish revolutionary outburst of July 1936, labeling it a "confused, hybrid, half-blind, half-deaf revolution." The last relations between Trotsky and Nin were broken after the POUM joined the Generalitat's coalition government of September 1936. Trotsky considered this a reactionary step, claiming that the real duty of revolutionary Marxism was to form a united mass party of all revolutionary elements to replace the vestiges of middle-class Republicanism.[12] In a subsequent reassessment of the Spanish revolution, he asserted,

> The Spanish proletariat displayed first class military capacities. In its specific gravity in the economy of the country, in its political and cultural level it stood in the first day of the revolution not lower but higher than the Russian proletariat at the beginning of 1917. On the road to victory, its own organizations stood as the chief obstacles.[13]

After its first direct confrontation with the Communists, the POUM's central committee explicitly rejected organized Trotskyism. To clarify the party's position, in a meeting of mid-December 1936, it resolved that

> The Second and Third Internationals are not, and cannot be, the instrument of worldwide revolution. Neither can the Fourth International founded by Trotsky, which because of its sectarian character lacks roots among the masses.[14]

(This last limitation was of course true of the POUM as well.)

The Comintern was determined to crush the POUM not because the latter was "Trotskyist," but because it was the only united, well-organized anti-Stalinist revolutionary party determined to use coherent political means to carry out a fully independent Spanish revolution. Its first blow was struck early in November 1936 when the POUM was denied representation on the Madrid Defense Junta formed to defend the erst-while capital after it was evacuated by the Largo Caballero government. Though Russian assistance shored up the Madrid front, the

---

12. Pierre Broué, *Trotsky y la guerra civil española* (Buenos Aires, 1969).
13. *The Lesson of Spain: The Last Warning* (London, 1938).
14. *Resoluciones aprobadas en el Pleno ampliado del Comité Central del P.O.U.M.* (Barcelona, 1936), quoted in Bricall, Chap. XX.

POUM's organ *La Batalla* warned on November 15 that the Soviet government should not be considered a devoted friend since "what really interests Stalin is not the fate of the proletariat in Spain or anywhere else in the world, but the defense of the Soviet regime through official agreements of certain states against others." Two days later, the first formal rupture between the PSUC and the POUM occurred when the Catalan sector of the JSU refused to attend a joint rally with the POUM's Iberian Communist Youth (JCI). The Russian consul in Barcelona subsequently issued a formal press release denouncing *La Batalla* as part of the "press in the pay of international fascism." Even the POUM, however, refrained from criticizing the great purges which were under way in the Soviet Union. Apparently the only protests against the first Stalinist purge trials to be published within leftist Spain came from the Anarchist Youth (FIJL) and from the CNT's *La Noche* (Barcelona), whose editor was a member of the ultra-anarchist society Friends of Durruti. In order to avoid antagonizing the Communists further, the Catalan regional committee of the CNT disavowed the editorial.

The Communist offensive against the POUM was launched by provoking a cabinet crisis in the Generalitat on December 13 to demand greater order and discipline. When the Generalitat was reorganized four days later the POUM was excluded on the casuistic grounds that in a revolutionary democracy the working classes should be represented by syndical organizations rather than by political parties. It was decided that the POUM's trade union federation was too small to merit representation alongside the CNT, UGT, and Rabassaires, though the Catalanist left would still provide the main executive leadership as representative of the democratic lower middle classes. The new ministry was composed of four representatives of the CNT, four from the Esquerra, three from the UGT, and one from the Rabassaires. Fàbregas was replaced by the PSUC leader, Comorera, as Councillor of Economics, and the authority of the revolutionary supply committees was largely ended, giving greater freedom to private shopkeepers (in what the Communists called a "Catalan NEP") but increasing inflation. The POUM's central committee replied by calling for a new constituent Cortes to be chosen by revolu-

tionary committees of workers, peasants, and soldiers. This reflected the POUM's determination to copy as much as possible
of the nominal organizational pattern of the Russian Revolution,
though Nin had already expressed his opinion that in Spain
there was no need to form "soviets."

At a big rally on December 20 the PSUC spokesmen admitted
they had forced the reorganization, stressing that there were still
too many committees and too much confusion in Catalonia. One
of them, Antonio Sesé, declared that support for the lower middle
classes was a necessary expedient in the short run, but that "the
liquidation of the lower middle classes will come in due time"
after their cooperation was no longer needed to win the war.
PSUC leaders emphasized that theirs was the only effective
revolutionary party in Catalonia because it was the only one
whose policy was capable of laying the foundations for victory.
Comorera concluded the rally by promising, "On the day after
victory we Catalans will be the first Iberian nationality to
establish a full-fledged Socialist Republic." [15]

The anarchists grudgingly acquiesced in the government
change. *Solidaridad Obrera* editorialized on December 19 that

> Frankly we must confess that the scolding refrain of "first win the
> war" pains us. This is a desiccated slogan, without substance, almost
> without nerve, without fruit. First win the war and make the revolution
> at the same time, for the war and the revolution are consubstantial
> like sun and light. *That* is the slogan.

The CNT could accept neither the independent Marxism of the
POUM nor the totalitarian Russian Marxism of the Communists,
and became increasingly disturbed about the latter. On January 24, 1937, *Solidaridad Obrera* warned of excessive foreign influence and insisted that "Our revolution must be Spanish of an
ethnic and psychological type, which has lived for many years in
the heart and soul of our race."

Further measures were taken during the winter of 1937 to
increase government authority and to moderate revolutionary
pressure in Catalonia. On January 12 the Generalitat's Councillor
of Finance put into effect 58 decrees to restore government con-

15. Antonio Sesé, José del Barrio, and Juan Comorera, *Nuestra situación
política actual* (Barcelona, 1936).

trol over finance. New taxes were levied and, in a further concession to the liberal middle classes, the Generalitat recognized
the right of every resident who was not a supporter of Franco
to be indemnified for property losses suffered since the beginning
of the revolution. The remaining syndical supply committees of
the CNT were also dissolved, their functions to be assumed by
the commercial syndicate of the UGT. In February the Generalitat stopped further efforts at collectivization of agrarian smallholders and several previously formed collectives were broken up.

Once having accepted the principle of collaboration, the
CNT was forced to surrender one revolutionary conquest after
another. The Confederation had become a virtual member of the
Popular Front, and its official leaders both inside and outside
the government counseled continued compromise so long as the
war lasted. Juan Peiró, the CNT's Minister of Industry in the
Largo Caballero government, wrote in February:

> The road to follow is this: We must wage the war and, while
> waging it, limit ourselves to preparing for the revolution by means of
> a conscientious and discreet control of the factories, for this is equivalent
> to taking up revolutionary positions in a practical way for the final
> assault on capitalist society after the end of the war.[16]

The strongest opposition to the program of centralism, discipline, and revolutionary moderation came from the revolutionary youth movements. JSU secretary Santiago Carrillo engi-
neered a special national conference of his group in January 1937
to support the Communist position and announced that the Civil
War was being fought for "the democratic Republic," bringing
angry protests from ultrarevolutionary elements of the JSU in
Asturias and elsewhere. On February 14 a mass meeting was held
in Barcelona to set up a Revolutionary Youth Front of the FAI
and POUM youth (FIJL, JLC, and JCI). Joint meetings were
also held at Madrid and Valencia. On March 15 the executive
committee of the JCI launched a manifesto "To the Combatant
Worker and Peasant Youth of the Entire Country," stating that
"The reality is that during eight months we have achieved no
fundamental victories while suffering serious defeats." "The
fascist hordes have shown that they possess organization, disci-

16. *Política*, Feb. 23, 1937, in Bolloten, 166.

pline, audacity and decision," and according to the JCI could be defeated only by the adoption of a "revolutionary military policy" based on the following points:

1. No Separation of the War from the Revolution.
2. Forging of Revolutionary Unity of All Working Class Youth.
3. Mobilization of All the Youth.
4. Aid to the Combatant Youth Defending Madrid and Start of a General Offensive on Every Front.
5. Military Preparation of All Working Class Youth.
6. A Revolutionary Workers' Army.
7. Organization of a Powerful War Industry.
8. Establishment of Stern Wartime Discipline.[17]

Ruta, the organ of the Catalan anarchist youth (JLC), replied on March 25 to calls for discipline and subordination under the People's Republican government:

We cannot die for that pretty April democracy which deported us, dishonored and robbed us, singled us out as government prisoners, condemned us to hunger and beatings. WE DO NOT FORGET.

If there are some who are ready to forget, if there are some who get amnesia by dint of easy chairs, public offices and titles, we do not forget. The April Republic does not deserve one drop of our anarchist blood, does not deserve one small drop of sweat.

We have died for the democrats too many times. Now let the democrats sacrifice themselves for us. Let them sacrifice their "ideals" (which are the ideals of their pocketbooks) for us. . . .

And as far as those who obey Stalin are concerned, and seek to Stalinize us so that we become good little boys, we must repeat to them that we don't belong to that parish either: that we detest the red tyranny as we do the tricolor. . . .

The dilemma is not Fascism or Democracy. No. The tragic alternative is, as it was in the First Workingman's International: either State or Revolution.[18]

Five days later Rafael Fernández, secretary of the Asturian JSU, resigned from the JSU's national committee in protest against its Popular Front line, then promptly signed an agreement with the Asturian anarchist youth to create a joint Socialist-

17. JCI, *¡A La Juventud Combatiente Obrera y Campesina de Todo el Pais!* (Barcelona, 1937).
18. Quoted in Brademas, 424–25.

anarchist Revolutionary Youth Front in Asturias. Early in April the secretary of the Valencian section of the JSU also resigned from the national committee and several local sectors of the JSU announced their alliance with the anarchist youth.

Communist pressure against the revolutionary extreme left mounted steadily. One of the Comintern's most important tools was its own separate Spanish section of the Soviet secret police (NKVD), introduced by Alexander Orlov in September 1936. Using only a handful of Russians and relying mainly on Spanish personnel, Orlov and his colleagues quickly laid the basis for an entirely independent Russian police system. Branches were set up in nearly all the principal towns of the main Republican zone. In the December Catalan government shakeup, a pro-Communist Esquerra leader was made Councillor of Security in Barcelona. He in turn named the crypto-Communist Eusebio Rodríguez Salas Catalan police chief, making it easier to introduce NKVD organization in that region.

The first major police incidents with the anarchists occurred at the close of December 1936. In February 1937 the pace of Checa activity increased, provoking open protests from CNT and non-Communist UGT leaders. The anarchists later claimed that no less than 80 of their comrades were murdered by Communist police in the Madrid district alone between February and May 1937. In Catalonia the FAI responded vigorously; during the same three months 150 political street murders are said to have occurred in Barcelona, in addition to the continuing high rate of political executions.

By the beginning of 1937 the regular Republican security police had been reorganized and were beginning to function normally in many parts of the leftist zone. The Assault Guard had been increased in number to nearly 40,000 and the border guards (Carabineros) were being expanded from 15,000 to 40,000. One of the last acts of the Giral cabinet had been to rename the Civil Guard the "Republican National Guard," and it also was being expanded. By mid-1937 the Popular Front regime was devoting a greater proportion of its prime manpower to police activities than was the Franco regime in the opposing zone.

The first CNT newspaper shut down by the government was closed at Madrid in December. By April 1937 four more had been silenced and at the initiative of the Communists only one of the POUM publications (*El Comunista* of Valencia) was still being allowed to continue normal activities. The more the activities of the CNT were curbed, the more moderate became the attitude of most syndicalist leaders. "Syndicalist capitalism" and the pressure of civil war were pushing the CNT into all-out politicization. In general, the anarchosyndicalists' sense of reality was as dim as ever; most of their leaders in the spring of 1937 still did not grasp the configuration of forces building up in the leftist zone. They attributed government measures against them to the influence of "resurgent reactionaries" and obscurely defined forces of the "bourgeoisie."

On March 12 the Largo Caballero government issued a general order for all parties and syndicates to hand over their caches of weapons to the authorities. Nine days earlier the Generalitat dissolved the syndical- and militia-dominated "security junta" that had held responsibility for most police work in Catalonia during the past eight months. It ordered that all weapons held by political organizations be relinquished. Companys announced draconian measures against "uncontrollables" of the extreme left and the cabinet set up a new "security council" under its pro-Communist minister with power to abolish all local police and militia committees. Moreover, it was decreed that no functionary in any kind of official position could any longer be a member of any party or syndicate. Meanwhile, in Bilbao the Basque-Communist-Socialist alliance arrested the Basque regional committee of the CNT.

The CNT and POUM refused to turn over their weapons in Catalonia or obey the new orders regarding submission to the military draft or central incorporation of all administrative authority. On March 26 the CNT councillors walked out of the Catalan government, and the ensuing crisis lasted three weeks. The ministry was reconstituted in mid-April with exactly the same political composition as before. The CNT still kept its weapons, but the local police and militia committees were being abolished and the military draft for the new People's Army continued.

The extreme left could ultimately be repressed in Catalonia only so far as the Largo Caballero government was willing to support the campaign on the highest level. Stalin himself dispatched private letters to Largo in December 1936 and January 1937, urging conciliatory measures to woo the peasantry and the lower middle classes, and to assure the continued support of the middle-class Republican left, whose allegiance was necessary to maintain the appearance of a democratic Republic. Stalin observed in his first letter of December 21 that

> The Spanish revolution is marking its own route, which differs in many respects from that traversed by Russia. . . . It is quite possible that the parliamentary route will prove a more effective means of revolutionary development in Spain than in Russia.[19]

Though Largo's government did take steps to organize a People's Army and recognized the need for greater government authority and coordination of economic activity, the old Socialist refused to accept many Comintern suggestions and would not eliminate all the local committees set up by the extreme left. By the late winter of 1937 Largo's attitude toward the Communists had finally changed. Russian pressure, together with the Communist takeover of the JSU and PSUC, were the major factors in producing this alteration. Largo had come to realize that the strength and influence of the Communists, particularly in military power, had grown to the point where they jeopardized the future course of the Spanish left. He completely set his face against merger of the Socialist and Communist parties. In Asturias, where elections to the UGT's regional executive commission were held in April, the Communist "unity" ticket received only 12,000 votes compared to 87,000 ballots for the incumbent leaders who were already pledged to a "revolutionary alliance" with the Asturian CNT. On April 23, after increasing protests against NKVD activities in Madrid, Largo dissolved

19. The Russian text is in *Guerra y revolución en España*, I, 100. Cf. the French translation in Salvador de Madariaga, *Spain, A Modern History* (New York, 1958), 672–74.

the Communist-dominated Madrid Defense Junta and turned the city's administration over to a municipal council. A few days later there was a similar crackdown in Murcia, where the provincial governor was dismissed and several Communist police officials arrested. On May Day, Carlos de Baráibar, one of Largo's closest associates, addressed a joint UGT-CNT meeting in Valencia on the need to oppose Communist influence. The prospect of a broad UGT-CNT "revolutionary unity" alliance was raised, but Largo could not overcome his habitual strategic uncertainty and shrank from pursuing a clear-cut alliance with the extreme left in opposition to the Communists and middle-class left.

Despite the moderate position of Andrés Nin, the most vocal leaders of the POUM came out in April for complete revolutionary reorganization of the government. Juan Andrade wrote in *La Batalla* on April 4 that new revolutionary committees should be elected from the ground up. Subsequent articles— when allowed by the censors to appear—suggested that this would be the Spanish version of the Russian soviets. The JCI's intermittent *Juventud Comunista* demanded a new constituent assembly chosen by factory committees and assemblies of peasants and soldiers. Both Andrade and the JCI leaders insisted that true revolutionaries must have nothing further to do with the existing Popular Front regime.

It was clear by the end of April that the power struggle in the leftist zone—and most concretely in Catalonia—would soon reach a climax. On April 27 the Generalitat issued yet another decree that gave the FAI-CNT and the POUM forty-eight hours to hand over their private stocks of weapons. There was open skirmishing with the state police in Barcelona by the evening of April 30. On May 2 *Solidaridad Obrera* warned, "The proletariat in arms is the guarantee of the revolution. To try to disarm the people is to place oneself on the other side of the barricades. Let no one permit himself to be disarmed!"

The complete story of the internecine struggle that took place during the week that followed may never be known. An attempt by the regular police to seize the Barcelona telephone and communications center from the CNT on the afternoon of May

3 was another logical step in the restoration of government. POUM leaders, however, have said that this move was directly initiated by Gerö on Comintern instructions.[20] The move was somewhat premature for, according to Companys, the Catalan government still had only 2,000 armed police in the city.[21] They failed to carry their objective and by nightfall approximately 80 percent of Barcelona was under the control of armed workers once more in de facto rebellion against the nominal government.

The resistance of the workers seems to have been to a large degree spontaneous. Three groups were prepared to carry the situation to a climax: the POUM, the Catalan anarchist youth, and the extremist Friends of Durruti. After fighting began, POUM leaders asked their CNT counterparts if the latter were willing to participate in joint action to get rid of Stalinist influence in Catalonia once and for all.[22] They were not; the leaders of the FAI and CNT had no stomach for an uncompromising stand against the government. All they demanded of the Generalitat was dismissal of the pro-Communist security chiefs, Ayguader and Rodríguez Salas. The CNT national and regional committees considered the fighting a tragic mistake. The POUM, the Friends of Durruti, and the tiny Bolshevist-Leninist Section all called for a revolutionary change,[23] but after CNT leaders negotiated a cease-fire with the Largo Caballero government on the night of

20. Gorkín, *España, primer ensayo de democracia popular* (Buenos Aires, 1962), 70. This parallels Krivitsky, 108–11.

21. Companys, "Notes and Documents on the Fighting in Barcelona, May 3–7, 1937." (Bolloten Collection.)

22. Julián Gorkín, undated "Nota sobre las Jornadas de Mayo de 1937." (Bolloten Collection.)

23. The Bolshevist-Leninist Section printed a hasty circular on the evening of May 3:

LONG LIVE THE REVOLUTIONARY OFFENSIVE!

No compromises. Disarming of the reactionary Republican National Guard and Assault Guard. This moment is decisive. The next time will be too late. General strike in all industries not engaged in war production. Only proletarian power can assure military victory.

TOTAL ARMING OF THE WORKING CLASS!

LONG LIVE THE UNITY OF ACTION OF THE CNT-FAI-POUM!

LONG LIVE THE REVOLUTIONARY FRONT OF THE PROLETARIAT IN SHOPS, FACTORIES, BARRICADES: REVOLUTIONARY DEFENSE COMMITTEES!

May 4–5, they were too weak to resist and soon accepted the truce.

The result of the "May Days" was a partial victory for the Communists and the state; it was a defeat for the extreme left and also for Catalan autonomy. Sizable police reinforcements were moved into Barcelona and the central Republican government in Valencia announced the suspension of Catalan autonomy under the emergency provisions of the Republican constitution—a long-forgotten document that was dusted off only when convenient. A government minister for the affairs of Catalonia was named on May 6 and all military and security forces in the region were taken under central command. The cabinet of the Generalitat was allowed to reconvene several weeks later, but the scope of the Generalitat's administration was henceforth increasingly circumscribed.

Hundreds of POUMists and anarchists were arrested and scores were shot. The press and radio facilities of the extreme left were shut down, though some CNT newspapers were later allowed to reopen under strict censorship. Nevertheless, only a portion of the arms held by the CNT and POUM workers was seized, and POUM spokesmen later gave credit to the partial retention of weapons for preventing a more extensive bloodbath by the Communist-controlled police.

In the central government the Communists proposed that the defeat of the extreme left in Catalonia be exploited to carry out a win-the-war program of thorough centralization. Among other things they insisted on complete elimination of the POUM, the anarchist "uncontrollables," and the Bolshevist-Leninist Section. Largo Caballero refused to go that far. The Socialist *Adelante* (Valencia), a Largo organ, declared on May 11,

> If the Caballero government were to apply the measures of suppression to which the Spanish Section of the Communist International is trying to incite it, then it would come close to being a government of Gil Robles or Lerroux; it would destroy the unity of the working class and expose us to the dangers of losing the war and shipwrecking the revolution. . . . A government composed in its majority of people from the labor movements cannot make use of methods that are reserved for reactionary and fascist-type governments.

Largo Caballero rejected Communist proposals for centralization, state control, police terror, reduction of CNT membership in the cabinet, or Russian dictation of military affairs. On May 15, after the Communists refused further collaboration with his government, Largo resigned.

Though the non-Communists could not form a united front, the Comintern had no interest in a formal Communist takeover of the Republican government. This would have further excited western hostility to the leftist regime and made cooperation between the various parties even more difficult. What Russian policy sought was a more cooperative Socialist to serve as prime minister. The Comintern's choice was the finance minister, Juan Negrín, who had first won its notice for initiating the massive transfer of Spanish gold. By vocation a professor of physiology, Negrín had never been a formal member of the Communist party and did not figure among the crypto-Communists who had earlier infiltrated Socialist leadership. He had, however, played a temporary role in the formation of the first Spanish Communist party in 1920–21,[24] was married to a Russian woman, and had long been known as an admirer of the "great experiment" being conducted in the Soviet Union. That he was dedicated to the cause of a leftist victory irrespective of tactics or consequences seems without question. According to Jesús Hernández, who first tendered him the Communist proposal to serve as prime minister, Negrín was under little illusion as to what serving as Communist nominee would entail, but he was willing to go to the most extreme lengths for a leftist victory. To non-Communist Socialists who later protested his concessions to Communist policy, Negrín simply pointed to the fact that the Soviet Union was practically the only source of military support for leftist Spain. Alexander Orlov has judged Negrín "politically naïve," but that seems an oversimplification. He knew what he wanted—a military victory for the Popular Front—and he realized that there was only one course to follow in order to have a chance for that. The Negrín cabinet installed on May 17, 1937, was composed of 3 Socialists, 2 Communists, 2 left Republicans, 1 Catalanist, and 1 Basque Nationalist, with Prieto replacing Largo in the key post of Minister of Defense. During the two years that followed, the new

24. According to the anti-Communist Socialist Carlos de Baráibar, "La traición del stalinismo," *Timón* (June 1940), in Comín Colomer, III, 41.

prime minister rarely disappointed the Communists, and after the Civil War ended he remained closely associated with them in opposition to the non-Communist Socialists who eventually helped overthrow his regime.

Largo Caballero was shattered personally and politically by his experience with the Communists. He went into bitter, unremitting opposition and seemed more concerned to combat the Communists than to defeat Franco's Nationalists. Afterward he referred to the Civil War as a national tragedy rather than as the glorious revolutionary affirmation of the Spanish proletariat, and this was a more realistic attitude than he had shown in the years of 1933 through 1936. But in 1937–38 he was effectively silenced by the government and kept in political isolation. At the time of the May crisis, the executive commission of the UGT, still controlled by pro-Largo leaders, voted to support him as head of the government and Minister of Defense, but a meeting of the full UGT national committee was called by the pro-Communists and anti-Largo moderates at the end of that month. Though the pro-Largo revolutionary Socialists probably still had the support of the numerical majority of the UGT rank and file, since the beginning of the war the Communists and pro-Communists had organized new federations of nonindustrial workers with scanty membership that gave them control of many of the individual craft federations in the UGT. At the May 28 meeting the Communist-moderate alliance pushed through a vote of 24 to 14 rebuking the UGT executive commission for not supporting the Negrín cabinet.

Largo's followers on the executive commission took their revenge in August by expelling 29 of the 42 federations in the UGT on grounds of failure to pay dues and other organizational irregularities. These 29 federations dominated by Communists and anti-Largo moderates had scarcely half the UGT's total membership but held a strong majority of the votes on the national committee due to individual craft union representation. Consequently the anti-Largo forces called a new meeting in Valencia on October 1 to reorganize the UGT executive commission. By that time they had gained control of 31 craft federations and, with government backing, their new anti-Largo executive commission was imposed as UGT leadership.[25] An international commission headed by the French Socialist Leon Jouhaux came to Spain in January 1938 to patch things up. A new "compromise" national committee was then formed, still controlled by progovernment leaders.

Meanwhile, the POUM and the Bolshevist-Leninist Section were dissolved and their top leaders arrested. Disapproval of the other leftist parties prevented the Communist police from murdering any of them save Nin, however. The liquidation of Andrés Nin has been described by Jesús Hernández:

> The torture of Nin began with the "dry" method, an implacable inquisition lasting ten, twenty, thirty hours during which the inquisitors always ask the same questions. . . .
> Nevertheless, Andrés Nin resisted in unbelievable fashion. He gave no sign of that mental and moral collapse that led some of Lenin's old collaborators in Russia to the complete abdication of will. . . .
> His inquisitors grew impatient. They decided to abandon the "dry" method for "firmness": skin peeled off, muscles torn, physical suffering pushed to the limit of human endurance. Nin resisted the pain of the most refined tortures. After several more days his face was a shapeless mass of lacerated flesh.[26]

25. The case of the anti-Largo sector of the UGT is given in the *Memoria de la decisión de la destitución de la Comisión Ejecutiva de la Unión General de Trabajadores y fundamentos para elegir la que la ha sustituído* (Barcelona, 1937).

26. *La Grande trahison* (Paris, 1953), 103–05.
Nin was a sincere and courageous man who died a martyr to his cause. Yet it is well to remember where he stood on the question of revolutionary murder. There is no evidence that he did anything to limit the mass killings in Catalonia in 1936, and in 1922 he penned the following justification of the Bolshevist liquidation of the revolutionary extreme left in Russia:
> The Russian Communist Party is the only guarantee of the Revolution and, in the same manner as the Jacobins saw themselves obliged to guillotine the Hébertists, in spite of the fact that they represented a tendency to the left, in the same manner that we ourselves [in the CNT] have eliminated those who constituted an obstacle to the realization of the objectives we pursued, our Russian comrades see themselves inevitably obliged implacably to smother every attempt which might break their power. It is not only their right but their duty. The health of the Revolution is the supreme law.

Lucha Social (Lérida), Apr. 29, 1922, quoted in Gerald Meaker, "Spanish Anarcho-Syndicalism and the Russian Revolution 1917–1922" (USC Ph.D. dissertation, 1967), 249.
Like most of those who seek to justify revolutionary murder, Nin assumed that he was justifying the elimination of other people, not of himself.

It was finally decided to execute and bury Nin secretly, while announcing that he had been rescued by a special German Gestapo commando team.

Though the POUM's purported "Trotskyism" was one of the main reasons for its suppression, Trotsky, as was his wont, did not waste energy in shedding tears for it. In his *The Lesson of Spain: The Last Warning* (1938), written from exile in Mexico, he denounced the CNT and added, "Not much better is the record of the POUM." "Despite its intentions, *the POUM proved to be, in the final analysis, the chief obstacle on the road to the creation of a revolutionary party.*" (Italics Trotsky's.) He accused the late and, for him, unlamented POUM of isolating the "revolutionary vanguard" from the masses, rather than constructing a united mass revolutionary anti-Stalinist party.

After the suppression of the POUM, the second sector eliminated was the autonomous enclave in eastern Aragon. It was occupied by the Communist-controlled 11th and 27th divisions in August 1937; the Council of Aragon was deposed and several of its leaders murdered. Scores of anarchist collectives were broken up by force, hundreds of *cenetistas* arrested and an undetermined number killed. Though Communist writers have subsequently protested that the suppression was not carried out so brutally as the anarchists charged, such methods apparently provoked second thoughts even among certain Communist leaders at the time. After a few weeks there was a letup and many of the anarchist collectives were allowed to resume operations.

Perhaps the most surprising feature of political developments in the People's Republic in 1937 was not the growth of Communist power, but the relative meekness of most of the *cenetistas* and their willingness to suspend pure anarchosyndicalist principles in favor of cooperation with the Communist-statist regime. The FAI and CNT responded to the May Days with two months of pamphlet warfare and announced their willingness to support Largo Caballero against the Communists, but then made little effort to avoid their exclusion from the Negrín government and their expulsion from other multi-party coalition institutions of the People's Republic, such as the panels of the revolutionary courts. The great influx into the CNT during the first months of the Civil War had tended to swamp the anarchist elite within the CNT, and "syndical capitalism" and the pressures of the military struggle had brought out all the latent politicism that even the FAI had never totally overcome. As early as October 25, 1936, a FAI circular had raised the question of the desirability of converting the FAI into a regular libertarian political movement that would fulfill the same function vis-à-vis the CNT that the comparatively small Socialist party carried out regarding the UGT. This would give anarchosyndicalism the political representation and organization needed to protect its interests within the Popular Front coalition.

Between mid-1937 and the autumn of 1938 a series of concrete decisions came very close to converting the anarchist movement into a regular political party. A peninsular plenum of the FAI held at Valencia in July 1937 implicitly endorsed the notion of a multiparty revolutionary People's Republic, so long as the freedom of all members of the coalition could be preserved. It adopted the statement that

The FAI declares that our revolution must not be the expression of any totalitarian creed, but must be the exponent of all the popular sectors that influence political and social life. As anarchists we are foes of all dictatorships, whether of a caste or of a party; we are enemies of the totalitarian form of government and believe that the ideals of our people must be the result of the joint action of all sectors that cooperate in building a society without class privileges, in which the organs of administration, work and coexistence in a federal system must satisfy the needs of all the regions of Spain.[27]

The Valencia plenum voted to end the elite structure of the FAI, adopting more liberal membership standards to achieve an "anarchism of the masses." This was too much for some veteran anarchist individualists, who stamped out of the hall shouting *"¡Viva la anarquía!"*

Two months later, in September 1937, the anarchist youth federation established an "Antifascist Youth Alliance" with the official (that is, Communist) leadership of the JSU. The importance of this was mainly symbolic, for no move was to be made to merge the two organizations, but it signified the willingness

27. Quoted in José Peirats, *Los anarquistas en la crisis política española* (Buenos Aires, 1964), 286.

of most of the anarchist youth leaders to cooperate with the Communists in prosecuting the war and sharing political power. The only anarchist elements that publicly resisted the politicist, collaborationist trend were the Catalan federation of the anarchist youth (JLC) and a few remaining private anarchist societies, such as the "Irreductibles" in the industrial suburbs outside Barcelona.

A new CNT-UGT unity-of-action agreement was signed in March 1938 in the face of a powerful Nationalist military offensive in the northeast. This registered the CNT's acceptance of key goals of its rival, including a proposal to establish a Superior Economic Council under central state supervision, the nationalization of basic industries, sweeping government controls over labor in factories connected with the war effort, and, aside from the municipalization of public services, the limitation of the social and economic powers of local and communal governments by central state decree.

The first concrete step in the formation of an anarchosyndicalist political party was taken on April 2, 1938 when a regional conference of representatives of the FAI, CNT, and sectors of the anarchist youth set up an Executive Committee of the Libertarian Movement of Catalonia. The national committee of the CNT was bending over backwards to cooperate with the Negrín government, but the FAI still had reservations. The CNT national committee accepted Negrín's Thirteen Point Program announced on April 1 for ending the war on leftist terms, but the peninsular committee of the FAI denounced this proposal as selling out a genuine revolution. On April 8, to give an appearance of greater unity, Negrín restored token representation of the CNT in his government by handing the unimportant portfolio of Education to Segundo Blanco, one of the most moderate and compromising of the CNT leaders.

During the next six months, support for the formation of a coordinated anarchosyndicalist movement increased, and in late October 1938 there was held the first national conference of regional representatives of the Spanish Libertarian Movement (MLE), representing the CNT, FAI, and FIJL (anarchist youth). The CNT national committeeman Horacio Prieto, who seems to have had some influence on the CNT's moderate national secretary, Mariano Ramón Vázquez, proposed that the FAI be converted into an outright Syndicalist party, reviving the effort of the late Angel Pestaña that had collapsed two years earlier. All sectors of the MLE in Catalonia were opposed to this, as were other groups in the south and east. The only general decision on which the first MLE conference could agree was the need to maintain Popular Front unity and to continue to collaborate with the Negrín regime.

Most of the anarchist leaders apparently did not feel that they were going "reformist," but that they were simply making inevitable compromises under the pressure of military needs. Just as the Communists considered the wartime People's Republic a mere tactical phase, so the main anarchosyndicalist leaders considered collaboration a temporary expedient to facilitate the defeat of "fascism," after which they could concentrate on completing their revolution. Juan Peiró, the CNT's most influential ideologue, stressed that on the first day of military victory the struggle with the Marxists and the middle-class left would begin once more. Nonetheless, Peiró hoped to avoid another civil war among the left and agreed that the CNT should continue to collaborate in a Popular Front government after the war ended so long as by so doing it contributed to the realization of libertarian goals.[28]

AFTER HAVING ACHIEVED undisputed political power, the Negrín government implemented the economic program already outlined under the Largo cabinet: restriction of the scope of agrarian collectives; reduction of worker control to harmless proportions; centralization of state control of all important industry with the objective of concentrating "all technical direction under one person, with full powers to carry out completely his orders on production and with full responsibility." [29]

Government controls were steadily extended over factories

28. Peiró, *Problemas y cintarazos* (Rennes, 1946); "El Estado, el anarquismo y la historia," *Timón* (Oct. 1938), 65–73.
29. Juan Comorera, *El camino del Frente Popular anti-fascista es el camino de la victoria* (Barcelona, 1937).

and plans were made for the nationalization of basic industry, though deteriorating political and military conditions forestalled efforts to put them in practice. On the other hand, state policy toward the owners of industrial capital became increasingly moderate. By mid-1937 it had been established that the previous owners of expropriated property had the right to a formal hearing in which the legality of each expropriation would have to be proven. Late in 1938 Negrín announced that a program of compensation would be adopted after the war. In many cases, industrial properties outside Catalonia and the Levant that were nominally under state control nevertheless continued to be run by their original managers or owners.

The land reform was continued, but the general policy of the Negrín regime was to deny legal recognition to many of the anarchist collectives and restrict credit and equipment for those that had been legitimatized, while encouraging private property cooperatives among smallholders. CNT efforts to form an independent federation of agrarian collectives were stymied. The Ministry of Agriculture pointed to the achievements of its mixed policy in attaining a 6 percent increase in the amount of land sown in grain in the main part of the leftist zone during 1937.[30]

The major changes continued to occur in Catalonia, where the economic autonomy of the Generalitat and the CNT was steadily reduced. When the Communist Comorera replaced the

30. The following figures were given for wheat production:

	Metric Quintals		
Region	*1936*	*1937*	*Difference*
Catalonia	1,968,228	1,550,000	—417,628
Aragon	1,349,999	1,620,000	+270,001
Central Zone	5,236,721	6,090,238	+853,517
Levant	1,293,942	1,197,216	— 97,726
	9,848,890	10,458,054	+609,164

SOURCE: *Economia Politica,* in *Campo Libre,* Oct. 9, 1937, quoted by Hugh Thomas, *The Spanish Civil War* (1965 ed.), 472.

These figures are probably not fully accurate, if for no other reason than because of the irregularity of the districts involved. It would appear that production increased in approximate proportion to the extension in acreage sown. There is no evidence of notable improvements in technique; perhaps the reverse, since the grain output of the more productive areas of Catalonia and the Levant was, in contrast to that of certain other crops, altered by the turmoil of 1936–37 and registered a decline.

Catalanist Tarradellas as Councillor of Industry in the Generalitat in May 1937, he shook up the Catalan War Industry Commission to introduce greater Communist influence. Just as Indalecio Prieto, the Minister of Defense, appointed special delegates to supervise war production in various parts of the leftist
zone, Comorera named a special PSUC-dominated agency to
supervise the multiparty Catalan War Industry Commission.
CNT plans to form independent national federations of collectivized industries were blocked, and the degree of worker control
in the more important factories was progressively lessened. The
growth of UGT membership in Catalonia, which, it was claimed,
reached 550,000 by the autumn of 1937,[31] gave the Marxists almost as much numerical support as the anarchists had in Catalonia. Though the great majority of industrial workers remained
loyal to the CNT, UGT sections were expanded in some plants
and special Stakhanovite-type speed-up operations were attempted. Similarly, the UGT opposed the CNT's equal-pay policy
in favor of Russian-style skilled labor incentives and piecework
rates.

The agrarian reform in the Catalan countryside was extended during the latter part of 1937, but in most cases the interests of smallholders were still protected. Though the problem
of "bourgeois attitudes" in the Catalan countryside was recognized at the PSUC's first regular conference in July 1937,[32] the
need for cooperation in the war effort and the lack of technical

31. *Informe de José del Barrio, III Congreso de la U.G.T. en Cataluña*
(Barcelona, 1937). The Communist position on syndical problems was stated
in Del Barrio's *La labor de los militantes del P.S.U. en los sindicatos de cara
a la guerra* (Barcelona, 1937); Manuel Delicado, *Los problemas de la produc-
ción, la función de los sindicatos y la unidad sindical* (Valencia, 1937); and
Manuel D. Benavides, *Guerra y revolución en Cataluña* (Mexico City, 1946),
245–54.
32. One speaker divided the Catalan rural opposition into four categories:
(1) large owners; (2) middle holders of the Republican left who continued to
resist infringement of the private property principle; (3) former renters and
sharecroppers who gained control of land under the earlier reforms and were
determined to keep all of it (roughly analogous to the new class of Russian
kulaks of the 1920's); and (4) "Poor devils" who support anticooperative
and/or antisocialist attitudes. The membership of the FNTT in Catalonia
in mid-1937 was placed at 58,000, somewhat lower than the Rabassaires,
though "many" of the latter were said to have joined the PSUC. Victor
Colomé, *La terra i els seus fruits per a qui la conrea* (Barcelona, 1937).

facilities for a change in productive techniques resulted in continued emphasis on the family farm and private cooperatives.

A new decree of August 14, 1937, carried the agrarian reform in Catalonia farther than it had been pressed anywhere else save Aragon and Asturias, but expropriation was limited to what were, by Catalan standards, medium- and large-scale properties. For the first time it was declared that every Catalan peasant who applied for assistance was entitled to a minimal amount of land for personal cultivation. It was further stipulated that each landless laborer who did not apply for a plot of his own had to be guaranteed 20 percent of the net profit of the family farm on which he worked. The only owners of medium- and large-size properties entitled to indemnification were those who already cultivated part of their land personally; these might claim compensation for the surplus which they lost.[33]

The policy toward the lower middle classes of Catalonia, and in general toward those of the rest of the leftist zone, was perhaps most clearly explained by the Communist Estanislau Ruiz i Ponseti, Undersecretary of the Generalitat's Council of Economy, in a speech of September 9, 1937. He admitted that some former capitalists had been greatly victimized, for the social welfare system of the new regime was not well developed and some of those whose property had been expropriated were left entirely without assistance. Ruiz i Ponseti found the system of municipalization of housing as carried out in many Catalan towns to be more just because in that sphere the principle of compensation was recognized—at least to a degree.

I believe that if our land continues to have a mixed economy—a system of socialized property beside a system of private property—there will be no alternative to adopting eventually a solution in collectivized industry similar to that adopted in the municipalization of housing.

He also attacked the provisions for *agrupaments industrials* that made it possible for collectives to take over small competing firms:

33. *Decret d'adjudicació de terres i sistemes de treball* (Barcelona, 1938); Josep Torrents (agrarian secretary of the PSUC central committee), *La revolució democràtica i els camperols de Catalunya* (Barcelona, 1937). Cf. Vicente Uribe, *La política agraria del Partido Comunista* (Valencia, 1937), and the Instituto de Reforma Agraria, *Por una cooperativa en cada pueblo, dentro del Instituto de Reforma Agraria* (Valencia, 1937).

Revolutionary practice abused this principle. It interpreted the law of *agrupaments industrials* not only to combine large and small industries but to expropriate very small commercial establishments operated by only one person or a single family. This system has resulted in incalculable complaints, intolerable abuses and has subjected to undeserved misery broad sectors of our lower middle class, who have bitterly complained of these actions, thinking them to be the direct result of the system of collectivizations. It must be realized that this is not correct, . . . for it is an abuse of the system of collectivizations. The original system was not intended to destroy the lower middle class but to allow the workers in large industries to take possession of the tools of production that by rights were theirs. . . .

. . . When we want to establish the initial parallel between the transformation carried out in the Union of Soviet Socialist Republics and the transformation carried out in our land, we can say that the beginning of the transformation was about the same; the first steps were quite similar. There the evolution has been long and painful and has presented great difficulties at certain times. In our country we have tried to carry out the transformation in the most rapid way possible. It would be senseless not to try to profit by the experience of others. . . . And so since our Russian comrades after long years of war communism followed by misery and hunger finally arrived at the beginning of the NEP, . . . here we have tried to avoid that painful experience, . . . and leap in a single jump, . . . from the primitive war communism that we experienced during the first months to our own period of the New Economic Policy, to the period of subsistence . . . in good comradeship of socialized property side by side with private property.

It is clear that private property will be eliminated, and among us will be eliminated rapidly, by collectivized property. But it is also clear that no country in the world can afford the adjustments required by immediate total collectivization. That is such a costly step no one would recommend that total immediate collectivization be attempted.

. . . We are already under the New Economic Policy, trying to make the principle of private property compatible with the existence of collective property. This is the strongest, most sure and humane formula—and also the most efficient—to arrive rapidly at the collectivization of all property. It is also the most rapid formula with which to subdue private property, and to subdue it precisely with its own weapons.[34]

The Catalanists grew more and more anxious about the steady shrinkage of their sphere of autonomy. The new Generalitat cabinet chosen in the summer of 1937 was composed exclusively of Catalanists and Communists, but the elimination of the

---

34. Estanislau Ruiz i Ponseti, *Les Empreses Collectivitzades i el nou ordre econòmic* (Barcelona, 1937).

CNT accentuated latent disagreements between the governing forces. The Generalitat assembly met for the first time since the start of the war on August 18–19, 1937, and immediately adjourned sine die. As pressure from anarchosyndicalism lessened, the Catalanists became increasingly conservative; they would have liked to restore private ownership of housing in towns where most residences had been municipalized, but the Communists refused.[35] More important was their dismay over the fact that Barcelona had become the center of NKVD activity since the May Days. Companys denounced the volume of arbitrary killings that continued in Catalonia even during 1938. The secret police remained busily at work, dumping new corpses on the edges of highways as had the militia at the beginning of the Civil War. In addition, the regular "popular tribunals" in Catalonia continued a high volume of "legal repression," handing down "nearly one hundred" death sentences in one week as late as the spring of 1938.[36] But after the seat of Republican government had been moved from Valencia to Barcelona, the function of Catalan autonomy had become little more than symbolic. Police operations were already under central control, and economic decrees of November 1937 and April 1938 established "total control" by the central government over certain industries and broadened its jurisdiction over others.

The last straw for the Catalanists occurred in August 1938, during the battle of the Ebro, when the Republican government brushed aside what remained of the authority of the Catalan commissions and assumed full control of all war-related Catalan industry. This was hardly so shocking as the Catalanists pretended, but removed the last symbolic illusion of autonomy. The two Basque and Catalan ministers in Negrín's government resigned. Though the regionalists were eventually persuaded to reenter the cabinet, the last phase of the war in Catalonia was one of gloom and frustration.

The Socialist party fared somewhat better than the regional-

35. PSUC, *Documents interessants: Esquerra Republicà, la C.N.T., la U.G.T., el Partit Socialist Unificat de Catalunya* (1938).
36. Companys to Negrín, Apr. 25, 1938, in documentary appendix to Pedro Bosch Gimpera, "Notas al libro de H. Thomas sobre la guerra civil española," *Ciencias Políticas y Sociales*, VIII:30 (1962), 523–65.

ists, at least in maintaining its separate institutional status. It continued to hold the largest bloc of representatives in the cabinet of any single organization and retained a large core of followers in the main part of the Popular Front zone. As prime minister, Negrín did not desert his own party, but discouraged Communist efforts to form a "unity party" with the Socialists. The fact that the government was formally a Republican coalition allowed the prime minister a degree of independence in some matters that the Communists had to respect, so long as it did not thwart their military and diplomatic plans. A "Program of Common Action" had been signed by the executive leadership of both parties in August 1937, but it guarded against piecemeal takeovers of sectors of the Socialist party by the Communists, and the premature formation of a Socialist-Communist *partido único* in Jaén province was immediately repudiated. Socialist antipathy to the Communists increased during 1938, and demands for fusion were dropped. Moreover, the Socialist leaders were in large part responsible for blunting Communist insistence on the holding of new elections. The Communist chiefs were confident that their great military and political influence, combined with their superior propaganda facilities, would enable them to achieve greatly increased representation in an exclusively leftist parliament, but precisely because of this they could not overcome the apprehension of the leaders of other parties.

By 1938 Soviet policy was to maintain a military delaying action as long as possible without requiring major Russian expenditure. This would provide continued leverage for Soviet diplomacy and might prove of strategic value should the Soviet Union become involved in war with Germany. Hence Communist concentration on military strength and the maintenance of discipline were redoubled. Complaints from the chastened extreme left were met with the forceful argument that without military victory there would be no revolution at all, and that the current domestic policy of state control and a mixed economy was the only truly revolutionary one, for it would maintain the productive balance needed for victory while laying the basis for a collectivist system through public control of industry.

Yet the Comintern became more and more concerned about

the lack of response of the western democracies to the leftist effort in Spain and strove to make the Republican government appear more moderate outwardly while inwardly the Communist hegemony waxed stronger. Indalecio Prieto, the last important independent figure in the government, was eliminated as Defense Minister after the collapse of the Aragonese front in March 1938. After helping the Communists dump Largo Caballero a year earlier, he had staunchly opposed Socialist political merger with the Communists and had made an effort, albeit largely ineffective, to avoid Communist control of the Republican military. Public charges against Prieto were based on his famous "pessimism," and pessimistic he had certainly been since the spring of 1936, though his work as Minister of Defense was reasonably efficient.

According to Hernández, the Comintern advisers instructed the Communist central committee to withdraw its representatives altogether from the new cabinet to be formed after Prieto's ouster. The intention was to mask the extent of actual Communist influence and allay the fears of the western democracies about a Communist-dominated Republic by forming a cabinet entirely of cooperative non-Communists who could be relied upon to work with Negrín in continuing the war effort. Such a maneuver proved too difficult to arrange; the cabinet was reconstituted with two Communist ministers and much the same representation as before, save that the vital Ministry of Defense was taken over directly by Negrín. This further reinforced the Communist military hegemony.

There have been many polemics pro and con about the nature of the "democracy" that obtained under the Spanish Popular Front regime of 1936–39. Its defenders have stressed the degree of freedom under a multiparty coalition compared with the tight single-party authoritarianism of Franco's Nationalist government. Its detractors have sometimes called it a regime of out-and-out police terror. Both views are incomplete, but both contain significant elements of truth. Even in the final phase of the Civil War, there was opportunity for a certain amount of public dissent—only by leftists, of course, not by independent liberals or conservatives—and this was not possible in the opposing zone. But in other respects there was less difference between the internal policies of the contending regimes, for under the People's Republic there were no elections, little or no attention to constitutional law, little attempt to achieve a government fully representative even of all the left. Specific domestic achievements, such as expansion of education in several areas under difficult wartime conditions, were not so significant as to obscure these fundamental facts.

It is still impossible to assess exactly the extent and effect of the wartime terror. The number of victims of the Franco regime in the long run was probably greater than that of the People's Republic and its revolutionary precursors, but only if the large volume of executions carried out after the war as punishment and vengeance for the Red Terror is included. During the early months the left probably killed more than the right, but moderated its practices after uninterrupted military defeat made it vital to try to conciliate moderate opinion both inside and outside Spain. It is legitimate to ask what the policy of the left would have been in this regard had they won the war. They showed little leniency during the early weeks when they believed things were going their way and later carried out a purge in Teruel on the occasion of their only military victory during the second half of the war. The way in which the leftists would have treated the Nationalists had they defeated them is perhaps best illustrated by the way they treated each other. There was nothing in Franco's zone to equal the almost constant interparty murder that went on under the People's Republic. For example, Joaquín Maurín, the chief founder of the POUM, was probably saved from death only by the paradoxical circumstance of being captured by the Nationalists at the beginning of the war; otherwise the NKVD would probably have liquidated him along with Nin.

Death sentences were nominally abolished by the People's Republic in September 1938, but that did not halt political killings by the police. In fact, during the latter months of 1938 the government relied mainly on police repression and censorship to sustain discipline. This was a major factor in the final collapse of morale within the People's Republic.

FOURTEEN *The Republican*

People's Army

DURING THE SPRING OF 1936 one of the few things all the
revolutionary parties agreed upon was that the regular
Spanish Army and its professional officer corps should
be replaced by some sort of revolutionary militia. Yet, though
the Republican left and the officer corps were mutually hostile
because of the manner and substance of Azaña's army reform of
1931–32, the Azaña government of 1936 shrank from a drastic
reorganization of the armed forces. It did not want to run the
risk of directly provoking a military revolt and its leaders were
also probably reluctant to place themselves irremediably in the
power of the revolutionaries. The only change was to switch
most command assignments, so that by July 1936 nearly all
sections of the Army were led by senior officers known to be
either proliberal or at least respectful of the established authority.

The rebellion that precipitated the revolution and Civil
War was not a "generals' revolt" but a rising by the active middle
strata of the officer corps that in many cases dragged senior
generals along with it. Most officers in senior command positions

refused to take personal initiative, but the conspirators gained control of the only first-rate section of the regular Army, the 25,000 troops in Morocco, and managed to spark some sort of revolt in most garrisons. These were successful in little more than one-third of the peninsular posts, mainly in the areas where the civilian population was politically conservative.

A significant portion of the armed forces remained loyal and at the orders of the newly formed Giral ministry of July 19. The nominal government retained most of the First, Third, and Fourth Infantry divisions, as well as parts of the Second, at Málaga, and and of the Sixth (the Santander regiment and the Bilbao brigade), and nearly all of Spain's munitions factories. According to a memo of the First Section of the Nationalist General Staff, dated July 15, 1937, the division of forces that occurred in the first week of the conflict was approximately as follows:

	Popular front	Nationalists
Regular Army in the Peninsula, Balearics and Canaries	36,685	23,595
Army of Africa	341*	24,400
Civil Guard	20,120	14,200
Assault Guard and Armed Police	22,000	9,200
Carabineros (border guards)	8,750	6,040
TOTALS	87,555	77,435

* (on leave in the Peninsula)

This seems roughly correct for the organized forces available to the left, but apparently does not include all the troops reincorporated in the Nationalist military units. It would probably be accurate to raise the figure for the latter by 25 percent to a sum slightly greater than those of the progovernment forces, though of course the addition of many tens of thousands of militia soon gave the loyalists a great numerical advantage.

Despite the success of the revolt in several regions and the desire of the revolutionaries to abolish the regular army, the Popular Front regime was not left without a significant number of organized military units of its own. Some of the army forces that remained nominally loyal in leftist territory were rendered of little value by internal conflict, but others were immediately mobilized and the first columns sent out against the Nationalists on July 20–22 were composed primarily though not exclusively of regular army units. In the northeast, these scored the principal victories against the small rebel forces in Aragon (at Caspe, Alcañiz, and Huesca) before being submerged by leftist militia.

Moreover, approximately 75 to 80 percent of the Air Force and most of the Navy remained loyal[1] to the Popular Front regime, so that the preponderance of force in the early stages of the fighting was clearly on the side of the left, had there been unity and leadership to exploit it. The proleftist sections of the Navy were, however, gravely incapacitated by the slaughter of officers that they carried out; some ships were partially crippled for lack of discipline and leadership. This was not the case in the Air Force, which had always been more sympathetic to the left than other sectors of the armed forces, nor was it necessarily the case in the regular Army.

Proleftist apologists have tried to explain the incoherence of the Popular Front's military effort by the notion that almost the entire professional officer corps deserted to the rebels at the beginning of the Civil War. This is not correct. There were 8,000 officers on active duty in 1936, plus 8,000 to 10,000 on the retired list but still under 65 years of age. At least 70 percent of the officers on active duty were to be found in the leftist zone, and of these no more than one-third had actively participated in the rebellion. Altogether, a pool of approximately 10,000 professional officers who were not committed to the rebels was available in the leftist zone. Had there been intelligent and imaginative leadership politically, these men might have been used militarily to decisive effect.

The revolutionary onslaught that erupted after July 19 largely precluded this possibility. "Arming of the people" meant the hasty formation of scores of disparate, poorly organized, ill-led, untrained, often completely undisciplined militia units which within a few weeks swamped what was left of the regular

1. The eventual lineup of the respective fleets by September 1936 was:

Nationalists	Popular Front
1 battleship	1 battleship
2 cruisers	4 cruisers
1 destroyer	16 destroyers
2 gunboats	6 torpedo boats
	9 submarines

Army. A Militia Bureau was set up in the Ministry of War to try to coordinate these elements. The Bureau was directed by professional officers, the most important of whom were Communist party members, but at first such authority as it had was limited to the greater Madrid region.

On July 28 the Giral government announced the call-up of the military contingents for the years 1933 and 1934 as a first step to rebuild a regular Army. This met with opposition from all the revolutionary groups save the Communists. The CNT was the most vociferous in its resistance. When the call-up was repeated by the Catalan Generalitat, 10,000 anarchosyndicalists attended a protest meeting in Barcelona on August 4. Militiamen receiving enlistment notices were told by the CNT to ignore them and return to militia groups. *Solidaridad Obrera* declared on August 5: "The CNT cannot understand or defend the need for a regular uniformed Army. . . . If you do not want to be obligatory soldiers, the CNT sustains your judgment." And the anarchist *Boletín de Información* said on the same day: "We will go to the militia. To the front as well. But to go to the barracks as before, soldiers subject to discipline and orders which do not come from the popular forces, No."

On August 2 the government tried an alternate tactic when it announced a plan to form "volunteer battalions" led by professional officers, though the official call for regular army volunteers did not go out until August 17. Because of leftist opposition it was announced that the "Volunteer Army" would be composed of volunteers from the First Reserve (meaning men who had previously served in the regular Army from 1931 to 1936) to be led by retired professional officers and NCOs whose political loyalty could be vouched for by a Popular Front organization. This was a revival of an old nineteenth-century Spanish Republican idea, but it was too much for most of the revolutionaries. On behalf of the revolutionary Socialists, *Claridad* declared on August 20 that "To think about any other kind of Army to substitute for the present militia that might in some way control their revolutionary action is to think in a counterrevolutionary manner." Within a few days the idea of forming a "Volunteer Army" had to be dropped.

Throughout the summer of 1936 military affairs went from bad to worse for the leftists. The first phase of the war was lost by the inability of the loyal sections of the fleet to blockade the straits of Morocco and prevent the passage of the elite Army of Africa, backbone of the rebel offense. Not merely was the leftist naval superiority employed ineffectively, but the nearly four-to-one superiority in aircraft during the first days was also squandered. No serious effort was made to provide air support for the fleet, which was easily scattered by a handful of Italian aircraft sent to assist the rebels.

By August most remnants of the regular Army had been submerged, and the entire military effort rested on the militia. Formation of the volunteer militia represented a spontaneous outpouring of enthusiasm and sometimes of bravery on the part of the revolutionary groups. Even the parties of the middle-class left organized small detachments. Altogether, by the end of 1936 the militia bureau tallied a total of 146,936 men who had been enrolled in the disparate militia battalions and columns,[2] and this figure was undoubtedly incomplete. The Giral government made an effort to control the disorder and indiscriminate seizure of property by the militia through a decree of August 13 that awarded the militiamen a daily wage of 10 pesetas—$1.25— which made them the best-paid common soldiers in the world in 1936. In addition to being the best paid, they were among the most poorly organized and militarily ineffective. The successive columns sent south to oppose the advance of the Army of Africa were chewed up in turn by the small veteran Nationalist forces. The Catalan Anti-Fascist Militia Committee sitting in Barcelona accomplished even less. The Catalanists eagerly packed off the most incendiary anarchist elements to the militia in Aragon, where 30,000 leftist militiamen could do little more than hold their own against a thin line of no more than 10,000 Nationalists, many of whom were also militia, but from the antileftist parties. The other major enterprise of the Catalan militia, an effort to invade and occupy the Nationalist-held island of Mallorca, ended in failure.

The leftists persistently complained of lack of equipment, but in the early stages of the war they were no more poorly

2. Comandancia General de Milicias, *Un esfuerzo en 1936* (Madrid, 1937).

equipped than the rebels.[3] The latter did control about five-eighths of the artillery, but the small Spanish armored units were equally divided and the leftists had great superiority in munitions and secondary supplies. In the northeast, the militia were probably better equipped than the scattered Nationalist forces on the Aragonese front.

It was above all else the military struggle that brought Spanish communism to the fore. Even before the Civil War began, the Comintern recognized the importance of providing a well-organized military base for the party in Spain. Under the Republic, the Socialists insulted army officers and the FAI occasionally carried out isolated guerrilla raids on military barracks, but the Communists built up their own separate organized military apparatus as well as a network of cells within the armed forces proper. Such planning and organization paid off as soon as the fighting started. A nucleus of Communist or pro-Communist professional officers was ready to work in the government Ministry of War. Communist military leaders such as Juan Modesto and Enrique Líster (Liste), who had studied briefly in the Frunze Academy at Leningrad, were already active in the Communist militia (MAOC).

Using the MAOC as their base, the Communists built up at Madrid the only well-organized and partially professionally led militia cadre in leftist Spain—the so-called "Fifth Regiment," labeled thus to designate the "People's Regiment" that would take the place of the four regular infantry regiments that formerly made up the capital's garrison. Under the chief Comintern military adviser in Spain, Vittorio Vidali (Carlos Contreras), the Fifth Regiment imposed discipline and gave its members regular training. It built its own reserve cadres, its own supply system, and its own artillery and support units. Communist leaders have since claimed that the political origins of Fifth Regiment volunteers were:

Communists	50%	Left Republicans	15%
Socialists	25%	Without party	10%

3. Leftist writers have been reluctant to recognize this fact, but consider the remarks of the Socialist leader Romero Solano: "The battle at Oropesa [in August 1936] was a disaster similar to that at Mérida. And all for lack of organization and discipline, since in those days we had as much equipment as the enemy." *Vísperas de la guerra de España* (Mexico City, 1947), 310.

Altogether, during its five months of existence, the Fifth Regiment purportedly trained nearly 70,000 men,[4] though this figure is not confirmed by the available records of the People's Army. Thus the Communists made the greatest single contribution of any individual party to the formation of the militia columns that tried to stave off the northward advance of Franco's forces; their losses were correspondingly heavy.

The Communists made a "regular, disciplined army" one of their main goals by the middle of August 1936. The need had always been acknowledged by the middle-class left and the revolutionary Socialists began to accept this fact by the end of August, after the loss of much of Socialist Extremadura to the rebels. One of the two principal objectives of the Largo Caballero government was the formation of a regular organized People's Army to defend the revolution.

The creation of the People's Army may thus be dated from the month of September 1936, and the initial leaders were Largo's own chief military advisers, Col. José Asensio and Gen. Martínez Cabrera. On September 11, approximately one week after becoming prime minister and defense minister, Largo appointed an official military commander-in-chief, together with a regular General Staff section, for each main theater of operations. Even though the authority of the new leaders of the People's Army was at first respected only in the central area around Madrid, this was a beginning. In a series of three decrees between September 29 and October 22, Largo officially militarized all the militia, placing them under regular army discipline. A General Militia Command was established to transform these volunteer battalions into regular army units.

During September and October plans went forward to create organized brigades, and this at a time when the Nationalist battalions still functioned on an ad hoc basis. During the entire first year of the war, the staff of the People's Army surpassed the Nationalists in the scope, if not the quality, of its planning and mobilization. Before the end of October, the call

4. Enrique Líster, *Nuestra guerra* (Paris, 1966), 62, and *La defensa de Madrid batalla de unidad* (Toulouse, 1945); A. Samarin, *Borba za Madrid* (Moscow, 1940), 25–28.

was officially resumed for all the former recruits of the classes 1932–35. On October 10, the best of the militia units in the Madrid area were reorganized as the first six regularly constituted brigades of the People's Army. Two-thirds of these troops came from the Fifth Regiment volunteers, four of the first six brigade commanders were Communists from the Fifth Regiment and altogether "more than sixty percent of the commands of the first units of the People's Army were given to the Communist Party." [5]

As a revolutionary military force, the People's Army adopted the insignia of its only counterpart, the Red Army of the Soviet Union, to make the red star its official emblem on uniforms, decorations, weapons, and so forth. In place of the normal military salute, the clenched fist of the Communist cadres became the official army salutation.

The two crucial problems were equipment and leadership. The former, for better or worse, was provided mainly by the Soviet Union. The latter would have to come mainly from the thousands of professional officers in the Popular Front zone, and from the best of the militia chiefs. Soon after the start of the fighting, the Ministry of War had appointed a special officer classification committee, the central figure of whom was the Communist Major Díaz Tendero, who had been the chief organizer of the leftist officer association, UMRA. The committee's task was to classify all available officers according to political reliability. Three grades of classification were used: F (ascist), I (ndifferent), and R (epublican). The committee's labors were influenced by the general hatred of professional officers that pervaded the leftist zone and the sectarian animosities of its own members, who as UMRA militants had been among a small minority and seemed eager to wreak vengeance. There is no reliable information as to how many officers were originally classified in each category, but it seems that at first very few "Rs" were assigned. Loyal officers who had taken part in leading militia columns were sometimes held suspect; several who had been wounded fighting for the Popular Front were pulled out of their columns and shot. Factors such as this must be kept

5. Segismundo Casado, *The Last Days of Madrid* (London, 1939), 53.

in mind when noting the tendency of some of the erstwhile loyal officers to desert their leftist units in the summer and fall of 1936. Conversely, some of the officers who later most distinguished themselves in the People's Army were first classed as "Fs" because of their lack of proleftist zeal.

After the formation of the People's Army, classification was relaxed, for the need for competent leadership was sorely felt. The Communists then showed themselves more understanding than any other revolutionary group in accepting professional officers and making use of their talents. The aim was to reproduce Trotsky's feat of the years 1918 to 1920 in using the old-style professionals to help build a revolutionary army, but because the pressure of the extreme left was much greater in Spain, the policy worked out less successfully than in Russia. Furthermore, the notion that the Communists were purely and simply interested in military efficiency is misleading. The Communists themselves frequently rejected professional officers in order to promote party members from the ranks into positions of influence. Moreover, as they later showed, the Communists would use professional officers as scapegoats for their own political purposes, and in this respect were scarcely superior to the anarchists.

Altogther, the records of the People's Army are said to indicate that approximately 3,000 officers from the active list of July 1936 actually served, plus at least 1,500 more from among the retirees. But they were always resented by the leftist militants and most had to be assigned to staffwork, training, supply, and other appointments in the rear. Perhaps no more than 500 ever held active field command of troops.[6]

The burden of field leadership thus fell on militia officers and new candidates risen from the ranks. This fact alone had grave consequences, for the handful of trusted professional officers and the militia chiefs, who, together with their Red Army advisers, composed the upper echelon of People's Army

6. C. Liubarskii, *Nekotorie operativno-takticheskie vivodi iz opita voini v Ispanii* (Moscow, 1939), says that ultimately 70 percent of the professional officers were purged or went over to the Nationalists. The figure is perhaps a trifle too high.

leadership, never solved the problem of developing a corps of capable junior- and middle-rank officers. The Fifth Regiment had already begun its own officer training school, and the military schools at Madrid were the best the People's Army had until mid-1938. The Catalan Anti-Fascist Militia Committee, though it long resisted the incorporation of its forces into the People's Army, also opened an officers' school in Barcelona. Attached to the "Bakunin Barracks," it turned out some 2,000 officers during its first eight months. Finally, in late November and December, the central command began the formation of special schools for each branch of the armed forces and for the northern zone as well. A People's Staff College for senior officers was announced, and later a People's General Staff College, but the quality of instruction and facilities was wanting, and the length of time devoted to training was insufficient. The leadership of most units of the People's Army proved mediocre at best.

Another important decision taken in October, at the suggestion of the Russians, was to set up a regular corps of political commissars, assigning one to each unit at the level of company and above to provide political indoctrination and improve security and morale. The commissars, based on the Red Army system, were also to watch over the well-being of the troops, supervising supply, food, clothing, furloughs, and the like. As in the Russian system, most battalion-level orders were to be countersigned by the respective commissar. The first Inspector General of Commissars was the crypto-Communist Alvarez del Vayo; it was not surprising that a large majority of the commissars appointed were either Communists or directly pro-Communist. Many had received their training in the Fifth Regiment. Though the officer development system never functioned effectively, the political commissars played an important role in the People's Army. The Nationalist forces had no regular system of political indoctrination, and in the first year or so of the war this cost them a number of desertions,[7] though

7. A report by the commander of the Nationalist 52nd Division in the Calamocha region (Aragon), June 1, 1937, claimed that the enemy was astounded at the absence of indoctrination in the Nationalist Army and recommended that a series of political lectures be organized for the troops to lower the desertion rate. (Bolloten Collection.)

there is no evidence that the number of desertions from the Nationalists was markedly higher than the flow from the opposite direction.

During August and September few military supplies were received by the Popular Front forces from abroad. Stocks steadily dwindled, and the matériel problem became extremely critical (and for the Nationalists as well—in some Nationalist sectors during October 1936 orders were given not to fire unless fired upon because of the shortage of ammunition).

Direct Russian military assistance, as distinct from Comintern activity, first became important in October 1936. As indicated in Chapter 12, there is some evidence that a small group of Russian aviators and planes arrived about the first of August, and another small detachment may have been sent in September,[8] but nothing substantial appeared until October, when large shipments of arms arriving in the ports of eastern Spain temporarily gave the People's Army superiority in matériel once more. During October and early November at least 50 heavy tanks and 100 planes were received, with at least one Russian crewman for each tank and one pilot for each plane.[9] Records of the People's Army are said to indicate that another 36 Russian fighter planes and aviators were sent directly to Asturias. Other shipments followed; by the first of January 1937 a total of 13 Russian squadrons (156 planes) had been committed to the central front around Madrid. This quickly

8. German Consul Report from Barcelona, Sept. 16, 1936, *Documents on German Foreign Policy* (Washington, 1950), Series D, III, 89.

9. Soviet Army Archives, in K. L. Maidanik, *Ispanskii proletariat v natsionalno-revoliutsionnoi voine* (Moscow, 1960), 179.

During the first three and one-half months of the war, prior to the arrival of the German Condor Legion, the left had either retained or received a total of at least 300 planes, compared with approximately 128 for the insurgents. The Popular Front forces began the war with at least 160 planes, received 94 from France between August and October (the Nationalist military historian Col. Priego says 98, beginning on July 25), and approximately 100 planes from the Soviet Union by the end of October (Priego claims 200). The Nationalists began with only 44 planes and received a total of 84 from Germany and Italy up to November 1, but used theirs more effectively. The balance was righted for them by arrival of the Condor Legion in November and further Italian shipments in December.

brought counterescalation by Germany and Italy that erased the temporary advantage of the People's Army.

By the time of the first major Russian arms shipments, the Soviet military mission had also been fully organized in the leftist zone. It consisted of a relatively small corps of observers, advisers, and technicians charged with making detailed reports on military activities and the use of new weapons and tactics, providing advice and planning assistance to all units of the People's Army at least from the size of brigade upward, helping develop military schools, and aiding in the training of Spaniards for the specialized branches of the armed forces, particularly in aviation and armor. The most extensive study of this matter concludes that there were probably not more than a total of from 500 to 700 Russian military personnel in Spain at any given time, amounting to no more than 3,000 throughout the span of the war.[10]

Of all sectors of the People's Army, the one most thoroughly dominated by the Russians was the Air Force. The chief Russian "adviser" had almost complete control, drawing bitter complaint from such disparate Popular Front leaders as Prieto and Largo Caballero.[11] The Air Force was conducted with great independence [12] and Prieto has written that during his tenure

10. Robert L. Plumb, "Soviet Participation in the Spanish Civil War" (Georgetown University dissertation, 1956), 275.
11. "The Air Force was directed by a Russian, though officially there was a Spanish commander. The Republic paid for the matériel but the Russians believed they had the right to direct training and even decide whether or not orders to send aircraft to any sector of the front were to be obeyed. The General Staff would order the transfer of planes because they were planning an offensive or had to stop an enemy advance; Prieto would communicate this to the Air Force commander and the latter to the Russian chief. There were numerous cases in which the Air Force did not obey, preventing our own units from advancing or stopping the advance of the enemy." Largo Caballero, *Mis memorias*, 206.
12. Casado, *Last Days of Madrid*, 54, has written: "I can state clearly that during the whole war neither the Air Force nor the Tank Corps was controlled by the Minister of National Defense, nor in consequence by the Central General Staff. The Minister and his staff were not even aware of the quantity and types of their machines and only knew the situation of those which were used in actual operations. In the same way the Minister and his Staff were not aware of the situation, and even of the existence, of a great number of unknown 'flying fields' (aerodromes) maintained in secret by the 'friendly

as Air Minister of Defense his orders were constantly counter-
manded. The Spanish Communist commander-in-chief of the
Air Force, Gen. Ignacio Hidalgo de Cisneros, told Burnett
Bolloten "that Soviet pilots were relieved every few months
and that altogether one thousand flew in Spain during the
war."[13] It appears that in the early part of the war approximately half the pilots were Russian, though this proportion
steadily declined.

The first important fully organized foreign units to enter
the fighting were the Communist-prepared International Brigades, two of which were sent into combat at Madrid early in
November 1936. The first individual foreign volunteers were
not those recruited by the Communists, but small numbers of
anarchists and others from France and other western countries
who joined the CNT militia in Catalonia during the first
week of the war. Easy access to the French border also made
it possible for the PSUC to form several loosely organized
companies of foreigners in August 1936, but neither of these
groups amounted to fully equipped, organized, and trained
foreign units. The original decision to form an international
volunteer force that might serve as the nucleus of an international Communist army was taken by the Comintern meeting
in Prague on July 26, and the first major contingent consisted
of a group of German Communist refugees who were shipped
out of the Soviet Union to Spain in September. From the
beginning it was planned to take advantage of the groundswell
of sympathy for the Spanish Popular Front among leftist and
progressivist elements throughout Europe and America to build
Communist military strength in Spain. Recruiting for the
International Brigades remained under Communist control
throughout and in most cases no one of suspect political background was sent to Spain. The largest number of volunteers
came from France, because of its geographical proximity, but
standards also seem to have been lower among the French
recruiters. The French contingent seems to have included

---

advisers' and certain of the aviation chiefs who were entirely in their
confidence."
13. Bolloten, *The Grand Camouflage,* 125.

more adventurers and more of the shiftless, and achieved a less distinguished record than most sectors of the Brigades, in contrast to the almost uniformly high performance of the smaller group of French rightist volunteers who made up the Jeanne d'Arc battalion serving with the Nationalists. At first International Brigades were not fully integrated with the People's Army. As a separate Comintern military machine they had their own general staff, training schools, commissariat, supply system, and even their own military intelligence network. After mid-1937 recruitment dwindled and during the second half of the war more and more Spanish troops had to be enrolled in the Brigades to keep them up to strength, as also happened in the Italian Volunteer Corps serving with the Nationalists. There has been much controversy about the total number of foreign volunteers who served in the Brigades. The only detailed statistics are from the Soviet Army Archives and are reproduced in Table 14.1.

Controversy over the total numbers of foreign participants on both sides in the Spanish Civil War has amounted to one of the more heated "numbers games" played by recent historiography. The main question mark still refers to the International Brigades. Evidence points to about 35,000; there is no guarantee that the number was not larger, but the claims of Spanish Nationalist historians are undoubtedly exaggerated. Even if the total number of volunteers in the Brigades amounted, as some think, to 50,000 or 60,000 (and there is no direct support for such a figure), the total number of foreign participants on the leftist side would amount to approximately half the sum of those assisting the Nationalists.[14]

14. The foreign participation on the Nationalist side was composed of four categories: German special units, the Italian Corps (plus aviation and artillery), the Moroccan battalions, and volunteers from other European countries. The only figure that has ever come from a Nationalist source regarding the number of Moroccan mercenaries is 70,000, but since only 75 battalions of less than 500 men each were formed, the figure may be too large. Concerning the Italians, the Historical Service of the Spanish Army's General Staff acknowledges the presence of as many as 40,000 Italians in the spring of 1937, which may indicate that as many as 50,000 altogether served. The German contingent was, however, only slightly larger than the Russian one, and the total number of foreign volunteers on the Nationalist side from other coun-

TABLE 14.1. *National Composition of the International Brigades (Based on figures at the end of April 1938)*

Nationality	Total enlistment	Remaining in April 1938	Killed up to March 30, 1938
French	8,778	2,700	942
Polish	3,034	1,212	466
Italian	2,908	1,310	526
Americans	2,274	740	276
Germans	2,180	1,030	308
British	1,806	735	124
Belgians	1,701	701	185
Czechs	1,046	610	133
Austrians	846	430	138
Yugoslavs		300	
Bulgarians		166	
Rumanians	2,056	109	—
Albanians		—	
Greeks			
Latvians			
Lithuanians	862	—	179
Estonians			
Finns			
Danes		200	
Swedes	662	173	91
Norwegians		84	
Dutch	586	170	42
Hungarians	510	195	56
Canadians	510	181	71
Swiss	406	110	78
Misc.	1,072	—	960
TOTALS	31,237	11,156	4,575

SOURCE: Soviet Army Archives, in Maidanik, 206.

The first important victory for the People's Army—and there were not many—was the defense of Madrid against the Nationalist attack in November-December 1936. This was undoubtedly a human victory as well as a military triumph, attributable in part to the enthusiasm, determination, and self-sacrifice of the defenders. They had the advantages of numbers, interior lines,

tries besides Italy and Germany may not have even reached 10,000. In toto, this would indicate a minimum of 125,000 foreigners on the Nationalist side compared with an absolute maximum of 60,000 (probably less) serving with the People's Army.

a good defensive position, and superiority in armor thanks to the Russian tanks.[15] In 1936 the Red Army possessed the only heavily armored cannon-bearing tanks in regular use anywhere in the world. The Nationalists had only a few light English and Italian tanks armed with machine guns, and at first completely lacked antitank weapons. Yet, though Russian tanks and the International Brigades provided important assistance, the defense of Madrid was basically the achievement of the leftist militia of central Spain, for the most part still loosely organized and not yet properly formed into People's Army units.

Defensive fighting proved to be the People's Army's strong point, for it exploited the basic stubbornness and tenacity of the Spanish character without calling for the more complex organization needed in offensive operations. Yet defensive fighting rarely wins a war, and during the winter months of 1937 the People's Army command struggled to complete the transformation of the militia and build up a strike force. They planned to have 15 brigades (approximately 50,000 men), 50 heavy tanks, and 100 pieces of artillery ready for a counteroffensive south of Madrid in mid-February, but were forestalled by the Nationalists' pre-emptive attack along the Jarama on February 6. The two-week battle that followed was the first sustained large-scale engagement of the war.[16] It ended in a bloody draw, providing a foretaste of what was to come.

Red Army advisers expressed satisfaction with popular response to the buildup that followed, for 80 percent of the new draftees were said to have appeared at their assigned recruitment centers on the first day of their mobilization periods during the spring of 1937.[17] By the beginning of April the Popular Front forces totaled more than 350,000 (compared with 280,000–290,000 under Franco's command), and of these at least 110,000

15. The Russian military writers Samarin, 36–37, 51, and Liubarskii, 20, are more frank in this regard than Spanish leftist commentators.
16. Perhaps because of weak firepower on both sides, casualties were not particularly heavy in the early battles around Madrid in November-December 1936. Surviving documents of the People's Army are said to list less than 300 combat deaths at Madrid for the month of November 1936. Servicio Histórico Militar, *La Marcha sobre Madrid* (Madrid, 1968), 158.
17. Soviet Army Archives, in Maidanik, 302.

were being organized in the regular People's Army brigades of the central front.[18]

When the first fully organized units had been established in the preceding October, Russian advisers had begun to structure the People's Army on the basis of a new unit—the mixed brigade. The mixed brigade was intended to constitute a versatile formation that could be militarily self-sustaining, capable of handling most of its own communications, transportation, engineers, light artillery, antitank support, munitions, supplies, and medical assistance. Each of the People's Army officers who has written about the mixed brigade has given a slightly different description. It was theoretically composed of approximately 3,700 men, organized into four infantry battalions, one cavalry squadron, one antitank battery, one communications company, one hospital company, one company of sappers, one munitions section, one motors section, and one company of reinforcements. On paper the total armament was approximately 2,200 rifles, 120 machine guns of varying caliber, 104 mortars, and 24 pieces of light artillery. However, few units of the People's Army ever achieved full strength. After a year or so, the mixed brigade was modified, in part because its hodgepodge formation left it scarcely able to put half its men on the firing line. The brigades in turn were incorporated into regular divisions in the main sectors of the Army by the close of 1937.

Formation of unified brigades had the political purpose of breaking up the individual-party militia groups or at least including them in a larger whole subject to impersonal discipline. Soviet military observers sent back the following figures

---

18. The former Communist staff officer, F. Ciutat, gives the following numerical breakdown by regions:

	Republican forces	Nationalist forces	Ratio
Center	110,000	80,000	1.3:1
North	110,000	80,000	1.3:1
Northeast	80,000	30,000	2.6:1
Extremadura	15,000	10,000	1.5:1
Andalusia	45,000	40,000	1.1:1
		plus 50,000 Italian troops	
	360,000	290,000	1.26:1

"Voina na Severnom fronte," *Ispanskii narod protiv fashizma*, 229.

on the political and social composition of some of the new
brigades on the central front as of March 1937: [19]

Brigade number	Communists	Socialists	JSU	UGT	CNT	Workers	Peasants
1	526	52	179	762	142	732	474
2	662	85	316	1054	116	591	1030
18	770	50	397	1458	625	1156	1361
29	783	78	541	1386	180	877	854
32	391	63	456	1308	145	1295	781
36	970	192	813	1788	626	812	2082
24	605	183	832	2324	391	1045	1939
40	587	240	385	1350	230	1474	539
41	488	112	404	1955	262	936	1056
42	1284	211	694	1538	273	1756	715
43	796	107	725	1453	400	1291	1025
67	193	70	159	1683	327	1484	406
77	31	27	88	311	2555	730	2173

This table shows the political limitations on brigade mixing.
Since the CNT was in a minority in central Spain, in many
cases it was not difficult to form largely Socialist-Communist units,
with a minority of anarchosyndicalists, but in some brigades, such
as the 77th, CNT militia battalions seem to have been incorporated wholesale.

Communist influence in the People's Army increased *pari
passu* with its numerical expansion. Communist leaders proudly
announced at major meetings that an extremely large proportion of the party membership had already volunteered for the
People's Army. At the March 1937 meeting of the central committee, José Díaz declared that 131,600 of the 249,140 party
members were currently serving,[20] and it was asserted that an
additional 16,000 members of the PSUC were also in the military.[21] A JSU memo of July 1937 claims that 141,000 JSU members were at that time in the People's Army (5,000 of them
officers) and that 10,000 more were in the police.[22] By 1938 it
was claimed that JSU members in military service numbered
300,000,[23] or more than one-third the total manpower in the

19. Soviet Army Archives, in Maidanik, 171.
20. José Díaz, *Por la unidad, hacia la victoria* (Valencia, 1937), 50–51.
21. Cited in Maidanik, 170.
22. Bolloten Collection.
23. In the article by Arconada cited in the previous chapter.

armed forces of the leftist zone. It is a moot point how seriously such statistics can be taken; at any rate, the duplication of membership between the Communist party and the JSU must be kept in mind.

What is perfectly clear, however, is the overwhelming emphasis placed by the Communist party on military affairs. Whether or not the preceding statistics are exaggerated, the party's organizational chief, Pedro Checa, was probably not overstating the matter when he declared that the People's Army "absorbed 80 per cent of the attention of the party." [24] Furthermore, greater stress was placed upon recruitment of new party members from among the non-Communist members of the military than from among any other social or professional element.[25] The Communists also realized that they must pay the necessary consequences of their military elitism, and boasted of their heavy losses.[26]

The proportion of party members in leadership positions was, moreover, two or three times as great as the proportion of

24. Pedro Checa, *A un gran partido, una gran organización* (Barcelona, 1937).
25. Point Three of the JSU Militia Secretariat's booklet for JSU members in the armed forces directed: "Through work and propaganda convince the soundest comrades to join the party in charge of the revolution—the Communist Party." Quoted in Carlos Hernández Zancajo, *Tercera etapa de octubre* (Valencia, 1937), 13.

P. Clavego's Communist manual, *El trabajo de los comisarios políticos* (Madrid-Barcelona, 1937), listed among the "Duties of the Commissar":

7. The political commissar should be the organizer of the Party in his unit, carrying out a bold and systematic labor or recruitment among the best combatants, nominating them for positions of responsibility.

26. At the March 1937 central committee meeting, the following casualty figures were given for commissars on the central front from October 1936 to March 1937:

	Number of commissars	
Party	killed	wounded
Communists	21	31
JSU	3	15
Socialists	3	3
Republican left	1	1
UGT		1

(At that time there were no anarchist commissars on the central front.)

Francisco Antón, *Madrid, orgullo de la España antifascista* (Valencia, 1937).

the Communists in the armed forces as a whole. By an undetermined point in 1937 the Communists purported to hold 90 percent of the officers' commissions in the People's Air Force.[27] According to the claims of *Mundo Obrero,* 80 percent of the commissar posts on the central front in the spring of 1937 were held by Communists. At approximately the same time, Col. Vicente Rojo, the chief of staff of the central front (and, by the way, a Catholic moderate, not a leftist), was quoted by the Russians as saying that "80 percent of the Army was under Communist influence" and that any attack on the Communists would lead to severe weakening and demoralization of the Army.[28] Young party members, especially if from the working class, won rapid promotion. Russian reports indicated that approximately three-quarters of the first 55 brigade commanders were members either of the party or the JSU, and over half less than 30 years of age.[29] There were 20-year-old brigade commanders, and later a 25-year-old divisional commander, as well as 18-year-old brigade commissars and 20-year-old divisional commissars—all from the JSU.

The People's Army at first took shape only in the central and southern sectors of the leftist zone. The northern sector and Catalonia-Aragon remained militarily autonomous despite coordination of command on paper. The CNT's original position advocated formation of a National Militia Committee to coordinate the military effort in place of a central government or a Regular Army. Yet, despite the CNT's resistance to "militarization," its more capable leaders could not ignore the ineffectiveness of their militia. At a meeting on the Aragon front in September 1936, Juan García Oliver, the Catalan Anti-Fascist Militia Committee's chief of military operations, ruefully observed:

It is a phenomenon of this war that when towns held by the fascists are attacked they hold out for a long time and that [when we are attacked] we do not resist at all. They surround a small town and

27. Maidanik, 170.
28. *Ibid.,* 280.
29. *Ibid.,* 234–35.

after a couple of days it is taken, but when we surround one we spend our entire lifetime there.[30]

The CNT's entry into the Catalan government at the end of September 1936 marked the dissolution of the Militia Committee and the first efforts to bring militia forces in the northeast under unified control. On October 5 the CNT issued new "Rules for Confederal Militia" which stated that they must unquestioningly obey the orders of superiors. The CNT's national committee admitted, "We paid dearly for remaining faithful to our ideals for so long." [31] However, even after entering the Largo Caballero government in November, the CNT showed little inclination to accept a regular People's Army. Though militia groups in Catalonia were supposed to be subject to formal military discipline after November 1, their behavior in fact remained little changed.

Throughout the first year of the war the manpower of Catalonia-Aragon was considerably undermobilized compared with that of the central zone. Little more than 50,000 militiamen were provided for military duties, of whom 30,000 were sent to Aragon and approximately 10,000 to the Madrid front. The latter sometimes contributed little to the military effort because of their insubordinate attitude. A middle-class Catalanist officer assigned to an anarchist column has written that his unit's anarchist commander made a speech to the men assuring them that

after winning the war against Franco, which was just like blowing bubbles, the war against the Republicans, Socialists and Communists would begin with the goal of establishing anarchism, and once this second war had been won, they would shoot us, the "technicians" [as anarchist militia called officers], because we would no longer be needed.[32]

Though the commander afterward explained that such speeches were only made for rhetorical effect, they had obvious impact on military attitudes. To criticism from the Marxists and the

---

30. "Verbatim Report of Meeting of Political and Military Leaders on the Aragon Front in September 1936" from the files of Col. Villalba, nominal commander of the Aragon front. (Bolloten Collection.)

31. *Boletín de Información C.N.T.–A.I.T.–F.A.I.,* in Brademas, 408.

32. "Peripècies d'un alferes de l'Exèrcit de Catalunya." (Bolloten Collection.)

middle-class left, the CNT pointed to the fact that in October 1936 their Councillor of Economics in the Generalitat had called for the general military and economic mobilization of all men between 18 and 45 under the existing system of revolutionary dualism. The Communists had rejected that proposal because it was still designed to avoid centrally controlled government and a regular army.

The POUM was equally insistent in rejecting a traditional army. *La Batalla* declared on December 16, 1936, that "The working class cannot permit that under pretense of military necessity an Army is reconstructed that tomorrow would be the instrument with which to destroy it." The POUM proposed a "revolutionary" Red Army not dominated by Stalinist central-ism but based on regular army organization controlled by a commissariat representing all the revolutionary parties and by soldiers' soviets that would constitute an army board of review.

In January 1937 the Generalitat began a paper reorganiza-tion of the militia battalions and columns within its territory to form regular divisions, but at its meeting at the end of that month the CNT regional plenum still rejected the notion of a regular, hierarchical, fully organized People's Army. It did ac-cept the principle of "obligatory military service," but only in a militia system coordinated by a central militia command.

In the winter and spring of 1937 the ultimate responsi-bility lay with the reconstituted government but, as explained in the previous chapter, Largo Caballero refused to force matters to a conclusion. Though his military appointees had begun organization of the People's Army, he was reluctant to bring heavy presure against the anarchist militia. Moreover, he insisted on retaining personal authority as Minister of Defense, and was more and more inclined to resist Communist demands in top military policy, though he made little effort to interfere with Communist initiative in the main organizational cadres of the Army.

There is little doubt that the indiscipline of the CNT militia was a major factor in the loss of Málaga in February 1937. Communist pressure became so strong that Largo saw himself forced to give up one of his two chief military aides,

Gen. José Asensio, the Undersecretary of Defense, who was made the scapegoat for the continuing deficiencies in military organization during the winter of 1937.[33]

The defeat of Franco's last direct attempt to seize Madrid in March 1937 (the Guadalajara offensive) proved the mettle of the elite elements of the main part of the People's Army and of the Russian-organized Air Force, which dominated the skies over the battlefield. It eased the threat to Madrid, but only briefly interrupted the political quarrel about military and government policy.

Largo Caballero had taken revenge for the ouster of Asensio by shipping off to Bilbao the Communist Major Díaz Tendero, former head of the vital Information and Control Department of the Army, responsible for officer classification and promotion. In April Largo finally decided to do something about the Communist preponderance among the commissars. Whereas officer appointments were approved by the Ministry of Defense on the recommendation of the Political Commissariat, the Communist-controlled Commissariat was completely independent in the choice of commissars. By April 1937 125 of the 186 battalion commissars and 28 of the 62 brigade and divisional commissars on the central front were members of the party or the JSU.[34] On April 17 Largo finally curbed the powers of the Commissariat and imposed his personal control over all commissar appointments.

The last major military policy conflict between Largo and the Communists concerned the proposed Republican offensive

33. Asensio's side was given in the pamphlet, *El General Asensio. Su lealtad a la República* (Barcelona, 1938).

The personal "Declaration" of the Málaga commander, Col. José Villalba, dated Feb. 17, 1937, stressed lack of material and manpower in addition to the absence of cooperation. Commissar-Inspector Alberto F. Ballesteros' report, "Lo Ocurrido en Málaga, Actuación del Comisario del Sector," Jaén, Feb. 18, 1937, concludes that the loss of Málaga was not primarily due to the failure of leadership there, but to local disorganization, lack of equipment, and the dominance of the CNT among the militia and their refusal to cooperate. (Bolloten Collection.)

34. Soviet Army Archives, in Maidanik, 310.

On May 15 *Mundo Obrero* claimed that of 89 commissars killed or wounded thus far on the central front, 54 were Communists and 24 were from the JSU.

for the late spring of 1937. Largo and his military advisers preferred a southwestern offensive to break the thin Nationalist lines in Extremadura, cutting Franco's territory in two. The Communist leaders and Russian advisers insisted on an assault near Madrid, using the Communist core of the central sector of the People's Army to strike at the main part of Nationalist territory. Both arguments were partially influenced by political considerations, and the military advantage of either may not have been easy to determine. Largo's position was entirely defensible, for an offensive northwest of Madrid, as proposed by the Communists, that would indirectly threaten Salamanca (Franco's headquarters) and the communications of the main part of the Nationalist zone, would also meet more rapidly and directly concerted resistance in an area to which Franco could more quickly shift reinforcements. These drawbacks were not sufficient to deter Communist insistence on retaining the military initiative in the hands of the most heavily Communist sector of the Army.

The question was solved immediately when Negrín replaced Largo Caballero and Prieto took over the Ministry of Defense. Prieto was willing to cooperate with the Communists in the spring and summer of 1937 in a last effort to stabilize the situation of the Popular Front zone. Thus he relaxed some of the restrictions on Communist influence and appointments recently imposed by Largo and let plans for the Madrid offensive go forward. Colonel Vicente Rojo, chief of staff of the central front, who had cooperated completely with the Communists and Russian advisers, was made chief of staff of the entire Army. He was the military counterpart of Negrín.

During the second half of 1937 the conversion of existing units into regular forces and the expansion of the People's Army was carried on apace. The policy of trying to avoid brigades of one single political background was continued. Russian-derived statistics in Table 14.2 indicate how the political mix worked out in a selected number of units.

Though the Communists held absolute control of the Air Force (reconstituted as a separate unit on March 30, 1937) and general, though not absolute, hegemony in the Army, they

TABLE 14.2. *Party Origins of Members of Certain Republican Army Brigades (Summer 1937)*

(in either absolute figures or percentages)

Brigade number	Troop total	Communists	JSU	Socialists	CNT	Republican left
6	3200	35%	25%	8%	5%	5%
16	—	1000	700	800	50%	—
17	2356	20%	15%	4%	13%	1%
20	—	30%	—	—	25%	—
25	2607	500	800	120	230	54
26	3195	456	610	87	104	126
27	2415	384	584	89	111	57
28	2948	908	629	71	252	169
34	2609	850	—	—	—	—
36	3355	1064	502	235	34	771
40	3528	801	—	—	—	—
42	—	1600	129	17	60	28
46	2270	395	240	185	308	97
47	—	40%	—	—	—	—
50	3091	1035	—	—	—	—
51	3114	50%	—	—	—	—
52	—	50%	30%	15%	2%	—
54	2981	50%	—	20%	10%	—
55	1600	60%	—	—	—	—
57	3109	900	—	—	—	—
62	1779	20%	—	60%	—	—
63	—	60%	—	20%	—	—
73	—	50%	15%	10%	15%	—
74	2339	40%	15%	10%	27%	—
78	2714	532	525	130	320	78
79	—	45%	—	—	40%	—
85	2941	40%	—	40%	3%	—
86	—	85%	—	8%	5%	2%
88	—	4%	—	2%	85%	3%
91	—	15%	—	20%	20%	—
92	2497	700	—	—	—	—
106	3425	222	429	53	508	151
109	—	10%	15%	5%	10%	—
110	2998	125	338	24	509	44
130	2924	40%	—	30%	—	20%
131	—	55%	—	—	10%	35%
132	—	55%	—	—	10%	35%

SOURCE: Soviet Army Archives, in Maidanik, 172–73.

were much less successful in their attempts to dominate the Navy. The party had developed a network of cells among ordinary sailors before the war began, but CNT affiliates were more numerous. Unlike the Army or the Air Force, the Navy had a resolutely non-Communist commissar general, the Socialist Bruno Alonso. The Communist weakness in the Navy may also have explained why the Navy remained relatively inactive. The Soviet Union sent comparatively little maritime equipment and the number of Russian advisers was proportionately lower than in the Army or Air Force, though apparently two Republican submarines were commanded by Russian officers.[35]

In general, Russian military supplies flowed fairly steadily from October 1936 through the middle of 1937. Material was shunted away from the anarchosyndicalist northeast and concentrated on the central front, giving the People's Army air control there for much of the winter and spring of 1937,[36] continued superiority in armor and for several months approximate parity in artillery, in addition to their continued superiority in manpower. Anti-Communist leftists later charged that the Soviet military material was not only in the long run quantitatively inferior to that provided the Nationalists, but qualitatively inferior as well. The evidence on both counts is incomplete and complicated. The common contention that the total amount of German and Italian assistance was greater than that of the Russians appears fully valid in general, but not for every period of the struggle. Apparently some obsolescent Russian equipment was shipped to Spain, and some of the material obtained by the NKVD-purchasing agencies from other countries may also have been second-rate, but much of the Soviet military equipment—particularly in planes, tanks, and artillery—was the very best that the Red Army had to offer in the years 1936 to 1938.

The success of the People's Army in defensive fighting on the central front during the winter of 1937 led Franco and his

35. Bruno Alonso, *La flota republicana y la guerra civil de España* (Mexico City, 1944), 47.

36. The Servicio Histórico Militar, using the captured People's Army records, reports that the Nationalists employed a total of 1,122 planes in the war and the leftist forces 1,807. This may well be true, and it is not inconsistent with the overwhelming air superiority generated by the Nationalists in 1938, for the leftist losses were always considerably greater. Moreover, Russian air tactics were defensive-minded and cautious in the extreme, so that full use was rarely made of the air strength available.

advisers to break off further efforts to seize Madrid. The Nationalist command was correct in doubting the ability of the leftists to develop an effective offensive force, and therefore ran the risk of going over to the defensive in the center while employing the best sections of the rapidly expanding Nationalist Army in the conquest of the secondary Republican zone in the north, which included Spain's other main industrial complex. Franco's strategy in the spring and summer of 1937 proved completely successful.

The first large-scale offensive of the People's Army, at Brunete just to the northwest of Madrid in July 1937, revealed deficiencies of military organization which were never altogether remedied during the remainder of the war. The fervent young Communists and Socialists who filled the command positions may have been brave and dedicated, but they lacked adequate training or experience. Military administration and coordination were poor; junior officers lacked initiative and vigor; even the best assault brigades showed little mobility. Against weak enemy units, the offensive achieved little, and Nationalist reinforcements soon turned the tide. Reconcentration of air power on the central front restored aerial superiority to the Nationalists, and with the assistance of German supplies they never again lost it. When operations were suspended, the Republican striking force was completely exhausted.

The failure of the Brunete offensive doomed the northern zone. There the leftist forces were much weaker than in the central area, in part because of a lesser degree of Communist activity and much less Russian assistance. Nevertheless, leftist writers have to some extent exaggerated the supply shortages in the north as well as in the main zone. Apparently very little was transshipped from the main Republican zone to the north,[37] but not insignificant shipments were sent directly, especially to Asturias. The main deficiency in the north was the absolute lack of unity, for the zone was divided into three autonomous sections—Vizcaya, Santander, and Asturias. Lack of military

37. From the main Republican zone Aguirre acknowledged receipt by the Basques of only 200 machine guns, 15,000 antiquated rifles, a few cannon, and 15 new Russian fighter planes with Russian pilots.

training and leadership and supply shortages compounded this weakness.

As far as Vizcaya was concerned, under the Popular Front tactic it had originally been Communist policy to support Basque nationalism as a device to weaken central unity and authority in Spain, but after the war began this policy was found to be counterproductive. On January 13, 1937, the new Basque president, José Antonio de Aguirre, is supposed to have written the government that "All matters concerning the war, the utilization of human and military resources within the territory of Euzkadi, except for the command of military operations, are the exclusive jurisdiction of the government of Euzkadi and its Minister of War." [38] Though the Basque section of the MAOC was the only effectively organized paramilitary force in Vizcaya at the start of the war,[39] the Basque Communists were unable to use this advantage to establish Communist military hegemony similar to that achieved in the central zone. Instead they exceeded instructions and collaborated with Basque nationalism to the extent of ignoring the dictates of the party hierarchy itself.

A power struggle over the question of military authority went on between the Basque government and the central government throughout the winter and spring of 1937. For three months the central command tried to get rid of the Basque chief of staff, Lt. Col. Alberto Montaud, not because of incompetence but for political and disciplinary reasons. The Basques resisted this as long as possible. When a single commander, Gen. Llano de la Encomienda, was appointed for the entire northern zone, in May 1937, he found it almost impossible to establish integrated authority over the three separate districts involved. Each sector was defeated separately by superior Nationalist skill and firepower.

The Basques put up a stiff fight, but the same could not be said of the leftist militia in Santander. This was a moderately conservative province which had cast a majority vote for the

38. According to Ibarruri, 275.
39. According to the former Basque defense minister, José Rezola. Discussion in St. Jean de Luz, Oct. 22, 1962.

right in the 1936 elections. Part of the militia battalions had been raised by conscription and little desire to resist was apparent when the onslaught of the Navarrese and Italian units began in August 1937.

The military record in Asturias was different, however, for the Asturian miners were the revolutionary elite of the Spanish working class. By mid-1937 some 75,000 militia had been recruited in Asturias and the left-controlled sector of León, and their valor was unsurpassed by any group. They were, however, little affected by the organization of the People's Army and, though there was a small munitions industry in the province, it was not prepared to turn out quantities of finished arms. An officers' school of sorts was eventually established, but the Asturian militia leaders were in general untrained and their operations were poorly planned, organized, and coordinated. The worst mistake was probably to insist in battering away at the well-defended Nationalist enclave of Oviedo, which threw back persistent frontal assaults. The Asturian militia attempted to make up in numbers and impetus what they lacked in skill and organization. Losses were high, especially among the officers.

The Nationalist conquest of the northern zone, completed in October 1937, decisively tilted the balance of power. Of the 200,000 recruits that the People's Army had raised in the northern zone, perhaps as many as 33,000 were killed [40] and approximately 150,000 were captured or disarmed. Little more than 10,000 men could be evacuated to the central zone. The loss was all the more grave because of the steadier combat potential of the Basques and Asturians. [41] At the time of the

40. According to the former Communist leader, Enrique Castro Delgado, *Hombres made in Moscú* (Mexico City, 1960), 580. He also claims that more than 45,000 of the prisoners were later incorporated into the Nationalist Army, and this seems to be more or less correct. Russian reports indicated that the bulk of the deserters from the Nationalist Army in 1938 came from among former prisoners who had been enlisted. General Staff, Soviet Army, *Upravlenie voiskami i rabota shtabov v Ispanskoi Respublikanskoi Armii* (Moscow, 1939).

41. According to one of the leading psychiatrists in the People's Army, "Soldiers from the north were more resistant to nervous breakdown than those from the south, but once the northerners developed a neurosis, recovery was far more difficult." Emilio Mira, *Psychiatry in War* (New York, 1943), 73.

Guadalajara battle (March 1937), the Nationalist zone included little more than 25 percent of Spain's prewar metallurgical industry; eight months later this proportion had risen to about 65 percent.

The command of the People's Army responded with new plans and increased mobilization. By the time the war ended, it had mobilized 24 classes of troops (1919 to 1942), roughly from ages 17 to 40, though in the final campaigns boys of 15 and men of 45 could sometimes be found. According to the records, this eventually amounted to a total of 916,677 men,[42] to which figure must be added at least 40,000 older men drafted for fortifications work, a certain number of teen-aged boys who volunteered or were impressed in emergencies, possibly as many as 100,000 police, and very likely a certain number of militiamen in the northern sectors and elsewhere who may not have been included in the totals. Altogether, well over 1 million men were organized in the leftist zone, or more than 8 percent of a steadily shrinking population base. The mobilization of the Nationalists was not quite so extensive. The latter called up nearly 1 million men from beginning to end, but out of a steadily expanding population base that also incorporated many enemy prisoners. Though the Nationalists did not have to go beyond the class of 1927, the whole effort was an enormous strain on a country of less than 25 million.

After the loss of the north the most important single source of manpower and supply for the People's Army was Catalonia. Catalanists claimed that 260,000 men from the region had been mobilized by the end of 1937 [43] and there was further heavy recruiting in 1938. If the original Catalan militia compiled a poor combat record, some of the draftees incorporated into the better units of the People's Army in 1937 and 1938 gave a superior account of themselves.

---

42. General Staff, Soviet Army, *Katalonskaya operatsiya* (Moscow, 1940), 19.
43. According to Jaume Miravitlles in *La Humanitat* (Barcelona), Dec. 12, 1937. Perhaps as noteworthy is the fact that at least 30,000 young men, mostly from the middle classes and the peasantry, escaped Catalonia to serve in the Nationalist Army. There were more than 1,000 Catalan officers in the Nationalist Army Officer Corps. José María Fontana, *Los catalanes en la guerra de España* (Madrid, 1956), 262–63.

The record of Catalan war industry was at best mediocre. The chief of staff, Rojo, wrote soon after the final defeat:

Notwithstanding lavish expenditures of money on this need, our industrial organization was not able to finish a single kind of rifle or machine gun or cannon, succeeding only, when there were proper materials, in manufacturing one [kind of] airplane. Nonetheless it was politically necessary to sustain at the head of the Undersecretary of Armaments an eminent obstetrician, whose good will, intelligence and effort were not sufficient to avoid industrial disaster.[44]

In defense of Catalan industry it is customarily pointed out that before the war the latter had been based on textiles, chemicals, light metallurgy, and finished goods. During the first five months of the conflict syndicate-controlled Catalan industry produced few military supplies [45] and when a more serious effort at reconversion for war production began output declined 35 to 40 percent in March and April 1937.[46] War goods production did not significantly rise until the autumn of 1937. Workers in Catalan war industries were very well treated by comparison with other labor groups and Catalonia always remained the center of leftist war production, but by the beginning of 1938 the ammunition output of factories in the Valencia region had in several categories surpassed that of Catalonia. Perhaps the major achievement of Catalan war industry was to have constructed 169 fighter-plane engines on Russian designs during 1938.[47]

44. Vicente Rojo, *¡Alerta los pueblos!* (Buenos Aires, 1939), 270.
45. A certain amount of ammunition, 294 ambulances, 385 trucks, and 147 crudely armored cars, according to José Peirats, *La C.N.T. en la revolución española* (Toulouse, 1952), II, 145.
46. *De Companys a Indalecio Prieto: Documentación sobre la industria de guerra en Cataluña* (Buenos Aires, 1939); *Nuestra Bandera*, no. 6 (1950), 448, in José García, *Ispaniya narodnogo fronta* (Moscow, 1957), 174.
47. According to Soviet Army records, in December 1938 the monthly arms production of what remained of the leftist zone amounted to:

10,000,000 rifle bullets
700,000 hand grenades
300,000 artillery shells
80,000 mortar grenades
1,000 rifles
100 mortars
18 armored vehicles
plus a number of airplanes and a few cannons

(*Katalonskaya operatsiya*, 12.)

Thus the burden fell upon the Soviet Union, and after mid-1937 Russian supplies also began to decline. Red Army advisers remained with the commanders up until the very end, but in slowly decreasing numbers. They continued to send back reports on military performance, though sometimes the wrong conclusions were drawn.[48] Russian and Comintern experts also directed the formation of guerrilla bands behind Nationalist lines. This work began rather slowly despite the fact that modern guerrilla warfare had been born in Spain 130 years earlier. By 1937 the number and size of partisan units operating in Nationalist territory had reached considerable proportions,[49] but they seem to have had a measurable impact on the war only in the region of Asturias after the fall of the northern zone. There the depredations of large irregular forces delayed Franco for a month or more in fully disengaging his shock units and regrouping for another major offensive.

The intelligence and counterintelligence activities of the People's Army were also supervised by the Russians.[50] Prieto

48. The classic example concerns the use of armored forces and the failure to appreciate the German-style *blitzkrieg* (though the Germans did not have full opportunity to experiment with this in Spain, either). Soviet Army reports indicated that Russian tanks never operated more than 500 meters in front of the Spanish infantry. (*Katalonskaya operatsiya*, 128–29.)

49. Alexander Orlov, who had organized Red partisans during the Russian Civil War, was also in charge of this operation. He writes:

The Russians regarded Spain as a testing ground for perfecting the Soviet guerrilla science accummulated since the October Revolution and for acquiring new experience. We started from scratch and within ten months [that is, by July 1937] we had 1600 regular guerrillas trained in the six schools which I organized in and around Madrid, Valencia and Barcelona, and about 14,000 regular guerrillas, who were trained, supplied and led by our instructors on the territory of Franco, mostly in the hills from which they could descend to harass moving enemy columns, attack supply convoys and disrupt communications.

(Orlov mss.)

It should be remembered that much of the Nationalist zone was originally based on politically conservative territory, and that the leftist bands often did not receive enough civilian support to attain maximum effectiveness. Furthermore, it might be pointed out that antileftist guerrillas were active among one sector of the conservative peasants of northern Catalonia in 1938.

50. According to Orlov,

In Spain the Soviets tested the system and methods of their military intelligence, which proved effective beyond all expectations. With the help of the Soviet long-standing network of spies in Berlin and Rome and with my own network on the territory of Franco, I was able to organized an independent Servicio de Inteligencia Militar (SIM) within the People's Army in mid-1937, but the proportion of Spanish Communist appointees increased during 1938 until the SIM also formed part of the Communist-controlled espionage network. Yet the Communist intelligence system never became absolute because of the enormous distrust and resentment between the various leftist groups and between rival branches of the government and armed forces. Manuel Ulibarri, one of several temporary commanders of the SIM, has recounted the proliferation of espionage and counterespionage groups under the People's Republic:

Everyone in our rear guard carried on counterespionage. The political parties and the trade unions. The ministers of nearly all ministries and their subordinates in every sphere. And as if that were not enough, every kind of political or security organization, even the border guards, preferred above all else to get involved in this activity. . . .

When I took over direction of the SIM, in Barcelona alone there were the following intelligence services:

The official one founded by Prieto.

That of General Rojo (of the General Staff), commanded by Colonel Estrada which, under the guise of collecting military information, practised intensive, surreptitious espionage.

That of Lieutenant Colonel Lacalle, with extra official influence from the Foreign Ministry.

That of the International Brigades, a direct offshoot of the GPU, and off limits to us.

The so-called DEIDE (Special Department of Information of the State), commanded by a lad of great personal ability and antifascist enthusiasm, but too young and inexpert not to fall into the formidable snares of the Gestapo. That was a function of the Ministry of the Interior.

That of the Catalan Generalitat, commanded by another young man of great ability, vision and good will, Fernando Meca.

That of the General Director of Security. . . .

The Basque Government also had its intelligence service. . . .

The Undersecretary of the Ministry of Defense also had another little bureau of military counterespionage. . . .

---

provide Prime Minister Negrín and his Chief of Staff Vicente Rojo with the strategic plans of the Nationalist High Command and with the *Order of battle* [italics Orlov's], before and during each important engagement with the enemy.
(Orlov mss.)

There are at least nine and I think I must be leaving some out. . . .
In Madrid it was just as bad. A veritable centipede. Chaos.[51]

This points up the fact that the unity and centralization
achieved by the Negrín regime had to do mainly with the
central government itself and the central organization of the
Army. Local government, local affairs, and local branches of the
government ministries were by no means fully coordinated, and
even some of the local sections of the Army were only nominally
integrated within the whole. There were limits to what could
be done in a brief time under heavy stress.

In the People's Army, the emphasis throughout was on the
main Communist-led units that had been formed on the central
front. In the late summer and autumn of 1937 these were shifted
to the northeast for the first time, apparently for two reasons.
One was to bring the non-Marxist northeast under better
control, and the second was to launch a People's Army offensive
against a weaker section of the Nationalist front, slightly northeast of Zaragoza. The Belchite offensive that resulted was a
final effort to divert the Nationalists before the latter's conquest
of the north had been completed, and it was the first to include
sections of the newly formed Catalan Army of the East, which
contained many CNT members and former militiamen. Despite
some initial success in the hilly terrain east of Zaragoza, the
same deficiencies that had stood out at Brunete reappeared.
Lack of professional leadership led to what one Russian military
writer criticized as an extremely "bureaucratic" command structure in the People's Army. Minutely detailed orders were
prepared by the Republican general staff for both offense and
defense so that subordinate officers would not have to make
decisions on their own, but this frequently had a paralytic effect
on operations.[52] Even the best-prepared sections of the People's
Army were unable to develop or sustain offensive momentum,
or concentrate forces effectively, nor did the command seem
capable of moving its reserves in time. Nationalist reinforcements and reconcentration of firepower soon forced the operation

51. Manuel Ulibarri, *El S.I.M. de la República* (Havana, 1943), in García
Venero, *Internacionales*, III, 334–35.
52. Liubarskii, 69.

to be suspended.

By that time the main question for the Nationalists was simply how to achieve the final victory most quickly. There is some indication from the German documents that Franco's German advisers wanted him to launch a knockout blow against the key leftist center, Catalonia, that would end the war. By the last months of 1937 the German military were becoming nervous about continuing a major commitment in Spain, and warned that developments in central Europe might soon require their full resources. Franco was not, however, a general of great imagination; he was a stubborn and determined leader mesmerized by the centuries-old political dominance of Madrid, the importance of key cities, and the myth of leftist resistance in the capital. Moreover, the German advisers in Salamanca were indeed merely advisers, and lacked the political influence to impose their decisions that the Russians held in the People's Army. Franco decided instead to launch another major offensive through Guadalajara at the end of 1937 with the aim of outflanking and capturing Madrid.

There is no information as to whether or not this decision was taken with the knowledge that the next move planned by the Republican command was to be yet a third offensive effort, this time reviving the "Largo Caballero plan" of slicing across the Nationalist corridor in Extremadura to the southwest, where the enemy forces were second-rate and numerically weak. Extremadura had been a proleftist area and there was considerable unrest in the Nationalist rear. As it turned out, this plan was soon shelved for the second time after Republican intelligence learned of Franco's preparations for a renewed Guadalajara offensive. Each side was eager to seize the initiative and the Republican command decided on a pre-emptive attack at Teruel, east of Guadalajara, to throw the Nationalists off balance before they could launch their own offensive. This required rapid redeployment of the elite divisions, but a quick buildup led to the largest Republican offensive operation of the war in mid-December 1937. It beat the Nationalists to the punch and managed to capture the provincial capital of Teruel—the Republicans' only noteworthy offensive prize of the war—before bogging down.

Franco's response has been much criticized, for he canceled plans for the Nationalist Guadalajara offensive and began to prepare a full-scale counteroffensive in the Teruel district. He has been accused of allowing Republican initiative to dictate his strategy and of failing to capitalize on the fundamental offensive weakness of the People's Army by not continuing his original plan after the best Republican units were committed elsewhere. This was weighty criticism; on the other hand, Franco was keenly aware of the importance of politicopsychological factors in civil war that made it dangerous not to annul immediately any leftist triumph, and he may have had intelligence reports on subsequent Republican plans. According to some memoirs,[53] the Republican command intended to shift its forces to the southwest once more and launch the Extremadura operation after having pinned down the main Nationalist forces in the northeast. The fact that Franco was unable to launch a full-scale counteroffensive during January 1938 is said to have led the Republican commanders to decide that they could retain the initiative by pulling their main units out of the northeast and going ahead with the Extremadura plan. When the major Nationalist counteroffensive did come in February it caught the enemy at least partially by surprise, with key Republican units in transit elsewhere and unavailable for rapid recommitment. When they were redeployed, it became a matter of too little and too late. By the end of February 1938 superior Nationalist firepower had once more ground down the best units in the People's Army. Moreover, the war was now concentrated in the northeast where the Republicans had previously developed less military strength and where defeat might be even more decisive.

The Nationalists had then only to regroup in March for a spring offensive through Aragon to the sea, isolating Catalonia and dividing the remaining leftist zone in half. During March and April front-line units of the People's Army—Communist and non-Communist alike—sometimes broke up with little re-

53. Castro Delgado, 593–94; Pérez Salas, 177–78.

sistance under heavy air bombardment and infantry assault.[54] From March 8 to April 15, 1938, the People's Army lost 100,000 men in the northeast,[55] mainly prisoners, while the casualties of the advancing Nationalists were extremely light. The shortage of equipment was so grave that it raised doubts about the ability to resist for more than a few months.[56]

Some units in the northeast suffered such a crisis of discipline that the section for reporting the number of deserters was apparently dropped from brigade commissar reports; the statistics were too demoralizing. Draconian measures were taken to insure discipline and keep the troops in line. Mutinous companies were literally decimated; in some brigades as many as 70 or 80 troops were shot as a disciplinary measure. Even after the initial rout had been stayed, commissar reports from frontline brigades indicated that in some units as many as four or five soldiers were being shot daily for "wanting to pass over" to the enemy.[57]

It was against this background of disaster that the final break came between the Defense Minister, Prieto, and the cabinet of Negrín. According to Prieto, he told his fellow ministers on March 29, 1938:

> Gentlemen, in view of the lack of combat spirit shown by our troops, their disorder and disorganization, in view of the enormous matériel possessed by our adversaries, I foresee that the rebels will reach the Mediterranean; I hold this fact inevitable and that necessary measures ought to be taken.[58]

54. The report of General Sebastián Pozas, commander of the Army of the East, March 17, 1938, is fairly frank about this, though blaming it on lack of equipment and reserves. (Bolloten Collection.)
55. *Katalonskaya operatsiya,* 9.
56. According to Russian statistics, the People's Army's strength on May 1, 1938, stood at:

	Troops	Rifles	Submachine guns	Machine guns	Cannon
Catalonia	197,618	56,993	1,320	506	261
Central Zone	491,511	198,402	3,185	3,072	457
	689,129	255,395	4,505	3,578	718

(*Katalonskaya operatsiya,* 16.)
57. According to the research of Lt. Col. Ramón Salas Larrazábal.
58. *Cómo y por qué salí del Ministerio de Defensa Nacional* (Montevideo, 1939), 52–53.

Prieto was sick of the war; he had foreseen it and dreaded it, and by the spring of 1938 believed that it should be ended as soon as possible, even though that might entail fundamental concessions to Spanish conservatism. Yet he had been a loyal and largely efficient Defense Minister, and had not allowed his fundamental anticommunism to interfere with the expansion of the People's Army. Proof of this is the fact that Communist influence in the military actually increased during his tenure in office. He had been less adamant there than in his resistance to Communist domination of the Socialist party. He was eliminated, not merely because of his "defeatism," but in order to isolate a scapegoat for military disaster, get rid of the most influential anti-Communist leader remaining, and reduce the next cabinet to even more manageable terms.

What followed within the People's Army during the spring of 1938 was nevertheless by almost any standard an impressive achievement. The People's Army still had some margin of strength to work with, for the miscalculation concerning Franco's plans had left some of the better units strung out in the reserve and never fully committed during the disaster. A nucleus for resurgence remained. Nearly 200,000 recruits were called up and a major reorganizational effort was begun under the shadow of final defeat. Since functional illiterates were holding commands at the batallion level and occasionally above, a major effort was made to develop a crash officer training program. Up to that time the best schools had been those of the central zone, but training centers at Valencia and Barcelona were improved, and a new staff school was hastily opened in the latter city. The mixed brigade system had already given way to incorporation into divisions, but the structure was further altered by addition of one special machine-gun batallion per division, at least in the better-equipped units. The refurbishing of the People's Army was made possible in part by changes in the international situation, for the formation of the second Blum government in Paris in March 1938 led to the complete reopening of the French frontier (though only for sixty days), facilitating an increase in Russian (and also to a lesser extent in French) military supplies.

During the process of reorganization, care was taken to preserve Communist predominance in the command structure, which already amounted to about 70 percent of the officers' commissions in the Army as a whole.[59] Though many thousands of new troops were recruited from CNT milieux, promotion of *cenetistas* was kept to a minimum, while during May there were said to have been 1,280 promotions in the Communist 27th division alone, most of these being appointments to commands in other units.[60] The new resources were mainly concentrated on two key forces: the Army of the Levant, defending the Valencia region, and the Armies of the East and of the Ebro in the Catalan zone. The latter were overwhelmingly Communist-officered, though a large proportion of the troops were Catalan. Com-

59. *Cómo y por qué sali*, 106–07; Jesús Hernández, *Yo fui un ministro de Stalin* (Mexico City, 1960), 144.

60. According to a report of the Military Section of the FAI to a plenum of the peninsular committee, October 1938, in Peirats, *Los anarquistas*, 356–59. This report stated that of a total of 7,000 promotions in the People's Army from May to September 1938, 5,500 had gone to Communists. Listing the paucity of command positions held by *cenetistas* and *faístas* in the People's Army, it reported that they commanded only

1 division and 5 brigades of the 9 divisions and 27 brigades of the Army of the East.

Only 2 brigades in the overwhelmingly Communist Army of the Ebro.

3 divisions and 13 brigades of the 20 divisions and 55 brigades of the Army of the Levant.

1 division and 3 brigades of the 12 divisions and 45 brigades of the Army of the Center.

1 division and 1 brigade in the overwhelmingly Communist Army of Andalusia.

3 divisions and 9 brigades of the 11 divisions and 31 brigades of the Army of Extremadura.

1 of the 19 Centers for Recruitment, Instruction and Mobilization.

None of the 20 to 23 Rearguard Battalions in the special strategic reserve.

The totals were:

Level of command	Number	Libertarians	Communists or pro-Communists
Army Groups	2	0	2
Armies	6	2	3 (1 "neutral")
Army Corps	21	6	15
Divisions	70	9	61
Brigades	196	33	163

munist influence was less in the Army of the Levant,[61] which
had become militarily one of the best-organized sections of the
People's Army, under an apolitical chief of staff, the professional
officer Matallana.

Thus the weak forces that had seemed to be nearly finished
at the end of April managed to put up stiff resistance during
June and July as Franco stubbornly tried to battle his way
southward by means of frontal attacks against the crucial hinge
of Valencia, whose loss might seal the fate of the central zone.
The People's Army, re-expanded to more than 700,000, rebuilt
its reserve, while Franco committed nearly all his reliable units
in exploiting the breakthrough and in trying to slug his way on
the ground to Valencia.

The last Republican offensive, a sudden amphibious attack
across the Ebro from Catalonia, came as a genuine surprise.
It forced Franco to suspend his own offensive operations for
the second time, and regroup his entire army for a slow,
painstaking reconquest of the small bulge of territory seized by
the Republicans southwest of the Ebro. All of August, September,
October, and part of November were devoted to a series of
limited engagements as each subsection of newly won leftist
territory was pulverized by air and artillery, then reoccupied
by bayonet. As in the case of Teruel, Franco has frequently
been attacked for abandoning his own plans once more and
committing his forces to a struggle of attrition along the Ebro.
In October he explained to the German military attaché that his
forces were not well enough equipped to enable him to fight
both a major defensive and a major offensive operation at the
same time. Since he had not the means of preparing an adequate
reserve, he did not want to run the risk of failing to respond to
any major effort of the enemy.[62]

---

61. For example, the political affiliation of the staff officers of the Army of
the Levant was

Communist,	36%	Republican left,	12%
Socialist,	22%	No party,	16%
CNT-FAI,	14%		

(*Upravlenie voiskami*, 43–44.)

62. Memo by the Head of Political Division IIIa, Oct. 20, 1938, *German
Documents*, Series D, III, no. 685, 775–76.

Fighting a battle of attrition against the best portion of the People's Army may not have been the most imaginative strategy, but since Franco's superiority in firepower, air strength, and numerical weight grew steadily, it was an effective one. Franco used only small forces, heavily supported by air and artillery, in concentrated attacks. Though the initial Republican offensive force had not been large, over a period of three months most of the reserves in the northeast were fed across the river in the forlorn hope of maintaining a foothold. The struggle was waged largely on Franco's terms. When the last Republican forces withdrew northeast of the Ebro in November, nearly all combat value had been pounded out of them. The meatgrinder along the Ebro cost the People's Army 75 percent more casualties than it did the Nationalists [63] and destroyed what had been built up during the spring and summer of 1938. It had been the last great military effort of which the People's Army was capable. The end was at hand.

63. Nationalist casualties totaled 41,414, with a rather low percentage of dead. Republican dead and wounded may not have exceeded 50,000, but 20,000 prisoners were also lost, and all these casualties came from the best remaining units.

FIFTEEN *The Defeat*

T HE FIRST FORMAL EXPRESSION OF Soviet reluctance to continue the struggle in Spain came during diplomatic remarks at Moscow in June 1938. Though the Soviet Union had temporarily accelerated arms shipments in the spring of that year, Hitler's diplomatic offensive in central Europe increased Russian caution; this was heightened by the failure of the Ebro operation, whose last stages coincided with the Anglo-French capitulation to Hitler at Munich. Yet, as long as leftist resistance could be sustained at slight cost, it provided a useful counterbalance to the growing isolation of the Soviet Union. The foothold in eastern Spain might prove a major strategic asset if Stalin could not avoid being drawn into a war against the fascist powers and it could also provide a useful card in arranging an understanding with Germany, should that become feasible. Hence, despite the hopelessness of the military situation in the peninsula, the Comintern's instructions were to fight on to the very last. More than ever before, the Spanish Communists became the backbone of resistance. They were told that the Spanish left must hold out until a general continental war began, after which they would be directly supported by the Soviet Union and presumably by France. Some of the Spanish Communist leaders believed that, if worst came to worst, the Soviet Union would intervene unilaterally to stave off total defeat.

Negrín was a distraught man, torn by conflicting sentiments. He wanted to end the war, and knew there was almost no logical hope of victory. He made several direct and indirect efforts during 1938 to open the possibility of a negotiated settlement, and at one point was ready to resign the burden of leadership altogether. On the other hand, he was reluctant to make fundamental concessions to the Nationalists and was deeply involved both politically and emotionally in the policy of resistance at all costs. Though direct evidence is lacking, there is some indication that extremely heavy pressure was exerted by the Communists to convince him of his indispensability and to warn that he simply would not be permitted to resign. At any rate, despite his inner doubts, Negrín became the political personification of the will to resist and adopted the Communist policy of continuing the war desperately with the sole hope of being saved by foreign assistance once a general European conflict broke out.

Negrín was a determined leader, but not a persuasive or efficient one. He paid less and less attention to the other leftist parties, and often simply ignored their complaints and suggestions. He lacked the energy or capacity to administer the Defense Ministry well, and left most matters to subordinates, nearly all of whom were either Communists or professional officers. He ignored details and wasted his energy on personal indulgence that sapped his strength and capacity for leadership. No effort was made to construct real unity in government and administration. So long as the Socialists and the CNT did not interfere with the functions of the government executive and the central command of the Army, they were left to administer local affairs, local economic operations, and some local sections of the military.

Of the three major revolutionary parties, the most disgruntled was the CNT. Ultra-anarchist influence was clearly on the wane in 1938; during that year the CNT endorsed the notion of central state economic planning (though not of state control) and propounded a kind of syndical corporatism, together with the idea of hierarchies of salaries, disciplinary norms, and the rational integration of syndical industrial federations. But the increasing moderation and desire to cooperate worked both ways, for the whole Civil War came to seem less significant to the anarchosyndicalists. They had less and less hope for a productive outcome to the fratricidal struggle and resented Russian and Communist influence more and more as military conditions worsened and civilian privation became extreme. Since the spring of 1938 sectors of the FAI and CNT had contemplated some sort of negotiated peace, as attested by both Peirats and Abad de Santillán. This tendency was increased by the growing moderation of the Negrín government's position on property expropriation, which encouraged the notion that the "bourgeoisie" was using the Communist party and the current regime to destroy the economic achievements of the revolution while the war decimated the revolutionaries and Spanish blood was sacrificed to Russian policy. A compromise with the national syndicalism of Franco might be no worse and possibly better in the long run.

The situation of the People's Army was desperate in both material [1] and moral. After the withdrawal beyond the Ebro, spirits sagged irretrievably. According to one account, the proportion of "psychogenic alterations" in the People's Army was approximately twice as great as among the Nationalist forces,[2] though this would not necessarily be surprising. The Nationalist troops were rather better cared for and had enjoyed an almost uninterrupted series of victories. The tone of religious exaltation and the emphasis on traditional moral values in the Na-

1. The only branch to register a slight improvement was the Air Force. On July 1, 1938, it had only 188 planes. Between that date and December 25, it lost 135 planes in combat and 56 through accidents and breakdowns, but 95 new planes were shipped in—mostly from Russia—and 63 new fighters were assembled by Catalan industry, so that the Republican Air Force numbered 197 planes on December 25, 1938. (*Katalonskaya operatsiya*, 29.) But this was scarcely one-third the strength of the Nationalists.

2. The percentage was said to be 9.98, according to one captured Republican report in J. J. López Ibor, *Neurosis de guerra* (Barcelona-Madrid, 1942), which gives the corresponding figure in the Nationalist forces as 4.75. Mira, 73, says only that no more than 1.5 percent of the Republican troops were temporarily discharged because of neurosis, probably referring to combat fatigue.

tionalist zone provided an easily understood and accepted credo
that helped maintain psychic and emotional stability. The
revolutionary morality inculcated in the leftist zone may not
have taken root so easily, to which was added the moral conflict
engendered by the great wave of blasphemy, sacrilege, church-
burning, and priest-murder that had swept the leftist zone during
the first year of the war.

But perhaps most important of all in lowering morale were
the catastrophic living conditions that prevailed in much of
the leftist zone by the end of 1938. The ordinary civilian population of Madrid was subsisting on little more than 100 to 150
grams of bread per day. The average rations of the Republican
troops had shrunk steadily: [3]

Normal rations	1936	1937	1938
Bread	700 grams	600 grams	400 grams
Meat or fresh fish	250 "	200 "	150 "
Fresh vegetables	200 "	250 "	180 "
Butter and fat	60 "	60 "	50 " (margarine)
Wine or beer	.5 liter	.25 liter	.25 liter
Field rations			
Biscuits	500 grams	500 grams	300 grams
Canned meat	250 "	200 "	150 "
Fat	30 "	25 "	20 "

Morale was even lower in the rearguard and on the inactive
fronts than in the combat units.[4] The non-Communist officers
at the Cartagena naval base, who had for the most part been

3. *Katalonskaya operatsiya*, 10.
4. Mira, 73, wrote, "It was striking that the amount of war neurosis observed
among front-line troops was slightly smaller than that observed among second-
line troops or those at the rear." Even the commissars on the relatively inactive
southern front were less vigorous and determined than those in the key areas.
An unsigned report to Alvarez del Vayo on "El Ejercito del Sur y los Comisarios," Aug. 21, 1937, had called them so ineffective as to be "counterproductive." (Bolloten Collection.)
    A report to Negrín by Alejandro Garcia Val, a Delegate of the Under-
secretary for the Land Army, on the problem of the rear guard in September
1938 called for a purge of all the recruitment and training centers, because
of rampant espionage, conspiracy, and general unreliability. The situation
was labeled as particularly bad in Alicante and Jaén, where anti-Communist
Socialists and the CNT were strong. *Sur*, the organ of the Army of the South,
was said to be controlled by the CNT and to be calling for the demobilization
of inactive troops. (Bolloten Collection.)

sitting out the war, are said to have passed a vote of no confidence in the Negrín government at a meeting in October 1938, asking that a new independent, moderate ministry be formed that could win British and French assistance in ending the war.[5]

The final Nationalist offensive against Catalonia, that began in late December, was a slow but almost uninterrupted advance which the People's Army was powerless to halt. Russian military commentators have pointed out the lack of vigorous momentum in this offensive, and its failure to achieve dramatic breakthroughs or to trap large sections of the Republican troops. There was, however, no need for spectacular achievements so long as the main objective of eliminating the principal remaining sector of the People's Army was accomplished. The Nationalists completed that task within sixty days.

Ricardo del Río, wartime director of the Republican news agency Febus, afterward wrote in a French concentration camp, "In Catalonia, where people had been particularly accustomed to living well throughout the war, not even five percent were willing to undergo the short rations demanded of them by the government."[6] After the Nationalist offensive began, the regime raised the draft age to 45 in Catalonia, but merely succeeded in calling up third-rate recruits for whom there were no arms. Lack of general interest in responding to the emergency call for volunteers to build fortifications was painfully clear from the start. The Catalanists, who had yet again discussed the possibility of a "separate peace" after walking out of the cabinet in the crisis of August 1938, re-entered Negrín's government in January 1939, but this was a hollow gesture without effect.

Rojo wrote,

For the spirit of resistance there had been substituted the idea of salvation. Everyone was afraid of being cut off. The soldiers knew the significance of the enemy's movement and were dominated above all else by the desire not to fall into his clutches. In fact, morale was only sustained in the leaders.

Barcelona was a city of the dead. The cause of death was demorali-

5. *Katalonskaya operatsiya,* 17.
6. Ricardo del Río, "Account of the Political and Military Situation in Catalonia During the Last Few Months of the Civil War," 4. (Bolloten Collection.)

zation, caused by both those who fled . . . and those who stayed in hiding, without the courage to leave their houses. . . . It is no exaggeration to assert that Barcelona was lost purely because there was no will to resist either in the civilian population or in some of the troops who had become contaminated by its atmosphere. Morale was at rock bottom. With a few honorable exceptions, all those who used to give encouragement to the troops had disappeared. Though not exhausted by suffering and hunger, the people were tired of the war and, long before the enemy's arrival, had only hoped for a sudden end to it. Therefore they remained shut up in their homes, which also served as a refuge for deserters fleeing from the front, who did not want to fight either, converting that urban concentration of a million souls into a wasteland spiritually deserted.[7]

The battle front approached Barcelona silently because it was not necessary for the Nationalists to use their artillery to open the advance. The port of Barcelona

was defended by a few soldiers who threw down their guns as soon as the first enemy forces approached. They were not taken prisoner, but, after having their Republican Army weapons confiscated and being given new rifles of the Nationalist Army, were placed in the vanguard of the Nationalist advance.[8]

In effect, the Republican forces in Catalonia were simply herded across the border for the French to worry about. According to the Servicio Histórico Militar, approximately 60,000 regular troops were taken prisoner and 209,000 pushed into exile, all at minimal cost to the Nationalists.

Unless some dramatic change occurred in the international situation, the end of the war was merely a matter of time. Though nearly 400,000 troops were still nominally under arms in the central zone, the best units of the People's Army had been destroyed, and the bulk of the best remaining equipment had also been lost in Catalonia. Some commanders had warned against the danger of overconcentrating matériel in the northeast, but the Republican command had seen no alternative. After the fall of Catalonia, there were only 50 or 60 operational warplanes and less than 100 tanks left in the central zone, which was also seriously short of automatic arms and artillery of every caliber. Even rifles were lacking for nearly half the troops.

7. *!Alerta los pueblos!*, 169, 172–73.
8. Del Río, 21.

The Catalan collapse also provoked a crisis in political and military leadership. Azaña, for long impotent and eager to resign the Republican presidency, seized the freedom given him by French exile to do so. The chief of staff, Rojo, who had fully cooperated with the Communists militarily but had preserved his personal independence, also resigned and indicated that he would not return to the central zone. A few months later he wrote, "*In the social and human order Franco has triumphed: . . . Because he has achieved moral superiority at home and abroad.*" [9]

During February Negrín apparently made a final attempt to negotiate an end to the war without reprisals. In the face of Franco's intransigence, he found no alternative to returning to the central zone with the sole hope that outbreak of a general European war would rescue what remained of the leftist cause. On February 26 he called a meeting of top army commanders in the central zone at Albacete to encourage resistance, promising that large shipments of matériel would soon arrive. Meanwhile, plans were drawn for the defense of three concentric lines of resistance in the remaining leftist zone. The innermost was to be a well-munitioned redoubt at the Cartagena naval base, where the People's Army would make its last stand. [10]

At present it is not possible to resolve the question of whether the Soviet Union did attempt to send a large shipment of war matériel to the People's Army in the winter of 1938–39. Anti-Communist leftists deny it, yet the memoirs of Regina García, Ibarruri, and the customarily honest Hidalgo de Cisneros, who claims to have negotiated the shipment with Stalin, report that a large quantity of equipment was sent by the northern route to Bordeaux but did not reach Catalonia because of that region's collapse. Pérez Salas wrote of a shipment of arms that entered Catalonia just before the evacuation and had to be left behind. Rojo and Casado refer vaguely to quantities of matériel in France that could not reach the central zone, and also to shipments of arms that were canceled because of the

9. Rojo, *¡Alerta los pueblos!*, 274–75. (Italics Rojo's.)
10. Col. J. M. Martínez Bande, "El final de la guerra. La semana comunista en Madrid (febrero-marzo 1939)," *Ejército*, no. 306 (July 1965), 15–28.

fall of Catalonia. At any rate, most of the commanders in the central zone no longer had confidence in Negrín, doubted that they would receive any further assistance, and had little stomach for continuing the struggle.

Only the Communist party remained staunchly behind the resistance, but Communist power had been weakened by the collapse of Catalonia. A large proportion of the officers driven across the border into exile had been Communists, and the best Communist units had been eliminated. The degree of Communist influence in the divisions remaining in the central zone was not so great as in the Army of 1938. Both Pérez Salas and Rojo have written that plans were made early in February to fly several hundred top Communist officers out of the fast-shrinking zone of northern Catalonia to take up commands in the center, but time and air space were lacking. Moreover, as military strength was depleted, so was general Communist control, for the party did not have the influence in the rear guard and among the proleftist population as a whole that it had developed in the armed forces.[11]

Defeatism and opposition reached a peak in the non-Communist groups. Many Socialists willing to cooperate with Negrín and the Communists so long as there was a chance of victory turned against the government after the situation became hopeless. In a belated gesture to encourage unity, several leading anti-Communists (such as Largo Caballero, Besteiro, and Lucio Martínez) had been reappointed to the executive commission of the Socialist party in August 1938, but this only increased the tension with the Communists. The anarchosyndicalists, in their new "Libertarian Movement," went even further. In a closed meeting at Valencia in January 1939, MLE leaders discussed the feasibility of an anti-Communist rebellion that would overthrow the Negrín regime and negotiate a settlement with the Nationalists.

The initiative was finally taken in the Communists' former military stronghold, Madrid. Since mid-1937, the main part of

11. Ibarruri wrote, "In general, the party's work with the masses was inadequate, since we stressed the importance of the fronts to the neglect of the work in the rear." *They Shall Not Pass*, 316.

the central front had been relatively inactive. Its commander, Miaja, was a circumspect, elderly general who usually followed the path of least resistance. Left in command of tottering Madrid when the government had first evacuated it in November 1936, he provided resolute leadership in resisting the Nationalist onslaught. He had had little choice, for after his equivocal relations with the Nationalist military conspirators in Madrid at the start of the Civil War, he would have been shot had Madrid fallen. Communist propaganda quickly converted him into the People's Army's first great hero at a time when it had profound need of popular leaders. From that time on Miaja jealously guarded his preeminence. He refused to cooperate with the Republican operation at the Jarama battle until his personal authority was further increased, and during the crucial engagements in the northeast in 1938 the central front was conducted almost like an independent entity. After the elite Communist units had been moved, Miaja refused to commit any of his own troops to a secondary supporting action that might have taken pressure off the main fronts. It is difficult to resist the conclusion that by 1939 his main interest was simply in saving himself. Many of his troops felt the same way, for, as the General Commissariat admitted in February, "After the fall of Barcelona and the loss of Catalonia, desertions have increased considerably." [12]

The local commander of Madrid was a professional officer, Col. Segismundo Casado, who was extremely hostile to the Communists and eager to end the war. He was in contact with leaders of the non-Communist political groups, most of whom felt that the struggle was being continued in the interest of the Soviet Union, and not of leftist Spain. For nearly a year such feelings had been spreading. As the professional soldier Pérez Salas wrote:

No one could be sure of what would become of Spain's political future if we won. While some—a minority—hoped to reconquer the democratic Republic of 1936, others feared that wartime changes had gone so far that they verged on Communism, and still others—the most

12. Comisariado General de Guerra, Ejército del Centro, *Orientaciones a los Comisarios sobre el trabajo en relación a las evasiones* (Madrid, 1939).

pessimistic—believed there would be direct Communist rule. Whether right or wrong, what is certain is that in the face of such fears there could not exist a determined will to sacrifice.[13]

Moreover, though direct evidence is lacking, it seems fairly certain that the Nationalist agents who had infiltrated the Republican command assured non-Communist military leaders that it would be much easier to negotiate a satisfactory peace with Franco after they had eliminated Soviet influence in Spain.

On March 4 Negrín made a series of moves to try to assure the loyalty of what was left of the People's Army by assigning several top Communist commanders to key positions. Galán was given command of the garrison at Cartagena, where the naval forces were becoming openly insubordinate, and Manuel Tagüeña was placed in charge of Murcia. Furthermore, it was rumored that Etelvino Vega was to be in charge of Murcia, that Líster was to be promoted and given command of the Army of Extremadura and that Modesto, who had just been promoted to general, was to be made commander of the Madrid front. According to the Socialist naval commissar, Bruno Alonso, "Everyone judged these nominations to be a veritable coup d'état by which the Communist Party would take over all the levers of power. . . ."[14]

Not the least of the ironies of the Spanish Civil War was that it ended the same way that it began: with a revolt by a large minority of the Republican Army against the current Republican government on the grounds that the latter was dominated by the Communists and about to give way to a Communist dictatorship. The Casado revolt, which established a "National Defense Council" (approximately the same term used by Mola in 1936), began in Madrid on March 5. Its success was dependent on a groundswell of defeatism and anti-Communist feeling, for three of the four Army corps in the Madrid area were led by Communists. Moreover, nearly all the remaining armored forces as well as all four of the special reserve divisions behind the central front were also commanded by Communists. These units were, as usual, better equipped and organized than

13. *Guerra en España*, 231–32.
14. *La flota republicana*, 136.

most other remaining sections of the People's Army, whereas Casado only held personal command of 11 understrength battalions in the city itself. Had the Communist forces received firm, cohesive leadership, the revolt could have been crushed. The Comintern advisers, however, accepted the situation for what it was. While instructions were sent to the Communist commanders near Madrid to smash the rebellion, the Comintern advisers, the remaining Soviet military personnel, and the top party leaders hastily burned their papers, packed their bags, and fled in the few remaining planes. Negrín went into exile within twenty-four hours.

Nevertheless, Communist military discipline on the central front held firm, and a vicious six-day battle was waged for control of Madrid. If the Communist units had not also been responsible for defending the battlefront against the Nationalists, they would probably have conquered. As it was, they occupied all but the center of the city and would soon have captured the rest had not the Defense Council finally received reinforcements from the anarchist Cipriano Mera's non-Communist army corps in Guadalajara province. That took the spirit out of the Communist units, but not before 2,000 troops had been killed and a brief round of political executions had been carried out by both sides. The result was hailed by *El Socialista* on March 12 as a patriotic victory that enabled what remained of leftist Spain to avoid becoming "a colony of the Soviet regime."

Of the 7 civilians on the Defense Council, 3 were from the CNT, 2 were Socialists, and 2 represented the Republican left. Their principal leader was the Marxist moderate Julián Besteiro, intellectual dean of Spanish socialism, who had retained his moral rigor and personal integrity undiminished throughout the war. Largely withdrawn from Socialist party politics since 1933, he had strongly disapproved of the excesses of the Spanish revolution, which in its existing form be believed to be doomed from the beginning. Yet he had never fled abroad as did many others who looked toward a "third Spain" of law, orderly development, and justice, nor had he abandoned the working classes of Madrid in the autumn of 1936, when the professional rhetoricians of revolution had fled the capital in desperate haste. He insisted that his place was with the common people and remained in Madrid throughout the war in a minor post of municipal government. Already in 1937 the more moderate Socialists and members of the Republican left had begun to look to him as one of the few alternative leaders remaining. He had made soundings in London in 1937 concerning a negotiated peace and had traveled to Barcelona at Azaña's behest in mid-1938 to search for a political alternative to the Negrín regime.

Appalled by the deeds of Communists and "Bolshevized" Socialists between 1934 and 1939, he failed to understand the nature of the reaction that had developed behind the Nationalist lines. Independent-minded people in the leftist zone knew that the current propaganda about Franco being a puppet of Hitler and Mussolini was exaggerated. Some of the anti-Communist leaders hoped that by putting an end to what had become a Communist-led struggle against the other half of the Spanish people they would make it possible for most patriotic Spanish groups to participate, at least to some degree, in building a strong, progressive new Spain.

Besteiro's viewpoint was precisely expressed in a private memorandum written immediately after the National Defense Council was formed:

> Open the people's eyes to the truth, but only carefully, so that they will not be too irritated by the light after such a long period of darkness.
> The real truth: we have been defeated by our own sins—though of course to consider these sins mine is pure rhetoric. We have been defeated nationally for having let ourselves be dragged along by the bolshevist "line," which is perhaps the greatest political aberration known to the centuries. International Russian policy in the hands of Stalin, perhaps as a reaction against its own domestic failure, has become a monstrous crime that exceeds the most macabre conceptions of Dostoevsky and Tolstoy. The reaction against that error of the Republic in letting itself be dragged along by the bolshevist "line" is genuinely represented by the Nationalists, who, whatever may be their defects, have waged a great anticomintern crusade. But the greater or lesser share of people who have suffered the consequences have a right, which is not something merely to be demanded, but possess a store of experience, tragic experience, if you like, but for that very reason more useful. And that experience cannot be scorned without grave harm for the

development of Spain in the future. That experience and the reaction of the subsequent liberation represent the only legality remaining in the collapse of Republican Spain—the resignation of the president has made clear the collapse which existed even before. Moreover, the National Defense Council came at the right time. Previously it would have clashed with that Himalaya of lies that the bolshevist press had deposited in simple souls and would have shattered. All the same, the shock did occur, but it has not been against a hard, massive mountain— only against a heap of sand built by a desert hurricane. In this situation the misfortune has not been so grave and has been overcome. If the action of March 4 had not been taken, the complete domination of the remains of Republican Spain would have been a fact and the inhabitants of this zone would probably have had to suffer a few months more, not just the prolongation of the war, but the most frightful bolshevist terrorism, the only means of maintaining such an artificial fiction, manifestly contrary to the desires of the people.

The drama of the citizen of the Republic is this: he does not want fascism, not for what it has of reaction against bolshevism, but because of the passionate, sectarian atmosphere that accompanies such a justified reaction (racial theories, myth of the hero, exaltation of a morbid nationalism and a spirit of conquest, resurrection of historical forms that have no meaning today, antiliberalism and anti-intellectualism in the social order, *enragés,* etc.). The citizen of the Republic, with his rich and tragic experience is not, then, fascist. But neither is he in any way bolshevist. He is perhaps more antibolshevist than antifascist, since he has suffered bolshevism personally, but fascism, no. How can this interesting state of spirit and this rich experience contribute to the building of tomorrow's Spain? That is the great problem. For to think that half of Spain can destroy the other half would be a new madness that would end all possibility of affirming our national personality, or even, would completely destroy our national personality, a danger that we have run and from which we have escaped, it seems, little less than by a miracle.

To build Spain's personality tomorrow, Nationalist Spain, the conqueror, will have to count on the experience of those who have suffered the enormous errors of the bolshevized Republic, or lose itself on erring paths that only lead to failure. The useful mass of Republicans cannot, without degrading itself, ask for a share in the booty. But it can and must ask a place in the ranks of constructive labor.[15]

15. Andrés Saborit, *Julián Besteiro* (Toulouse, 1962), 411–12.
    Besteiro's attitude may be compared with that of his former arch-enemy, the disillusioned ex-revolutionary Luis Araquistain, whose articles on "Communism and the War in Spain" were published in *The New York Times* in May and June 1939. Araquistain declared that "Aside from other factors, the defeat was due to the unprecedented moral deterioration of the Republican

This memorandum was penned under the shadow of Munich. Besteiro was, in general, ill informed about the actual development of international relations during the Civil War, and went on to posit the construction of a compromise national syndicalist Spain as a part of an harmonious western Europe united in opposition to Communist totalitarianism. This more nearly described the Europe of 1949 than that of 1939, for Besteiro misunderstood the real character of the Franco dictatorship and seemed largely ignorant of the nature and aims of Nazi Germany. The Defense Council had no chance of negotiating peace, but was forced irremediably into unconditional surrender. After Franco's forces occupied the remainder of the leftist zone at the close of the month, Besteiro was imprisoned and sentenced to virtual life imprisonment—basically on the charge of having failed to initiate an active revolt against Socialist party policy prior to 1939. Already nearly seventy years of age, he died in prison the following year.

The counterrevolution of 1939 was not that of 1934 or 1936. It had become an iron-fisted military dictatorship that immediately incarcerated more than a quarter-million opponents, prosecuted and sentenced most of them to prison terms, and, during the next few years, brought tens of thousands of them before the firing squad. Many were guilty of common crimes, but some had only been involved in political activities. The goal of this repression was to exact vengeance and to drown the revolution in its own blood.

---

leadership." Better informed than Besteiro on international affairs, Araquistain was certain that Stalin would soon make a deal with Hitler, and warned that "For the western powers, or at least for France, a defeat [by Germany] without the assistance of Russia would be no more disastrous than a victory with its assistance. This apparent paradox can currently only be understood by Spaniards loyal to the Republic, who know what the Communist dictatorship was like during the war and what it would have been like after a victory." (From the Spanish version, *El comunismo y la guerra de España*.)

SIXTEEN *Conclusion*

I T HAS BEEN CUSTOMARY to describe Spanish society as extraordinarily backward and narrow, incapable of coming to grips with modern challenges save through convulsive transformation. A standard cliché is that the middle classes of Spain are very feeble and have never been able to take charge of their country's affairs, yet that is more or less what they did throughout the greater part of the century stretching from 1833 to 1936. A great deal of social change occurred during the latter part of that period, and during its span Spanish middle-class society usually supported the most advanced form of representative government consonant with the country's cultural and economic development. It would be difficult to find another land at a similar stage of socioeconomic development that sustained as much civil liberty so long against as many difficulties.

In retrospect it is clear that the governing system which permitted the freest development of national affairs was constitutional monarchy; its stagnation after 1917 and short-circuiting in 1923 made the re-establishment of an orderly developmental polity very difficult. The civic discipline of the middle classes was well demonstrated in 1931, though the vacuum left by the dictatorship made it difficult to reorganize well-structured representative groups quickly. By that time, however, the disparity of civic values between differing political sectors may already have become too extreme for a cohesive democratic representative system to function. There is no guarantee that a liberal democratic Republic in the 1930's would have succeeded even if it had begun with a broader base than the sectarianism of the factions of the middle-class left. Yet the initiative fell to the latter and the choices of the moderate right subsequently mirrored those of the moderate left.

The first major step in the breakdown of the tenuous Republican polity was the revolutionary insurrection of 1934. The more extreme apologists for the latter have claimed that this was nothing more than the counterpart of the conservative Sanjurjo revolt of 1932—a somewhat absurd comparison since the *sanjurjada* involved only a few hundred monarchist conspirators and did not receive the support of any other important political group. The argument that the left was trying to avert a "fascist takeover" would be more credible were it not that there was no significant organized fascist movement in Spain at that time and had not the insurrectionists indicated their determination to overturn the existing constitutional system.

The idea that the dominant political concerns in Spain in 1935 and 1936 were negative—fear of "fascism" and fear of "communism"—contains a measure of truth, but is not wholly accurate. It does not explain the wave of destructive activity after the left had already rewon control of the government. If the main concern of the revolutionary groups had been to ward off "fascism" rather than to destroy existing institutions, they would have rallied in support of a government of the moderate left during the spring of 1936. They did not do this because, as a reading of their newspapers makes clear, such was not their primary concern.

Given the refusal of the middle-class left to compromise with moderates or conservatives, the representative system could only have been preserved from the revolutionaries and their equally determined but much weaker opposite number on the extreme right by the emergence of a strong constitutional party or coalition among the moderate liberals or moderate conservatives. Thus the failure of the CEDA to develop into a Christian democratic republican party was second in importance only to the role of the revolutionaries in frustrating the continuation of representative government.

The revolutionary left was prepared to destroy the Republican system, but not to prosecute thoroughgoing revolution. They found it easy to belabor existing institutions and to try to wreck the capitalist economy, but were not certain where to go from there. Hence the paradox that the revolution was precipitated in the final instance not by the revolutionaries but by the counterrevolutionaries. The former revealed themselves to be disunited and uncertain. The anarchosyndicalists proved once more that theirs was Spain's mass movement of revolutionary spontaneity, but they could not readily mobilize themselves for constructive work. The Spanish Socialist party followed an equivocal course. Earlier considered one of the best disciplined and most unified of European Socialist parties, it broke down under the conflict between ideology and reality. The "bolshevization" of Spanish socialism was in part a response to Russian example and pressure, but it also reflected an effort to remain true to revolutionary Marxism. The concern not to go the way of revisionist German social democracy had the effect in Spain not of saving revolutionary socialism but of eliciting a reaction that destroyed it.

All the revolutionary leaders underestimated the Spanish middle classes. The latter displayed considerable tolerance amid the disorders of 1931 to 1936 but when the chips were finally down had no more desire to be led away to the slaughter than did the left to submit to the "fascism" it discovered in middle-class parliamentary government. The left ultimately lost the struggle because the balance of foreign assistance went against it and also because in Spain the middle classes were too numerous and the established institutions of Church and Army too strong to permit the country to be taken over easily by the revolutionary movements. It may also have been that the mythology of proletarian utopianism and materialist anticlericalism proved less potent than did the old-time religion of the Nationalists. The old myth conquered the new; many Spanish Catholics showed greater discipline, determination, and self-sacrifice than did a large number of the secular utopians.

The great contradiction of the Spanish revolution was that the very revolutionary measures taken by the extreme left dissipated their energies and frustrated their chances for success in the crucial arena, which was not social and economic, but political and military.[1] In these circumstances the Communists went far to prove their claim that only they had a policy and discipline capable of achieving victory. The official Communist history of the war and revolution declares:

> It is worth noting that bourgeois historians currently dedicate them-selves to defining what was "revolutionary" and what was "counter-revolutionary" in the Spanish war. The basic falsification here can be easily pointed out: The struggle to put an end to efforts at anarchist "libertarian communism" was not waged to reestablish the "old order" of the landowning bourgeois oligarchy. It was not an attempt to return to the Republican institutions that existed before July 18, 1936, . . . but to rebuild them with a completely new content that responded to the demands of the antifascist war and to the democratic character of the revolution that was developing in Spain. The suppression of the "committees" was not a step backward but forward. It served, on the one hand, to fortify the people's unity in the war; and, on the other, to secure a new type of democratic Republic; to structure a people's democracy, that was emerging for the first time in Europe; to develop the Spanish democratic revolution with its own specific characteristics through its own original channels.[2]

Stripped of Communist rhetoric, the fundamental point here—that the Communists were attempting to guide the Popular Front regime toward a viable new revolutionary system—seems accurate. The anarchists and Socialists could break up the parliamentary Republic—with the assistance of left Republicans and ultrarightists—and wreck much of the economy, but they could not win an all-out revolutionary struggle. Only the

1. Cf. the succinct catalog by the left Catalanist Antoni Rovira i Virgili of the flaws that undermined the Popular Front effort:
> the unjustifiable excesses of the uncontrollables during the first stages of the struggle . . .; the confusion in the formation of the militia, due in large part to the predominance of elements without any preparation and often with extravagant ideas; the obstacles presented, for supposedly ideological reasons, to the building of a genuine and efficient army; the indiscipline of certain sectors of the people; the disorientation in industrial and agrarian labor; the persecution of small artisans and small businessmen; the scandalous incapacity of many Republican and labor leaders; the depressing spectacle of the disagreements and clashes—some-times bloody—between the parties and labor groups that were fighting against Franco; the vain diplomacy of Alvarez del Vayo, . . . always futile and sometimes counterproductive; the war policy of Negrín, espe-cially in the last months, which gave the impression abroad of being dictated by Moscow, even though that was not true.

Els darrers dies de la Catalunya republicana (Buenos Aires, 1940), 211–12.

2. *Guerra y revolución en España,* II, 271.

Communists were able to provide the leadership, discipline, organization, and military support for that.

After 1945, when occupation by the Red Army, the disappearance of the old order, and the discontent of large sectors of the population made it possible to establish hybrid Communist-Socialist dictatorships in all the Russian-dominated lands of east central Europe, reference was sometimes made to the Popular Front regime in Spain as the first instance in which special conditions had made it possible for relatively weak Communist political cadres to form a transitional "People's Republic" or "People's Democracy." When Georgi Dimitrov defined the goal of the new regimes as "a people's republic and not a capitalist republic, . . . a people's republican government and not a bourgeois republican government," [3] it recalled to some José Díaz' definition of the Spanish People's Republic in March 1937. There were definite similarities between Popular Front Spain and the first phase of the new east European Communist regimes: fused Socialist-Communist movements and front organizations; elimination of "nonprogressive" political parties; establishment of a new People's Army; nominal extension of new regional autonomies that were largely ignored in practice; broad land reform; nationalization or state control of basic industries; a façade of workers' control in the factories; and Communist domination of police, propaganda, and foreign policy. The central leader of Spanish communism, Dolores Ibarruri, said in March 1947 that "Spain was the first example of a people's democracy." [4]

Such flat assertions are nonetheless misleading. Insofar as they are true, the comparison refers only to the first phase—the pretotalitarian phase—of the east European regimes in 1945–46. Most of the other leftist parties in Spain were allowed to continue their separate political activities to a considerable degree, as were many of the independent liberal and leftist parties of eastern Europe during the first year or so of Communist domination. The Spanish war did not develop to the point

3. In a speech of September 8, 1946, quoted by Félix Montiel, "España fue una República popular, y volverá a serla," *Nuestra Bandera*, no. 23 (Dec. 1947), 1027–49.
4. *Ibid.*

where outright Communist dictatorship was feasible. On the other hand, the political process was much the same. Matyas Rakosi once termed this the "salami tactic" of slicing off the other political elements one at a time. The Communist meatcutter moved steadily along until it was stopped just before the end of the war. It is difficult to resist the conclusion of David T. Cattell that

the Communists had attracted by the end of the war almost a half million adherents and had secured a dominant position in the most important ministry of the government, the Defense Ministry, controlling all the armed forces of the country. From the evidence it seems clear that the party was in a position to seize absolute power in the Loyalist government when and if it wanted to.[5]

Military and diplomatic conditions made it neither possible nor desirable that an overtly Communist regime be established, but the general Communist hegemony that did develop—what some anarchists and Socialists called the "Communist dictatorship" *tout court*—created a fatal dilemma for the non-Communist left that, combined with uninterrupted military defeat, sapped the will to continue. Joaquín Maurín wrote a quarter century later, "From the moment in which the alternative was posed, beginning in June 1937, between the Communist party, at the orders of Moscow, or the opposing military regime, reactionary but Spanish, the conclusion of the Civil War was predetermined."[6]

A not insignificant number of commentators hold that liberal democracy is inapplicable to Spain and that an authoritarian solution to its problems was inevitable. Heretofore, however, the record of revolutionary leftists and right-wing authoritarians is less impressive than that of the constitutional liberals. Dominated by futile myths and debilitating doctrinairism, the Spanish left was unable to achieve unity and progress in the 1930's. Its failure was another chapter in the disasters of twentieth-century revolutionary maximalism. If liberal democracy is ever to function in Spain, it will not be sufficient to turn the clock back to 1939 or 1936.

5. *Communism and the Spanish Civil War* (Berkeley–Los Angeles, 1955), 211.
6. *Revolución y contrarrevolución en España* (Paris, 1966), 289.

Bibliography

THE PRINCIPAL social history of Spain is Jaime Vicens Vives, ed., *Historia social y económica de España y América* (Barcelona, 1957–59), 5 vols. Juan Beneyto Pérez, *Historia social de España y de Hispanoamérica* (Madrid, 1961), may also be consulted. The best individual effort at an economic history is Vicens' *Historia económica de España* (Barcelona, 1959; rev. ed., 2 vols., 1963–64). The first attempt to sketch an historical account of the Spanish lower classes was the *Historia de las clases trabajadoras* (Madrid, 1870) by Fernando Garrido, a social-minded leader of the Democratic party.

Heretofore the most energetic historian of the working-class movement in Spain has been Maximiano García Venero. His *Historia de las Internacionales en España* (Madrid, 1956–58), 3 vols., is the only comprehensive, detailed account of the revolutionary movements and his *Historia de los movimientos sindicalistas españoles (1840–1933)* (Madrid, 1961) is the only general treatment of Spanish trade unionism. Gerald Brenan's *The Spanish Labyrinth* (London, 1944) has become a standard analysis of social conflict and the origins and politics of the left, to which it is sympathetic. Two brief general interpretations of social and political class evolution are José Mariá Jover, *Conciencia obrera y conciencia burguesa en la España contemporánea* (Madrid, 1952), and Octavio Gil Munilla, *Historia de la evolución social española durante los siglos XIX y XX* (Madrid, 1961). Renée Lamberet, *Mouvements ouvriers et socialistes. L'Espagne (1750–1936). Chronologie et bibliographie* (Paris, 1953), is a useful tool.

The most extensive history of Spanish anarchism is Eduardo Comin Colomer, *Historia del anarquismo español (1836–1948)* (Madrid, 1950), but this work is in considerable measure vitiated by gross bias. Diego Abad de Santillán (pseud.), *Contribución a la historia del movimiento español. I: Desde sus origenes hasta 1905* (Mexico City, 1962), is a work by the onetime propaganda chief of the FAI that provides considerable detail. The German anarchist historian Max Nettlau has published *Miguel Bakunin, la Internacional y la Alianza en España (1868–1873)* (Buenos Aires, 1925) and *Documentos inéditos sobre la Internacional y la Alianza en España* (Buenos Aires, 1930).

A chronological outline of the working-class movement in northeastern Spain is provided in Emili Giralt, Albert Balcells, and Josep Termes Ardèvol, *Els moviments socials a Catalunya, Pais Valencià i les Illes: Cronologia, 1800–1939* (Barcelona, 1967). Two important studies of the initial phase of the anarcho-syndicalist movement are José Termes Ardèvol, *El movimiento obrero en España: La Primera Internacional (1864–1881)* (Barcelona, 1965), and Casimiro Martí, S. J., *Orígenes del anarquismo en Barcelona* (Barcelona, 1959). There are three earlier general accounts of the modern social conflict in Catalonia: Manuel Raventós, *Els moviments socials a Catalunya durante el segle XIX* (Barcelona, 1925); F. de Solà Cañizares, *Les lluites socials a Catalunya (1812–1934)* (Barcelona, 1934); and Josep Ma. Vilà, *Els primers moviments socials a Catalunya* (Barcelona, 1935). José Llunas Pujols, *Organización y aspiraciones de la Federación de Trabajadores de la Región Española* (Barcelona, 1883) is one of the first early syndicalist statements, and Anselmo Lorenzo's *El proletariado militante* (Barcelona, 1901; Toulouse, 1946–47), 2 vols., has been the most widely read autobiography by a Spanish revolutionary leader.

The land problem has been treated in Pascual Carrión, *Los latifundios en España* (Madrid, 1932); Carmelo Viñas Mey, *La reforma agraria en España en el siglo XIX* (Santiago de Compostela, 1933) and, by far the most thorough, Edward

Malefakis, "Land Tenure, Agrarian Reform and Peasant Revolution in Twentieth Century Spain" (Columbia University Ph.D. dissertation, 1966). There is only one thorough and detailed study of peasant unrest in a region of Andalusia: Juan Diáz del Moral's *Historia de las agitaciones campesinas andaluzas— Córdoba* (Madrid, 1929 and 1965), an outstanding work that has long been recognized as something of a classic. Other works of some usefulness on rural problems include Julián Zugasti, *El bandolerismo* (Madrid, 1876–80), 10 vols.; Constancio Bernaldo de Quirós, *El espartaquismo agrario andaluz* (Madrid, 1919) and *Los derechos sociales de los campesinos* (Madrid, 1928); R. Sancho Brased, *Organización de los trabajadores agrícolas* (Zaragoza, 1908); Eloy Vaquero, *Del drama de Andalucía: Recuerdos de luchas rurales ciudadanas* (Puente Genil, 1923); J. Polo Benito, *El problema social del campo en Extremadura* (Salamanca, 1919); Prudencio Rovira, *El campesino gallego* (Madrid, 1904); and the Instituto de Reforma Social's *El problema de los foros en el noroeste de España* (Madrid, 1923) and *La rabassa morta y su reforma* (Madrid, 1923).

The best general work on Catholic syndicalism is José Ma. García Nieto, *El sindicalismo cristiano en España* (Bilbao, 1960). Other accounts include Severino Aznar, *El catolicismo social en España* (Zaragoza, 1906); J. A. Meliá, *Sindicatos católicos y sindicatos revolucionarios* (Madrid, n.d.); Maximiliano Arboleya Martínez, *De la acción social: El caso de Asturias* (Barcelona, 1918) and *De la acción social: Los sindicatos obreros* (Oviedo, 1918); Florentino del Valle, S.I., *El P. Antonio Vicent y la acción social católica española* (Madrid, 1947); and Montserrat Llorens, *El P. Antonio Vicent, S.I.* (Barcelona, 1954). On the cooperative movement, see Juan Reventós Carner, *El movimiento cooperativo en España* (Barcelona, 1960), and Joan Ventosa i Roig and Albert Pérez i Baró, *El moviment cooperatiu a Catalunya* (Palma de Mallorca, 1961).

Joan Connelly Ullman, *Spain's Tragic Week* (Cambridge, 1968), provides an excellent, comprehensive study of the disturbances at Barcelona in 1909. From the turn of the century, the contemporary literature on the working-class movement became more abundant. Angel Marvaud, *La Question sociale en Espagne* (Paris, 1910), provides considerable data, though some of it is inaccurate. F. Tarrida del Mármol's booklet, *Les Inquisiteurs d'Espagne* (Paris, 1897), was a widely publicized denunciation of police repression. On the Barcelona underworld and the bomb-throwing wave of the first years of the century, see a well-researched contemporary essay, Juli Vallmitjana, *Criminalitat típica local* (Barcelona, 1910), and a more recent booklet, Enric Jardí, *La ciutat de les bombes* (Barcelona, 1964). Contemporary publications of those years include: Vicente Santamaría de Paredes, *El movimiento obrero contemporáneo* (Madrid, 1893); Andrés Borrego, *Historia, antecedentes y trabajos a que han dado lugar en España las discusiones sobre la situación y el porvenir de las clases jornaleras* (Madrid, 1890); Concepción Arenal, *La cuestión social* (Madrid, 1895); Comisión de Reformas Sociales, *Información oral y escrita* (Madrid, 1899–1903), 4 vols.; Ramón Sempau, *Los victimarios* (Barcelona, 1900); José López Monte-negro, *La huelga general* (Barcelona, 1901); a series of four volumes by Miguel Sastre on *Las huelgas en Barcelona*, which cover labor disturbances in the Catalan capital from 1903 to 1915; Práxedes Zancada, *El obrero en España* (Barcelona, 1902); Juan Alvarez Buylla, Adolfo Posada, Juan Uña, and Luis Morote, *El Instituto del Trabajo* (Madrid, 1902); J. Puyol, R. Salillas and C. Sanz Escartín, *Informe referente a las minas de Vizcaya* (Madrid, 1904); Gustavo La Inglesia y García, *Caracteres del anarquismo en la actualidad* (Madrid, 1905); Antonio Ma. de Mena, *Del anarquismo y su represión* (Madrid, 1906), on the legal and administrative difficulties of repressing political crimes; J. A. Torrents, *Història de l'Associació obrera* (Barcelona, 1907); Juan Uña Sarthou, *Las asociaciones obreras en España* (Madrid, 1910); José Cascales Muñoz, *Los conflictos del proletariado* (Madrid, 1912); Baldomero Argente, *La esclavitud proletaria* (Madrid, 1913); Rafael Altamira y Crevea, *Cuestiones obreras* (Valencia, 1914); Cristóbal de Castro, *Catálogo de documentos y resumen de debates parlamentarios sobre cuestiones sociales* (Madrid, 1910) and *Duración de las jornadas en los distintos oficios y términos geográficos de España* (Madrid, 1919); Juan G. Acebo y Modet, *Origen, desarrollo y trascendencia del movimiento sindicalista obrero* (Madrid, 1915); Instituto de Reforma Social, *La jornada de trabajo en la industria textil* (Madrid, 1914); Jacques Valdour, *La Vie ouvrière: L'ouvrier espagnol. Observa-*

tions vécues: Catalogne (Paris, 1919), describing the living conditions of Catalan workers in 1913; and Palmiro Marbá, *Origen, desarrollo y trascendencia del movimiento sindicalista obrero* (Barcelona, 1931), an early account that was actually written in 1913.

There are a number of published volumes that help to clarify the Catalan social turmoil of 1917 through 1923. Albert Balcells, *El sindicalisme a Barcelona (1915–1923)* (Barcelona, 1965), is a recent essay that provides some new data. One of the few accounts by a CNT leader is Manuel Buenacasa, *El movimiento obrero español (1888–1928)* (Barcelona, 1928), which, though sometimes inaccurate on the earlier years, is informative on certain key developments after 1917. E. G. Solano, *El sindicalismo en la teoría y en la práctica. Su actuación en España* (Barcelona, 1919), sheds some light on the Canadiense strike. R. Pla y Armengol, *Impresiones de la huelga general de Barcelona, del 24 de mayo al 7 de abril de 1919* (Barcelona, 1930), contains the observations of a Catalan Socialist. The text of the key CNT national congress was later published as *Memoria del Congreso celebrado en el Teatro de la Comedia de Madrid, los días 10 al 18 de diciembre de 1919* (Toulouse, n.d.). Gaston Leval, *Conceptos económicos en el socialismo libertario* (Buenos Aires, 1935), is useful for the development of anarchosyndicalist ideas. On terrorism, the most useful books are José Ma. Farré Moregó, *Los atentados sociales en España* (Madrid, 1922); F. de P. Calderón, *La verdad sobre el terrorismo (Datos, fechas, nombres e estadísticas)* (Barcelona, 1932); and Manuel Burgos y Mazo, *El verano de 1919 en el Ministerio de Gobernación* (Cuenca, 1923). Other publications worth noting are Francisco Madrid, *Las últimas veinticuatro horas de Francisco Layret* (Buenos Aires, 1942); Pedro Foix, *Los archivos del terrorismo blanco* (Barcelona, 1931); Mauro Bajatierra, *¿Quiénes mataron a Dato?* (Madrid, 1929); and Diego Abad de Santillán and E. López Arango, *El anarquismo en el movimiento obrero* (Barcelona, 1925). Quintiliano Saldaña y García Rubio, *El atentado social* (Madrid, 1927), analyzes legal problems arising from political crimes. On the Free Syndicates and the Catalan middle-class militia, see Feliciano Baratech Alfaro, *Los Sindicatos Libres de España* (Barcelona, 1927), a memoir by one of their first secretaries, and A. Delvillar, *El Somatén* (Barcelona, 1919).

There are two early Socialist histories of the origins of the Spanish Socialist party: Francisco Mora, *Historia del socialismo obrero español* (Madrid, 1902), and Juan José Morato, *El Partido Socialista Obrero* (Madrid, 1918), the latter being more trustworthy. To these may be added two hagiographic biographies of Iglesias: Morato's *Pablo Iglesias, educador de muchadumbres* (Madrid, 1931), and Julián Zugazagoitia, *Una vida heroica: Pablo Iglesias* (Madrid, 1926). Iglesias' speeches and articles for 1885–87 were later collected and published under the title *Reformismo social y lucha de clases* (Madrid, 1935). Largo Caballero's *Presente y futuro de la Unión General de Trabajadores de España* (Madrid, 1925) gives the text of some of the UGT's negotiations with the CNT during 1918 to 1920. Harry Feldman, "The Socialist Movement in Spain (1917–1930)" (Columbia master's essay, 1958), is a useful research essay written from a Marxist viewpoint. By far the most informative memoir on the Socialists in 1917 is Andrés Saborit, *La huelga de agosto de 1917* (Mexico City, 1967). Fernando Soldevilla, *Tres revoluciones: Las Juntas de Defensa, La Asamblea Parlamentaria, La Huelga general* (Madrid, 1917), is a chronicle, and *Acción de la minoría socialista* (Madrid, 1918) a collection of speeches by Socialist Cortes deputies on the events of 1917. An accurate account of early Asturian socialism to 1931 is given by David Ruiz González, *El movimiento obrero en Asturias* (Oviedo, 1968). Antonio L. Oliveros, *Asturias en el resurgimiento español* (Madrid, 1935), provides some information on UGT relations with Primo de Rivera; the attitude of the anticollaborationists was expressed by Gabriel Morón, *El Partido Socialista ante la realidad política de España* (Madrid, 1929). Eduardo Aunós, *La política social de la Dictadura* (Madrid, 1944), is a defense of the labor policies of the Primo de Rivera regime by its Minister of Labor.

There is an official *Historia del Partido Comunista de España* (Paris, 1960), but the principal study of the early development of Spanish communism is Eduardo Comín Colomer's *Historia del Partido Comunista de España* (Madrid, 1965–67), whose first three volumes cover developments to July 1936. There are memoirs by two of the first secretary generals of the party in Spain: Oscar Pérez Solís, *Memorias de mi amigo Oscar Perea*

(Madrid, 1929), and José Bullejos, *Europa entre dos guerras 1918–1938* (Mexico City, 1945). Fernando de los Ríos, *Mi viaje a la Rusia soviética* (Madrid, 1921), is a skeptical report by one of the original Spanish Socialist delegates to Moscow. *Setenta días en Rusia* (Barcelona, 1924), by Angel Pestaña of the CNT, is more ambiguous. Among the favorable reports on the Soviet Union by leading Spanish Socialists are Julio Alvarez del Vayo, *La nueva Rusia* (Madrid, 1929); Rodolfo Llopis, *Cómo se forja un pueblo* (Madrid, 1930); and Julián Zugazagoitia, *Rusia al día* (Madrid, 1932). Aspects of early Spanish Socialist differences with the Communists are revealed in *Cien cartas inéditas de Pablo Iglesias a Isidoro Acevedo* (Madrid-Barcelona, 1938) and Indalecio Prieto, *Entresijos de la guerra de España* (Mexico City, 1953). Andrés Nin's *Las organizaciones obreras internacionales* (Madrid, 1933) is a dissident Communist's analysis of the rival internationals.

Three general histories of the Second Republic may be recommended. The most concise, Gabriel Jackson's *The Spanish Republic and Civil War* (Princeton, 1965), is favorable to left Republicanism. José Pla's four-volume *Historia de la segunda República española* (Barcelona, 1943) is a moderate account devoted almost exclusively to politics. The most detailed treatment is Joaquín Arrarás, *Historia de la segunda República española* (Madrid, 1957–67), 4 vols., written from a conservative point of view. Rhea M. Smith, *The Day of the Liberals in Spain* (Philadelphia, 1938), is a somewhat superficial study of the drafting of the Republican constitution. Luis Jiménez de Asúa's *Proceso de la constitución de la República española* (Madrid, 1932) is the memoir of the chairman of the parliamentary constitutional commission. Policies of the first Republican biennium are discussed in Alvaro de Albornoz, *Política religiosa de la República* (Madrid, 1935); E. Isern Dalmau, *Política fiscal de la República* (Barcelona, 1933); Marcelino Domingo, *La escuela en la República* (Madrid, 1932), which gives the texts of many laws and regulations, and also in Domingo's superficial sketches of the events of 1931, *La libertad en España* (Toulouse, n.d.). Labor regulations are studied in a published dissertation by Robert Barreau, *Le Syndicalisme en Espagne* (Toulouse, 1934). Juan Marichal has edited the *Obras completas de Manuel*

Azaña (Mexico City, 1966–68), 4 vols.

The most extensive studies to date of Spanish socialism and the other revolutionary parties under the Republic are L. V. Ponomareva, *Rabochee dvizhenie v Ispanii v gody revoliutsii 1931–1934* (Moscow, 1965), and those of her former student Svetlana P. Pozharskaya, *Sotsialisticheskaia Rabochaya Partiya Ispanii 1931–1939 gg.* (Moscow, 1966), and "Taktika ispanskoi sotsialisticheskoi rabochei partii v pervye gody burzhuaznodemokraticheskoi revoliutsii (1931–1933)," in *Iz istorii osvoboditelnoi borby ispanskogo naroda* (Moscow, 1959), 263–307. The principal contemporary Spanish Socialist accounts dealing with the first years of the Republic are Manuel Cordero, *Los socialistas y la revolución* (Madrid, 1932); Gabriel Morón, *La ruta del socialismo en España* (Madrid, 1932); Antonio Ramos Oliveira, *Nosotros, los marxistas* (Madrid, 1932); and Margarita Nelken, *Por qué hicimos la revolución* (Madrid, 1936). Jules Moch and Germaine Picard-Moch, *L'Espagne rèpublicaine* (Paris, 1933), is an interesting early analysis by two French Socialists.

The principal study of the anarchosyndicalist movement during the Republican years is S. John Brademas, "Revolution and Social Revolution: A Contribution to the History of the Anarcho-Syndicalist Movement in Spain, 1930–1937" (Oxford dissertation, 1956). Statements by revolutionaries dissenting from the main movements include Joaquín Maurín, *La revolución española* (Madrid, 1932); César Falcón, *Crítica de la revolución española* (Madrid, 1931); and José Antonio Balbontín, *La España de mi experiencia* (Mexico City, 1952).

There are interesting observations on the effects of the Republican polarization in a small rural Aragonese community in Carmelo Lisón-Toledana, *Belmonte de los Caballeros: A Sociological Study of a Spanish Town* (Oxford, 1966). The only analysis of labor disturbances under the Republic is Casimir Martí, Jordi Nadal, and Jaume Vicens Vives, "El moviment obrer a Espanya de 1929 a 1936 en relación amb la crisi econòmica," *Serra d'Or* (February 1961). Blas Infante Pérez, *La verdad sobre el complot de Tablado y el Estado Libre de Andalucía* (Seville, 1931), is a defense of Ramón Franco and other Radical Socialist conspirators of 1931, and Enrique Villa, *Un año de República en Sevilla* (Seville, 1932), is a conservative's account of the disorders of 1931 in Seville. Two of the major scandals of the last year of the biennium are treated from opposing viewpoints in Luis Jiménez de Asúa's *Castilblanco* (Madrid, 1933), an account of a political crime by the defense attorney involved, and M. García Ceballos, *Casas Viejas* (Madrid, 1965).

The outstanding memoir by a moderate liberal is Miguel Maura's *Así cayó Alfonso XIII* (Mexico City, 1962). On Melquiades Alvarez, see Maximiano García Venero, *Melquiades Alvarez: Historia de un liberal* (Madrid, 1954), and Mariano Cuber, *Melquiades Alvarez* (Madrid, 1935). Manuel de Burgos y Mazo, *De la República a . . .?* (Madrid, 1931), is a bitter critique by a conservative Republican. For the Radical Socialists, there are the collected speeches of Félix Gordón Ordás, *Mi política en España* (Mexico City, 1964), 3 vols., and the three volumes of *Texto taquigráfico* for the Radical Socialist congresses of 1932–33 (Madrid, 1932–33). On Alejandro Lerroux and the Radicals, see Lerroux' anecdotal *La Pequeña historia* (Buenos Aires, 1940); José Rodríguez de la Peña, *Los aventureros de la política: Alejandro Lerroux* (Madrid, 1915), a hyperbolic denunciation of Lerroux in an earlier period; and Miguel Carmona, ed., *Trayectoria política de Alejandro Lerroux* (Madrid, 1934), a collection of speeches and writings.

The only history of Catalan nationalism is Maximiano García Venero's *Historia del nacionalismo catalán* (Madrid, 1944; rev. ed., 2 vols., 1967), which is in part based on an earlier work by the left Catalanist writer and historian Antoni Rovira Virgili. L. V. Ponomareva, "Natsionalnyi vopros v Ispanii i osvoboditelnoe dvizhenie katalontsev v 1931–1933," in *Iz istorii osvoboditelnoi borby ispanskogo naroda* (Moscow, 1959), 55–122, is the principal Marxist interpretation.

Lluis Creus Vidal, *Visió econòmica de Catalunya* (Barcelona, 1934), 2 vols., provides a perfunctory description of the region's economy during its brief period of autonomy. Economic problems are discussed in Jaume Alzina, *L'economía de la Catalunya autònoma* (Barcelona, 1933); Felipe Ferrer Calbetó, *Los factores económicos y el momento político catalán* (Barcelona, 1933); Pedro Gual Villalbí, *Temas candentes de la vida económica y social* (Barcelona, 1934); and Vicenç Bernades, *Perspectives econòmiques* (Barcelona, 1935). Josep Planes Mundet, *Superestat:*

Projecció d'un sistema d'Orgànica Social (Barcelona, 1936), is a proposal for a semitechnocratic Catalanist welfare state. The leader of the Lliga has been the subject of three useful books: Josep Pla, *Cambó* (Barcelona, 1929–30), 3 vols.; Maximiano García Venero, *Vida de Cambó* (Barcelona, 1952); and Jesús Pabón, *Cambó, 1876–1918* (Barcelona, 1951). On the other hand, there are no biographies of Macià or any of the left Catalanist leaders with any substance or pretense of objectivity. The sketches by Lluis Aymamí i Baudina, *Macià* (Barcelona, 1933), and Angel Ossorio y Gallardo, *Vida y sacrificio de Companys* (Buenos Aires, 1943), are about as helpful as any.

Catalanism produced a large bibliography under the Republic. For the attitude of the liberals, see Jaume Bofill, *Una política catalanista* (Barcelona, 1933); Joan Estelrich, *De la Dictadura a la República* (Barcelona, 1933); and Lliga Catalana, *Un partit, una política* (Barcelona, 1933), and *Dos anys d'actuació* (Barcelona, 1935). The position of left Catalanism is explained in Jaume Aiguader i Miró, *Catalunya i la revolució* (Barcelona, 1931); A. Rovira i Virgili, *Catalunya i la República* (Barcelona, 1931); Artur Perucho, *Cataluña bajo la Dictadura* (Barcelona, 1931); and Rafael Campalans, *Política vol dir pedagogia* (Barcelona, 1933). J. Casals and R. Arrufat, *Catalunya poble dissortat* (Barcelona, 1933), is a critique of the rule of the Esquerra by two leaders of the dissident Partit Nacionalista Català that split off from Estat Català. On the role of the Catalanists in the coming of the Republic, see, in addition to Aiguadé, M. Carrasco i Formiguera, *El pacte de San Sebastián* (Barcelona, 1931), and José Gaya Picón, *La jornada histórica de Barcelona* (Madrid, 1931).

On the agrarian reform in Catalonia, see Albert Balcells, *El conflicte agrari a Catalunya 1890–1936* (Barcelona, 1968), and Emilio Giralt y Raventós, "El Conflicto Rabassaire y la cuestión agraria en Cataluña hasta 1936," *Revista de Trabajo,* no. 7 (1966). Three hostile Catalan critiques of the agrarian reform law are Joan Garriga Massó, *Contribució a l'estudi de l'actual conflicte agrari de Catalunya* (Barcelona, 1933); Aureli Joaniquet, *La reforma agrària a Catalunya* (Barcelona, 1933); and Emilio Saguer y Olivet, *De la cuestión agrària* (Barcelona, 1933).

Enrique de Angulo, *Diez horas de Estat Catala* (Barcelona,

1934), and J. Costa i Deu and Modest Sabaté, *La veritat del 6 d'octubre* (Barcelona, 1936), are detailed, critical narratives of the 1934 revolt in Catalonia, the first concentrating on events in Barcelona and the second on affairs in the rest of the region. There are several left Catalanist explanations of the rebellion, its causes and consequences: Jaume Miravitlles, *Crítica del 6 d'octubre* (Barcelona, 1935); Lluis Aymamí i Baudina, *El 6 d'octubre tal com jo l'he vist* (Barcelona, 1935); and Joaquim de Camps i Arboix, *Desprès del 6 d'octubre: Política d'esquerra a Catalunya* (Barcelona, 1935). Josep Dencàs wrote an apologium for his fiasco, *El 6 d'octubre des del Palau de Governació* (Barcelona, 1935). R. Closas, *El problema del règim transitori de Catalunya* (Barcelona, 1935), deals with the juridical problems created by the defeated Catalanist revolt.

The question of Catalan regionalism in comparison with other nationalist and regionalist problems in Spain and Europe is considered in Joaquim Cases-Carbó, *El problema peninsular 1924–1932* (Barcelona, 1933); M. Casas Fernández, *Proceso del catalanismo* (Madrid-Barcelona, 1932); and Joan Estelrich, *La Question des minorités et la Catalogne* (Lausanne, 1929) and *Catalanismo y reforma hispánica* (Barcelona, 1932).

B. Pou and J. R. Magriñá, *Un ano de conspiración* (Barcelona, 1933), narrates conspiratorial contacts between the CNT and the Republican left in Catalonia during 1930–31. The *Pensamiento de Juan Peiró* (Mexico City, 1959) presents a number of articles written by Peiró under the dictatorship that help to explain his notion of revolutionary syndicalism. Pedro R. Piller (Gaston Leval), *Problemas económicos de la revolución española* (Barcelona, 1933), is a representative general statement of anarchosyndicalist economic ideas in the early 1930's. An interesting account of local politics and labor affairs in Barcelona in 1931 is given by Francisco Madrid, a talented journalist sympathetic to the left, in *Ocho meses y un día en el gobierno civil de Barcelona* (Barcelona, 1932). Madrid's *Film de la República comunista libertaria* (Madrid-Barcelona, 1932) mainly provides an impressionistic description of the January 1932 revolt in the Upper Llobregat valley. The CNT's *La barbarie gubernamental* (Barcelona, 1933) is its official account of police brutality attending the suppression of its next major attempt at insurrection

(January 1933). Manuel Buenacasa, *La C.N.T., los Treinta y la F.A.I.* (Barcelona, 1933), gives the position of the FAI-CNT leadership.

The evolution of Angel Pestaña from apolitical revolutionism to political syndicalism can be traced in his pamphlets: *Acción directa* (Barcelona, 1924), which is highly critical of the anarchosyndicalist concept thereof; *Sindicalismo. Su organización y tendencia* (Valencia, 1930); *Sindicalismo y unidad sindical* (Valencia, 1933); and *Por qué se constituyó el Partido Sindicalista* (Barcelona, 1936). To these may be added his booklet *El sindicalismo, qué quiere y adónde va* (Barcelona, 1933). Pestaña's autobiography, *Lo que aprendí en la vida* (Madrid-Barcelona, 1934), is perhaps the most interesting memoir ever written by a Spanish working-class leader.

Joaquín Maurín's *Revolución y contrarrevolución en España* (Paris, 1966) is an important book that provides keen analysis of the early years of Spanish communism and the development of the revolutionary movements in Catalonia. To this may be added two contemporary pamphlets, Maurín's *El Bloque Obrero y Campesino* (Barcelona, 1932), and Jaume Miravitlles, *Perqué soc comunista* (Barcelona, 1932). Angel Estivill, *6 d'octubre. L'ensulsiada dels jacobins* (Barcelona, 1933), is a Communist critique of the Catalanist left.

The split in Spanish socialism is to some extent revealed in Julián Besteiro's *Marxismo y antimarxismo* (Madrid, 1935), a collection of his articles and speeches during 1933, and Francisco Largo Caballero, *Discursos a los trabajadores* (Madrid, 1934). Andrés Saborit's *Julián Besteiro* (Toulouse, 1962) is a well-documented biography, and his *Asturias y sus hombres* (Toulouse, 1964) is somewhat helpful on the background of socialism and progressivism in Asturias.

Rafael Salazar Alonso, Minister of the Interior in 1934 until a few days before the insurrection, published a partially documented volume of memoirs, *Bajo el signo de la revolución* (Madrid, 1935). The principal leftist accounts of the Asturian revolt are, for the BOC, Manuel Grossi, *La insurrección de Asturias* (Barcelona, 1935); for the FAI-CNT, Manuel Villar, *El anarquismo en la insurrección de Asturias* (Buenos Aires, 1936), and Solano Palacio, *Quince días de comunismo libertario en Asturias* (Barcelona, 1936); for the Communists, Maximiliano Alvarez Suárez (pseud. of Manuel Navarro Ballesteros, editor of the Communist daily, *Mundo Obrero*), *Sangre de octubre* (Madrid, 1936); Manuel D. Benavides, *La revolución fue así* (Barcelona, 1935); and José Canel (pseud.), *Octubre rojo en Asturias* (Madrid, 1935). The Spanish government's *La revolución de octubre en España* (Madrid, n.d.) and "Reporteros reunidos," *Octubre rojo* (Madrid, 1935), give critical narratives. Ignacio Corral, *Por qué mataron a Luis de Sirval* (Madrid, 1935), provides some fairly objective material on the repression.

There are four memoirs by Communist leaders of these years that possess some importance: *El comunismo en España* (Madrid, 1935), by Enrique Matorrás, a former secretary of the central committee of the Communist Youth, is one of the best sources on Spanish communism during the first years of the Republic; Jesús Hernández, *Yo fui un ministro de Stalin* (Mexico City, 1952); Enrique Castro Delgado, *Hombres made in Moscú* (Mexico City, 1960); and, by far the least honest and useful, Dolores Ibarruri, *They Shall Not Pass* (New York, 1966).

On Spanish Trotskyism, see G. Munis, *Jalones de derrota, promesa de victoria* (Mexico City, 1948) and *Qué son las Alianzas Obreras* (Madrid, 1934); Pierre Broué, *Trotsky y la Guerra civil española* (Buenos Aires, 1966); and Juan Andrade, *La burocracia reformista en el movimiento obrero* (Madrid, 1935).

Among the better contemporary accounts of politics during the moderate-conservative biennium are Juan Castrillo Santos, *Cuatro años de experiencia republicana 1931–1935* (Madrid, 1935) and *Ante el drama de la Reforma constitucional* (Madrid, 1935), and Salvador Canals, *El bienio estéril* (Madrid, 1936). José Samblancat Salanova, *El odio a Lerroux, el mejor amigo de la República* (Barcelona, 1935), is composed of a series of articles by an old-style, period-piece Barcelona Radical in defense of Lerroux. Joaquín Pérez Madrigal, *Memorias de un converso* (Madrid, 1952), offers a few interesting notes by a temporary supporter of Lerroux. Jaume Alzina, *Els pressupostos de les corporacions públiques* (Barcelona, 1936), provides interesting material on public expenditures. Unió de Rabassaires, *Els desnonaments rùstics a Catalunya* (Barcelona, 1935), indicts the agrarian policy pursued by the government in Catalonia after the revolt, and Alardo Prats, ed., *El gobierno de la Generalidad en el banquillo* (Madrid, 1935), gives the text of much of the trial of the Catalanist leaders. Ramiro Gómez Fernández, *¿Por qué se calumnia a Azaña?* (Madrid, 1935), defends the left Republican chief.

There were a considerable number of polemics by the leaders of the working-class parties in 1935. Indalecio Prieto's articles were collected in his *Del momento: posiciones socialistas* (Madrid). Three major statements by the revolutionary Socialists are Carlos de Baráibar, *Las falsas 'posiciones socialistas' de Indalecio Prieto* (Madrid); Carlos Hernández Zancajo, *Octubre: segunda etapa* (Madrid); and Segundo Serrano Poncela, *El Partido Socialista y la conquista del poder* (Barcelona). Antonio Gascón and Victoria Priego, *Por hoy y por manaña (Leves comentarios a un libro firmado por Carlos de Baráibar)* (Madrid), is pro-Prieto. The executive commission of the PSOE published its official account of the resignation of Largo Caballero in a pamphlet, *Por la unidad y la disciplina del Partido Socialista. Historia de una dimisión* (Madrid, Jan. 1936). The best contemporary critique of the "Bolshevization" was Gabriel Mario de Coca, *Anti-Caballero (Crítica marxista de la bolchevización del Partido Socialista* (Madrid, 1936). Communist goals and tactics are reflected in the official *Las lecciones de los combates de octubre en España* and in Jesús Izcaray and Nicolás Escanilla's partially fabricated *El socialismo español después de Octubre* (Madrid, 1935). The position of the CNT was stated in the resolutions of the *Pleno nacional de Regionales, celebrado en Zaragoza el 26 de mayo de 1935 y días sucesivos.* Diego Martínez Barrio, *Orígenes del Frente Popular Español* (Buenos Aires, 1943), is an attempt by one of the key leaders of the middle-class left to explain the hybrid Popular Front alliance.

Partial analyses of the elections of 1936 have been made in José Venegas, *Las elecciones del Frente Popular* (Buenos Aires, 1944), and Carlos M. Rama, *Ideología, regiones y clases sociales en la España contemporánea* (Montevideo, 1963). Ricardo de la Cierva, ed., *Los documentos de la primavera tragica* (Madrid, 1967), is an able collection of materials dealing with the spring of 1936 and interpreted from a conservative viewpoint. Aside from volumes previously mentioned, there is little other useful memoir literature dealing with the last months before the war. Two partial exceptions are the work of a Socialist, L. Romero Solano, *Vísperas de la guerra de España* (Mexico City, 1947), and the memoirs of a former Communist activist, Rafael Pelayo de Hungría (Rafael Pelayo Aunión), *Rusia al desnudo,* ed. by Ramón Moreno Hernández (Madrid, 1956). Baldomero Díaz de Entresotos, *Seis meses de anarquía en Extremadura* (Caceres, 1937), is a hostile personal description of the revolutionary swell in southwestern Spain during the spring of 1936.

Bibliographical references to the Spanish Civil War abound. The most systematic list is R. de la Cierva et al., *Bibliografía general sobre la guerra de España (1936–1939) y sus antecedentes históricos* (Barcelona, 1968). There are extensive references to the literature on the left in Hugh Thomas, *The Spanish Civil War* (New York–London, 1961), and in Burnett Bolloten, *The Grand Camouflage* (New York, 1961). All sources of particular importance for the years 1936 to 1939 that I have used and are not mentioned in other general bibliographies have already been listed in the notes.

The largest collections of material on the Spanish Civil War to be found in the United States are located in the Library of Congress, the Bolloten Collection of the Hoover Institution, and the Southworth Collection of the University of California, San Diego. The largest pamphlet collection on the Civil War has been assembled at the Unidad de Estudios sobre la Guerra de España in Madrid, and is supplemented by the holdings of the Biblioteca Nacional, of which an annotated bibliography has been edited by Vicente Palacio Atard. The most complete newspaper files for the Civil War period are in Madrid's Hemeroteca Municipal. Captured documents of the People's Army are held under restricted access by the Spanish Army's Servicio Histórico Militar in Madrid. A large mass of undigested documentation on all the leftist parties is kept under similarly restricted access in Salamanca.

I have treated the opposing side in the Civil War in my books on the *Falange* (Stanford, 1961) and *Politics and the Military in Modern Spain* (Stanford, 1967).

Index

184, 188, 195, 197, 206, 216, 230, 307, 312; *general references:* 166, 167
Primo de Rivera, General, 57, 77–78, 80, 83–84, 114, 117, 152, 262, 263
Progressive party, 12, 13, 14, 89, 101n, 103, 184
Provincial Peasant Federation (FPC), 282–83
PSOE, *see* Spanish Socialist Workers' party
PSUC, *see* Unified Socialist party of Catalonia
Publicitat, La, 212n

Qué son las Alianzas Obreras, 148

Rabassaires, *see* Unió de Rabassaires
Radical party, 69, 85, 87, 89, 97, 100, 102, 103, 110, 111, 131–32, 141, 143, 148–49, 150, 158, 160, 161–63, 175, 180, 184
Radical Republican party, 33, 67, 69, 103
Radical Socialist party, 85, 87, 89, 102, 103, 111
Rakosi, Matyas, 374
Rama, Carlos, 221
Ramos Oliveira, 194–95
Red Army, 322–23, 329, 335, 339, 345, 373
Reformist Republican party, 69, 83, 85
Regional Federation of Catalonia, 250
Renovación Española party, 184, 213
Republican Action party, 85, 89, 103
Republican Antifascist Military Union (UMRA), 205, 212, 321
Republican Left party, 163, 184, 202–3
Republican National Guard, 293, 297n
Republican Union, 67–72, 163, 177, 184, 202–3
Reverter, Andreu, 286
Revolutionary Youth Front, 291, 293
Rezola, José, 341n
Río, Ricardo del, 359
Ríos, Fernando de los, 87, 100
Rodríguez Salas, Eusebio, 293, 297
Rojo, Col. Vicente, 333, 337, 344, 346, 359, 361–62
Romero Solano, 319n
Rosenberg, Marcel, 233–34
Rovira i Virgili, Antoni, 372n
Ruiz i Ponseti, Estanislau, 308
Russia, comparison with Spain, 31, 55, 71, 107–8, 146, 148, 165–66, 188, 193, 198, 224, 240, 248–49, 260, 295, 309, 373; influence felt in Spain, 35, 47, 73–76, 139, 179, 307, 371; involvement in Spanish affairs, 79–81, 167, 194, 233–34, 271–72, 275–76, 278, 288–89, 299, 312, 333, 342n, 355–56, 357, 363–64, 366, 368n; sends arms to Spain, 264–65, 267–70, 273–74, 287, 311, 319, 321, 323–26, 327n, 329–30, 336–37, 339–40, 344–45, 347–48, 350n, 351; *general references:* 119, 122, 290, 301
Ruta, 292

Sabadell, 120
Sagunto, 200n
Salamanca, 10, 111, 337, 348
Salas Larrazábal, Lt. Col. Ramón, 350n
Salazar Alonso, Rafael, 142
Salazar, Dr. Antonio de Oliveira, 263
Sama, 156
Sánchez Román, Felipe, 149, 158–59, 163,

177, 202–3, 218
Sanjurjo, 370
San Sebastián, 163
Santander, 182, 183, 221, 230, 237, 315, 340, 341–42
Santiago, Enrique, 78n
Schacht, Hjalmar, 272
Seguí, Salvador, 41, 42n, 56–57, 69, 73, 74
Serge, Victor, 41n
Serrano Poncela, Segundo, 146
Servicio de Inteligencia Militar (SIM), 346
"Servicio de la República, Al," 89
Sesé, Antonio, 290
Seville, 10, 25, 26, 53, 80, 118, 141, 170, 207, 222
SIM, *see* Servicio de Inteligencia Militar
Sindicatos Católicos-Libres, 52n
Sindicates Libres (Free Syndicates), 51–52, 53, 54–57, 77, 116, 201
Sindicatos Únicos, 45, 50, 51, 54, 78, 94, 199, 245
Social Democratic party, 68
Socialista, El, 64, 68, 74, 94–95, 108–9, 135, 146, 186n, 209n, 230, 365
Socialist party of Spain, agrarian programs of, 95–99, 106, 142; attitude toward military, 319, 340; beginnings of, 63–64, 66–67; in Catalonia, 113, 121, 126, 138–39; and communism, 73, 74–76, 93, 108, 166–67, 371; in the Cortes, 68, 89, 102, 167–68, 184, 195; in defeat, 365–68; membership of, 77, 167, 210, 222, 281; militia of, 205–6; Popular Front and, 177–79, 197–98, 210–11, 311; propaganda of, 110, 135, 146, 164, 171–72, 229–30, 298; revolutionary elements in, 136–38, 142, 146, 148–49, 189, 193, 198, 209–10, 215–16, 231, 232–33, 282, 300, 317, 320; in the Second Republic, 85, 87–89, 92–100, 109, 118; strikes of, 38, 40, 69–71, 149, 155–56; trade unions of, 57, 64–65, 222–23; UGT and, 65, 66–67, 94, 102–3, 111, 132–33, 135, 169, 188, 303; under Negrín, 356, 358n, 362; union with Communists, 145–46, 154, 167, 169–70, 172, 187–89, 287, 295, 298–99, 351, 373; the Worker Alliance and, 138–39, 143–44, 146, 154, 172; youth groups in, 75, 107–8, 132, 142–43, 149, 167–68, 171, 194, 205; *general references:* 33, 62, 84, 90, 157, 163, 191, 203, 218, 237, 262, 334, 374
Socialist Youth, *see* Federation of Socialist Youth
Society of Friends of the USSR, 154
Sol, El, 101n, 126–27n, 143, 191, 203, 206, 207
Soldevila, Cardinal-Archbishop, 57
Solidaridad Obrera, 43, 46–47, 116, 117–18, 206, 227, 286, 290, 296, 317
Solidarios, Los, 53
Somatén, 47, 53, 150
Soviet Union, *see* Russia
Spain, agrarian reform in, 87, 95–99, 106, 109, 115, 122, 124–26, 133–34, 141, 143, 150, 160–61, 176, 186, 190–92, 238–41, 244, 256, 258–60, 305–9; *see also* land distribution; anarchism in, 17–20, 23–29, 31–35, 38, 40–46, 51–54, 62, 64–66, 70, 72–74, 77, 79, 82, 90, 94–95, 100, 113, 116–20, 132, 151, 191, 200–1, 222, 226, 229, 231, 233, 237, 243–44, 248, 251–52, 281, 284–86, 293–94, 298, 302–4, 306, 317–18, 322, 326, 334, 356–57, 362, 365,

398   INDEX